The Secret Story of Steven Spielberg, Warner Bros. and the Twilight Zone deaths.

FLY BY NIGHT

STEVE CHAIN

Fly By Night: The Secret Story of Steven Spielberg, Warner Bros, and the Twilight Zone Deaths
Copyright ©2021 Steve Chain. All Rights Reserved

Published by:
Trine Day LLC
PO Box 577
Walterville, OR 97489
1-800-556-2012
www.TrineDay.com
trineday@icloud.com

Library of Congress Control Number: 2021949524

Chain, Steve, J
Fly By Night—1st ed.
p. cm.
Epub (ISBN-13) 978-1-63424-366-7
Cloth (ISBN-13) 978-1-63424-364-3
Trade Paper (ISBN-13) 978-1-63424-365-0
1. Landis, John, -- 1950- -- Trials, litigation, etc. 2. Spielberg, Steven, -- 1946- -- Trials, litigation, etc. 3. Trials (Homicide) -- California -- Los Angeles. 4. Morrow, Vic, -- 1931-1982. 5. Twilight zone (Motion picture). 6. Motion picture industry -- Accidents -- Investigation -- California. 7. Motion picture industry -- Accidents -- Investigation.
Trials (Homicide). I. Title

Photography by Ben Swets

First Edition
10 9 8 7 6 5 4 3 2

Printed in the USA
Distribution to the Trade by:
Independent Publishers Group (IPG)
814 North Franklin Street
Chicago, Illinois 60610
312.337.0747
www.ipgbook.com

CONTENTS

PROLOGUE

Indian Dunes
Friday, July 23, 1982
2:20 A.M.

Frank Marshall looked on as the cameras rolled. They were filming scene 32, a night scene, a tricky shot involving a military helicopter with a powerful searchlight beaming down on the Vietnamese village below. He watched Vic Morrow slog through the water of a shallow, sluggish stream loomed over by a dark bluff. The helicopter hovered just overhead. Marshall had worked with children before on movies like *Poltergeist* and *E.T.*, and Morrow, he saw in the brightness of the beam, was holding two children, a boy and a girl, precariously under each arm. The little girl was also holding something in her arms. It was a naked broken barbie doll.

One of the first large special effects went off in the Vietnamese village. Marshall became aware of a loud explosion, followed by a blinding light and searing heat. The blast seemed to rock the helicopter, and that instant, looking for cover, a shield against the onrushing disaster, Frank Marshall ran from the river, flinging himself beneath a truck as two more explosions, close together, rocked the earth.

A fire storm instantly leapt up.

Marshall saw that the helicopter was in trouble.

It began to fall.

About 50-60 feet to Marshall's left, on a finger of land that looked like a small island in the middle of the stream, John Landis, a crouched bearded figure clutching a bullhorn, was directing the action. Marshall watched as the director with frantic gesticulations and shrill yells of "Fire! Fire!" lowered the helicopter into the scene. Just a few feet behind the shaggy movie director stood Elie Cohn, the assistant director. Immediately flanking Landis and Cohn were two special effects men: Jerry Williams who had a blanket wrapped around him to keep debris from getting into his eyes and face was to his left, and to the director's right, closest to the action, Mike Milgrom, a long-time friend of Landis, was firing what looked like a rifle.

Ordinarily, Milgrom was the show's propman. Just before the action he had completed his last job for the night, giving the little girl the prop-the barbie doll--as called for by the script; minutes before the final shot, however, Landis and the special effects chief, Paul Stewart, discovered they were short-handed, and so the propman was drafted to operate the special effects gun that fired marbles simulating bullet hits.

Taking his cue when the machine guns on the helicopter opened fire, Milgrom took aim--the marbles impacted near Vic Morrow and the kids and made it seem as if the machine guns were really strafing the water.

But suddenly the marble-gunner was grabbed by the director from behind and abruptly pulled back. John Landis ordered him to stop. Vic Morrow had stumbled, dropping the little girl into the river.

Milgrom looked up.

He screamed.

The whole set scattered.

"It's falling!"

Richard Sawyer, the set designer, 20 feet behind Landis on the same spit of sand, turned and ran and slipped and fell in the water. Jerry Williams, a potbellied bearded giant, also turned and ran, holding the blanket as a shield. George Folsey, the film's associate producer, grabbing the two parents of the children, dove into the bushes.

The huge roaring object which just a moment ago appeared to have been mounted on a pillar of light in the dark night sky sat silently on the water. Tilted sideways, it blocked the view of the Vietnam village set on the opposite shore. Vic Morrow and the kids had disappeared.

Andy House, the second assistant director, was first to discover Vic's body. Believing that Vic was unconscious, he began pulling him from the water. Then he dropped the body in shock.

Landis, after running around the chopper, was standing a few feet away in the river.

"He's dead!"

The director lost control. He cried hysterically. He waved his arms and beat the water. "Oh, shit! Oh, shit!" He was helpless and wandered aimlessly in the shallow stream.

Amidst the pandemonium, Frank Marshall, the show's executive producer, handpicked by Steven Spielberg, took command. On the side of the craft facing the smoking Vietnam village set he spotted the body of the little girl. Running to her, Marshall gathered up the crushed body, and carrying it from the river to the shore, placed it on the ground on a green furniture pad. He then returned to the water where John Landis was still walking aimlessly.

As Marshall waded John Landis back to the shore everything looked like some filmic disaster -- hazy scenes, distant cries, vague milling figures.

But it was not a movie.

It was real.

There were shouts.

The shouts were real.

"Call the police!"

"Get on the radio!"

* * *

Richard Sawyer's eyes met Marshall's. They looked at each other. Both were white with shock.

"OK. Richard, you've done enough. OK!" Marshall said. "Everything is under control. Go home."

Marshall turned to Andy House and told him not to bother with the "wrap," to leave everything where it was, to send everybody home, to make sure the film was on the truck--as Marshall left he instructed House, "You're in charge now."

Some of the crew couldn't wrap right away. With millions of dollars of camera gear lying around, the cameramen stayed until they finished taking care of their equipment.

Special effects chief Paul Stewart and his crew hurriedly worked at sorting out their mortars and cables. They wrapped up all their equipment and loaded the trucks. It took no longer than ten minutes.

Andy House – dazed, sickened – watched the powdermen drive off.

George Folsey Jr., the film's associate producer, saw Ms. Chen, the girl's mother, on hands and knees wailing hysterically, cradling the girl's limp body that Frank Marshall had placed on the furniture pad.

She flailed her arms. She sobbed. She shrieked.

"You killed my daughter."

Ms. Chen resisted fiercely when Folsey and Marshall tried to help her into a waiting car.

She struck at the driver.

"You killed my daughter."

At last the car took off with the frantic figure inside it.

The boy's father clung to a tree, crying softly, "I saw him, I saw him."

Another car took off to take away Frank Marshall, George Folsey Jr., John Landis, and the dead boy's father Dr. Daniel Le ...

1

COLD TO THE TOUCH

In the very early morning hour of Friday, July 23, 1982, the phone rang at the county sheriff's department in downtown Los Angeles. The slow pace of the graveyard shift permitted a catnap now and then, and the sound woke up the deputy sheriff, Tom Budds. Alone on duty that night, Budds had been asleep lying on his desk covered by a blanket and his head resting on a pillow.

Picking up the phone, he registered the time by the illuminated dial on the wall. It was three A.M.

"Deputy Sheriff Budds, Homicide."

He sat down at his desk, cleared a space, and while listening to the deputy from the Santa Clarita Valley station copied down in his notepad: "Movie studio (Warner Bros.), helicopter crash. Three dead. Six injured. @0230 hrs."

The helicopter had been downed by special effects explosives in the making of a movie. The injured were taken to a hospital in nearby Valencia. Three dead bodies were still at the scene. Budds took instructions on how to get to Indian Dunes. It was a good forty miles north from county sheriff's headquarters in LA's Civic Center.

Before leaving, Budds followed procedure. He notified his supervisors. He made a routine call for the arson-explosives man. He asked the Sheriffs Investigative Division for graphics people, an artist-illustrator and photographer. He would himself give the written account of the homicide scene. It would be read by detectives later in the day and then go to the district attorney.

When Budds got into his sheriffs' car and headed out of the Civic Center complex it was close to 4 A.M. At this forlorn hour there was hardly any traffic; skimming from the Hollywood onto the Ventura Freeway and into the Interstate and down the offramp at 126, he headed west into the scrub above Newhall, rough, rocky, brush-and-desert country.

The LA county sheriff enforced the law in vast, largely empty and unincorporated tracts outside the city limits, desert spaces with few people and not many homicides. If in the tail of the night Budds was called out it was to a scene of family murder, a suicide or the vehicular manslaughter caused by a drunk on a dark country road. But this time his dispatch promised something out of the ordinary. The combination of Hollywood and disaster fascinates everybody, and Budds, a native Angeleno, was not immune.

The entrance at Indian Dunes was guarded by an old man who sat in a small trailer by a tiny light. The trailer served as office for the Newhall Land & Farming Company which owned the grounds, originally a sacred Indian burial site and more recently a motorcycle parkway and movie location spot. In the dark, two female security guards were already busy sealing off the site.

The homicide man showed his badge, drove down a little way, parked the car and after getting out found himself at the edge of a narrow stream, the Santa Clara River, looking across the water to the south shore at a 90-ft.-high cliff. Along the cliffs base ran a 50-ft.-wide strip on which sat a village comprising eleven native huts. One row of four huts was at the water's edge; another seven were slightly back of the shoreline. A sampan was tied peacefully to a pier. A dam was built about 220 feet downstream from the village.

It looked an altogether peaceful little settlement in Southeast Asia. But on closer look it came as a shock to see that the huts stood charred and shattered, empty, as if the inhabitants had fled or died.

Some huts were partially burned, the nearby foliage was singed. One prominent hut at the water's edge had its floor and roof blown away. Inside that hut stood a strange-looking metal pot, the like of which Budds had never seen before. Scanning the movie-set village, he spotted several more of the heavy metal pots scattered throughout the eerie landscape. A few feet downstream another pot was standing alone, and although its shape was slightly different from the one inside the hut, he paid little attention to it at the time.

Budds was unfamiliar with the arts of illusion practiced by Hollywood filmmakers. The burnt and blackened ruin he took to be the effect of the explosions. Smoke burns showed on the face of the cliff, two distinctive bands which Budds estimated at approximately 60 and 80 feet in height. Broken scorched bamboo, mud and debris were strewn everywhere.

Opposite the village the shallow Santa Clara contained a spit of sand that looked like a small island in the current. There Budds saw the Vietnam-era Huey helicopter with machine guns and bands of empty cartridges lying on its left side. The tail assembly was submerged; the main rotor blades were shattered, bent and also in the water. The rear rotor area of the broken metal hulk showed a deep patch of burned, bubbled paint; the rear rotor blade was missing from the hulk and lying on the ground covered with black soot. Visible on the nose of the helicopter was a colorful logo showing an eagle with spread wings and extended talons and over it the legend, "FLY BY NIGHT."

The quiet scene gave no hint of having harbored a charge powerful enough to knock the massive gunship out of the sky, and then almost immediately Budds was struck by a most interesting clue. On the side of the cliff just outside the hut area he spotted a bunch of beer cans.

He picked up a can. The film people must have left not too long before his arrival. The sheriff recorded in his notebook that the beer can was still "cold to the touch."

Robert Sinclair and William Strait, two Santa Clarita Valley deputies, were on the scene when Budds arrived. They told him that during the filming the helicopter had been hovering at about 50 feet when hit by two explosions that damaged the rotor blades so that the craft went out of control with six people aboard, killing three on the ground. LA County paramedics had already picked up the body parts out of the water and collected them ashore. The deputies spelled out for Budds the names of the victims. In his notebook he wrote down the dead as Le Myca Dinh, male, oriental, 7; Chen Renee Shin Yin, female, oriental, 6; and Vic Morrow, male, white, whose age was given as 50.

In his report Budds was required to specify the location and condition of the bodies. Designed against future tampering or any external disturbance of the evidence, it put the investigator in the hideous necessity of looking at the dismembered and decapitated remains.

Sinclair and Strait led him under the cottonwood trees on the shore northeast of the sandspit. Two deputy coroners materialized at the site, and before the eyes of the sheriff's man they delicately lifted a quilt-like cover from a rubber pad on the ground.

The lifeless body of the girl was lying supine, showing blood around both ears and back of the head and chest; her left leg had snapped like a twig and the ankle was broken. A small bundle next to the girl indicated the body of the little boy. The two coroner deputies repeated their gruesome ballet of uncovering the quilt over the headless Myca. The fragile torso was also supine. Missing were the parts, the right arm and shoulder, for which Budds had already learned the paramedics dredged in vain. Myca and Renee were both dressed in Vietnamese peasant dress, black sarong-type pants and a paisley shirt with a thermal top under it.

At the foot of the rubber pads by the water's edge stood a brown plastic bag in which the paramedics had put the heads of Vic Morrow and Myca. Shaken, Budds gazed inside the bag. One head, stripped away in its entirety from below the eyeline, containing solely one eyeball, was larger than that next to it in which the small, innocent features were still intact. Both heads appeared to have been sliced clean from the neck as if by the same knife in a single chopping motion.

The paramedics had left Morrow's torso on the "island," and Budds was led back to the spit of sand.

Dawn light revealed the mound. Beneath the green-brown quilt, a few feet from the crashed gunship, lay the actor's headless trunk. The quilt was lifted. Budds noted that the trunk wore a blue plaid suit, jacket and pants, white shirt, brown socks and shoes.

2

A SCRIPT IS BORN

In the early summer of 1982 Hollywood film director John Landis finished writing a new script at his Universal Studios office in Los Angeles. There had been a problem with his initial screenplay for a new production called *Twilight Zone: The Movie*. The main character, Bill, an angry racist bigot, had been drawn too harshly. After reviewing the script with Steven Spielberg and Warner Bros. executives, Landis was persuaded that Bill required an empathetic human dimension for the audience to identify with. As he came through in the early drafts Bill was too negative; and so, in the new draft, his third, Landis thought he had solved the problem. He gave the handwritten pages in which Bill had undergone a human transformation to his secretary, Alpha Campbell, to be typed.

Alpha Campbell, in distinguished suits, fluent in French and German, looked the middle-aged patrician secretary. Slim and discreet, with a finishing-school air, speaking with a husky German accent, she was doyenne of the Hollywood script-typing pool. She had typed scripts for famous directors like Alfred Hitchcock and Clint Eastwood. Landis' script was for a single segment of the *Twilight Zone* (TZ) movie.

Like all studios, Universal kept archives where scripts were stored. Some of the bundles on the shelves ran to encyclopedic size, revision upon revision. Scripts typed by Alpha were in the archives. With some surprise, therefore, she heard Landis, upon receiving the immaculate pages, enjoin her categorically that no one was to be given a copy. In its final form the script bore on the cover the director's additional note: "Per John Landis. All existing copies of script should be thrown away."

Alpha thought the procedure irregular. The young director, in his early thirties, bearded, hyperkinetic, longhaired with raven locks and thick glasses, was a far cry from the old-time directors and scriptwriters she had known. If asked, "Are you John Landis' secretary?" her feeling for the young director was contained in her prim reply, "I'm not his secretary. I just work as his secretary."

She followed her instinct. She did not throw away all existing copies of the script. She kept several for the archives.

The script Alpha Campbell had typed was called simply the "Landis segment." The TZ movie was an unusual venture for American film makers in that it followed a format of four "minimovies," four different sections within a single movie, each with a different director and different plot and cast. But even more remarkable than the unusual format was the participation in the venture of Steven Spielberg as co-producer and director.

That Spielberg was willing to share credit with lesser directors at first caused some surprise. Among Joe Dante and George Miller, the other TZ directors, John Landis had the highest visibility next to Spielberg due to a few movies: *Kentucky Fried Movie*, a college humor movie which made some money and brought him to the attention of Universal Studios; *Animal House*, then the highest-grossing comedy movie in Hollywood history, bringing the young director wide recognition; *Blues Brothers*, a movie that was a critical and financial failure, and *American Werewolf in London*, a so-so remake of the cult classic noted primarily for the work of the special effects transformation specialist. On the Hollywood scale Landis was a grade below top-of-the-line money makers like George Lucas with *Star Wars*, or Steven Spielberg with *Jaws*. But his latest project with Spielberg suddenly put Landis in the league of Hollywood's hottest properties!

If it was a triumph, John Landis shared it with his longtime business partner, George Folsey Jr., known in the industry simply as "Folsey." Fastidious, in natty English and Italian suits, with a Palm Springs tan, Folsey was ten years older than Landis. Together they represented the current Hollywood marriage of business and creativity. Among the new generation of Hollywood film-makers the combination made practical sense. For the producer in his natty suits to be in league with the wild-locked, bearded, jeans-clad director, his junior by more than a decade, was not at all uncommon in the new Hollywood of the 80s. A similar relationship existed between Steven Spielberg and his business partner Frank Marshall. Both sets represented the new brash younger Hollywood-products of TV and advertising culture, masters of film technology, unidealistic, clever, "bottom-liners."

Like John Landis, George Folsey Jr. had experience in every facet of movie making and film production. Both men could work the cameras, edit film, and even act (Folsey was the hapless jogger on *Laugh-In* who keeps crashing into walls). Folsey was still in his early forties when he and Spielberg's partner Frank Marshall worked out the business end of the TZ production. The two teams hoped that with the movie they could revitalize a TV classic with the same success as other TV-revival motion pictures like *Star Trek: The Movie.*

The Landis segment followed the "Twilight" theme familiar to millions of Americans from the successful 60s TV series. It's about a person taken from their workaday reality into another dimension. In the Landis script this person is Bill Connor, a beer-swilling bigot who, wandering drunkenly out of a bar, steps into the "Twilight Zone" where the bigot becomes the persecuted victim – a "kike," a "nigger," and finally a "gook." As a Jew he's chased by Nazis in wartime France, then he's a black man led by hooded KKK men to a burning cross, and in the climactic episode he's an American mistaken for Viet Cong by American helicopter gunners.

The problem with Bill in the first two scripts was that he came across as an unpleasant, vicious juvenile. In Landis' first draft Bill appears in the opening scene with his friends in a cocktail lounge conducting a conversation that consists of a stream of racial slurs. He offends a black patron. He says, "Niggers in my neighborhood, kikes taking my job? Sure, sure, I'm a lucky guy." Bill was not a character but a cartoon. He sounded moronic. "Scuse me lady, you got slant eyes? Pow!"

After the second script it was clear to the Warner people involved in the TZ production that a person like Bill was too bigoted to make good box office. Landis also came to realize that his character had absolutely no redeeming value whatsoever. He had to somehow "soften up" the bigot, and so in the third script, guarded by Alpha Campbell, Landis added a couple of children in the film's finale. Bill rescues two Vietnamese children while being chased by a machinegunning Huey. He's in a Vietnamese village – it's the "Twilight Zone" –and the village is being bombed by Americans. This episode, which did not appear in the previous scripts, ends dramatically:

> Suddenly LOUD NOISE and WIND as a HUEY HELICOPTER hovers over the village. Bill stands as both kids cling to him in terror.
>
> Bill (shouts) Help us! I've got children down here.
>
> Bill waving his arms.
>
> The machine gun mounted in the copter opens fire on Bill. He grabs the kids and runs for cover.
>
> Bill (screaming) Stop it! I've got children here! Stop it! Stop!
>
> Bill clutching the kids crouches behind one of the huts. The helicopter turns on a powerful spotlight and hovers over the village sweeping it with its beam.

Bill (to kids) I'll keep you safe, kids. I promise. Nothing will hurt you. I swear to God.

The helicopter makes another pass over the village and then one of the huts EXPLODES in a spectacular fireball. One after another the buildings blow up in flames...

Finally Bill, holding a child in each arm, makes a herculean effort and runs for the shallow river.

With the village burning behind them Bill runs as best he can across the river.

* * *

With the helicopter chase scene involving Bill and the kids and an exploding village, Landis in his third draft had achieved the missing human element. This climactic scene was not scheduled to be filmed until the end of the 12th and final shooting day of the Landis segment- Wednesday night, July 21, 1982. That night had been declared crew night by Landis and Folsey because it was the "wrap," the traditional wrapping up of the shooting.

The wrap never came off that night because of delays. There was a problem with a dolly shot and problems with the children selected for the job of "softening" Bill, six-year-old Renee Chen and seven-year-old Myca Dinh Le. Mrs. Chen, the mother of Renee, grew concerned towards midnight. Together with her husband and the parents of Myca, she looked on at the mysterious business of the set. In broken English she asked Folsey, "When they start filming our two children?" He replied, "Just be patient. When the time comes, I'll let you know." Folsey then took the two sets of parents in tow to John Landis' trailer where they met Belinda Folsey, his wife, with their son and one of the son's friends. The Chens and Les were introduced to Deborah Landis, the show's costume designer and director's wife, and to Rachel, her two-month-old baby.

When the children were finally called it still took several hours before they were done. Not being professional studio children – they belonged neither to the Screen Actors Guild nor to the Screen Extras Guild – this was their first experience on a motion picture set – and they were shy because of all the novelty and strangeness. The two little amateurs were unimpressed by the gravity of the clock that ticked away production time. Giggling and smiling, they did the scene again and again, finally getting it right as the clock ticked towards dawn at 4:30 A.M.

The Landis script required night for night shooting, that is, a night scene shot not in the artificial night of a studio but in actual night-time.

The director in his drive for authenticity may have been able to create the illusion on an indoor set but would have found it impossible for his galaxy of special effects. As the children shyly smiled and giggled and other production problems piled up, the Wednesday night ran out of "night," and the production schedule was extended by an additional day.

In the director's mobile trailer about a mile from the set the children's parents had already been waiting some ten hours. Christopher Le, Myca's little brother younger by two years, was there as backup. The spectators at crew night, including the Folsey and Landis children, had gone home disappointed.

Just before the studio driver took the children and their parents home, around 5 A.M., Folsey returned to the trailer and gave the father of Myca an envelope with the names Daniel and Kim written on it; inside the envelope were five $100 bills. Mrs. Chen received an envelope with the name of Mitsui Manufacturers Bank of Beverly Hills on it; inside were also five $100 bills. There were no receipts or stubs indicating dates or hours worked. Folsey instructed the parents not to tell anyone they got paid and just say, if asked, that they were helping out a friend. Would they please allow him to bring the children back to finish the filming the following night?

After initial reluctance, the parents agreed. Myca's little brother could stay home, they wouldn't need a backup.

Folsey said, "Thanks for coming, see you tomorrow. Someone will pick you up Thursday evening."

3

NIGHT FOR NIGHT

The filming schedule was crowded on the rolled-over final night of shooting at Indian Dunes, Thursday, July 22, 1982. The four scenes remaining to be filmed included three that were key to the whole film. They comprised the second part of the Vietnam sequence. The first, partially filmed the night before, had seen Bill, after a first encounter in a snake-infested swamp with GIs mistaking him for Viet Cong, emerge injured in the Vietnamese village; there he meets for the first time the two children and the girl gives him the naked broken barbie doll. He then begins his second encounter with Americans as a helicopter appears over the cliff with a terrifying spotlight. The sequence that night ends with Vic stashing the children in a hut while alone he faces the descending helicopter. The shooting of the rest of that sequence was pushed over to Thursday.

Three shots were filmed that Thursday night. They took place at 9:30, 11:30 and the last, the biggest shot of the entire Landis segment, did not occur until 2:20 in the A.M. of the following day, July 23. The first shot that evening was the "rescue" sequence in which Bill goes back to the hut, picks up the kids one under each arm and begins his dash across the river while being chased by the Huey. The 11:30 shot saw Bill's "rage" when he realizes that the descending helicopter has not come to rescue him but to attack him as the enemy, showering him with rockets and machine gun fire. The 2:20 shot saw Vic with the kids, still under fire from above and with the village exploding behind them, complete his dash across the river by running out of the frame. In the editing room the rescue scene would be spliced onto the final shot, so that in the completed film movie audiences first saw "rage," followed by "rescue" and then the dash across the river against the backdrop of the "exploding village."

There was actually a final scene 33 to be shot that same night – the fourth scene – a flashback to an earlier Nazi chase scene in which Bill, while hiding inside a wooden shed with the kids following their escape from the helicopter, is pulled out of the Vietnam war zone, a la "Twilight Zone," by Nazi hands reaching inside the shed. It was a very brief sequence.

Because of the necessity of capturing the film's spectacular shots – both complex as well as dangerous, involving the maneuvering of a giant Huey helicopter and super realistic special effects explosions, two extra crews of cameramen had been added for the Vietnam sequences to the three already there.

Landis felt the pressure to get all the footage he needed. With the shooting schedule already forced by one day, tens of thousands of dollars rolled over with every delay. Each minute spent idly by a crew member meant a loss of production time.

Four new FSOs, fire safety officers, appeared on the set for the last day of shooting, joining two FSOs already present. The additional officers had been specifically requested by Paul Stewart, the special effects (SFX) co-ordinator on the Landis segment. Short, balding, with gold-rim glasses, Paul Stewart seemed perennially preoccupied behind a vaguely wistful smile. Stewart had 22 years' experience in the business. He was holder of the highest-level pyrotechnic-explosives license granted by the state of California, the A-card, as it was called, which allowed him to operate in the hazardous field of Hollywood special effects.

Stewart was concerned that the original two FSOs would be inadequate to control the fire fallout, and together with Landis' location manager, Dick Vane, he made a scouting trip to the Indian Dunes location before shooting started. To create the illusion of military-like explosions the movie makers planned to use fireballs ignited from oddlooking metal containers called "mortars"-thick metal-walled pot-like contraptions that come in two types: round, which gives the explosives a straight-up effect, and square, which gives a scattered dispersal effect. Whether the fireballs went straight up or fanned out was important to the visual canvas Landis wished to create on film. At the location Stewart described the destruction his combustibles would rain on the village and Vane had agreed that the size and volume of the explosives called for by the script required substantially more firefighting muscle than two FSOs could provide.

At the LA fire department, DeWitt Morgan, a seasoned observer of hundreds of incendiary movie sets, issued the fire permits for the use of SFX on movie locations. Earlier Vane had obtained from Morgan the fire permits for the Landis segment, as well as the two FSOs, retired firefighters that the studio paid $15.75 an hour to be on special effects locations. But Vane returned to the fire department after his talk with Stewart about the size of the fireball explosions expected to go off in the mock village. DeWitt Morgan agreed to send an additional four FSOs. Four of the six

FSOs were to be stationed with their tanks, hoses and water trucks above the village atop the cliff with its mesa of dry, easily inflammable brush where the danger of a summer wildfire from fireballs leaping up to 150 ft. seemed greatest. The movie makers assured Morgan that no special effects mortars would be placed inside any of the huts in the village.

A retired fireman himself, DeWitt Morgan was curious to see the kind of SFX that needed six FSOs – an almost unprecedented number for a single shooting. He traveled to Indian Dunes and attended the aborted Wednesday night shooting in the hope of being taught something. The huge gasoline explosions would be the "first really big ones" in his experience. But like the guests at crew night with whom he mingled, DeWitt Morgan went home disappointed very late that evening as the promised fireballs, due to "production difficulties," failed to materialize.

The next night, Thursday night, July 22, at 11:30 on the dot, the shooting call for the "rage scene" went out from the 1st assistant director. For the evening's second shot the voice of Elie Cohn, rich in guttural inflections of his native Hebrew, once again barked over the walkie-talkies at scattered points in the night.

"Turn 'em!"

The call for the 11:30 rage scene set in motion hundreds of hands to create the illusion. On the TZ set the two Hollywood stuntmen with combat-blackened faces, the camera operators with their assistants, gaffers, gofers, grips and best boys, the script supervisor, the set designer and the location manager, Folsey and Frank Marshall, the director and the firemen, production assistants and assistant directors – an odd and voluminous lot, including some fifty spectators, was active in and around the village scene.

There were no stars in the conventional sense. As with the big Spielberg and Lucas blockbusters of recent years, the stars were spectacular visual effects. On the Landis set the stars were the five powdermen that encompassed the SFX crew under coordinator Paul Stewart, Harry Stewart (no relation to Paul), Kevin Quibell, Jerry Williams and James Camomile. They held panels-firing boards from which emanated wires. These firing boards gave the SFX crew the awesome power to make the earth erupt, to draw fire from the skies, to fire bullets, squibs and bombs like the wrath of Armageddon.

The helicopter pilot, Dorcey Wingo, was a Vietnam veteran who had flown Hueys during the real war in Southeast Asia. Prior to the 11:30 shooting call he was downstream at the dam with his UH-1B "Huey" military-type chopper. A makeshift helipad had been built by the dam where Wingo, wearing his military uniform with the captain's bars, waited for the mock battle to begin. The dam, like the Vietnamese village, was a Hollywood creation. Several days earlier it had arisen in the narrow, shallow portion of the Santa Clara River so that on film the meager stream would appear much larger, giving the impression in the climactic scene that Bill is crossing a broad body of water.

Like the pilot waiting at the dam, a number of people involved in the production were not visible in the immediate neighborhood of the village set. Two firemen, Jack Tice and Jack Rimmer, were posted at set level. The other four – Willard Major, Francis Groat, Richard Ebentheuer and their supervisor George Hull – had gone up the cliff with the water truck and other fire-fighting equipment.

Five camera crews were assigned to this second shot of the night, which was to see Bill's "rage" (the full complement of six would be in use at 2:20). At 11:30 Michael Scott on Camera D was up on the cliff, shooting down on the village. Shooting down from the helicopter, Camera E was operated by Roger Lee Smith, the helicopter cameraman from the *Air Wolf* TV series. Smith, assisted by Randy Robinson, had to aim his lens from the hovering chopper a mere 30-40 feet above the main character as he rages on the shoreline.

Camera C in the river was operated by John Connor with his assistant Lee Redmond. Both were standing in the water behind cameras mounted on tripods. Still-cameraman Morgan Renard, in position to aim his 35-mm. lens from directly across tide village, was standing by the Chapman crane, a 13-ton truck specially built for the movie industry with a giant arm, at the end of which a platform swings cameramen into overhead positions. The Chapman crane would be used to swing Steve Lydecker, Camera 'B', over the exploding village at 2:20. The crane was not needed for the rage scene and Lydecker, instead, stood knee-deep in water with his 'B' camera opposite the village, getting the broad frontal perspective, the "master shot," which established geographically all the visual elements in the frame; the explosions, the helicopter and Vic Morrow.

Set designer Richard Sawyer stood close by looking on. Sawyer with his greensman, Jerry Cutten, had prepared for the 11:30 scene by going around straightening the "eukie" (eucalyptus) poles and the matting on the huts. Earlier at 9:30 during the first shot that evening, the rescue sequence, the helicopter propwash had introduced considerable dishevelment in the arrangement of bamboo, palm fronds and bushes.

A youthful-looking art school graduate, Richard Sawyer belonged to the set's managing elite, but ironically, in the aftermath of the crash, it was largely through recollections from marginal employees like the greensman that the set at Indian Dunes was to become characterized as having been a strange and dangerous place. From the set's nameless ranks would come a spooky tale rife with near misses and brushes and narrow escapes, prefiguring the set's final doom, as if the spell of the *Twilight Zone* story had become fact. The greensman himself had a close call. Earlier during the filming, busy clearing some foliage obstructing the angle of a shot, he was cutting into some branches with a power saw when all at once he found himself inside a cloud of sparks; it was only because someone yelled out – as it were, breaking the spell – that he stopped cutting through the sizzling cable that connected with a high-power tension line, a mere quarter-inch short of electrocuting himself!

The greensman's boss, who had drawn up the jungle settlement, was perhaps more than anyone familiar with the look of the village, and any other detail of the film's scenic background. There were two rows of huts; seven in the back row built against the cliff and four at the shoreline, prominent among which was the "drying hut." Richard Sawyer had the village sketched out by his staff of artists in a series of illustrations and storyboards of the shots, very much like a series of cartoons, up to the huts exploding. Like the other departments on the film, his own had felt the squeeze of a tight budget. With ampler funds he might have built the village not out of hardwood but out of balsa, which he would have preferred knowing that explosions were going off. He tried to cut costs in other ways by having the illustrators do their sketches and storyboards out of his own crowded North Hollywood garage. Each of the eleven different huts was illustrated to scale, and from the set designer's garage a stream of visual representations, based on ideas from the script and talks with the director, had gone out to Landis' office.

Sawyer had seen the village grow from a series of sketches to a peaceful little settlement and later that night he was to witness its fiery destruction, like George Folsey Jr., Sawyer didn't have to be on the set that night. He came to help out in view of the fact that they had only one greensman, and to share, as well, the excitement of the spectacular fireballs and the wrap party afterwards. Some time ago he had missed his first opportunity of working with Steven Spielberg on *Poltergeist* because of another commitment. He was glad that with the TZ movie the opportunity had come again, in addition to working with Spielberg's co-producer, the famous director of *Animal House.* Not being needed for the 11:30 scene, Myca and Renee remained in the director's trailer with their parents, a mile or so distant from the hubbub on the set. In the trailer Hilary Leach, a young director-trainee from the Director's Guild working closely with the 2nd assistant director, took the wet costumes from the first shot off them to dry. During the 9:30 scene both Myca and Renee were surprised when they slipped from Vic Morrow's arms as he entered the river to create the establishment shot. This prompted the inexperienced young actors to cry, thinking they had made a mistake. After John Landis reassured his hidden cargo, the children were then allowed to rest until the trainee would awaken them and help them put on their dried costumes for the final shot. The children knew Hilary Leach as the "lady with the walkie-talkie."

At 11:30 Vic Morrow waited in the Vietnamese village for the director's cue. Though in a jungle setting, he was still dressed in the blue plaid suit, white shirt, brown shoes and brown socks, the same outfit Bill wore in the cocktail lounge scene opening the segment and worn subsequently through his vicissitudes as kike, nigger, and now as gook. Bill's disheveled, weary appearance resulted from the combined labors of Virginia Kearns, the hairdresser, and the makeup artist, Melanie Levitt. But under his square-jawed profile and blocky build, Bill was recognizable as Vic Morrow who during the 60s had portrayed Sgt. Chip Saunders, the gritty unshaven tough guy with a human heart in TV's successful *Combat* series.

Morrow had been happy about getting the role in the Landis segment. As a Hollywood actor he had never risen higher than a typecast GI in a string of unmemorable black-and-white B movies, mostly made in the 50s. Television had briefly resuscitated his career with *Combat*, but when the show went off the air in 1966 the jobs became scarce. He was grateful to Landis for giving him the part and the chance for a fresh comeback. His central role promised to give him a great deal of exposure.

Nevertheless, the job proved a punishing ordeal. He was 50 years old and he suffered through the action stunts, some of which he performed himself rather than Gary McLarty, his double, a professional Hollywood stuntman. Vic Morrow was without the power of the Hollywood star. The director made the case convincingly for authenticity, and Morrow, like his movie soldiers, groused but did as he was told. He did not want to be difficult. He wanted to strike up a good rapport with the wunderkind directors. These young men with their beards and spectacles and savvy, who were children when they watched him on television, were the rising power, he surmised.

The previous 12 days of shooting had been hard on him. The first week on the set he hurt himself in an action stunt where Bill, going into another dimension, turns into a Jew hunted by Nazis: Morrow gritted his square jaw and limped for a day. Also, his gums were bothering him all week and he suffered from a skin condition that was aggravated by the wet-suit he wore in a scene where he stood in snake-infested water during the first part of the Vietnam sequence. On the final night of shooting, he appeared to be worried. Having fought many movie battles, Morrow knew something about the fiery devices used on the set to simulate the look of combat. Earlier that Thursday night he was seen pacing the fake village front. He wandered around the huts. He looked down into the murky Santa Clara. He appeared to be nervously lingering at the foot of the cliff. It was as if he felt something wasn't right.

4

THE "VIETNAMESE"

When Dan Allingham hired on with Landis, George Folsey Jr. quickly filled him in on the overriding necessity of cutting costs. As unit production manager, Allingham's job was to make the deals, hiring, renting and leasing everything in the way of crews, props and vehicles. Folsey stressed to Allingham the "tightness" of the budget; even though budgeted by Warner, they had to use the cost-cutting techniques of an "independent."

Allingham had a non-studio background; having worked in many non-union productions, mostly commercials, he was used to the more "seat of the pants" type operations, and whether it was a generator, a honey-wagon or the Chapman crane, he always got the best deal. But on the *Twilight Zone* with both Frank Marshall, the executive producer, and George Folsey Jr., Landis' associate producer, looking closely over his shoulder he felt the extra pressure to keep spending down, part of a general frantic push to bring in the picture under budget.

Shortly after coming on board he had to line up the segment's major piece of equipment. Allingham first notified Clay Wright, a well-known helicopter outfit in Long Beach, much used by the film industry. Allingham represented himself to Wright as working for Fly By Night, the name John Landis had given his company that was to produce his segment of the TZ movie. Clay Wright had just done a helicopter scene in the James Glickenhaus-directed action film, *The Exterminator*, the model for all the Vietnam/helicopter movies, including Landis' own. In fact, the helicopter stunt Wright had performed in *The Exterminator* was not only shot at the same Indian Dunes location but was nearly identical to the one planned for the Landis segment. Wright sent in his bid to Landis' Building 71 on the Universal lot. He charged $ 1200 an hour with a three-hour minimum.

Not long after seeing Wright, looking for a better deal, Allingham approached another pilot, John Gamble. But after hearing Allingham describe how the director would go about blowing up the village directly below the helicopter, Gamble warned against it and declined the offer.

Allingham next went to National Helicopter's Dick Hart. Since 1957, Hart's company had provided helicopters, pilots and helicopter SFX to many Hollywood productions, including all the *Mash* shows, *Tora Tora Tora, Funny Girl, Thunderball, King Kong, The Graduate,* and its most famous client of all, Steven Spielberg for *Close Encounters.* Hart had previously supplied Allingham with helicopter equipment for some commercials; Allingham now asked him for rates on the chopper, a movie pilot, camera mounts and a Nite-Sun, a spotlight with a powerful glare used on police helicopters. Allingham told Hart the Nite-Sun was to be used to shine a light down on Vic and the kids in the dramatic exploding village scene. Hart happened to have the same Nite-Sun Spielberg used in *Close Encounters* in the famous shot where the light shines down on Richard Dreyfuss and his car gets lifted up.

Hart came in considerably under Clay Wright at $900-an-hour with a three-hour minimum; but in the end the aircraft lease agreement Allingham signed was neither with the experienced Wright nor the seasoned Hart, but with Dorcey Wingo, a Vietnam combat pilot who was inexperienced flying on a Hollywood set but anxious to do stunt work in movies. Dorcey Wingo wanted to bring more movie work to Western Helicopter, which felt it hadn't been getting its share and had been advertising in studio magazines. Western Helicopter came in with a rock-bottom bid of $800 an hour with the same three-hour minimum, including a standard SAG (Screen Actors Guild) contract for the pilot.

The day Allingham discovered the best deal was July 14, a Wednesday, exactly one week before the dramatic scene was to be shot. He went out to Western Helicopter's maintenance yard in Rialto, 60 miles southeast of Los Angeles, and met the VP, who was also the pilot with the fitting flying man's name. Dorcey Wingo had originally gotten into the Screen Actors Guild through one of Hollywood's most famous stunt pilots, Art Scholl, who had flown one of Western's helicopters in the movie *Blue Thunder* (and was to die three years later in a mysterious and still unsolved airplane accident during the filming of *Top Gun*).

Dorcey Wingo came from Oklahoma. He was of medium height, with sharp features, brown hair and a brown droopy mustache. He still had slow laconic country ways and made his own wry comments on humanity with his hobby of drawing caricatures and cartoons. Wingo had a license for flying rotorcraft, having logged 4,400 hours, including 800 in the UH-1 series Bell aircraft, mostly in Vietnam. Currently he had been relying mainly on heavy lift operations.

Allingham inspected the Bell UH-1B and gave his approval. It was a deal. They shook on it. Wingo was happy. He saw the opportunity of breaking into Hollywood. Allingham, on his way out of Western's office, spotted a display of snazzy Ray-Ban sunglasses for sale on the counter and picked up a pair, casually promising Wingo he would take care of payment at some other time. It was perhaps the price Western had to pay for getting in the movie business, because the snazzy Ray-Bans were never paid for.

The only problem with the Western deal was that it didn't come with the Nite-Sun. Only Hart's National Helicopter had that powerful searchlight available for movie work. Allingham came back to Hart and asked him to rent out solely the Nite-Sun. For Hart there was no money in it without the rest of the package, but he relented and Allingham finally got the deal. Allingham told Hart they were going to use the Nite-Sun to create the fear of the "police state" in the film with that light shining down. But as Allingham had no experience operating the Nite-Sun, Hart offered to do the job for a fee, a job he had done on many films before. The UPM, however, decided to operate the light himself in the critical exploding village scene, even though Hart insisted that to keep the light on one point with the helicopter moving took some practice.

Dan Allingham was in his early thirties and stood about 5 ft. 4. With a longish-in-the-neck pageboy and a mustache and beard, he had the look of an early Beatle. He grew up in San Pedro where his parents ran a mom-and-pop bar & grill. He drifted into the production end of film making after hiring out as an actor on the strength of a high school play. But after a brief struggle in Chicago confronted him with the choice between "acting and eating," as he put it, he got into film production in 1978 working on a TV movie called *Ishi* by Edward and Mildred Lewis, the makers of *Reuben, Reuben,* on which he had the job of UPM (unit production manager).

Oddly enough, his presence was not required on the final night of filming. Ordinarily, it was not part of the UPM's job. But like set designer Sawyer, Allingham showed up to cut costs; in this case by operating the Nite-Sun himself.

Dick Hart would later shake his head.

"They were penny wise and pound foolish."

Just weeks before the film was scheduled to begin production, George Folsey Jr., agreeing with his creative partner in the manner of softening up Bill, set out to find the two Asian children that were to realize the director's visual imagery on the screen. Typically, a film production turns to a casting agency for the filling of parts. However, as soon as the agency used by Landis and Folsey learned that they were required to cast children in contravention of child labor law regulations it forcefully declined. As the script read, the children would have to be involved in night for night shooting on location rather than in the studio. Landis and Folsey knew that in order to avoid problems satisfying the California department of labor's stringent requirements, they would have to hire the children without a labor permit, i.e., illegally.

At that point Donna Schuman, Folsey's production coordinator, came to the rescue. Donna's husband, Harold Schuman, a psychiatrist with the county's Asian Mental Health Division, was a longstanding family friend of the Folseys. It was not at all difficult for him to find a suitable boy and girl. The boy, Myca, was the son of Dr. Daniel Le, a refugee from Vietnam, and the lovely little girl, Renee, was the daughter of Shin Yin Chen, a Chinese accountant living in Pasadena. Like most parents, the Les and Chens were flattered and excited to have their children appear in a Hollywood motion picture.

The illegal employment of Myca and Renee was kept close to the chests of Landis and Folsey but, in order to keep it secret, they had to admit Dan Allingham into the plot. As UPM he was crucial in helping the movie makers circumvent Warner's no-cash-payment policy. He would keep the business of the illegally hired children from becoming known by omitting their mention in the production's paper-work Warner normally received for each day of filming. But by the time production got under way, Landis, Folsey and Allingham were no longer alone in their knowledge of the secret. The plan to conceal Myca and Renee had widened to include Andy House, the film's 2nd assistant director.

In terms of the set's power structure Andy House belonged to the above-the-line category staff, the talent and managers, as opposed to the below-the-line employees, the craftsmen, technicians and service personnel. As 2nd AD, Andy House was, after John Landis and 1st AD Elie Cohn, in command of directing the film. He gave cast calls, he communicated between the 1st AD and UPM, he inspected much of the production paper-work and supervised the crew at the wrap at the end of the production day.

Anderson Garth House II at 35 bore the unmistakable stamp of the 60s. He was bearded, with soft features and a somewhat professorial harrowed look. He seemed too mild and diffident for the crass industry which, nevertheless, had been his first love. At the University of Southern California in 1967 he was already acting in commercials. In 1970, while a graduate student, he was working at a news station. For much of the decade he worked in TV as an assistant location manager until getting his first big break working with Spielberg on *E.T.* The TZ movie was his next step up. He was very happy with the way his career was going.

He had been hired by Allingham and patiently listened to the UPM bragging about his deal-making. He learned that Allingham had worked on a lot of non-union commercials and knew a lot about getting around unions whose scales, Allingham complained, were too high. When he got the Western Helicopter deal, he bragged to Andy House about it.

House read the script in the last week of June and called Allingham back. Since it's part of the 2nd AD's job description to work with children, if there are any, particularly in making sure their permits have been properly secured, House expressed to Allingham his concern about shooting portions of the exploding village scene with children at night. The 2nd AD was not reassured by Allingham's flat reply that he need not worry about securing the proper permits because they planned to shoot the scenes without them. House suggested that instead the scenes be shot on stage, thus avoiding the need for illegality. Allingham merely reiterated that they were going to do the shooting as the script read, on location at Indian Dunes.

House called Allingham again a day or so later, still worried by what he saw in the script of helicopters and explosives in relation to the kids. House suggested the use of doubles or dummies for the children to avoid breaking the law. He told Allingham the studio would be in big trouble if they got caught working the children without permits.

Again, Allingham made flat reply that they were going to go on and do it, as he had told House previously. During a third call from House, he elaborated that in the several cameras, especially the close-up of Vic escaping across the river with one child under each arm, "the juxtaposition of dummies could never conform to the positions that a body would take." With finality he said, "It wouldn't work."

By going along with the plan, even though he opposed it, Andy House entered a kind of "Twilight Zone" of his own. For, as much as he wished to keep clear of the sordid little plot, he became burdened by additional knowledge which further compromised him.

The ordeal of Andy House began the night of the planned illegal shot with his discovery on the set of fire-safety officer Jack Tice. Having worked with him on other motion pictures in the past, he knew Tice on a first-name basis and he also knew that Tice wore two hats.

In addition to being a fire safety officer, Tice had the long, official and cumbersome title of "studio-teacher/labor law representative." House knew that upon finding children working without a permit, illegally, at night, near explosives, directly below a low-flying helicopter, Tice would have to take drastic action. At the time of the aborted Wednesday shoot, when he first ran into Tice, House was the only person on the set to know that if the fire-safety officer discovered the director's secret he would at once assert his dual capacity and shut the set down.

Andy House immediately scribbled a note to Dan Allingham, enclosing it in the production pouch routinely transmitted to the offices at Universal Studios. Later that day he spoke with Allingham by phone about the presence on the set of Jack Tice. That same night his two superiors on the set were told. Andy House came to his immediate superior, 1st AD Elie Cohn, to inform him that he recognized in the fireman a social worker who could cause problems. Cohn then went looking for John Landis and, finding him busy in the river, related the bad news. John Landis said, "You know, we must be careful and try not to be caught."

Meanwhile, Andy House plunged more deeply into the plot by suggesting to director-trainee Hilary Leach that she help conceal the children. Hilary was in charge of escorting the kids. Her stint on the set was part of an apprenticeship system by which the Directors Guild of America regulates the supply of directors to the Hollywood studios.

The film trainee scores points by obtaining hands-on experience.

Typically, a director-trainee like Hilary Leach works on the set with a second assistant director like Andy House who, in the context of the learning experience, acts as instructor to the apprentice.

From that particular point forward the surreptitious scheme intensified and ramified and deepened further. It became a conspiracy – a plot within a plot. No longer did it merely concern getting away with working the kids illegally. With the unexpected discovery of Tice, the inevitable next step was to make sure that he would not be anywhere near Myca and Renee during the filming. Allingham told House to enlist Richard Vane, the location manager who had applied for the fire and explosives permits, to keep an eye on Tice.

* * *

By the time the cameras started rolling for Vic Morrow's rage scene, the concealment plot had so far held up. The night before, Tice had been up in the mesa area of the cliffs edge which overhung the village below;

busily spotting generators, lights, safety lines, water tanks and hose lines. Unless he wrapped himself over the cliffs edge, Tice was unable to see the actual filming of the scene in which Vic first meets the children and receives from the little girl the naked broken barbie doll. Tice never knew that children were being used that night.

On the next and final night, Dick Vane convinced Tice that the best place for him would be at a distance upriver, far from the center of the action. Throughout the evening Vane checked with Tice three times, steering him to posts that shared the common feature of blocking Tice's view of the village and river areas where the children were to be filmed, while enabling him to spot fires on top of the cliff. The plot further ensured that he did not accidentally overhear mention of the children over his walkie-talkie. Andy House instructed Hilary Leach to refer to Myca and Renee over her walkie-talkie not as children but more cryptically as the "Vietnamese."

5

"Ladies and Gentlemen, Vic Morrow!"

O n the final night of shooting the pressures of the preceding 12-day filming schedule showed markedly on director John Landis. He appeared to be under tremendous strain. It was not just the tricky fireballs, the "illegal children," the looming threat of a set shutdown by the unexpected presence of Tice, nor the enormous drain on the budget of an extra day of filming of a scene shot on location late at night – all of them elements to rattle the steeliest Hollywood temperament; it was as much the fixation on authenticity, the obsession to capture the ultra-realism of exploding rockets, the drive to give cinematic incarnation to fire and destruction that harrowed his nerves to the point where they visibly seemed to crackle like a fuse before it blows, sparking a frenzy on the set that night.

Among the crew many observed a super-charged, raven-haired Merlin pushing and pressing to the limit, working himself and others late into the night. Those who had worked in the past with different directors put John Landis in the classification "screamer." Streams of profanity and abuse poured at high pitch from the young director; he seemed wound-up, overwrought. The crew watched him parade about the set with his still photographer constantly flashing snapshots of his personal antics. Everyone was discombobulated by the director's extreme mood swings, joking one moment and viciously berating the next. Just the day before, everyone had looked on in embarrassment as he mercilessly flayed a best-boy. The best-boy, filmdom's name for an electrician's assistant, had gotten very upset at being called "chickenshit" by the director and complained to 1st AD Elie Cohn; Allingham stepped in and the best-boy and the UPM walked away together, yelling back and forth.

So, things were tense at the 11:30 cue for the rage scene. Everybody on the set felt jittery about the explosives. Though the scene was not nearly as hazardous as the upcoming exploding village at 2:20 – at 11:30 there were no children and only a few mortars while the copter would not be flying as low to the ground – still the camera crews groused about the danger. John Connor on Camera C openly questioned within the director's hearing the safety of his position in the middle of the river in close proximity to the exploding special effects. In view of everyone present, Landis screamed that if Connor was queasy he would operate the camera himself. Camera operators had a provision in their contract permitting them to refuse to do a dangerous shot; they could not be fired for it. But Hollywood is a small town. You could say no, but you wouldn't work the next day.

The rage scene called for by the script begins with Bill charging wildly toward the hovering helicopter, believing that the aircraft is there to rescue him. But with his realization that the chopper perceives him as a Viet Cong, he starts pacing back and forth with angry, frantic gestures between the shoreline and the water. Director John Landis is standing opposite the village on the island. He's wearing waders, rubber boots attached to a rubber apron which, by virtually encasing him in a protective shield, allows him to enter the river. Though out of camera-range, his position is central to the action. As director he is supreme commander on the set. From makeup, wardrobe and SFX people to the camera crews, soundmen and technicians, everybody obeys instantly the commands he screams through his electronic bullhorn and walkie-talkie.

From the small island – actually a spit of sand extending into the narrow river – the director gestures and waves his bullhorn. It's the sign for Elie Cohn and through his walkie-talkie the 1st AD transmits the director's cue to Andy House, the 2nd AD, clad in a bright orange shirt next to him.

Although the scene should take no more than a few minutes of filming, it's a tricky shot. While Vic Morrow waves his arms and paces wildly in front of the hut he's also being machine-gunned and rocketed by the hovering helicopter. The director has to position the helicopter directly above Morrow without bringing the ship too close to the special-effects explosions. He must take care not to send the giant Huey crashing into the wall of the 100-foot cliff that rises above the village ... a hundred yards distant at the helipad by the dam, the helicopter receives the command over the walkie-talkie ... it takes off...

Along with a two-man camera crew, the two stuntmen and the pilot, Dan Allingham was aboard with the Nite-Sun. They were lifted upward together with a deafening whirl of the main rotor blades. Besides operating the Nite-Sun, Allingham maintained communication directly with Landis on the ground, relaying the director's orders to the pilot and crew aboard. Allingham wanted to make sure that the director would, in Hollywood parlance, get "his shot."

Aboard the chopper Allingham told E Camera operator Roger Lee Smith what kind of airborne shot the director wanted. Landis had to have in the frame part of the helicopter and a machine gun and the light. The husky veteran *Air Wolf* copter cameraman bracketed himself in the door while gripping the 40-pound camera, being helped by his assistant Randy Robinson. Dorcey Wingo received instructions from Allingham to fly in from the east side and position the helicopter half over the water and half over the village area.

Upon lift-off Wingo rose to near the top level of the cliff, making visual contact with the small bearded figure in waders hopping and gesticulating and waving an electronic bullhorn on the ground below. From behind the controls Wingo could see the intensely lit scene on the ground with its peaceful collection of little thatched roof huts. He lowered the gunship to 40 feet. His main worry was to maneuver the craft clear from the face of the cliff.

With the helicopter in position Vic Morrow took his cue. Storming toward the shoreline he could be heard screaming frantically. He ran from the land part of the village to the water and back.

As the colossal Huey hovered, creating an enormous propwash on the water and shoreline, Wingo could see everywhere around him the wind effect of the main rotor blade. Things were being blown all over the place. He could see the wind shaking the scaffolding erected by the grips and gaffers to support the giant arc lights which made it possible to see into the village at night. Suddenly he saw one of the lights fall over.

"Well, there went a light. That's going to cost," the pilot remarked laconically in his eerily-lit cockpit to no one in particular.

Smith crawled out with his camera on the chopper skids. Leaning over perilously, he kept his lens glued on Morrow's movements below. The cues were radioed from the ground. Allingham hollered. Wingo hollered. The assistant cameraman Randy Robinson tapped the two stuntmen for their cues and Gary McLarty and Kenny Endoso at the M-60 machine guns by the doors, in torn fatigues and made-up grimy faces, opened fire. The guns flashing in the sky signaled Landis to cue Paul Stewart and his crew to hit their firing boards. The powdermen on the ground, exploding their mortars, created the incredible illusion that the chopper was actually rocketing the village.

Several mortars went off. One on land, the other in the water, almost simultaneously hurled aloft a jet of water and a huge fireball.

The blasts shook everybody aboard the copter. The fireballs made directly toward them. The first to hit the gunship came from the water mortar, a short distance from the village shoreline. The spout burst upward as if shot from a cannon. The Huey was splattered with mud and debris, drenching the cockpit windows completely. Dorcey Wingo, temporarily blinded, thought only of the cliff. Fortunately, his right window was down and, moving a little closer to the window, he managed to restore his bearings. But just as he got his fix on the cliff another mortar roared below. A fireball flashed. In the window appeared a head of flames with radiant streaming hair. It scorched the pilot's face.

The flaming head threatened to thrust inside the ship!

Stuntman McLarty became conscious of a heat so intense that he leapt from the open door inside the helicopter to avoid being burned. It looked as if the fireball was going to knock the chopper out of the sky. Wingo shouted into his walkie-talkie, "That's bullshit!" In Vietnam he had never flown through anything like fireballs. "This is bullshit! This is bullshit!" In the instant he pulled away from the blasts, he saw glowing embers circulating in a cloud of debris that seemed to envelop him.

Flying back to the helipad he muttered over and over, "This is bullshit! This is bullshit!"

A few minutes later a badly shaken copter crew returned to the ground. The first to greet Wingo as he exited from the chopper, Harry Ferguson, the helicopter mechanic, a specialist on the UH-1B, was worried about damage to the rotor blades. He said he actually saw a fireball make its way through the helicopter's vital tail rotor system. Even in combat conditions in Vietnam Wingo had never had fire in his rotor system before. Ferguson wiped the mud and water from the aircraft's windscreen. He took a quarter out of his pocket and waited for the blades to cool off. By tapping the blades with his coin, he could get a fair idea, through the type of ringing sound made by the metal, how critically they had been seared by the heat of the blasts.

Unlike the copter crew, the people on the ground could actually see how the fire and water explosions affected the gunship. The tremendous fireballs exceeded by far what anyone had expected. Even George Folsey Jr. seemed unnerved, confessing to his assistant, Cynthia Nigh, how glad he was his wife and children had stayed home. Script supervisor Kathryn Wooten who stood just behind Landis during the shooting was said to have expressed alarm that if the helicopter got any lower there might be a disaster. Virginia Kearns, the hairdresser, was shaken to the core by the frighteningly real display.

A little earlier Kearns had worked her art on Morrow's graying hair, mussing it up skillfully to give it the appearance of neglect and disarray to be expected in jungle conditions. During the filming she sat in Morrow's chair near the village. After the roll'em call she watched the actor prompt-ly run out to do the scene in which the Huey plunges out of the dark sky and hovers over Bill on the shore. She saw Vic look up at the roaring craft. Anxiously she watched the helicopter drop lower and lower.

Beneath the ship's shuddering underbelly, the old movie soldier gave a brave performance. His face, showing the marks of combat prepared with grime and grease, expressed bewilderment, fatigue and hope. When the machine guns flashed, he became obscured by a sudden tongue of fire. Through the smoke and water explosions the actor hammed it up mag-nificently – unless he was not acting – and Morrow's realistic portrayal showed authentic fear and true rage at what he believed to be mortal dan-ger to his life!

The fireballs looked astonishingly real. Virginia Kearns had her hair singed. The enormous winds from the helicopter propwash blew her jack-et into the river. She had been on lots of movie sets but had never seen anything like it...

After completing his scene Vic Morrow heard the director call out to him and at the same time invite the crew and spectators through the bull-horn to join in an ovation.

"Ladies and gentlemen, Vic Morrow!"

Everyone stood. In the loud shouting and clapping that followed there was a relief of tension. Many among the crew were amazed that the actor was doing the stunts himself.

Vic took a bow and quickly disappeared inside his trailer where he intended to rest until his next call at 2:20. For the past few days he had not felt chipper. He was tired. These young directors of the wunderkind school were awfully hard on an old soldier's bones.

The "Vietnamese" alone remained undisturbed by the excitement. Be-ing kept with their parents in concealment in Landis' trailer a mile distant out of the view of Jack Tice, they were unaware that an inferno had briefly touched Indian Dunes. Seated in the trailer they heard only the sounds of a distant thunder.

Myca and Renee dug into hamburgers brought by the "lady with the walkie-talkie."

Their next call was not until 2:20.

Before going aloft in the rage scene, Wingo had dutifully briefed the movie people about the hazards of flying low in the kind of scene he had just completed. At a meeting with John Landis and Paul Stewart minutes before the flight, the pilot had been told that there were only going to be "two grenade effects along the shoreline"; and he had been satisfied with Paul Stewart's soothing reply that there would only be a loud report – "boom!" Somebody, Wingo felt, must have changed the scene from the way the director had explained it to him. He was mad.

"This is bullshit. This can't happen," he fulminated at Allingham. "We're talking about safety, and this crap comes up!" Wingo protested that he had not been told a word about there being water in any of the explosions.

Allingham seemed to be in complete agreement. "Hey, we're going to take care of it. I know what you mean."

But Wingo testily informed the UPM that there was going to have to be some discussion about the incident, especially in view of the big shot to be filmed later that night. Allingham urged him not to worry.

"We're going to have a production meetin.... No problem.... We're going to take care of this, so this doesn't happen again."

Allingham dissuaded him from attending the production meeting; the pilot cooled down; the two cameramen, Smith and Robinson, however, wouldn't hear of it. Vocal in the desire to be in on a discussion that concerned their own safety, they prompted Wingo to turn again to Allingham with a renewed insistence on being present at the meeting.

"Dorce, please, I'm your liaison. Let me take care of it," the UPM pleaded. Charitably, Wingo assumed that Allingham didn't want him at the meeting because of fear that the excitable director might be provoked into firing him.

Allingham made his lone departure from the helipad back upstream to the canteen area where midnight "lunch" was being served. Wingo remained behind near his craft with the cameramen and stuntmen. They were muttering the bewildered, disbelieving, half-articulated phrases of people who have shared a grueling ordeal.

"Hey, this has got to get cleaned up."

The show's stunt coordinator, McLarty, seemed to be talking to himself.

"Boy, we couldn't take much more heat than that."

Wingo's face was all red – in fact, the burning sensation from the fireball that had nearly consumed him still felt like he was standing next to a hot stove. Everybody was still muttering as a truck arrived at the helipad. It took them across to the canteen at base camp upstream about a quarter-mile from the village on the other side of the river.

A few minutes ride from the helipad, the canteen served cafeteria-style food which people ate at tables set on the ground. The talk around the lunch truck was loudest at the table where Cynthia Nigh was seated. She was a pretty young gofer, a production assistant to George Folsey Jr. as well as Dan Allingham's girlfriend. Joining the group at the table, the copter crew made no bones about their gripes. The two stuntmen who'd been through the fireballs looked menacing in their torn and tattered jungle fatigues. During the shot, standing with Folsey, Cynthia had heard him voice alarm at how dangerous the scene appeared. McLarty and Endoso were now actually telling her how hairy it'd been.

The pretty gofer didn't feel like eating that night. She herself had seen the copter engulfed in flames. After listening to the copter crew, she wandered away from the canteen. She went back to the river and crossed over to the village. As she approached the huts the air became heavily saturated with gasoline. In the village she could hardly breathe. She was not wholly unfamiliar with the powdermen – one of her jobs as a production assistant was to pay them – and standing by the SFX truck while chatting amidst the fumes with some of Stewart's crew she was handed a beer from the truck.

She couldn't help but notice the stock of hard liquor inside.

While most of the set personnel took the lunch break, the youthful director stayed behind in the village with the powdermen. Technically, according to contracts between the union and the studios, any work without a break beyond 12:30 A.M. would result in pay bonuses to the crew. And though John Landis would probably have preferred getting his shot and having the film in the can, he called the lunch break because Paul Stewart, at any rate, needed time to plant fresh mortars in the village for the final blowup.

Together with Paul Stewart and Jimmy Camomile he explored the ramshackle band of bamboo-and-eukie pole structures, the front row as well as the huts in back. They discussed with one of the powdermen placing round mortars at the dam. They stopped at different places in the village, paying particular attention to the "drying hut" on the shoreline closest to where the spectacular action was planned for 2:20.

The "drying hut," near which Morrow was shortly to charge running and screaming, consisted of a four-legged structure raised above the ground, open-sided, with a thatched roof. It differed from most of the other huts in that its floor was built from bamboo poles tied together with wire and elevated about 3-4 feet from the ground. Of the eleven huts on the set, it was the most elaborate. His research taught set designer Sawyer that the "drying hut" with its raised floor was used by village dwellers in Vietnam to dry fish because it provided "maximum aeration."

Ironically, following the rage scene, while Landis and the powdermen were discussing the best ways of blowing up the village, Sawyer was busy trying to put back together again what the most recent blasts and wind effects had undone. He was surprised to see the place so badly torn apart; the air, he noted, smelled strongly of gasoline. Some of the huts were almost in tatters. They were coated with "fire fuel," a rubber cement much used by Hollywood illusion-makers to give the impression that a whole structure is on fire while what's actually burning is the glue-like coating of rubber cement. Richard Sawyer and his solitary greensman began redraping the foliage over the huts, putting the bamboo and banana plants back to rights so as to maintain the continuity for the next shot.

Meanwhile, Dorcey Wingo and the rest of the copter crew had finished their lunch. It was around 12:15 A.M. Wingo and assistant cameraman Randy Robinson, a pilot himself, decided to walk down to the north shore where the Chapman crane was situated, directly across the river from the village set. As they came around the huge white crane they saw the director standing above them on the arm.

"What the hell are you trying to do?" Wingo shouted up. "Kill us!"

Randy Robinson grumbled deliberately so he could be heard by Landis up on the arm. "Do they realize how intense that blast was!"

"That's just a warm-up for what's to come," Landis shouted back.

Smiling into his beard while the outsized bifocals on his face glittered, he looked like a mad boy genius.

"Well, you ain't seen nothing yet," the shrill voice again came down from the arm.

Though to the combat-seasoned pilot it was plainly not a joking matter, he refrained from disputing the supreme commander. Pointing directly below the crane, all he offered was a timid, "How would you like a fireball under you right now?"

The little crowd gathered around chuckled. People thought that was funny.

"Now, don't be squeamish," the director chided him for all to hear.

6

SCHLOCK!

The progenitor of the Landises was Oscar Levitsky, of Chubner, a small Jewish town near Kiev, who arrived in Chicago at the turn of the century and changed the name to Landis. He was in the horse-and-carriage trade. He did well in Chicago and had five sons and two daughters who in turn had children, one of whom, Marshall Landis, went to college and became an interior designer. Marshall Landis married Shirley Magaziner of Zanesville, Ohio, and in 1950, living in Chicago, the couple had their third child, a son, John Landis. A few years later they cut their Midwestern roots and moved to Los Angeles.

The person who remained for many years a powerful influence in the boy's life was the family strongman he called Uncle Ben, though Judge Ben Landis was in reality his great-uncle; likewise, Uncle Ben called his great-nephew "nephew." A graduate of the University of Chicago law school, Uncle Ben won fame as a federal prosecutor in Chicago by serving on the team that nailed Al Capone. He came to California in the 40s and became a successful Hollywood lawyer, representing Eddie Cantor and what were to become his nephew's favorites, the Marx Brothers. During World War II, Ben Landis even ventured into theatrical production, producing *Winged Victory* with Hollywood's future super-agent, Swifty Lazar. In the 50s Ben Landis was appointed to the bench of the Los Angeles Superior Court under Republican governor Goodwin Knight and remained until his retirement a well-known name in Los Angeles public life.

Judge Landis kept an eye on his nephew after his father died. The death of Marshall Landis at the Mayo Clinic, after successful surgery for a bleeding ulcer suddenly turned into a fatal hemorrhage, came totally unexpected. John Landis, five years old at the time, responded to the shock by withdrawing into the fantasy life provided by television. He belonged to the first generation who had never known a world without television. Walt Disney dominated the medium, but it was also the heyday of 50s TV comedy and Landis' favorites were *The Three Stooges*, *Abbott and Costello*, *The Honeymooners*; the shows that made him laugh.

The other fantasy escape was through movies with stunts and adventure. They took him away from all the nervous tension in a middle-class, fatherless home and the first time he saw a "real movie," *The Seventh Voyage of Sinbad*, was decisive for his entire subsequent life. "I was fighting those cyclopses and stuff," he was to recall many years later. "I went bananas." From his mother he received the astounding revelation that these monsters were the creatures of the director.

His mother, Shirley, remarried and John Landis and his two sisters grew up with his stepfather, Walter Levine, who worked for the City Recreation Department. Both parents worked and they lived in a modest Westwood home where the center of attention was the only son who with all his brightness and precocity was restless, very active, loud and willful, with all the early makings of a problem child. He developed a serious speech impediment, a lisp, for which he received therapy at a speech institute near UCLA. The monsters remained an obsession and they joined morbid childhood preoccupations like watching funeral processions at the veterans' cemetery near his home. The monsters were apes and werewolves, and their nervous effect on the young boy so alarmed Walter Levine that he threw out his stepson's priceless collection of *Famous Monsters* magazines.

John Landis never forgot this incident and still talks about it with his mother. It was an indelible event because he never left behind him *Sinbad*, *The Three Stooges*, Walt Disney, the fixations of his early years. *Mad* magazine was another early fixation introduced in early adolescence. All these influences gave rise to a personal drive to entertain. Soon he learned to play guitar and sang with his sister for money at parties, printing up business cards, *John and Joanie Party Perfectionists*. When his lisp was cured, in gratitude, the "party perfectionists" returned to the institute to give a free concert.

At the same time, he was reading everything he could get his hands on about movies and seeing every movie imaginable. So powerful was the illusion that he could see himself, an awkward, gangling teenager with thick glasses, as part of this glittering world. Seeing for many years every picture that ever came out mentally equipped him with a film library of stock scenes. With a phenomenal visual memory, he would draw on this when in an astonishingly short time he did achieve his dream – and became a director.

As a TV child his reading matter consisted of fantasy, mostly sci-fi; he read all of C.S. Lewis, and *Dune*, Bradbury, Heinlein and Clarke. He wanted to become something more than a Hollywood director. "He wanted to become the great American novelist," his mother recalled of this stage. But for a while, as the 60s rolled on, Shirley Levine saw her son become a part of the great upheaval of the times. She and Walter faced the crisis when in grade ten John Landis left the private school he'd been attending under questionable circumstances.

John Landis adopted the long hair and radicalism of the countercul-ture; he took part in the anti-war and anti-Nixon demonstrations; he es-poused the new causes and arguments; but he never forgot Hollywood. If he saw every movie on the radicalized UCLA campus, he was still the consummate fan who would receive a pleasure from introducing himself to Buster Keaton in Santa Monica greater than any epithet hurled against Nixon. He had dropped out of school to devote himself completely to getting into Hollywood. At age 17 the miracle took place: he got a job at a major Hollywood studio.

While John Landis would always refer to this boon as his "first big break," it was Uncle Ben, according to a story mentioned by several of the director's intimates, who landed him the job by contacting 20th Cen-tury Fox's lawyers and threatening that if they did not give his nephew a job in the mail room (where, the judge reportedly said, there were too many minorities), the studio would be facing some legal issues. Working in the studio's mail room for almost a year gave his nephew the chance to observe his movie heroes, talk to directors, wander over sets and sound stages and, by his own account, read all the mail that wasn't glued shut. He managed to meet director George Stevens and later Alfred Hitchcock. Finding himself once in an elevator with Cary Grant, he said he almost fainted. It was paradise for the consummate fan.

The directors he sought out were the action directors, the second unit directors who filmed the stunts and action scenes. He learned that An-drew Marion, who directed *King Solomon's Mines* and the chariot race for William Wyler's *Ben Hur*, was hired to direct the second unit for MGM's *Kelly's Heroes* in Yugoslavia. Having dated Marion's daughter, Landis pleaded with him for a job and, undeterred by being turned down, he lied to his mother that he did have the job and followed Marion to Europe. Marion finally gave him a job as a gofer.

On the set of *Kelly's Heroes* the young movie buff realized his dream of appearing in a movie. One of the gofer's first tasks was to find four women to don habits and do a walk-by as nuns. Landis found three girls and put on the fourth habit himself and did the walk-by, which for the first time put him in front of a Hollywood camera. Though it ended up on the cutting room floor, he was also in a scene as a soldier.

These stints sparked the fresh desire to be an actor, in addition to director and writer, and the set of *Kelly's Heroes* was a magical place where everything seemed possible. He made two friends who were to have great influence on his career. Saul Kahan, *Kelly's Heroes'* short rumpled publicist and aspiring actor, would eventually introduce John Landis to his first important Hollywood connection. Jim O'Rourke, a tall, blond, strapping Californian who was Clint Eastwood's stand-in, taught Landis the ropes of stunt work, which gave him entry to the movie set. They shared the same dream, though none more so than John Landis; his boldness and energy were overwhelming and he quickly became the "director."

Landis and O'Rourke spent a year in Almeria in southern Spain doing stunt work, mostly on German and Italian productions; according to John Landis' later recollections, there were about 70 films with names like *El Condor* or *Once Upon a Time in the West*, a movie in which he said he got killed about seven times. Once he had the chance to work with the great French stunt driver Remy Julian on a picture being shot in Rome called *The Italian Job* in which, Landis says, he stood on the Spanish Steps and got "the hell out of the way of his cars."

A few times he came closer to his acting ambition by having a few lines, as in director Paul Bartel's *Death Race 2000* just before Sylvester Stallone ran him over. He was one of the people who went out of the window in *Towering Inferno*. In *Battle for the Planet of the Apes* he was a "human slave," the victim of Aldo the Gorilla.

After that year in Europe John Landis was back living with his mother and stepdad in Westwood. He was full of complaints. In Almeria he and O'Rourke had been getting $20 a fall while a Hollywood professional got paid $1,000. Hollywood, on the other hand, was not friendly like the magical set of *Kelly's Heroes*. Career-wise, he did some second-unit work on biker pictures. He took odd jobs. When he tried to work as an assistant director, he found himself barred by union restrictions. His two friends from Almeria were back in Los Angeles, too. Kahan and O'Rourke were in the same boat and they decided to create their own employment when Saul Kahan saw a script John Landis said he had written as a joke. It was named *Schlock!* Kahan thought it was funny; O'Rourke, according to Landis, "immediately said, 'Let's make this movie,'" and so at barely twenty, Landis became something he thought he would not be till he grew up, a real director.

The film maker's first venture had as its central figure an ape played by the director himself. The ape makeup and costuming job was the work of a young transformation specialist, Rick Baker, who was to become well-known in the industry. The movie's object was to capitalize on a fad. "Our theory was – which up until maybe 1981 was sound economic theory – that all monster movies made money," Landis reasoned. But he really made *Schlock!* because he had "always been partial to apes."

While putting together the venture John Landis made his decisive Hollywood connection when Saul Kahan took him and Jim O'Rourke to the house of George Folsey Jr., Kahan's fellow-alumnus from Pomona college. George Folsey Jr., then in his early thirties, was an older and more experienced film maker, a film editor with TV shows like *Laugh-In*. He had already to his name a low-budget picture, *Glass Houses*, with Jennifer O'Neal, which he put together for $100,000 and sold to Columbia.

Folsey grew up in the movie business with the well-respected name of his father, George Folsey Sr., one of Hollywood's original film-making pioneers; noted in film annals for innovative camera techniques and as founding member of the Motion Picture Academy. One of his techniques, since made standard, involved reflective lighting on a subject. Folsey Sr. worked with stars like Lana Turner, and one of his son's most vivid memories is of going at age 11 with his mother to Elizabeth Taylor's marriage to Mickey Hilton. With pictures like *Seven Brides for Seven Brothers, Meet Me in St. Louis, Executive Suite* and *Green Dolphin Street*, George Folsey Sr. won 13 Academy nominations in an illustrious career.

George Folsey Jr. was an only child raised by parents who were old enough to be his grandparents. His mother was of Syrian extraction. They were Catholics and their son was raised in obedience to the church. Not at all a robust child, he was subject to asthma attacks and had to be careful about exerting himself. When watching Laurel and Hardy on television he laughed so hard sometimes he'd throw up his food. It was not surprising that he "bonded" to an aggressive type like John Landis with his wild locks who had done horse falls in Almeria and appeared to be fearless.

Folsey appeared to be untouched by the 60s. At the time he met Landis he drove a BMW motorcycle and had a preppyish look. He had a pleasant pretty blond wife, Belinda, herself the daughter of a Hollywood electrician. He already had two children when he met the bearded, longhaired young radical with his far-out movie ideas. When they first got to know John Landis, George and Belinda would ride into Westwood on Folsey's BMW and take their new young friend out to dinner at Mario's. John

Landis promised to bring George into the seething youth scene for which he was just a bit too old, and perhaps not robust enough.

Kahan's introduction was a success. Ignited by Landis' hyperkinetic enthusiasm, Folsey fell in with the firebrands. They needed to raise $40,000 to make *Schlock!* Folsey used his connections. Genial Jim O'Rourke, who had more faith than anyone, put the touch on people he knew. John Landis got his family to put up some money. George Folsey's father contributed his camera work. But they soon ran out of the $40,000 and in the end Judge Landis again came to the rescue. He coughed up the rest of the money for his nephew.

The judge probably didn't know that by his nephew's own account the production stories on *Schlock!* were "insane." George Folsey Jr., with his strict moral upbringing, at the time must have questioned the ethics involved in some of the shenanigans but apparently said nothing. Landis boasted to one interviewer how he solved the expense of a car stunt in *Schlock!* "So, we rented a car from a major rent-a-car company – and wrecked it! Then we said, 'We're sorry,' and let the insurance take care of it." Landis boasted about getting away with things and breaking the rules with impunity. He told the interviewer that he was only able to tell the story because the statute of limitations on the crime had expired.

Not long after they finished making *Schlock!* Jim O'Rourke was dead at 24. One morning in the shower he made an alarming discovery that turned out to be testicular cancer. He died a few months later. John Landis was a pall bearer at O'Rourke's burial, one of the many funerals that, strangely, were to haunt his life and career.

Schlock! was made for $60,000. But despite the fact that monster movies always made money, according to Folsey, *Schlock!* never turned a profit. One strange notice following its release mentioned that John Landis had won the best actor award at an unknown comedy film festival in Chamrousse, France, for his portrayal of the ape. But there were no offers and around this time when two porn movies, *Deep Throat* and *The Devil in Miss Jones,* were making fortunes, the bearded young film maker convinced the fastidious Folsey that sleazy bars up and down the California coast would want the reels of "Sex and Violence," his title for a porn movie he started to write, produce and direct. Like the car-wreck, the enterprise again skirted the edge of legality. Eventually, however, Sex and Violence came to nothing; the bright ideas of the makers of *Schlock!* were not appreciated by the people who worked with sleazy bars and after being threatened by gangster types the madcaps beat a quick retreat from the serious reality of the porn business.

For a full year following the release of *Schlock!*, no one called and Landis was unable to land another job. This slack period saw him blossom as a self-promoter. His efforts were rewarded by two breakthroughs, one in print, the other on television. He was featured as an aspiring film maker in a *Los Angeles Times* interview which noted in the 23-year-old interviewee a mixture of abrasiveness and chaos, describing the stripling movie director as "given to conversational non-sequiturs, resolutely off-beat gestures and wild-eyed generalizations." Landis' exposure on television was more noteworthy, nothing less than a spot with America's top talk show host. In the latter part of 1971, the wild-eyed young director appeared on the *Johnny Carson Show*. George Folsey Jr. watched the show live. A clip of *Schlock!* was run. Carson thought it was silly.

Around this time John Landis let it be known that he wasn't too shy to solicit a directing job; he put out the word, characteristically, "I'm actually horny to do another movie." The offer reached two brothers, Jerry and David Zucker. The Zuckers ran LA's Kentucky Fried Theatre. They caught the young film maker pushing his low-budget *Schlock!* movie on Johnny Carson and got hold of him, proposing their own idea for a movie called *Airplane*. Landis, consulting his mental film archive, suggested a derivative, a "ripoff'" of a movie with Dana Andrews called *Zero Hour*. Instead, they ended up doing bits from the Kentucky Fried Theatre, LA's well-known counterpart at Pico and Beverly to Chicago's Second City and San Francisco's Committee, a rallying point for the young satiric underground. Financed by United Artists Theater Corporation's Naify brothers, San Francisco's first film family (in the 30s the Naifys brought the candy counter to American theaters), *Kentucky Fried Movie* was made on a $600,000 budget and became a "sleeper" on the college circuit. The Zuckers eventually bought *Zero Hour* and made *Airplane,* which became a monster success.

Kentucky Fried Movie was not released until the spring of 1977. In the meantime, the director continued to live unglamorously at home with Shirley and Walter Levine. He was one of the legion pounding the Hollywood pavement who, when asked what they did, said they wrote scripts for TV and movies.

An opportunity arose in 1975 when his agent recommended him to Steven Spielberg, another young director who was in Martha's Vineyard in New York filming a movie called *Jaws*. Spielberg was at the same time planning an upcoming science fiction project being written by Michael and Julia Phillips. The story about an alien visiting from outer space was still in early development and Landis was invited to contribute his ideas. The account of this meeting Landis gave friends was that he spent a week on the Vineyard with Spielberg trading ideas for the *Close Encounters* project and that in the end Spielberg had a different concept than he did. But while ostensibly they parted with no hard feelings, Landis was chagrined to see Spielberg go ahead without him.

The episode at the Vineyard marked the beginning of their strange relationship of both contention and collaboration, of competition and admiration. Three years later, in October 1978, after scoring big with *Animal House,* John Landis revealed the depth of his pain at Spielberg's early rejection.

The 27-year-old director was in New York and staying at the Sherry Netherland for the opening night of *Animal House.* As news of the film's success poured in, Landis was described that night amidst a crowded room of friends and well-wishers as being in a "hyper state," expressing himself with "squeals, bellows and exclamations," jumping around the hotel quarters "like he had frogs in his socks." To a reporter from *Interview* magazine the newly acclaimed director expressed himself about Spielberg in a bitter vein: "And Steven Spielberg, he's a fucking baby!"

On the set of *Kentucky Fried Movie,* John Landis met a number of people who would become important in advancing his career; one in particular was to become his powerful patron inside a major studio.

Bob Weiss, the rotund producer of *Kentucky Fried Movie,* would produce one of Landis' subsequent films. Friends had earlier introduced Landis to Deborah Nadoolman, the film's costumer, a UCLA graduate with a degree in textile design who would become Mrs. John Landis three years later. But the most important person he met in terms of getting into Hollywood was the film's script girl, Kathryn "Boots" Wooten, a brainy, leggy young woman who belonged to a genteel junta of counter-culture film people.

"Boots" Wooten introduced John Landis to her boyfriend Sean Daniel, a 1973 graduate from Walt Disney's California Institute of the Arts. All were of the 60s generation with strong political activism histories and much-manifesto-ed humanitarian commitments. Daniel, nevertheless, had landed a job as an assistant production chief at Universal Studios. His relationship with Kathryn eventually broke up but he became interested in the ideas of her friend, the director of the low-budgeted *Kentucky Fried Movie.* Around that time Daniel was about to sign an important deal with John Belushi's agent, Bernie Brillstein.

Sean Daniel was part of the new young Hollywood crop, the soon-to-be-styled baby moguls, the fresh young set that in the latter 70s crowded the executive ranks of the major studios. The studios were eager to exploit a whole new comedy youth market spawned by the immensely successful *Saturday Night Live* after its first airing in 1975. A migration of talent from that show, including John Belushi, Chevy Chase and Dan Aykroyd, was headed for Hollywood. Daniel's job at Universal was to bring in the youth-oriented vehicles for the new comedy stars. His deal with Brillstein was for Belushi to star in a film produced by *National Lampoon's* Matty Simmons with co-producer Ivan Reitman. They were looking for a director and Daniel managed to sell the producers and Universal on John Landis to direct *Animal House*, in which the 27-year-old director would be paired with the 28-year-old star of *Saturday Night Live*.

Animal House, made on an investment of $2.6 million, ended up making over $100 million. Despite critical panning, it was a phenomenal success. No Hollywood comedy had ever grossed as much and the movie director was a frenetic, squealing, radical-looking film maker no one had ever heard of before. The film would remain Landis' financially most successful movie, although as an unknown he was paid barely the $60,000 minimum established by the Directors Guild of America. What it did earn him, however, was the priceless ticket into Hollywood. Universal gave him a place to work on the lot, a secretary and other support in Building 71, the so-called Universal bungalow, the cost to be charged off, as was customary, against future earnings.

Working under the strict control of producer Matty Simmons, John Landis ran a comparatively trouble-free set. One of his few run-ins was with humorist Doug Kinney, one of the three writers who created the *Animal House* script. Meeting the highly excitable director of the movie he'd written proved a "culture shock" for Harvard man Kinney. There was trouble over some questions of authorship; in the end John Landis took credit for changing much of the script, although some of these changes were hardly to the studio's liking. The studio objected to a skit in which a bunch of white college kids end up in a black night club where one of the boys turns to a sorority girl with a question about the name of her major in college, and the girl answers with a none-too-subtle allusion to a black blues singer gyrating on stage, "Primitive culture." Differences with the studio over the script were to recur in future Landis productions, and typically they concerned a comic vision based on racial stereotyping, which the studio feared would be considered offensive.

Animal House was seen as a return to the good old days before the Vietnam war and radicalism. It was a movie about college hi-jinks, frats, food fights and toga parties. It was as if Vietnam and the 60s had never happened. It reproduced the age of 50s television, *minus the censorship.* The director filled the big screen with the quick action of the tiny screen which had nurtured his most impressionable years. Following the *Saturday Night Live* formula of juvenile outrageousness, the film with its short attention span was typical of the Landis movie-making style – a series of skits like segments fitted to commercial breaks.

Certain self-indulgent characteristics to become pronounced in his later movies were already fixed in *Animal House.* The director's habit of putting himself on screen first in *Schlock!* and then in *Kentucky Fried Movie* (where he played a TV director who got thrown around a room) continued in *Animal House* in which he played a cafeteria worker during the famous food-fight scene (though he cut himself out in the end). Another whim that became habit was to use the screen for private jokes. One of these was to become his early trademark, "See you next Wednesday," an ad-line used in the old *Coming Attractions* trailers; Landis, however, got it from Kubrick's *2001: Space Odyssey,* where it was a line uttered by a computer. It appeared in *Schlock!* and *Kentucky Fried Movie* as titles on movie theaters and in *Animal House* (according to Landis, "if you know where to look").

With *Animal House,* the director also began the practice of putting family and friends in his movies or involving them in other ways. To the annoyance at times of the cameramen, Universal's Sean Daniel, who supervised production on the film, was consistently treated to a flattering salute from the director in what came to be known on the set as "Hi, Sean!" reels. Clowning before the cameras, Landis would himself appear on film and make a dedication at the end of a scene or at the beginning of one, "This is for you, Sean." At one point a reel was put together with different crew members and people, including stars Belushi and Aykroyd, chorusing, "Hi, Sean!" One of the director's cutest bits was to face the camera when something had gone wrong. "Hi, Sean, like what can I do about this?" Daniel reportedly enjoyed his friend's antics as he made it a practice to view the production's progress on a daily basis.

As a result of the success of *Animal House,* Universal's Daniel and John Landis became the staunchest friends. Daniel joined Uncle Ben as bestman at the July 1980 wedding of John Landis and Deborah Nadoolman in a small ceremony at a downtown temple. Daniel stood godfather to

Landis' first child and remained at Universal something like the godfather in terms of his friend's career.

Despite the phenomenal earnings of *Animal House,* the movie did not bring John Landis as director the sort of acclaim that was Spielberg's or Lucas's. The credit went to the producer Matty Simmons and the comedy star John Belushi (even though Belushi got only $35,000 for his role as Bluto, the immortal slob). In the end Landis was given two net points that never earned the millions it made producers Simmons and Reitman but still gave him a taste of financial success. Matty Simmons, however, nearly came to blows with Landis on the night of the movie's premiere and Simmons failed to offer him the *Animal House* sequel, *National Lampoon's Vacation* with Chevy Chase. Landis also had a falling-out with *Animal House* co-producer Ivan Reitman over their scheduled collaboration on a movie with Harold Ramis; Landis called Reitman a "hustler" because he felt cheated out of the plan for that movie.

John Landis spent the following year preparing *Incredible Shrinking Woman,* which Universal's executives offered him next. Of course, he had seen the original *Shrinking Woman* as a kid and while preparing his remake he met frequently with the proposed star, Lily Tomlin, and her inseparable assistant, Barbara Wagner. Landis involved himself deeply in figuring out how to do the most dramatic shrinking process. He was most impressed with Disney's *Darby O'Gill and the Little People,* which he screened a number of times before deciding on how to apply the light and mirror shrinking techniques from that film to his version of the *Shrinking Woman.* All that time there was no money; Folsey took a job as film editor on a film called *Freedom Road* and in the end the budget for *Shrinking Woman* Landis submitted was rejected by Universal's executives led by Daniel's boss Ned Tanen. It was too expensive. Landis was indignant about the way he had been treated and the studio gave him instead a film it put together, *Blues Brothers.*

Meanwhile, one result of the success of *Animal House* was to usher in for John Landis a period of unusually warm relations with his rival and friend, Steven Spielberg. They could meet on something like an equal footing, for Landis, too, was now big box office. Both had their offices at Universal, though Spielberg, who had just released *Close Encounters,* was indisputably the king of the lot. After *Animal House,* Spielberg showed renewed interest in Landis, socializing with his fellow director in an almost fraternal fashion that was a far cry from the frosty times at Martha's Vineyard.

Steven Spielberg during this period succumbed to the competitive spirit with a disastrous attempt at comedy. He shared Landis' enthusiasm for *Saturday Night Live* and, naturally, after Belushi's success in *Animal House*, he also wanted to do a Belushi comedy. While Landis was doing his mirror and light experiments with the little people from *Darby O'Gill*, Spielberg filmed his Belushi comedy, *1941*, a film with a WW II setting. Like George Lucas' subsequent essay into comedy with *Howard the Duck*, Spielberg's *1941* turned out a humorless bomb.

At the same time John Landis got his future wife her first job with Steven Spielberg; after looking at her credits Spielberg recruited her and under her professional name of Deborah Nadoolman she did the costumes for *1941*. Folsey and Landis visited Spielberg on the tank set at MGM for the shot where the ferris wheel runs into Pacific Ocean Park. John Landis made an acting appearance in the movie. As an adjutant to Robert Stack he played a messenger who rode around on a motorcycle with a sidecar; according to Landis, he spent a lot of time while the filming took place covered from head to foot in some kind of dirt which, Landis said, "Steven" took great delight in throwing in his face before each take. "He'd yell, 'Makeup!' and then haul back and – POW! It was like The Three Stooges on that film."

Landis thought he would get his own back by having Spielberg play a clerk in *Blues Brothers*. Deborah Nadoolman, the costumer on the film, was instructed by her soon-to-be husband to make Spielberg look like a "nerd." "What's this?" Landis says he yelled at her when he saw Spielberg turn up looking marvelous. "Why should I let him look this good?"; to which Deborah replied smartly, "Hey, remember, I work for him, too." After *1941* Spielberg kept her on while doing his next film, *Raiders of the Lost Ark*, with George Lucas.

Deborah, however, had problems on the *Raiders* set in London. She wasn't happy and made several calls to her new husband in Beverly Hills to discuss her grievances. There were rumors that she didn't get along with certain members of the crew and that in one encounter she'd walked off the set. The problem was highly personal and they never told friends but it put a fresh strain on John Landis' complex relationship with Spielberg.

When Spielberg and Lucas' *Raiders* came out in 1980 it set a new record for box office receipts. At around the same time Spielberg began working on a movie called "Night Sky" which would become *E.T.*, Hollywood's highest-grossing movie ever. Spielberg had wanted Belushi for *1941* and got him, and naturally he also wanted Landis' friend from *Schlock!*, the same young man with long hair in flowering hippie clothes, Rick Baker, who had done the ape costumes for Landis. Spielberg put Baker to experimenting with some E.T.-like dolls in a North Hollywood warehouse. At the same time, Landis had Baker in a lab on the other side of the building doing werewolf mockups for a project of his own. The competition between the two friends again led to an anomalous situation. Apparently, it was a thorn in Spielberg's side that Baker had the werewolf commitment with Landis. At any rate, he didn't like Baker's E.T.'s and not only fired him but also locked him out and closed down the werewolf lab at the other side of the building. Spielberg had new locks put on the doors and Baker had to move to another place.

Compounded by Deborah's troubles on the set of *Raiders*, John Landis, hearing about Baker's lockout from his lawyer while he was in England in the middle of shooting *An American Werewolf in London*, was reportedly very upset with "Steven."

In the summer of 1978, at the end of its third season, *Saturday Night Live* ran one of its all-time most popular shows. Hosted by Steve Martin, it featured John Belushi and Dan Aykroyd trying out a new bit, Jake and Elwood Blues, the Blues Brothers. The release of *Animal House* in the fall of '78 made Belushi a household word and in the fourth season of *Saturday Night Live* the Blues Brothers attained something like cult status. Steve Martin used the Blues Brothers for his opening act at the Universal Amphitheater in Los Angeles. The two white soul brothers with their porkpie hats, narrow ties, shades and baggy blue suits started a fresh wave of 50s nostalgia.

Belushi and Aykroyd soon recorded an album, *Briefcase Full of Blues*, which, after its release in December 1978, sold a million copies in less than a month. And before the season was out the Blues Brothers were signed up by Universal for a movie. The Blues Brothers represented an ultimate fusion of the youth market – TV through *Saturday Night Live*, rock music through the *Briefcase Full of Blues* and the new movie, a musical about two hipsters and a blues band, to be directed by John Landis. Sean Daniel was again the executive in charge of production; Landis was reportedly paid a half-million dollars.

Before Belushi became even more famous through his incarnation of Jake Blues he had already been signed along with Aykroyd for Spielberg's *1941*. John Landis had to bide his time until Spielberg finished filming Belushi before he could begin using the comedian in *Blues Brothers*. Timing was essential in a business of fleeting fads and the studio had to promise the theatre owners that they would have a Belushi release by the summer of 1980. Spielberg finally turned Belushi loose, and by August of 1979, Landis started the *Blues Brothers* production with a $16 million budget and 16-week shooting schedule designed to bring the film to completion for post-production by December 15 of that year.

The picture fell three months behind schedule and was rushed to make the summer release date. Its original $16 million budget ballooned to $28 million and it was said that thanks to George Folsey Jr.'s day-and-night work in the editing room the film got into the theaters at all in a half-way decent form. "The movie was more complicated than anyone thought," Folsey recalled, giving a small hint of the drug-related anarchy said to have overtaken the set. Among the crew on *Blues Brothers* many were aware that drug use while filming was constant, even by production people close to the director. It became the despair of Universal executives. The snorting and sniffing on the set was widely reported in the press. It was an open secret that the sunglasses worn by Elwood and Jake Blues were to disguise the drug-dilated eyes of John Belushi. Folsey's work earned him both an associate producer title on the film and recognition as a key man in the Landis organization who could be depended on to clean up the young director's mess.

But there was little Folsey could do about the star whose monster success had bred a monster appetite for cocaine that was soon to kill him. Crew members on the film who witnessed Belushi stumbling all over himself found it excruciating to watch the overweight, drug-ravaged actor. It was said that John Landis alone was able to handle the "monster" on the set. Not a few wondered at the youthful director who pushed the actor regardless, it seemed, of his pitiful condition.

Drugs were just one of the problems besetting the *Blues Brothers* film. Another was the unwieldly, almost unmanageable, sprawling 300-page script by Dan Aykroyd, the wooden Canadian who played Belushi's straight man. With scissors and paste Landis shaved the script down to a hollow story that relied almost exclusively on explosions, stunts and helicopter maneuvers to replace Aykroyd's jumble. The special effects and stunts took on even greater importance when it became clear that Belushi's charismatic humor style was lost to drugs. With *Blues Brothers*, Landis established high-risk stunts and colossal special effects as his cinematic trademark. He had discovered that with stunts you didn't need a story, or even an actor, as the dysfunctional Belushi in *Blues Brothers* had shown. After the filming the director would speak of *Blues Brothers* in terms of a comedy epic, the biggest stunt movie of all time, "bigger than

Ben Hur, bigger than *Lawrence of Arabia*," because of its extraordinary helicopter and car-crash stunts.

The stunt coordinator on the film was Hollywood veteran stuntman Gary McLarty. He had once been unconscious for eight days after a jeep accident on a TV series. McLarty had coordinated hazardous stunts for Landis before while others took the credit. Of the well-known last scene in *Animal House*, for instance, where Belushi as Bluto swings down Tarzan-style on a rope, Belushi used to boast that he performed this hazardous exploit himself, while in reality McLarty had hired a local athlete who, "suited up" as Belushi's double, performed the stunt without any recognition. For *Blues Brothers* McLarty was told to employ "the most spectacular stunts ever."

McLarty saw the job as the highlight of his life. He supervised a mammoth stunt crew of 75 daredevils whose inner core of eight of the most fearless was a kind of commando-like unit on the set. With the director's blessing they called themselves the Hollywood War Babies. In many of the film's car chases McLarty drove the bullet car with a camera mounted into a point-of-view (POV) position at speeds in excess of 100 mph. As McLarty drove as fast as he could under Chicago's famed downtown L with the cameras rolling, his fellow stuntmen crossed perilously close in front of him. One of the cameramen noted to his consternation that Landis pushed the stunt people to go "faster and faster, closer and closer."

Because of the disorganization, the *Blues Brothers* shooting was plagued by pitfalls that more often than not made the set a dangerous and unsafe place. During one of the Chicago explosion scenes in which an authentic old gas station was to be blown to bits, Cliff Wenger, a highly-experienced special effects technician, seeing that the explosion might involve an overhead power line, stopped the action – even though it infuriated the young director. In the famous chase scene filmed in the abandoned Dixon Mall in Harvey, Illinois, Landis had the art department restore the mall that had been closed for ten years; real plate glass instead of the safer special effects "candy glass" was put in store windows for the cars to shatter as they zoomed into the shops. But it wasn't merely the super-real visuals of sharp flying shards, during which one stunt girl received a slight cut; in an interview just weeks before the fatal *Twilight Zone* crash, the director recalled with satisfaction the ghastly end to which they subjected the old Dixon shopping mall, boasting that it was "all (sic) real glass, 'cause it's cheaper."

Shirley Levine, the director's mother, appeared in *Blues Brothers* as a bag lady. Her son appeared in the scene where Elwood and Jake are chased into the mall by state troopers. John Landis played a cop whose car overturns and he had one line, a characteristic, "Oh, shit!" For safety reasons, the cameramen filming many of these hair-raising car chases in the mall, being in the front-line, requested to "undercrank the cameras" so that the driving would appear faster when the film was shown at the regular 24 frames per second speed.

Landis not only turned the request down. To everyone's dismay he had the stuntmen drive even faster!

All the elements of disaster on the TZ movie were present during the shooting of *Blues Brothers*. But nothing foreshadowed more hauntingly the scenario at Indian Dunes than the young director's dealings with the helicopter shots on that film. *Blues Brothers* had many roles assigned to a helicopter. It was crucial to several complex and inherently dangerous stunts. In one scene Landis wanted to drop the Bluesmobile from a helicopter at an altitude of 1,000 feet.

For feats of this nature the Landis people needed the best in the business and the first expert they called upon was Jim Gavin, a former military pilot known as tops in his field. Since he was already committed to another job at the time Gavin suggested one of his colleagues, Ross Reynolds, who, in addition to working as a helicopter stunt pilot for the movie industry, was also the chief pilot for the LA Fire Department.

The prospect of the assignment at first intrigued Reynolds. He contacted the Landis people and over the telephone was told of the intent to drop the Bluesmobile from the helicopter. Reynolds soon gave up trying over the phone to describe the different ways it could be done and instead decided to bend the rules a little and allow the movie people entry into the electrically fenced-in security hangar where the fire department's helicopters were housed, so they could see what they were dealing with. What followed after he let Landis and his people into the facility was a four-hour harangue by the director in which Reynolds heard his ideas described as "dumb" and his suggestions repeatedly dismissed with "won't fit the script." Reynolds afterwards called the Landis people back and politely excused himself, saying he had a scheduling conflict. He suggested, however, another pilot, Carl Wickman.

Wickman was younger than Reynolds and better able to deal with the young director's "highly opinionated" style. Once in Chicago, Wickman became the overall stunt coordinator for the film's aerial shots, in particular the Bluesmobile's spectacular drop from the sky. Wickman's initial job was to clear everything with the FAA.

51

At first Landis wanted to film the opening of the scene with the helicopter carrying the Bluesmobile while the two actors dressed in Nazi uniforms were actually inside. The original plan called for beginning the car-dropping scene by flying them over the city while cameras mounted to the car filmed them in flight with Chicago below as a backdrop. After Wickman priced out the cost of doing this shot safely ($500,000) just for bringing in the special helicopter equipment, these ambitious plans were soon scrapped. Landis decided to film it the conventional way by taking a background film of the Chicago buildings from the air and projecting the images behind the actors safely seated in a mocked-up car inside a studio. It seemed to Wickman that Landis couldn't understand why he, as a pilot, wouldn't do certain things for the sake of the shot.

Following the car-dropping stunt, the helicopter's next appearance was even trickier. It occurred in the movie's big finale when National Guard troops invade downtown Chicago's Daly Plaza and there's a close-up shot of the helicopter hovering above them at a height of between 10 and 15 feet; the height referred to in helicopter-talk as "dead man's curve" because, should the engine lose power, it's a straight fall down.

On the set in Daly Plaza that day was Jim Ventrella, one of the FAA officials assigned to oversee the *Blues Brothers* filming as it related to helicopter safety. It was his first movie set and he had occasion to observe his first Hollywood director. He found a shaggy young man who impressed him as "always moving, almost hyper." Ventrella told Landis and Wickman that the stunt planned for the plaza wouldn't be safe because, he explained, in such a low hover "if the helicopter lost power the public and extras could be hurt by the landing." Landis would have to film the shot, Ventrella insisted, with the helicopter flying in behind the people.

The director appeared to understand Ventrella's warning about the low-hovering craft and, with the FAA official looking on, the shot was promptly rearranged. A few years later, when Ventrella first heard of the *Twilight Zone* crash, one of the things that came back to his mind was the Hollywood director's apparent indifference to certain realities – how he "was just looking for the best possible shot."

After *Blues Brothers* fell flat some of the aura of *Animal House* was rubbed away and *Blues Brothers* was being billed in the business as "1942," in wry reference to Spielberg's flop with *1941*. With *1941* and "1942" in quick succession, Universal decided that it couldn't afford to do comedies with these directors any longer, and as a result, Sean Daniel couldn't sell the studio on Landis' next idea, a monster movie remake called *An Amer-*

ican Werewolf in London. The studio passed on it; Polygram, a smaller independent film company, ended up financing it.

Landis decided to do the *American Werewolf* after his old friend Rick Baker had been contacted by another new young film maker, Joe Dante, to do the werewolf masks in *The Howling.* Dante was being groomed as a Spielberg protege; the lore of the business had it that Dante's early Roger Corman movie, *Piranha,* so impressed Spielberg as the "best *Jaws* ripoff" that instead of suing he hired Dante. Fifteen years before in the setting of *Kelly's Heroes* Landis had written his own script called *An American Werewolf in London,* and by letting Baker work with Dante he felt that he ran the risk of jeopardizing his own longtime goal of doing a werewolf remake.

In the deal with Polygram, Landis ended up making the film for a reasonable $8 million. But *American Werewolf,* when it came out in the summer of '81, was neither the financial disaster of *Blues Brothers* nor a financial success, though it made Rick Baker famous, winning him an Academy Award for his werewolf transformation effects. The film drew crowds but not the big crowds Polygram had hoped for.

A stagnant reputation is fatal in Hollywood and after *American Werewolf* Landis' reputation failed to rise with any new projects or announcements of new offers. Landis hired a publicist, Warren Cowan, to improve his standing in Hollywood. In short order, an LA *Herald Examiner* article appeared calling John Landis the "definitive baby mogul." The baby mogul boasted to one reporter, "People are falling all over themselves to give me money," and complained, "In Europe I'm lionized, in America the press considers me a war criminal." He portrayed himself with already inflated self–importance as a victim of the press because he was John Landis, even suggesting that Spielberg's *1941* got dumped on because "with Landis in the movie, you get bad reviews." While Folsey was flying back from London in August '81 for the Chicago preview of *American Werewolf,* he read for the first time a script called *Into the Night.* Landis liked it, but during pre-production attempts in the last months of 1981, Keith Barish, the financier, fell through; there was no other financial backing and *Into the Night* was shelved for a new project that involved the team into the early part of '82. It was a comedy chase story called *Whereabouts* and Landis was trying to get Warren Beatty for it. Apart from *Whereabouts,* Landis told people he was busy on numerous other projects. He let it be known that he also had a version of *Dick Tracy,* again with Warren Beatty as a prospective star. But in reality his file of ideas was dwindling like a rummage sale – *Topanga West, Say Uncle, Monkey King, Troop*; and when John Belushi died in March of '82 Landis was working with Aykroyd on *The Blues Brothers Meet the Zombie Queen*, a throwback to their recent failure, this time set in New Orleans with the KKK and Ton Ton Macoute as villains. At this point the telephone call from Steven Spielberg inviting him to do the *Twilight Zone* film together could not have come at a better time.

Landis' agent, Mike Marcus, brought him the deal and Landis' lawyer, Joel Behr, put it together with Spielberg and Warner. After a year of flailing about, John Landis would be doing his first picture with a major studio again.

Spielberg revived the young director's stagnant reputation, it was said, to make up for the bad blood between them since Deborah's troubles on *Raiders* and Rick Baker's lockout from the werewolf lab. In this act of reconciliation, if that's what it was, Spielberg made a very generous gesture as acknowledged in the "deal memo," movie-ese for a contract, in which Spielberg tactfully seemed to recognize John Landis' known aversion to studio control. After making *Blues Brothers* Landis had complained, "I have to take Universal's Teamsters, I have to take their electricians, I have to go by the rules." It had been structured differently, he claimed, on *Werewolf*, where he and George Folsey signed the payroll checks, "And it was a pleasure." The deal memo with his new partner in the TZ movie not only promised Landis freedom from the rules but he was also given final cut, a privilege shared by neither George Miller nor Joe Dante, the other two directors.

The four film makers involved each received $1 million on a "negative pickup" basis, where the studio provides the money in return for the finished film. The deal allowed John Landis to operate as an independent and Fly By Night, his original name for the production company, reflected an early stage of his relationship with Warner. The legal entity in the deal representing John Landis was Levitsky Productions, Inc., a "loan-out" company; that is, it lent out the services of John Landis and received compensation accordingly, while another entity, Twilight Zone Productions, an umbrella organization covering both Fly By Night and Levitsky Productions, was simply a payment channel through which Warner funded the Spielberg-Landis co-production. However, as the deal developed and Warner in the end rejected the "negative pickup" arrangement, Twilight Zone Productions eventually usurped all of the Landis organs involved in producing his segment, so that the Landis people continued to use the name Fly By Night only as a joke privy to the initiated.

The deal memo called for Landis to "write and direct the prologue, epilogue, and one segment of the picture." In exchange for these services,

Levitsky Productions would receive $150,000 – $30,000 for writing, $30,000 for producing, $90,000 for directing. Included in the deal was a 50-50 split between the two co-producers. Landis' participation thus amounted to a very generous half of ten per cent of the gross receipts of the picture escalating to 12 1/2 per cent of the gross receipts in excess of cash break even not earlier than $15,000,000 of gross receipts, and then to 15% of the gross receipts in excess of initial break-even *plus 50% of 100% of the net profit...*

Frank Marshall, Spielberg's friend and partner, and the film's executive producer, in addition to a flat $100,000 fee, would get one- half of 1% of the gross after cash break even, and 3% net profit. Writer Richard Matheson and director George Miller would also get a tiny part of the net profit, apart from their fees for writing and directing, respectively, while Joe Dante received only his fees as a director.

John Landis' final cut on his segment was subject to one condition: that he deliver the film on schedule (within six weeks after completion of principal photography) and within the approved post-production budget. The pressure to bring in the film on budget was contained in the "contingency 10%" clause of the agreement. At bottom it meant that if the director exceeded his $1 million budget by more than 10% the studio was legally entitled to take his final cut away; in other words, he could bring in his $1 million picture for $1.1 million, but no more. John Landis would receive with Spielberg credit as producer; it was further stipulated that "John shall be entitled to receive credit as writer and director of John's segment," and that the letters in his screen credit would be of equal height to Spielberg's except for the "presentation credit," which was exclusively reserved for Spielberg. However, in what could only be interpreted as another generous act by the maker of *E.T.*, Spielberg permitted Landis to put ahead of everybody else's segment a short Landis had written called "Real Scary." In the film it appeared as the opening story, a kind of prologue before the credits in which the director got Dan Aykroyd to do him a favor and appear for a minimal $10,000.

For John Landis the deal with Spielberg assumed a call to extraordinary endeavor. He wanted to make a picture that would prove his creative superiority to his co-producer and prove to Hollywood that he could do it at a lower cost. He stressed that he alone, being both writer and director, was *auteur*, pointing out that George Miller, Joe Dante and Steven Spielberg were all doing reinterpretations of old *Twilight Zone* stories. Miller's segment was called "Nightmare at 20,000 Feet," Joe Dante's was a very personal version of "It's a Good Life," and Steven Spielberg's segment was based on George Clayton Johnson's old *Twilight Zone* episode, "Kick the Can."

Landis took pride in claiming for his script the unique and original attempt to "specifically do a very particular kind of *Twilight Zone* segment." He distinguished it as "the only political or moral episode in the film," and spoke freely of his ambition to out-Spielberg Spielberg. He showed frank delight in a contest in which he would dazzle with spectacular fireballs and stunts of an astonishing realism.

And prove that Steven Spielberg was a "fucking baby."

A "nerd."

CENTURY CITY

7

GHOSTS FROM THE TWILIGHT ZONE

By 6 A.M. of Friday, July 23,1982, the set at Indian Dunes had the stricken look after a disaster. In the dawn light a few people here and there stood quietly or talking in subdued tones. Deputy Sheriff Tom Budds, among the first to arrive on the scene, consulted with the local deputies and the coroner's men he found already at the site. There were one or two studio truckdrivers and a scattering of the land company guards.

One of the new arrivals was Adnon "Don" Llorente; an investigator with the National Transportation Safety Board, he was accompanied by an official from the Federal Aviation Administration. Their number was to swell in the succeeding hours as more investigators from different state and local agencies joined them. Some would still be poking over the grounds when evening fell. Middle-aged for the most part, unflamboyant, they made a very distinct contrast to the bearded young film makers who had preceded them on the set.

Don Llorente received his first report from the sheriff's homicide man. Tom Budds filled him in on the details as far as he knew them and mentioned one unusual incident which had occurred in the hour preceding dawn. It involved a mysterious straggler doing something furtive on the bank opposite around the huts. When he shouted the figure, instead of coming forward, had just turned and fled.

Don Llorente was short, sturdily built, mild-mannered, a good listener, and enigmatic like a priest. A pilot himself, he investigated air crash scenes, seeking amidst smoking rubble and twisted wreckage for clues to the causes that brought the aircraft down. The job required steel nerves. It was often macabre. Burned torsos fell on top of Llorente during one recent investigation.

The deserted village set, next to the sluggish stream, hardly impressed the federal official as the location where a major Hollywood movie had been in progress only a few hours before his arrival. Missing were the motion picture cameras, the cannisters of film, the evidence of sound recording machines and sound tracks; even the giant Chapman crane which had held some cameramen high above the violent action was gone. The rapid departure of practically all of the film's crew left behind only the scantest evidence that six cameras, two sound crews and nearly one hundred other film technicians had just recorded on film the ghastliest scene in the history of cinema.

With the arrival of Llorente, Budds' authority on the set was ended. The federal arm outreached the local, though Budds did not yield at once. The two men differed in the object of their investigation. Llorente focused on safety conditions at the time of the crash. Budds as a homicide man looked for foul play. The dispute quickly subsided when Llorente reminded Budds that he had the power to call in federal marshals and have him thrown off the set. They agreed to collaborate and in the months to come Llorente kept his word. At crucial times when Tom Budds was bogged down, a hint from Llorente would turn him around and put him back on track, until five years later their work would culminate in a sensational Hollywood courtroom drama.

* * *

The police understanding of what had brought on the Landis segment's deadly finale was to be flawed and finally crippled due to a train of errors which Tom Budds, simply by being first on the scene, had the misfortune of setting in motion. Earlier that night in the course of his lone rounds over the abandoned set, he received a report which, in the light of later events, would turn out to have contained a startling development. A vehicle loaded with explosives was trying to get through Warner's Burbank studio gate where guards, apparently terrified to let it onto the lot, had contacted the police with an urgent plea for instruction; in the dark desert dunes the request came over Budds' radio telephone as to what they should do.

"I don't know," Budds said. "I'm not in arson."

It was not his department. He hung up and continued taking notes for his police report, having deprived the police of a priceless chance to inspect the 10-ton special effects truck before it was swept clean. By seizing the powder bombs, the police could have obtained an indication of the explosive force that gutted the movie set. The information would have been of immense consequence to its subsequent investigation. The condition of the special effects crew's equipment and of the explosives would have helped dispel the early conviction which for a considerable time was shared by Budds, Llorente and other investigators that the crash in the dunes was purely the result of an unavoidable accident. Indeed, the possibility that negligence of a criminal nature might have played a role would not occur to the authorities until long after the initial phase of the investigation was over.

The escape of the SFX truck was unfortunately not to be the last of Budds' sins in securing the evidence. Before Llorente's arrival, while still the lone authority on the scene, Budds had sent one of the drivers down the Santa Clara with the order to break the dam in the hope of finding the missing shoulder and arm of "V #2," the second victim, for which paramedics had already dredged in vain. The flimsy dam, hastily thrown up, was as quickly broken, and just as Budds had surmised when the waters fell back one of the deputy coroners found parts cut from Myca's torso in shallows a few yards from the helicopter. The coroner came and fitted the shoulder and arm to the small headless trunk laid out on the furniture pad; a tag was tied to the ear of the seven-year-old's head and Myca's diminutive remains were briefly exposed for an identification picture before being covered again by the quilt.

But by breaking the dam, Budds had inadvertently posed a threat to the integrity of the site. The broken rotor blades and mortars had already been moved. The draining Santa Clara washed away debris from the village. Slowly the accident scene was being altered and when Llorente appeared on the scene his first official act was to preserve what was left of the set. He ordered the draining of the river halted and had the arson man go out to check the site for explosives.

By now it was past eight. More and more people showed on the set. For the investigators the most interesting of these were the eyewitnesses to the crash. They appeared on the set like ghosts from the "Twilight Zone," some to wander in unannounced and unnoticed, others as if driven by an inner compulsion. The first to come to the investigators' attention was a huge person with a potbelly and wild goatee in whom Tom Budds recognized the mysterious straggler who earlier had turned and fled when he tried to hail him. His name was Jerry Williams. Williams was shortly followed by the pilot, Dorcey Wingo.

Williams described himself as an independent special effects man – "No company name." During the filming the night before he had spent most of his time close by the side of the man who was both his friend and the special effects supervisor on the show, Paul Stewart. Although unknown to the investigating deputy, only a few hours earlier Williams had been seen hustling important evidence onto the SFX trucks which exited the scene before the police arrived. But all he could tell Budds was that explosions went off, after which the helicopter went out of control.

As to the mortars exploding around the helicopter, the plan was to "fire by observing action and firing when safe," and apart from the obvious, the helicopter coming down and killing the actors, he had surprisingly little to say. Williams said he stayed on the set a while, went home, and returned with the purpose of looking for explosives still buried in the ground.

After Llorente requested Williams to help "disarm the village," the potbellied powderman teamed up with the sheriff's arson man in examining the blasted huts. While leading the arson man through the village, Williams became the first of anyone directly involved in the crash to give an account of what had happened. He told how he and two other powdermen, Jim Camomile and Harry Stewart, were charged with setting up and detonating the special effects mortars during the filming. He himself, he indicated, controlled a total of six mortars; five mortars involved with huts on the east end of the set and one mortar in the water west of the bamboo pier with the sampan, the spot closest to where the helicopter was actually knocked down. Of his own six mortars, he acknowledged firing his first five furthest from the helicopter "in a random pattern"; the sixth, located in the water west of the bamboo pier, was not fired, as he felt the helicopter was "too close to the device."

Finishing up his conversation with Williams, the arson man was joined by the two graphic artists from the sheriff's department. At Budds' direction one went out with his sketchpad to make a to-scale drawing of the location and cliff. The photographer spent much time clicking on a black metal square pot inside the "drying hut," one of the most severely damaged structures of the eleven different hutches which the art department had built for the final sequence. The square-shaped mortar in that hut had cooked up a fireball that blasted through the drying hut's bamboo floor and thatched roof, engulfing the helicopter. Another object to draw the lensman's curious attention was the rear rotor blade covered with soot that had detached from the helicopter and like the broken part of a toy was lying on the ground.

While all this activity was afoot, the pilot appeared. Tom Budds first spotted Dorcey Wingo on the bank opposite the cliff just after he and Llorente finished interrogating Jerry Williams. Wingo identified himself by his striking flying man's name and stated his connection with the crashed 87701 Bell UH-1B. Wingo said he had been taken to the hospital in Valencia and was treated for minor bruises and released.

The pilot was still wearing his Vietnam combat fatigues under a bomber jacket and baseball cap. He was agitated and eager, as if a compulsion to talk had driven him back to the dunes. He offered no objection to Llorente's suggestion that their conversation be taped. Sheriff Budds also wanted a copy of Wingo's statement, so he went back to his car and returned with his own tape recorder.

Dorcey Wingo talked into the two machines, peppering in names and movie jargon that would only become significant later. It was apparent that he felt compelled to exonerate his own part and, to a lesser extent, that of Landis and others. In the air, Wingo said, he'd been following orders from Dan Allingham, an occupant in the left front seat next to him with the job of directing the searchlight on the actors below. The pilot explained that he had to come down low and shine the light on the actors, chasing them and staying on top of them as they simulated escape from the chopper's ominous flight. The movie script called for the pilot to fly at the escapees while the village exploded. Wingo said that he maintained a 35-40 ft. hover. He stabilized the craft at that altitude when he heard the order.

"Get lower! Get Lower!"

He confessed, "And I did," continuing, "And, uh, of course I knew nothing about the locations of the explosives." The first, second and third explosions went off without causing the pilot undue alarm. Then came what Wingo called a "real-humdinger," the fourth, and as the explosions continued, the pilot described to the cop and the NTSB man the horrifying instant every pilot dreads – when the craft, refusing to respond to control, obeys the law of gravity. That fourth explosion, the "humdinger," was a "large fireball," after which, in Wingo's laconic phrase, "things began to deteriorate rapidly." The ship began to turn to the left, it was dark, there were more fireballs, but as best as he could remember it was a 360-degree spiral nose-down.

"Everything was just a fairly fast blow," he recalled of the impact. "It was fairly hard, and at that point it was a mad scramble to get out."

In that panicked exit he remembered unbuckling and "diving," and probably stepping on Dan Allingham who was trying to get out through the skylight. He remembered running in confusion until, already halfway to the shore, he heard the dry, hacking noise of the Huey's bare spinning shaft that would grind down into sparks and eventually blow up the helicopter.

He ran back, he said, and "finally got the darned thing turned off."

While being questioned by Llorente the pilot described an earlier flight before the crash where a particular "gas bomb" was set off so close that he and the cameramen, as did some people farther away, felt the radiation of heat on their faces. Wingo was referring to the rage scene.

"When you got this blast," Llorente asked, "did you discuss it any further with the special effects men?"

Wingo replied that in talking about it with Dan Allingham he had mentioned his concern about debris interfering with the tail rotor and that before the final shot he, Wingo, went out to make sure that everything was well tied down. He pulled and tugged on the cardboard and straw material on the huts and discovered, Wingo concluded, that everything was nailed or stapled down.

"I was satisfied with that because I knew we were going to be down pretty low, but I had no idea that someone would be setting off blasts directly underneath the aircraft or directly underneath the rotor system. This had not been done in earlier runs."

Just a few hours separated the speaker from the fatal blasts he was describing, and, like a movie track, the memories of the chaotic aftermath overlaid with grisly sounds and images the quiet setting to which he had returned. They took the speaker back to the unearthly wail in the night, making again vivid that moment when looking across the river he saw dimly through the trees behind the Chapman crane the figure of the little girl's mother – "like somebody just lost their marbles" – being restrained by some other dim figure. Over this same placid shoreline on which the pilot stood facing his interrogators in the bright light of a new day, Steve Lydecker, the master-camera shot, had come loping in the darkness to address consoling words."Don't worry, Dorce. I got it all on film. Don't worry about a thing," just before Wingo made his bewildered way to the ambulance that was to take him to the hospital.

But in his account to Budds and Llorente the pilot made no mention of these instances that were still fresh in his mind. He confined himself to technical details. Cautious, circumspect, he didn't say anything about the surprise water blasts in the rage scene blinding him to the point where it nearly caused him to collide with the cliff, and he passed over the incident afterwards that had seen him bow to Allingham's request not to attend a critical production meeting; nor when, motioning to the empty beer cans scattered around the flank of the broken-down helicopter, Budds asked whether any special effects people had been drinking, did the pilot reveal anything about his numerous encounters with alcohol on the set. Wingo merely replied that he had seen only one beer can, suggesting that what Budds saw might have been left by bikers who used the park; he and his crew and anyone working around them, he insisted, only had soft drinks.

The pilot was similarly mild in his description of the manic character who, with his vituperative crew-bashing, would soon come to be regarded as the chief cause of the disaster. "We have the normal domineering genius aspect in the director," Wingo told Budds in reply to the officer's question concerning any personality conflicts on the set. "That is not uncommon at all," he indicated, "the man who pushes for what he wants, not uncommon in any movie-making process like this, but a man who would touch you and talk to you and console you. And I feel," he added, "that I had confidence in his ability to produce this film safely."

Wingo's evasiveness in his initial encounter with investigators had the probably unintended effect of putting him among the early makers of the cover-up. The speaker in the combat jacket and baseball cap kept his innermost feelings in a box with a tight lid. Only the coming months and years would expose the contents of that box as through subsequent interviews and confessions Wingo gradually lifted the lid. And when, six months hence in January 1983, investigators were to get their first glimpse of the contents it would enable them to look back and appreciate the pilot's dilemma during that first talk they had with him in Indian Dunes. For Wingo at the time had felt terribly isolated and alone. Over the years this feeling of abandonment would lead him to pry steadily at the lid of the box, revealing more of his true feelings with each retelling of the story.

Between the time he crashed and his reappearance at the site some six hours later the pilot had seen very little of the people on the set whose assurances of "safety first" had persuaded him to fly in the final scene. After his arrival at the hospital Wingo had no contact with Landis and Allingham, and the pilot learned only after talking to one of his own crewmen, a fuel truck driver who had followed him to the Henry Mayo Hospital, that Landis was not among the injured; the driver told Wingo that he saw the director weeping while talking on one of the hospital pay phones to "someone important."

The sense of abandonment, already apparent while Wingo delivered his cautious account to the investigators' tape recorders, would deepen and turn into frustration and anger in the succeeding days. That very weekend, the pilot tried to call Dan Allingham. It was only to say something innocuous like, "Don't you feel good to be alive?" Allingham's girlfriend answered the phone and promised that Dan would return the call – but Dan never did.

8

FLY BY NIGHT

News of the tragedy out at Indian Dunes had an immediate and profound impact on the studio which, as the film's financier, could be held ultimately accountable. In the succeeding months and years Warner Bros. would be preoccupied with the legal ramifications. In the process the studio would become intimately acquainted with the names of Tom Budds and Don Llorente. But mere hours after the crash the most imminent danger to the studio came from a small-time state bureaucrat who had already let it be known that the labor commissioner's office had no record of a permit that allowed Myca and Renee to work on a movie set. Among the representatives of the half-dozen federal, state and local agencies which swarmed the *Twilight Zone* set by mid-morning was the labor commissioner's man, Charlie Hughes.

Charlie's slight, rumpled, ineffectual appearance masked his power as a child employment investigator, whose findings would have the most immediate impact on Warner Studios in Burbank. Charlie Hughes' office, upon determination of a certain set of facts, had the power to revoke Warner's state-controlled labor license to use kids in motion pictures and television.

Kids were used in almost all films, television and advertising. No film company could stay in business in California with its supply of children cut off.

* * *

The big Burbank studio leased the site at Indian Dunes from the Newhall Land & Farming Company. Weldon Sipes, the land company's manager at Indian Dunes, was himself a former film locations man. Not long after the helicopter crash, he appeared on the deserted set, acting, in effect, at that early hour as the studio representative. Sipes posted guards and kept an eye on the property until John Silvia, Warner's own safety man arrived about 9 A.M.

Silvia's job at the Warner lot was to identify hazards on the set, such as heavy machines, explosives, dangerous animals and stunts. Typically, working from a script, Silvia marked the dangerous parts so that the special effects people or the assistant director might know the kind of animal or stunt the insurance people were likely to object to. Silvia had come out from Boston several years before with the dream of becoming a Hollywood writer, producer and director. Sneakered and bearded, he was in the current mode set by the new successful Hollywood producers and directors like Spielberg and Landis.

At mid-morning Silvia was relieved by Jim Miller, one of Warner's top studio lawyers. A vice president in studio business affairs, Miller usually worked behind the scenes in Warner's corporate complex. Learning of the accident as early as 3 A.M., he had called Warner's VP of production, Ed Morey. At Indian Dunes, Miller issued the statement that Warner had no explanation for the alleged child labor violations and did not know who hired the children or how they got paid. By then, more studio people had arrived on the set. Dick Vane, who had been on the set all night and had helped shield the children from Jack Tice, the fireman/welfare worker, went around politely soliciting the investigators for their business cards.

Meanwhile, Frank Marshall, Spielberg's junior business partner and the film's executive producer, was being quietly represented by a young man from the Spielberg organization named Dennis Jones; like Dick Vane, Jones had worked on Spielberg's E.T. and Poltergeist. Each faction within the studio compact appeared to have his representative in the dunes and John Landis had Saul Kahan from the early circle of young cutups bitten by the movie bug. Short, grown pudgy, balding, still in rumpled college clothes, Kahan never had the acting career he aspired to, nor anything like the success of his friend from Kelly's Heroes. Like Silvia, he had settled on Hollywood's fringes. He worked under Rob Friedman, Warner's chief publicist at the Burbank studio.

Kahan spent much of the early morning of the disaster on the telephone. Alpha Campbell, John Landis' personal secretary, was the subject of an early call he placed to Friedman, urging that she be kept quiet over at Universal Studios. Minutes later Kahan personally called Alpha. She was expeditiously told to get hold of the black-and-white photographs taken at the crash site by the film's still photographer, Morgan Renard. They were wanted by Frank Marshall.

Some reporters, like the wire service boys who never sleep, had been waiting at Indian Dunes to be admitted to the set since shortly after the report of the crash came over the police radio band. Blocked at the Cyclone gate by the old man in the trailer, their early outpost had grown to a media mob.

Reporters enjoy paradoxes and in the succeeding days they would be quick to note *Twilight Zone* parallels in the young director known for his loud liberal notions who worked children in dangerous situations without a permit; in the actor killed while making a Hollywood comeback in his old role as a movie soldier; or in the Vietnamese boy born in Saigon three days before its fall and his death in California seven years later in a Hollywood-created Vietnam War battle. As well, a historic precedent gave a sensationalist twist to the story: normally actors didn't die on Hollywood sets because stunt people took the fall. Stunt people sometimes died. Special effects people were sometimes blown up by their own devices. It went with the profession. It went on in the industry. But now for the first time in Hollywood history a Hollywood actor had been killed on a Hollywood movie set.

The newsmen gathered at Indian Dunes would not learn the most salient facts until considerably later. For hours they were kept at the confines of the set. Studio guards brought in by John Silvia kept most of the milling crowd at bay. Location manager Dick Vane personally inspected the places where he thought news people might try and crash the scene in order to take pictures, and when one TV crew actually jumped the fence and got close to the crash site, Vane and his men radioed other security people: "Stop the trespassers."

As the morning wore on two news helicopters raised a clamor in the sky. In the scrub stood a glittering caravan bristling with antennae, news vans and jeeps dusty from beating up the dunes. The throng, tired of lounging in the dust and heat, felt relieved when the long-awaited publicist arrived at noon. But hopes of seeing the set were dashed for the time. It was past two o'clock that Friday afternoon when Landis' close personal friend finally permitted the gate to be unbarred. Kahan led the news corps to the gutted scene dominated by the large green crippled hulk of the helicopter.

Someone from the studio had come earlier and erased the legend from the helicopter nose cone. Where the FLY BY NIGHT legend had been boldly painted, someone had scrubbed the water-soluble paint away, leaving only an empty space. The eagle was still there, as if dug in the cone by its talons, but the words had vanished, never to be heard from again, never to be mentioned in all the years of testimony and trial, as if literally flown away by night. The curious press crowd had no reason to suspect that the bare metal strip over the eagle was the erasure of a joke which apparently in someone's mind had turned embarrassing. The erasure of the self-deprecating logo was one of the very first acts in a cover-up that persisted for 5 years.

Among the movie trade papers and LA dailies it was the custom to send young cubs to fast-breaking Hollywood stories. Not yet grown cynical and slow like the old war horses, they were quick off the mark and enthusiastic. At Indian Dunes the youngest reporter was Andy Furillo whose name had a certain ring in Los Angeles in connection with his father Bud Furillo, a well-known sports columnist, and his uncle, Carl Furillo, who played for the Brooklyn and LA Dodgers. Andy was starting his journalistic career at the *Los Angeles Herald Examiner*. On account of his flaming red thatch he was to become known during the protracted TZ trial as the "carrot-top cub" (to which he would invariably respond, "a carrot top is green not red"). The TZ disaster was Furillo's first big Hollywood story and when Kahan admitted him to the set he had not the least idea that the story would involve him for the next five years.

The most interesting knowledge Furillo obtained on the set was the name of Steven Spielberg whom Kahan mentioned while describing the format of the film. Furillo's interest was understandable in light of the fact that in the summer of 1982, due to the almost simultaneous release of two Spielberg movies, *E.T.* and *Poltergeist*, everybody knew the name of the young director who looked like an optometrist in a suburban shopping mall while turning out movies that made more money than any in Hollywood history. *Variety* ran a "Spielbergmania" headline three days before the deaths on the TZ set. In terms of news value, the name John Landis meant less than that of the new king of Hollywood. Andy was eager to follow up the Spielberg angle when he got back to the office.

But back downtown the cub quickly reconciled himself to the realization that getting hold of Steven Spielberg would probably require an executive order from the White House. He learned from Warner publicist Friedman that John Landis, after being taken to the Henry Mayo Hospital in Valencia, had left for an unknown destination. After a few more fruitless calls to the studios Andy wrote the story.

The story in the next day's *Herald* edition identified the accident as having occurred during the filming of a new "Steven Spielberg film." The other dailies, too, for about a week continued to identify the crash as having occurred on a segment directed by John Landis for a "Steven Spielberg film." But something curious happened without anyone, not even Andy Furillo, being aware of it at the time. They stopped calling the movie "a Steven Spielberg film." And as Steven Spielberg suddenly ceased being associated with the film and the fatal crash, his co-producer became more prominently identified. The new "Steven Spielberg film" was now linked exclusively with John Landis.

It was his baby.

9

THE UNIVERSAL BUNGALOW

Donna Schuman was married to Dr. Harold (Hal) Schuman, a psychiatrist employed by LA County. At one time Donna was an aspiring starlet. She also seriously wrote stories and scripts. Like everybody in Hollywood she waited for the big break. In the meantime, she drifted into TV production. She had no movie experience apart from one film she worked on, on which George Folsey, Jr. was editor. She was bright, efficient, a hard worker; she called herself "Flash" – and with these qualifications in mind, rather than her film experience, George Folsey Jr. called her up in the spring of 1982 to ask her to work on the TZ movie.

Donna felt obliged to point out that there was much she didn't know. But Folsey said that he and Allingham didn't think that would be a problem.

Donna had worked for John Landis previously in a film which never got beyond the pre-production stages. Folsey promised that the new movie would be short and simple and that because John didn't want to spend money on offices or on a move to Warner the picture would be done out of a bungalow on the Universal lot, Building 71; a single-story structure that looked more like an army barracks than a Hollywood facility. It was going to be a little cramped, Folsey admitted. They were not going to hire a production coordinator or 1st AD, either. The director felt that she and Dan Allingham could handle things if she worked closely with him and was given plenty of backup people. In film where everything seems to have the word "production" before it – production reports, production schedule, production charts – Donna Schuman hired on as production coordinator on a salary at less than the union rate.

On arrival at the Universal bungalow on her first day of work she entered a jerry-built maze of tiny hallways connecting some four or five offices. There were *Schlock!* and *Werewolf* posters everywhere on the walls. But soon she got the feeling of being in the wrong office. When George Folsey arrived she pointedly mentioned that things were not quite as she had expected. Folsey had a soothing rejoinder. The lines of communication had broken down. He promised to take care of it.

"While he was taking care of it," Donna recalled, "the office ran amok for a few days."

The subsequent weeks brought no improvement. The chaos increased as everything was being compressed into a very tight schedule. The senior staff members coordinated most of the administrative, logistical, technical and operational needs of the Landis segment. The bungalow was headquarters for the daily shooting schedule, graphics and all photography needs, for set design and construction, scheduling, location decisions and contracting use of aircraft and pyrotechnics, as well as for dealings with civil authorities. The office was always crawling with people. Donna worked with Dan Allingham. Sometimes seventeen people, including herself, were waiting in the tiny hallway outside Allingham's office.

She worked in Allingham's office for approximately one week until the 2nd AD, Anderson House and Hilary Leach, the DGA trainee, arrived. Under conditions in this office which Donna described as ranging "from silly to quite serious" she had to vacate her office and let Andy and Hilary have that space. Folsey helped her search for an appropriate place to work and at last offered his own desk and chair; he completed his work off the end of his desk. But about the pandemonium Folsey could do very little. Donna complained to him daily about the incredible disorganization in the office. Invariably, she was told that he would talk to the director about it. But nothing changed for the good reason that much of the chaos, the jarring tone, an atmosphere often close to hysteria that sent little waves of frenzy beating through the Universal bungalow, emanated from the director's personality.

Donna watched in amazement as Landis tore around the office like a hyperactive adolescent, awkward, loud, boisterous, with a piercing falsetto. One of his favorite "schticks" was a loping gait a la Groucho Marx, yelling something buffoonish, with hands held high. John Landis, Donna discovered, was a tireless joker, and as her husband noted, his jokes usually had some anti-ethnic orientation.

The universal confusion that reigned in the bungalow was due to the director's striving to cut costs all along the line, the result of the way Warner had structured the film budget. Andy House was shocked when he saw the state of the office. He told Donna he found it hard to believe that at the stage of production he had been brought in, still no shooting schedule had been prepared. As a day-to-day description of the sets, scenes, props, special effects, makeup and cast requirements, the shooting schedule is the blueprint for the filming action. And at an unusually late point in the production it fell to Andy House, with the assistance of DGA apprentice Hilary Leach, to prepare this vital document.

It was with patch up, stopgap and even illicit measures that people in the bungalow tried to cope with mounting confusion. But everything was already too late once the production got rolling within its tight 12-day schedule. Even George Folsey, realizing that it was "just too much" for Dan, in the end was forced by Warner's administrators to hire the 1st AD that they had hoped to do without. He was Elie Cohn, an Israeli film maker who had met John Landis before. More gofers were hired. But at that point Landis was so far into the production that the chaos increased proportionately. Every day packages containing call sheets, which tell what the production is doing from day to day, were spread across Folsey's couch for lack of any other place to put them.

The film's SFX explosives were a sensitive issue around the office. In the final days of shooting, it was on everybody's mind. Even Dan Allingham complained to his production coordinator that the director was spending a lot of money on explosives. Donna Schuman got the feeling that Landis wanted to do "something bigger and better than Spielberg." Someone close to the director even told her that Landis was "a madman around Spielberg." Everyone in the office knew about the illegal hiring of the kids.

And when there was talk in the bungalow of stunts and explosives a kind of silence fell, because everyone in the office was involved in the dirty little secret. The person most deeply affected was Donna Schuman. It was common knowledge in the business that you couldn't work kids under 18 at night. But she was pulling for the team, caught up in the spirit which Landis with his frenzy sparked about him, of pushing yourself and going beyond the call.

* * *

About 4:30 A.M. Friday, July 23, Donna Schuman was awakened by a call from George Folsey Jr. He was at the Henry Mayo Hospital in Valencia.

"You can't believe it," she heard him say. "The worst possible thing has happened. Vic and the kids are dead."

Donna remained silent.

"A helicopter fell on them."

Donna cried out what in God's name they were doing underneath the helicopter. Folsey said he didn't know. He said the helicopter "was way,

way overdoing some stuff," the pilot lost control, "and the helicopter just started careening around and fell on Vic and the kids."

Folsey asked if she wanted to go with him to tell Mrs. Le, Myca's mother.

"I don't want to," Donna said.

She broke down. She was inconsolable. Her husband was aghast.

About an hour later the phone rang again. A slurry voice, thick with sedative, announced itself as Cindy Nigh, Allingham's girlfriend and Folsey's production assistant with whom Donna was friendly. Cindy was on Valium. Her voice sounded slow and fragmented. She talked about her fear earlier on the set when the explosion hit. It was so big that even though she had been standing on a hill with some other people far away the explosion headed toward them and she ran for her life.

The Valium made her drowsy. She said Dan Allingham had asked her if she wanted to go up in the helicopter for the final scene.

"Are you crazy?" Donna heard Cindy drawl through her thickly sedated tongue.

"You guys almost got blown up in the last explosion. I'm not going up there..."

* * *

Vic Morrow reminded Alpha Campbell of the Hollywood she had known – and which was past and gone. In the new Hollywood, Alpha found that few people thought of a secretary as a human being. John Landis, when meeting famous stars in the office, would omit introducing her. But when Vic Morrow introduced himself his handshake was strong and real. He was polite and respectful and when Alpha was kind to Trudy, his young model girlfriend from Britain, he called back twice to thank her. Alpha thought Trudy was good for the middle-aged actor who was coming out of some very bad years. In a letter Alpha wrote Trudy a few months after Vic's death she called Vic a "real Mensch," and as Trudy in England might not know Hollywood-Yiddish argot Alpha wrote in brackets, ("human being").

Alpha Campbell had spoken to Vic Morrow on the night of his death and upon learning the shocking news she could only think, "If only he had called in sick." For Vic a few hours before the final scene had called her up to complain about a tooth problem, grousing that the pain was unendurable. Feeling sorry for Vic when she heard him accuse his tooth in that gruff, gritty way of Sgt. Chip Saunders, she had even suggested, "Can't you just stay home and take care of yourself?" Apparently, Alpha assumed, Dan Allingham got the pain killer to him, for at 2:20 A.M. Vic took his place under the helicopter with a child under each arm as the scene called for.

Alpha Campbell was already in the office when Donna Schuman reported for work at the bungalow that Friday morning at 9:00 A.M. Both had a cry. For the rest of the day Alpha hung in like a trooper, with all the newspapers and television stations, good and bad callers, as she put it, trying to get something out of her. It had begun the moment she arrived and sat down at her desk. David Sargent called from NBC News. Then John Landis called.

Everyone was to "freeze" in place, talk to no one, nothing goes in or out of the office, Alpha alone to answer calls, take names and numbers only, send nothing over to Warner and say nothing to anyone.

A siege mentality gripped the office. Alpha "froze," rooted to her telephone, automatically refusing people or being non-committal.

One of her very earliest callers was Lucy Fisher, the young president of Warner's creative division who was also one of Hollywood's rising female powers. Lucy Fisher spoke to Alpha from New York and called again a few hours later to say that she was flying home that night. A lot of the calls were from media – *People* magazine, *Entertainment Tonight*, the *Herald Examiner*, *Hollywood Reporter*; NBC News called again. Alpha fielded questions from Landis' father and stepfather and his mother-in-law, Mrs. Nadoolman. Carole Serling, the widow of *Twilight Zone* creator Rod Serling, called. Sesame Street's cookie monster, the creator and director of Miss Piggy movies, Frank Oz, called from Hawaii; Bemie Brillstein, Dan Aykroyd's agent, called from Century City, and Jamie Lee Curtis called from her apartment in West LA: "I love him very much and I am behind him. If he needs something, please call." Steven Bishop, the musician, and John Candy, the comic actor from SCTV, called; young Hollywood kept Alpha's switchboard lit. Her last message of the day was from Sean Daniel.

Alpha kept in touch with Indian Dunes through Dennis Jones, Frank Marshall's man, who reported on the police activity on the set. Meanwhile, Warner publicist Friedman asked Alpha to help Saul Kahan get a "bio" out of the trailer on the set. Frank Marshall personally called asking for a raft of things. Everybody wanted lists or sheets or copies of papers and documents.

It was ironic that John Landis, by insisting on working on a competing studio lot, forced Warner to petition the bungalow at Universal Studios for papers and information which would be ready at hand if, as was done normally, the director worked on the premises of his employer. As the

TZ movie's financial backer, Warner was actually Landis' employer; but the young director was indulged by the old guard that ran the studio system. The studios bent over backward to please the young film maker who seemed to read what kind of movies people liked, and when John Landis wanted to house his whole operation in a cramped bungalow on the Universal lot Warner assented, even though it effectively removed Landis from control and meant complications which at one point even included having two of Warner's financial watchdogs work out of a trailer on the Universal lot. It also forced the first showdown between Landis and the studio following the crash, resulting in the intervention of Landis' chief legal strategist and a suspension of the "freeze" order.

Just before Donna Schuman arrived in the office, Warner's executive, Ed Morey, asked Alpha for copies of all the call sheets and shooting schedules for the entire week. A vice president and executive production manager, Morey worked under Fred Gallo, Warner's production chief. Morey called at least six times in the next thirty minutes, each time more irate, and driving Alpha nearly mad. At last Donna stepped in and got hold of George Folsey, explaining the director's "freeze" instruction. Folsey knew as well as Donna that Warner wanted the call sheets and shooting schedules to see if they called for children. They both knew that neither Morey nor Warner's lawyer Jim Miller, nor anyone else, would find any trace of the kids in them.

About a half hour later Folsey called back. He told Alpha to give Morey everything he wanted and to cooperate fully with Warner. The decision was made by John Landis' personal attorney, Joel Behr, the junior partner in the Century City law firm of Silverberg, Leon, Rosen & Behr, whom Folsey consulted about Morey's request.

A rising Hollywood lawyer, Joel Behr was entrusted by his senior partners with the legal well-being of an important client. Behr was the first person John Landis called from the Henry Mayo Hospital and eventually Behr would devote himself fulltime to the Landis case. When the legal problems of the director would require a half-dozen lawyers to fight on every front, including one of the highest paid criminal lawyers in the country, Joel Behr remained in the background. As Landis' closest counselor and confidant, he was the architect of the director's legal phalanx and even of the shape of his public behavior.

10

SILENT SCREENING

When George Folsey made his early morning call to Donna Schuman to acquaint her with the catastrophic outcome of the segment's final shoot he used an outdoor telephone by the beat-up old trailer at the gate to the set area. A studio car was taking him and a small distraught party to the Henry Mayo Clinic in Valencia. Mrs. Chen, Renee's mother, was already on her way to the hospital. Dr. Dinh Le, Myca's father, was in Folsey's car with John Landis.

Dr. Le babbled disjointedly. With exquisite delicacy he expressed concern over how John Landis felt. He spoke of things he planned to do in the future. A small, frail man with almost dainty habits, he had the look both benign and remote which indicated a state of shock. He held John Landis by the hand.

As Folsey spoke to Donna from the rustic telephone the police had not yet arrived. The scrub desert dunes lay silent under a wash of moonlight. George Folsey hung up and got back into the car where, in the back seat, Dr. Le still sat with his dainty hand in the grip of the traumatized Hollywood director. The driver of the car was a young, pretty Teamster driver employed by Warner who wanted to be an actress; on the set there'd been rumors about her relationship with the director.

George Folsey was usually thought of as indecisive, content to coast, by not troubling the director. In part that was so because his partnership was not one of equals. Folsey, unlike Landis, had actually grown up in Hollywood, yet he looked up to his younger partner as a "genius," a "voracious reader" with a tremendous knowledge of film that outstripped his own. But more concretely, as associate producer of the TZ segment, his relationship with the director was defined by the terms of the deal they received. Folsey's earnings as associate producer were pegged to his partner's, and according to their deal with Warner, George Folsey received only 10% of Landis' portion of the profits. In the immediate crisis at Indian Dunes, however, with the director incapacitated, Folsey emerged as the main source of support.

Dealing with Mrs. Chen, the mother of Renee, had required all of Folsey's strength. "She was crazed," Folsey remembered. Everybody on the set, as high up as the 100-ft. cliff, heard the unforgettable wail of the mother who saw her daughter disappear beneath the plunging helicopter, the wail reaching an unbearable pitch when next she saw Renee on the furniture pad with blood streaming from her nose and the frail bones glistening through the skin. The reassuring thin-voiced producer who had just told the mother that the explosives were merely Hollywood special effects was now himself tottering over the sobbing figure who hopelessly attempted to bring back life in the girl's limp body. As Mrs. Chen had a panic attack she kicked and struggled while Folsey tried to hold her up. Afterwards, Folsey turned to Dr. Le who stood quietly gazing up at John Landis next to him.

Dr. Le said, "I saw him." He'd obviously seen his son's decapitated torso, Folsey understood.

* * *

Dorcey Wingo had been on the set only two days and it was in the hospital that for the first time he saw George Folsey. The pilot walked around the lobby in confusion. The two E-cameramen, Robinson and Smith, were still dazed. John Landis was hysterical with grief. Craig Wooten, the fuel truck driver for the helicopter, standing next to the director while both were making telephone calls, heard Landis bawl into the phone while describing the story to what Craig Wooten took to be either a close friend or lawyer.

The rapid series of telephone calls going in and out of the hospital at this hour was responsible for a lot of the commotion. Handed down from a bewildered nursing staff to any available movie person, the telephone calls became part of the confusion. The tangled messages created situations where it was possible for Howard Sanders, a production assistant, a mere gofer, to confer with Steven Spielberg's personal attorney, Bruce Ramer, a most influential entertainment lawyer of the famous Gang & Tyre firm; the phone inexplicably ended up in Sanders' hands. Ramer appeared informed of the disaster and warned Sanders about an *Entertainment Tonight* crew which he had heard was on its way to the hospital.

By daybreak the movie people stayed one step ahead of the authorities by departing from the hospital. After apparently calling Steven Spielberg, Frank Marshall quietly vanished. Jackie Compton, Landis' pretty Teamster driver who had waited faithfully in the hospital lobby, did not drive her employer home. In a car driven by another production assistant, Barry Penner, with Howard Sanders in the back, the distraught passenger in the front seat was taken to the Universal bungalow in Studio City.

Folsey remained behind to deal with the children's parents. Dr. Le at first was indisposed to call home where his wife waited up with their youngest son. He asked Folsey, who begged off. After ages searching through his address book Dr. Le finally rang a friend in the neighborhood. He asked that he tell Kim, Dr. Le's wife, only that something terrible had happened.

Folsey took a breather and left Myca's father briefly in a room for a medical examination. But walking back to the lobby with the hospital chaplain, Folsey suddenly encountered Mark Chen who lunged out of a room. Little Renee's father had been on the set the previous night but had not come that night due to an important office meeting the next day. He had rushed to the hospital from Pasadena after receiving the shocking news.

"You killed my daughter!" Chen screamed at Folsey. "You murdered my daughter!"

Folsey heard Mrs. Chen wailing inside the room. The chaplain put his arm around Folsey and led him back to the lobby.

The opening of another hot summer day in Los Angeles saw George Folsey drive 50 miles east of his home in Bel Air. His Rolls pulled up at a modest residence on a quiet street. It was about 6 A.M.

"She knew," Folsey recalled of the young "oriental" woman who opened the door.

Kim Le was told that her son had been killed. After a long silence she managed, "How did he look, peaceful?"

There were some other people present, friends from the neighborhood. Myca's younger brother Christopher clung to his mother. Neither Folsey nor her husband could bring himself to tell her how Myca had died, and it was not until several weeks later, after stumbling on a strange word in a news story about the crash, that she found out by looking up in a dictionary the meaning of "decapitation."

The important, well-dressed American film producer hugged the frail young Asian woman.

She started crying...

Among the people and things on the set that melted away into the night were the film and soundtracks from the cameras used in the final scene. However, unlike other vanishings, the film could be traced, at least through its early hurried stages. It turned up in North Hollywood at the giant Technicolor labs at just about the time Folsey arrived on the doorstep of the Le's in Cerritos. Two couriers handed the film in cans sealed with tape around the outside to the shipping clerk at the plant a little after 6 A.M. The clerk instantly rang upstairs to the plant foreman, Bill Galloway.

Galloway had been expecting the film. Sometime earlier, just as the late shift was finishing up before going home, a call had come in from Warner. The plant was put on alert. Something really "hot" was coming in from the *Twilight Zone* movie. The shift was held over, and as soon as the film arrived Galloway took the can to Technicolor's processing machine. There, the "negative-cutter," Del New, became the first person to see the motion picture recording of the crash.

One of Del New's jobs was to check the quality of the negatives after being processed. But before the processed film could be viewed on a projector a print had to be made, the so-called "dailies," where the print is rushed through the process without any augmentation from the film lab, giving the film makers a "rush," or what the processors refer to technically as a "one light daily." As soon as the first prints came out of the processing machine Del New locked himself in his viewing room.

His immediate reaction to the rushes was relief that the scenes were not more graphic. New had been somewhat unnerved by the prospect of viewing a bloodbath but from the rushes he couldn't really see the violence in any detail. Afterwards, at the specific request of Fred Talmadge, Warner's chief of post-production, Del New personally hand-carried the prints from Technicolor over to Warner's offices a few miles away. New arrived at Warner around 9:00 A.M. Talmadge was the first at Warner's to see the film.

After Talmadge, the film's trail became obscured and investigators were never able to completely reconstruct its path. Only a few studio insiders directly involved in monitoring the film's progress were aware that the studio's top brass permitted the prints to be released to John Landis on the same day of the crash. Along the studio's executive row the story circulated that Landis was in possession of the film prints during the entire morning and early afternoon of Friday, July 23, 1982, at which time the studio, perceiving a potential public relations disaster in the disclosure of its handling of key evidence, sent two members from its camera department to Landis to retrieve the film.

A chem machine, a device used for viewing 35mm film on a small screen, had been humming that morning, presumably as the director viewed the crash footage for the first time.

George Folsey Jr. enjoyed only a few hours' respite from the nightmare. He slept briefly and woke in the early afternoon of the same Friday, July 23. He got up, dressed, and drove to a large rambling house high up in Beverly Hills on 139 Lloyd Crest Drive. There, at the home of the director, he joined John Landis and the director's personal lawyer Joel Behr who now represented them both. They discussed the meeting scheduled to begin in a few short hours when Warner executives and their lawyers would view the footage from Indian Dunes. It was decided that Folsey and Behr would attend the viewing. John Landis remained at home in what was officially described as a state of shock.

The viewing was held in the complex known as TBS, The Burbank Studios, the studio lot and executive office complex owned jointly by Columbia and Warner Bros. Folsey and Behr met there in the early evening with Terry Semel, president of the Warner film division; Jim Miller, Warner's top lawyer; and Spielberg's man, Frank Marshall. In this same complex several weeks earlier Semel, Folsey, Marshall and Warner's Lucy Fisher had met under more cheerful auspices, expecting to make a financially successful Spielberg movie on a relatively small ($4-5 million) investment.

The film jumped considerably because of the rough cuts from six different cameras. But the fatal scene was definite and clear.

The helicopter appeared to be nearly inside the fireballs about 30 feet over the exploding village. The two children, being carried northward across the river, were most of the way across when suddenly Vic stumbled and struggled to keep the little girl from going under in the water. The stumble prevented him from getting out of the way of the blades of the helicopter which quickly came down sideways with the main rotor spinning. The cuts showed the helicopter flipped over on its side; John Landis in his waders was seen flitting across the screen, the 1st AD in a white shirt splashed in the water – it was full of rushing action but somehow innocuous-looking.

Of the six camera angles covering the fatal moment only the master shot, the B-camera, showed the blades that sliced into Vic Morrow and the two children. The viewers saw the action unroll without the benefit of one of the two soundtracks which had apparently gone missing. The blades seemed to do their work cleanly, as noted in the tone of relief by one of Landis' lawyers. "From the standpoint of the potential to inflame a jury," the lawyer was to write in summarizing the impact of the master shot, "it is fortunate that the details of the injuries inflicted on the three actors are not very easily observed in the film."

Among the small audience in the screening room Folsey and Marshall alone had seen the actual carnage. As they relived the frightful reality presented by the images, the only fear of criminal prosecution they could have had would have been the knowledge that children were on the set illegally without permits. But since there was no soundtrack with voices to help elucidate the mystery it was impossible to tell what had caused the crash and the meeting was short.

* * *

After the lights came on it appeared that the studio executives had already seen the film before Behr and Folsey arrived. No one would have been more astonished than Don Llorente had he known this, as earlier on the same day he had been told by Warner that it had no knowledge of the film's whereabouts. Llorente, then still at Indian Dunes – he did not leave until midnight – threatened to issue a subpoena

11

EULOGY FROM A STRANGER

George Folsey Jr. had known the actor who played Bill only for the few weeks he spent with him on the shoot. But he knew his ex-wife, Barbara Turner, a Hollywood writer and actress. He also knew Barbara's second husband, Reza Badiyi, a director for whom he had once worked. Barbara and her two daughters by Vic, twenty-one-year- old Carrie Morrow and fifteen-year-old Jennifer Jason Leigh, were at Barbara Turner's home when Folsey arrived in the afternoon on the day following Vic's death, Saturday, July 24. He came with Belinda, his wife, to pay condolences. The actor's funeral would be held the next day.

"It was an emotional scene. Their father had been killed. They asked if I could do the eulogy speech," Folsey recalled.

After his initial surprise he sat down and wrote the tribute. He read it to Barbara, Carrie and Jennifer. After making a few changes Folsey called John Landis, presumably under doctor's care at home. Landis, Folsey remembers, had him convey a request to "Barbara and the kids," and Folsey turned to the mother and the two girls.

"John asked if he could have a few words."

They thought it would be okay, was the way Folsey recalled their agreement.

The director shortly called Folsey back to read a short speech; adolescent in tone, chaotic, painfully straining after high emotion, the praise seemed to be not so much for Vic as for the speaker who helped a has-been make a comeback:

> I met Vic for the first time in my office one month ago. Having always admired his acting I was delighted to learn that Vic's performances were the result of a keen intelligence and deep emotions. Vic was a professional, and his role as a lead in our story was brilliantly realized. There is no way to express my feelings at this overwhelming time. Just before the last take Vic took me aside to thank me for this opportunity. He knew how wonderful his performance was and wanted me to know how happy he was with the work. Tragedy strikes in an instant, but film is immortal. Perhaps we can take some solace in the knowledge that through his work in stage, television and film Vic lives forever.

* * *

Vic Morrow's funeral was not the first to involve the young film maker in a controversial Hollywood death. Less than five months before the *Twilight Zone* fatalities John Landis had attended John Belushi's funeral. Hollywood had been shaken by the drug overdose death of the comedy sensation from *Saturday Night Live*. Belushi's death put the spotlight on the personal habits of the new film personalities and at the time of Vic Morrow's funeral Hollywood's cocaine culture was under widely publicized scrutiny by the DA's office. Assumptions were rife that drugs were involved in the crash on the movie set. A question mark still hung over the cause of the actor's death. No one knew what had happened that night in Indian Dunes, except that it had been violent, gruesome, even grotesque.

The service took place at Hillside Memorial Park Chapel in Culver City. The interval between the death and the burial, two days, satisfied the Jewish law according to which a body must be interred two days following its demise. The service was simple, lasting a little over a half hour. Rabbi Morton Wallack spoke, then Folsey gave the eulogy, and John Landis spoke his eulogy next.

The chapel was crowded with hundreds of mourners. Barbara Turner wore a black veil. With her daughters Carrie Morrow and Jennifer Jason Leigh she listened to the speech which she had heard Folsey recite in her living room the day before. Jennifer was said to have been estranged from her father; siding with her mother after the messy divorce, she was said to have vowed never to want to see her father again. Jennifer was pretty and looked like Vic. Aspiring to an acting career, she had already acted in a few small movie roles and had recently won accolades as a nude sensation in *Fast Times at Ridgemont High*. Her older sister would never be an actress; Carrie was plump and sweet and confused and after the divorce had tried to remain close to the stormy man who drank too much and was her father.

A cross-section of the film industry stood in the hot sun around the plain brown wood casket: fellow actors and showbiz friends Ray Walston, Peter Lupus, Joyce Van Patten, Pat Harrington Jr. and Rick Jason who co-starred with Morrow in *Combat*; Steve Shagan, the Oscar-winning screenwriter, and director Richard Donner; Morrow's lawyer, Al Green, and lots of film people, including members of the TZ set, and, most prominently, the wild-eyed, longhaired, raven-bearded *wunderkind* with the glittering bifocals who, in his obsession with special effects, was looked upon by some mourners as the cause of the actor's death.

John Landis was accompanied by his wife. Six feet tall, gazelle-like, with strong Nefertiti features, she craned an immensely long neck over the crowd. As Deborah Nadoolman, with the costuming credit on her husband's segment, she had outfitted Bill for what was to become his shroud-the blue polyester suit and the brown socks and the brown shoes in which he died.

Landis' presence at the funeral, especially as the unkempt eulogist in what seemed like a double bill with Folsey, struck the wrong note. Instead of solemnity there was near hysteria. The mourners listened in rising anger to two banal, feelingless speeches in which strangers to the dead man appropriated his memory. The eulogists were not old friends of Vic's like Steve Shagan, who had known him for some three decades. Vic's friends at the funeral were offended to hear Folsey and Landis portray themselves as having personally suffered a loss, well aware that in terms of Hollywood reality the friendship the speakers had for the actor was contained in the "deal memo."

The director and his business partner were Morrow's employers who had hired him because he fitted into the low-budget limits of the production. Morrow had taken the job because, as his attorney put it, "Vic was not turning down any work." The fact that it was a production "spearheaded by Steven Spielberg," according to Morrow's agent, had a great appeal to the actor, for the $40,000 salary was low by the standards of what Hollywood paid a leading man for 14 days – two days rehearsal and 12 days of filming. For a two-day appearance earlier in the Landis segment Albert Brooks received $5,000 a day, on a per diem basis almost twice as much as Morrow was getting on a daily basis, and Morrow was the star!

And so Vic Morrow, whose film career had consisted of a number of forgettable roles, went out of life with a B-script. Strangers spoke his eulogy. It was Hollywood glitter, superficial and cold. In the audience were his ex-wife behind the black veil and his estranged daughter and the baby granddaughter he hardly knew and Carrie who'd never really gotten to know her dad as well as she would have liked to.

Carrie had written a song for her father. It was sung at the end of the service. It was called "Time Together."

You were here, I was there We were happy when we were together You are here,/am somewhere We are laughing because we'll always remember our time together...

Carrie Morrow had wanted to know her father and understand him. But the gruffly sentimental dogface fighter was a Hollywood creation. Vic remained this creation at his own funeral where some people got the impression that Folsey was paying tribute to his creative partner rather than the dead actor.

In his speech at graveside Folsey reminisced how upon meeting Vic Morrow for the first time on the *Twilight Zone* set he was "bitterly disappointed" to learn that the actor was not a registered stock or commodities broker, "since he was more knowledgeable about the market than any broker." The eulogist continued in this talk-show vein. "We spent a lot of time comparing notes on how each of us had fared in the market during the day, and it was easy to see that anything he was involved in became a total commitment." Folsey continued, "Just take his acting. In every *volt, Blackboard Jungle, Deathwatch, Combat,* the power and integrity are so evident. This is why John chose Vic to be the star of the *Twilight Zone* segment he had written and was directing."

The names of the three movies Folsey mentioned belonged to Morrow's early years. *Deathwatch* belonged to the period of the 50s when, after studying at a small Florida college, Morrow got into stage work and directing off-Broadway productions. He had a role in another off-Broadway production, *A Streetcar Named Desire,* the play that made Marlon Brando famous in the film version. Morrow's stage career faltered and he went to Hollywood to try his luck on-screen. In 1955 he played a knife-wielding psychopathic punk in *Blackboard Jungle,* directed by Richard Brooks. A half-dozen movies followed this mild success in which he became typecast as a soldier in movies like *Tribute to a Dead Man* and *Men in War.* His film career ended in a 1961 flop in which he played the lead, called *Portrait of a Mobster.*

Vic Morrow, according to the brief entry in the *Encyclopedia of Film,* had one character, the "vicious heavy of occasional films." When from film he got into TV, the "vicious heavy" became the "unshaven tough guy with a warm human side" in his role as the hard-driving Sarge in ABC's *Combat* series. *Combat* ran three years and afterwards, for much of the 70s, Morrow was out of work. He had roles in a few TV movies, the *Glass House* in 1972 and the 1977 drama *Roots.* At one point in the 70s his career appeared to be reviving with a role he landed opposite Walther Matthau in *The Bad News Bears,* in which he played a win-at-any-cost coach who wins the league series but loses the moral victory by slapping his pitcher. The promise didn't materialize. He returned to playing the vicious heavy in a movie called *Funeral for an Assassin* and did a Japanese film, *Message from Space.*

During these barren years Morrow's personal life was a shambles. A bitter and painful marital breakup with Barbara Turner, the mother of his two girls, brought him to the edge. He drank more than ever. He got heavily into drugs. "Hollywood's first cocaine casualty," a friend recalled the Vic Morrow of those cheerless years. The floundering actor grew overweight, lazy and depressed. He took to challenging the town that had dumped him without ceremony. At the Polo Lounge where he hung out with his best friend, Billy Fine, Vic Morrow became known as a boozer and brawler, as if the "unshaven tough guy" had stepped out of the script into combat at Hollywood's choice meeting place for stars and deal-makers. He saved himself by getting away from Hollywood. He went to Scandinavia, returning sober, slimmed down and to fresh hope when one of the hot young directors offered him his first leading role in a feature film since *Portrait of a Mobster* more than two decades ago. In his eulogy, Folsey did not neglect to remind the mourners that the makers of the Landis film gave a broken-down actor the chance of a comeback.

> "Vic and I did not *always* talk about stocks and such," Folsey read with his high choirboy voice from his speech. "He often told me how happy he was to be playing this part. We all thought he was terrific, and he was – but what was really wonderful was that Vic knew it. He felt that it was one of the best parts he had ever played. We thought he was giving the performance of his life."

Hollywood hype could mean anything and nothing – even that Vic Morrow's senseless death was a noble sacrifice. There was a striking correspondence between Folsey's eulogy and Landis'. Both paid tribute to the TZ movie, a trivial film that would quickly sink into oblivion, as Vic's bid for immortality. Folsey ended:

> "If there is one consolation in this terrible situation, it's that the film is finished. There is nothing more to be shot to make the film work. Thank God, because his performance must not be lost. It represented for him something seldom attained – the culmination of all his idealistic dreams when he was first starting out in acting school in New York. It's Vic's last gift to us."

Already on the very day the accident occurred, Dan Allingham began mobilizing crew members to attend the funeral. He had production assistants call people from the set that night and urge them to attend the ceremony. But if the ostensible purpose was to present the crew in unity, it failed with a number of cameramen. Randy Robinson attended the service still terribly upset over the deaths and his own narrow escape. Seated next to him, Roger Smith, the *Air Wolf* veteran, felt that John Landis was getting away with not having to face up to the responsibility for Vic's death. Like Robinson, Smith was revolted by the director's behavior during the ceremony at the Jewish burial ground in Culver City. "It was silly, too light-hearted," Smith fumed to Robinson over the disrespect shown the deceased.

In the chapel Smith was seated directly behind John Landis and his wife. Deborah was in a plain black dress that emphasized her elongated limbs and strong features. Her husband beside her was characteristically hyper. His hair appeared to be uncombed, his beard untrimmed. Smith saw Landis turn a shaggy profile to his wife and make "some flippant and sarcastic remark." Roger could see her "sort of laughing." He considered this the height of disrespect and inexcusable.

The revulsion shared by the camera operators became widespread among the mourners after John Landis pushed himself forward to speak. No one outside of Folsey and the Morrow children and their mother knew that as a speaker the eulogist was self-invited. In his piercing falsetto Landis repeated the speech he had read to Folsey over the phone the day before. He stated how happy Morrow had been as an actor. But when he came to mention how just before the last take Vic took him aside to thank him for the "opportunity," there were ripples of protest.

Al Green, Vic Morrow's longtime lawyer and friend, wanted to shout: "Murderer!"

Landis went on and flung out the terribly embarrassing canard that film was immortal and Vic lived forever.

There were audible titters, impatient shushing of hands, and cries of, "Enough! Enough!"

After the funeral Roger Smith drove from the cemetery to a nearby pay telephone. From the corner of Sepulveda and Centinella he placed a call to fellow cameraman Steve Lydecker. Smith was revolted that Landis would take an opportunity such as a funeral to give Vic Morrow's last performance some sort of creative justification. Smith knew how deeply unhappy Morrow had been on the set, though trying not to show it.

Over the phone Smith and Lydecker vowed to each other not to let the director get away with it.

12

Lunch at Hampton's

Alpha Campbell, quietly, efficiently, continued to run the Landis office. On the first day of the new week she sent off the papers requested by Warner Bros. She even drove over to The Burbank Studios that Monday to pick up some boxes said to contain papers pertaining to Vic Morrow and the accident. She escorted the boxes back to the office at Universal, and as she performed these tasks, in her forbearance of all the shady goings-on, she might have been one of those quiet middle-aged ladies with excellently observant eyes and ears in a movie by her former boss, Alfred Hitchcock.

Alpha did not contribute to the speculations in the office. Saying she had heard so many versions of the accident she would rather not comment, she stayed out of the discussions. But she felt terrible and beneath her efficient demeanor she was very angry at the man she called "J.L." Vic's belongings had been brought from the set to the office and in the pathetic bundle she discovered an envelope containing a photograph of the actor. She swore to herself that one day she would talk honestly about what she thought and how she felt about the accident.

She was heartbroken for Trudy, Vic's nice English girlfriend, and never knew anyone so devastated. Trudy had told her that Vic knew something was wrong that night. Alpha sometimes said that what Trudy had gone through "could drive people to drink or to use drugs to forget." The nice English girl seemed to be reproaching herself for having permitted Vic to do the scene. And the same might be said of Donna Schuman's feelings in regard to the kids.

Like Landis' personal secretary, Donna Schuman had been too distraught to go to Vic's funeral, but the next day she showed up at Twilight Zone Productions at her regular time. Regardless of the tragedy the film had to be finished. But Donna was unable to concentrate that Monday. She waited for midday. Folsey had promised to take her to lunch. What Donna really wanted to know from Folsey at lunch was how far they were responsible for what had happened. She clutched at the hope of some assurance that would absolve her.

The question was the extent to which they were tainted by the miserable affair. Dr. Schuman did not know the Chens, he only briefly met Dr. Daniel Le. But he knew that the children would be working without permits. Nor could his wife avoid hearing in the days before the final shooting all sorts of talk around the office about helicopters and explosives in the scenes where the kids were being used. After the children were hired she even asked Folsey about the penalty for working them without permits on the set, and heard Folsey's flippant repartee, "Oh, nothing much. A slap on the wrist and maybe a little fine unless they find out about the explosives, and then they'll probably throw us in jail." It was hardly comforting, but she silenced her own alarm.

One of Donna Schuman's jobs was to distribute the call sheets to the production watchdogs at Warner, and the day before the shooting she believed she heard Allingham give her strange instructions not to send the paperwork over to Warner until everyone had left their offices for the location. Was it because they had the names on them of Renee and Myca? Her doubts and ambivalence told her that she was not quit of responsibility for the children, and so she was not at all amused when just a day or so prior to the final shooting she saw the director with gangly legs and milling arms and heard him shriek in reference to the film's final scene, "It's going to be BI-I-I-I-G!"

Once Donna Schuman had asked Folsey if Landis was a coke user. Folsey absolutely denied it and Donna believed him. The director's hyper behavior appeared to be the result of something unsettled and chaotic in his makeup that made him mad for action of any type. He appeared to be under a compulsion to be always asserting himself, even if only to pop his head into the door of the office and startle everyone by shouting, "Bi-i-i-i-g!" On one occasion, "in one kind of sick joke," as Donna recalled, John Landis was scurrying down the hall throwing his hands up in the air and shouting about the illegal hiring of the kids, "We're all going to jail! We're all going to jail!"

That the children would be exposed to danger was perhaps hardly to be thought of by those in the office, who, like Donna Schuman, were chiefly bothered by the illegality. But Donna heard Folsey in a telephone conversation reassure the parents of Renee, "It's nothing – it's just like fireworks," and she was awakened to the possibility of danger to the children. It became clear to her that a massive deception was on foot. She heard about changes in the script and how the last scene had been added and the character of it changed. And after learning that Alpha Campbell kept the scripts locked in a desk she gathered that the kids were to be kept concealed from the Warner people; and she felt powerless to influence the events which she herself had helped set in motion.

When at about noon George Folsey Jr. walked into the office an alteration was evident in him, too. Like John Landis and Donna Schuman and everyone else involved in the wretched affair, George Folsey suffered. There was the effect on his octogenarian father who was ailing, and on his mother. Folsey grew up a happy child in a warm, supportive family. As an only child he was afforded the very best. He graduated from one of Southern California's most prestigious schools, Pomona College. Along with a happy marriage, one fine son and a daughter, he had a bona fide name in the film industry. He was an Anglophile, a little snobby, a "small" millionaire with one extravagant hobby, collecting Rolls-Royces – and over this sunny life now fell the shadow of Indian Dunes.

At the office that Monday he talked briefly with Donna Schuman about where they would go for lunch. They decided to eat and talk at Paul Newman's restaurant in Toluca Lake, Hampton's, a breezy upscale hamburger restaurant.

As soon as they sat down at a table Donna said, "I really would like to know why three people are dead."

"It was an accident," Folsey said.

"I don't understand. How can you have that kind of accident? Tell me what happened."

"Well, God," Folsey said, "we rehearsed it and rehearsed it about 30 times, and everybody was in place and we went to shoot it and there was this – this crash! And it was like a million-to-one shot that it could happen again. And it – we just had this accident, like an act of God."

Donna could only murmur, "How did you have this accident?" and heard Folsey explain lamely, "You know, it's like – it's just like two cars coming over a center divider."

Donna lost her temper.

"No, it's not like two cars going pow!"

It was not an act of God. It was not like that at all. It was the act of a young director with a manner she found grating. It was not an accident. It was the "shot." The special effects. The budget.... No one had really cared very much about the kids and the broken-down actor.

13

The Burbank Studios

About midday on Monday, July 26, while George Folsey and Donna Schuman lunched at Hampton's, a discontented crowd of reporters could be seen milling in a glaring sun before the monolithic building known as TBS, The Burbank Studios. Among the media men and women, the "carrot-top cub" looked on with his freckled face as a small party of people from the different investigative agencies entered the building. Only the party of officials was authorized to go up to the Warner screening room for the first semi-public viewing of the film of the "Twilight Zone" crash. The press was excluded from this special screening, a denial that also excluded the reporters from welcome drafts of climate-controlled air. They wilted in the heat. Andy Furillo waited an hour before he saw the same party file out again. He spotted Charlie Hughes. The crusty labor investigator had just dropped a subpoena on Warner Bros., for their contracts with the children.

"Can't talk about it, sorry." He waved Andy off.

Furillo had to wait for the announcement from Charlie's boss, Colleen Logan, the area administrator for the state's labor standards enforcement division. His luck was no better with other officials.

"Can't talk about it, sorry."

Clearly, they were under instructions not to talk to the press. But if the journalists went home disappointed, feeling cheated of their time, it was thanks only to Don Llorente, the NTSB investigator, that the film was being shown at all.

It had taken an immense amount of doing on Llorente's part. Early on Monday he was at TBS, meeting with Stanley Belkin, Warner's Hollywood corporate counsel. In the name of the NTSB Llorente had already taken possession of the crippled aircraft at Indian Dunes and now he had with him a subpoena for both the film of the accident and the negative of the film which had already been in the studio's possession, processed and all, mere hours following the accident.

"Has anybody seen it?" Llorente asked that Monday.

"No," Belkin replied disingenuously, "it was processed over the weekend."

Llorente decided to use diplomacy. He wanted Warner to cooperate and he needed a trade-off. He fixed on the knot of press people outside the studio gate. Knowing how worried the studio must be by their presence, Llorente promised Belkin to exclude the media from seeing the film. But even more appealing from the film company's standpoint was Llorente's further offer not to talk to the press at all until he made his findings public.

At this early point in the investigation, a mere three days after the accident, Warner Bros., already faced a formidable host of legal problems. Ready to pounce upon it at any moment with subpoenas were a half-dozen state and local agencies. The studio faced the possibility of criminal charges to be filed by the DA's office, wrongful death actions, administrative proceedings and the possibility of one or more jury trials in the future. The deal with the NTSB man was one the studio couldn't refuse. Llorente's offer to exclude the press guarded against possible leaks in the media. At the same time it insulated the film from further subpoenas, since the NTSB as an arm of the federal government superseded all the other agencies involved in the investigation.

Fear of their exposure to allegations of a cocaine cover-up helped explain why the studio accepted Llorente's offer and agreed that the film be shown that very afternoon. Even in the earliest phases of the investigation, the NTSB man was faced with overwhelming news coverage pointing directly to the widespread use of drugs – specifically cocaine – on many Hollywood film sets. In that summer of 1982, headline stories fixed on rampant drug use in the film industry, underscored by the overdose death of John Belushi, reinforced the feelings that drugs may have been involved.

It turned out that Llorente told reporters that he was investigating the possibility that cocaine was being used prior to the crash. The celebrity news chatter carried stories on cocaine used by many Spielberg stars, in particular, *Jaws* star Richard Dreyfuss, who rolled his car on a Beverley Hills street and was charged with possession of cocaine; or producer and former business partner Julia Phillips who produced *Close Encounters of the Third Kind,* admitted spending over 1 million dollars on her cocaine habit. She said it all started on location on *Close Encounters.* And, due to John Belushi's death, the L.A. Grand Jury called Robert De Niro and Robin Williams to testify about their admitted escapades with the comedian the night before his overdose and death. A *NY Times* article quoted police authorities describing Hollywood's cocaine distribution rings as being as common as ice cream trucks in delivering drugs to movie sets. Other celebrities made the news with their cocaine habits, including Robert Evans, producer, and Linda Blair and McKenzie Phillips.

Under the NTSB procedure Warner was given assurance that no one would see the film except those with a legitimate interest. The film's first "semi-public" screening included Llorente's team, consisting of assistants deputized and sworn in hastily over the past few days. They were joined in the TBS screening room by investigators from the FBI, FAA, the LA County Sheriff's Department, the California Labor Commissioner and Cal/OSHA, the California office of the Occupational Safety and Health Administration. The viewers also included representatives from several unions, as well as experts from the Bell Helicopter Company and Western Helicopter, the manufacturer and owner of the helicopter, respectively.

These were the members of the party, about 20 in all, that Andy Furillo saw file into the TBS building's long shady corridors. On the hot sidewalk he had reason to reflect that it was a sad day when the press was "excluded." Yet, unbeknownst then to either, Don Llorente would make ample amends and not forget the likable young cub with the freckled face and flaming thatch.

Before the year was out, he would leak to Furillo amazing facts of his *Twilight Zone* investigation. Warner Studios had not yet been charged with anything. The NTSB investigation only focused on an industrial accident and had no criminal bearing. These were thought of as problems of the longer range. At the moment the studio sought only to contain the damage that grew out of its involvement in the illegal hiring. Its entire film production might be forced out of California by the suspension of its permit to hire children.

In those first few days Warner's corporate office was still as much in the dark as to the cause of the crash as the investigators were. Without more information the company's officers feared revelations that could be even more damaging than the illegal employment of children on a movie set. They knew about the cocaine binges associated with Landis' Belushi movies. Some among the studio brass envisioned a worst-case scenario; a Belushi-type drug orgy on the *Twilight Zone* set ending in decapitation and dismemberment. Bracing itself, the studio adopted a siege mentality; it, too, "froze."

At stake for the studio, apart from the future of the TZ film project itself, was something more than the reputation of John Landis. The studio's nascent relationship with the TZ film's famous co-producer, Steven Spielberg, represented much more than John Landis did, a precious asset with lucrative economic potential.

Warner's high hopes were relevant to the mood of that strange summer of '82 when Hollywood, in the grip of Spielbergmania, felt like the Klondike. Every studio wanted "Spielberg product," including Warner. *E.T.* from Universal and *Poltergeist* from 20th Century Fox put competing Spielberg product in rival movie houses, an unheard-of break with Hollywood practice in film distribution. Through its deal on the TZ movie Warner joined the other two studios by having Spielberg product on the shelf. Only Steven Spielberg could make films for two different studios and have them released simultaneously, while at the same time a third studio was financing another of his movies in the making. Moreover, on paper it looked like Warner had Spielberg product at a bargain-basement price.

In terms of the rising costs of movie-making Warner had made an astute deal by getting some of the top directors to work on the project for a reasonably small investment. At the time, Spielberg was a $2 million-plus-per-picture director; Landis $1 million-plus, and George Miller, the Australian director of *Road Warrior* fame, and Joe Dante who had made *The Howling* and *Piranha*, received slightly less than Landis. Yet the whole Spielberg-Landis co-production was budgeted for $5 million! The well-known directors involved in the film would ordinarily have absorbed the film's total budget. Hollywood offered few bargains like that.

Warner was able to keep the up-front costs low because it did not have to pay the high directors' fees. Eventually the TZ movie was to earn $34 million dollars on an $8 million-dollar investment, yielding a not very shabby $2.5 million dollars each for Landis and Spielberg; but in the immediate aftermath of the tragedy at Indian Dunes it looked briefly as if the movie might never get *off* the ground.

To protect Spielberg, the TZ project, and perhaps its own ability to make films in California, everything depended on how quickly Warner Bros., acted to defend itself. And by the end of the first Monday, working in a crisis atmosphere, the studio had ready a formidable legal team to safeguard the movie's financial future, as well as every other flank to which the actions of the brash director had exposed it.

The in-house legal team Warner mobilized consisted of Jim Miller, Stanley Belkin and John Schulman. In addition, the studio engaged one of LA's most noted lawyers, William Vaughn, of O'Melveny & Myers, assisted by an outside criminal lawyer, Douglas Dalton. It was not lost on the beleaguered movie company that the labor commissioner's office had no less than three investigators, including Charlie Hughes, at the NTSB screening that afternoon. Warner's greatest fear must have been that Colleen Logan, Charlie's boss, would turn over the results of the investigation to the DA's office for the filing of criminal charges against the famous studio.

Meanwhile, another phalanx was being formed across town in the Century City law offices of Silverberg, Leon, Rosen & Behr. Eventually John Landis would consider America's top lawyers to join this defense team. By that Monday afternoon, a mere three days after the disaster, Joel Behr in his Century City office had already introduced John Landis to one of LA's top criminal lawyers, a tallish, blond, high-flushed person in his early forties with a reputation for winning acquittals by trying his cases in the press.

His name was Harland Braun. Known as the king of LA's high-profile media lawyers, he had come highly recommended to Behr by an associate who suggested that Braun's ties to the DA's office might be helpful. Having previously served in the DA's office himself as deputy district attorney and prosecutor, Braun was still an active Democrat – the Democrats' "consiglieri" – at the time when the office of District Attorney John Van de Kamp was heavily Democratic.

Braun had discovered the secret of being quotable. He could toss off a pithy remark, a biting sarcasm, an hilarious analogy. He could make a statement of astounding erudition or give a summation so masterfully concise that the courthouse journalists in high-visibility cases would always make room in their reports for one of his lines. Outside the courtroom, in the hallway where the media people swarmed with their hurried questioning, Braun was patient and genial. But the courtroom transformed him. He was no longer genial. He was hardly patient. He had a relentless style, stubborn and dogged, and once committed to an issue, a line of attack, a strategy, he followed it unswervingly with the absolute singlemindedness of a hammer.

And so, Behr settled the urgent question of Landis' criminal defense after marathon discussions with Braun the weekend following the crash. At the time Braun was with his wife and two children up in his family hideaway at Lake Arrowhead, 60 miles east of Los Angeles. Up in his mountain retreat, Braun spent the weekend listening to Behr in Los Angeles narrate long-distance the story of the bigot who redeems himself in Vietnam by saving two children from a village that's being rocketed by Americans. Braun learned that while shooting the scene Landis, after seeing the helicopter suddenly drop from the foreground, went around the helicopter and saw that the children had been killed. The authorities, Behr informed Braun, "knew almost immediately that the kids did not have papers." Landis did not get the permit because of the night-hours violation, Behr said.

At Braun's first meeting with John Landis in Behr's office the following Monday he also met Dan Allingham and George Folsey Jr. So far no one had been questioned by police. Braun recalled, "Everybody seemed so quiet, very humiliated, almost as if before an indictment."

At the request of the NTSB's Llorente, an interview with John Landis was agreed to and scheduled for Wednesday, the day following the funerals of the two children. The NTSB was merely a fact-finding team, concerned only with determining the probable cause of the accident. It published its findings but had no power to lay charges or enforce the law, nor could it compel anyone to testify. John Landis could have easily refused to be questioned by Llorente. But as Braun put it, Landis would be made "to look like complete horseshit." The lawyers discussed with the crestfallen film makers what posture to take.

According to Braun, the only strategy that really made any sense in terms of public opinion was that of cooperating with the investigators in the hope that when all the facts came out it would be shown that John Landis had not been reckless. Braun said that he felt that they had a shot at avoiding an indictment on the manslaughter charges because it was an "accident." Technically, the violations of child labor laws were only misdemeanor criminal violations. By joining in a conspiracy to break those laws Landis and his associates could face felony charges. But still all this was on the assumption that the damage could be controlled and there would be no criminal violations worse than the conspiracy to break the laws; that is, Braun felt, they would have been charged with hiring the kids illegally.

The meeting broke up on a slightly more hopeful note than it had begun.

* * *

Harland Braun returned to his office, which was just down vast sun-drenched Century Plaza. Its horizon was bounded by towering buildings. The population of Century City, dominated by the Century Plaza Hotel where the president stayed on his visits to Los Angeles, was made up of lawyers, and everywhere, figures could be seen sunk in thought like Harland Braun pondering his new case. He was to meet with Joel Behr again that evening at Warner's Burbank office to see the film of the accident.

Behr had promised Braun there'd be "no gore – no details of blood and guts."

14

MORE FUNERALS

At Vic Morrow's funeral on Sunday the press was said to have been reasonably "behaved," whereas during the funerals on Tuesday of Renee and Myca, it was roundly denounced. The deaths of the children on a movie set brought out strong emotional reactions. By Tuesday, a lot more was known about the crash. The ceremonies saw a great amount of elbowing and jostling by the media people. At Renee's funeral in the morning the crush was so intense that one of the family members was almost pushed into the little grave.

Again self-invited, Landis and his Hollywood entourage burst upon the private grief of the Asian mourners. John Landis looked as if since the carnage at Indian Dunes he had stopped troubling himself about his hair and beard; he looked unshaven and uncombed. With appalling lack of delicacy this bohemian figure faced Mark Chen, the Chinese accountant, who looked upon him as the murderer of his little daughter. The presence of John Landis turned the ceremonies into a fracas. During the funeral of the little girl he fled around the chapel hotly pursued by TV cameramen, his wife Deborah in tow, along with his two longtime friends, Sean Daniel and Saul Kahan.

Someone shouted to ask whether he ordered the helicopter in too close to the special effects. Another shot a question about the illegal use of the child actors. In the eagerness of the reporters to get to the director he was elbowed and shoved while George Folsey Jr. was almost knocked over.

The media people found outside the chapel a mini-press conference in progress. It was conducted by Donna Schuman. Her husband Hal stood at her side. Both were grim and white-faced. They quickly drew attention from Universal's Sean Daniel, who with Landis' wife, friends and publicists formed a defensive flank around the director. Donna Schuman shouted at the slight-built ashen figure:

"You're a puppet for John!"

She then turned to the reporters, asserting that John Landis and Warner would do anything to protect themselves, and when Sean Daniel tried to intervene, she again turned on him, shouting:

"You'll do anything for John. You're his best friend. You don't care about the truth. You're only here to protect John."

* * *

Six-year-old Renee Chen was certainly pretty enough to be in a Hollywood movie. Her parents were quiet, industrious immigrants from Taiwan. They loved their daughter and felt proud that she was already a Hollywood star. The little girl was even more excited than her parents. She couldn't keep her innocent wonder to herself and kept talking about it to all her little friends on the quiet Pasadena street where the family lived.

During the services for Renee the eulogy was continually broken by her mother's sobbing, the unearthly sound of which neither Michael Scott on the cliff nor Steve Lydecker on his crane four days before could ever forget.

The Chinese minister read from scriptures and said that Renee "must have gone to heaven."

Afterwards Renee's mother was led outside to one of the eight canvas chairs that had been set up near the small grave just outside a line of trees. It was dug in a hillside and laden with flowers. Renee's father watched aghast as the metal coffin was lowered. Peter Chen, his brother, caught him as he stumbled towards his wife, crying, "She was the only child I had! Now she is gone!"

Renee was a happy child, people said, and very, very loving...

George Folsey Jr. had arranged for a Warner car to take the Schumans to the children's funerals. It so happened that their chauffeur had been on the set the night of the crash and after attending Renee's funeral he became so emotionally distraught that Hal Schuman ended up taking over the wheel; as the Schumans took the chauffeur home the rest of the Hollywood cortege hurtled on down the Golden State Freeway to Cerittos, a 30-mile drive southeast into LA's sea of suburbia.

Unlike the Chen funeral, with its emotional trauma, that of Myca Le was restrained. The Hollywood entourage trailed by the press fell into the subdued mood of the Lutheran church in Cerritos. Prayers were offered in Vietnamese. The choir sang Myca's favorite hymn, "Jesus Loves All the Children of the World."

Myca had been a member of the choir. Everyone remembered the little boy's goodness, obedience and religious devotion. "I know only two languages now," the pastor in his eulogy quoted one of Myca's sayings as remembered by the dead boy's first grade teacher, "but I want to know as many languages as I can, because some day I want to go around the world and tell people that God so loved the world that he gave his only begotten son." It was also remembered that once in class when the children were asked which among them was most like Jesus, everyone as with one voice chorused, "Myca."

Both Myca's parents were social workers. They went through the services, after quietly receiving condolences, with a bearing of disciplined dignity. The sadness was replete with ironies personal to themselves. Myca had been named in gratitude for the countries where Daniel and Kim had studied for their degrees, "My" for the United States and "Ca" for Canada, countries where they "remembered kind people." While still living in Vietnam, Myca's father used to watch regularly Vic Morrow in *Combat*, a favorite on Saigon TV.

The Les left their country just before the fall of Saigon. Both had large families still there and before the service began the pastor announced that it was being recorded for Myca's relatives in Vietnam. The country was now Communist. It took many weeks for the mail to get there. But finally, when his relatives got to listen to the recording, one doubts they wondered how different Myca's life would be if he had stayed in Saigon instead of coming to Southern California.

15

LA Law

In the four years following the *Twilight Zone* deaths, John Landis directed five more film projects: *Trading Places, Thriller, Into the Night, Spies Like Us* and *Three Amigos*. The films featured top box-office stars like Eddie Murphy, Chevy Chase, Steve Martin and Michael Jackson.

All that time the busy movie maker followed to the painful letter Joel Behr's instructions not to speak publicly about that night. To the world the young director gave the impression that, buried in moviemaking, bringing the world his rambunctious comic vision, he had left behind this dismal period in his career. Throughout the years he made public his understanding and feelings about the tragedy a total of no more than three times, always with lawyers at his side, sometimes as many as four, like a string quartet led by a longhaired, bearded conductor. John Landis spoke most fully about the events at Indian Dunes at his trial in the spring of 1987. The only other times were during the NTSB interview five days after the crash on Wednesday afternoon, July 28, 1982, and briefly to an *Los Angeles Times* reporter regarding a controversy in the case that briefly flared up in December that same year. Conducted by Don Llorente, the NTSB interview was held in the Century City offices of attorney Joel Behr.

Landis' personal lawyer had completed assembly of the legal phalanx to protect his client within 72 hours from the time of the crash. From the standpoint of priorities, the criminal attorney was the most important. Harland Braun's bailiwick consisted of all the criminal issues likely to be prosecuted by the district attorney's office, primarily the illegal hiring of the children. But the accident touched many agencies, not just the DA's office. To deal with agencies on the California state level like Cal/OSHA and Charlie Hughes from the Labor Commission, Behr engaged a specialist in labor questions, Andy Peterson, of the firm of Paul, Hastings, Janofsky and Walker. Anticipating many millions in damage claims from the grieving parents and the heirs of Vic Morrow, Behr also hired Martin Rose of Kern & Wooley for the civil side. Thusly insulated by his lawyer and confidant Joel Behr, in addition to the buffers of some half-dozen additional lawyers (eventually to include Landis' own private eye), the director was from the very beginning well-cushioned against an increasingly curious public and an army of investigators. Already at this early stage a half-dozen law firms were being kept busy just by Warner and John Landis alone; and their number was to grow as the crash became a controversy involving more and more people. By the time the trial commenced four years later they constituted an entire industry, absorbing enormous sums, spread over the towers of Century City.

When he sat down for his first public comments on the case the Wednesday following the crash, Landis' problems were not merely confined to the investigative bodies. Public opinion was being shaped by forces over which, at least initially, he had no control. Among the TZ crew there was a universal feeling of dismay about the way the investigation was going in its opening phase. Crew members spread rumors about Landis' relationship with the pretty female who was his personal driver on the production. Others like Roger Smith, the helicopter cameraman, and Steve Lydecker, the master shot, had openly begun to speak their minds. Even Steven Larner, Landis' director of photography (he would later win an Emmy for the TV film *Winds of War*), made some very pointed remarks about the safety on the set. Cameraman Randy Robinson repeated to the press the by now notorious "lower, lower" quote, and the pilot's description of the fire-engulfed helicopter was quotably pungent-"It felt like being shot out of the sun."

But fortunately for John Landis, his NTSB interview occurred at a time when the news people and investigators were as yet unable to contact most of the crew who had been closely involved in the set. Paul Stewart was off getting drunk with Jerry Williams, who had a boat. Others were scattered to distant points. Hilary Leach was in London. Dan Allingham and set designer Richard Sawyer were together in Hawaii. Even 2nd AD Andy House left for France the day after the disastrous wrap.

From the very first, Andy House appeared to be the person who might break the case wide open. Still wearing the bright orange shirt he'd worn on the set, the 2nd AD had gone home from the Indian Dunes disaster and cried. When Allingham in an effort to recruit him for the funerals called the next day, House had explained that his wife was waiting for him in Paris for a brief vacation that had been planned long in advance. Just before boarding the plane, House stopped at Elie Cohn's office on the Paramount lot to pick up a jacket the 1st AD had borrowed from him on the set.

The feelings Andy House had for his former boss were understandably ambivalent. Cohn had continued to reassure him right up till the moment of the crash that they were still considering the dummies or small people instead of children, which House had suggested.

House found Cohn in his office. The 1st AD was brisk and truculent. He was angry at the newspapers and insistently denied that Landis gave the cue for action with "lower, lower" as the press had reported.

House flew off to Paris with the painful awareness that neither Vic Morrow nor the kids had known what was coming.

After Universal and Paramount, Warner Bros. Inc. ranked third in revenues among the big three Hollywood studios at the time of the crash. Its golden shield consisting of the two WB initials was an indelible logo in American brand-name culture, setting off in people's minds Looney Tunes and movie titles with all-American heroes and heroines like Humphrey Bogart and Ingrid Bergman. The obviously undesirable effects on public opinion of the fatalities on one of its movie sets worried the studio. Its fate was now hitched to that of the young director. The dead children bound them together. From a legal standpoint, Landis and his group were agents of Warner and the studio as financier of the film could be held responsible for the actions of its stunt-happy director.

On Tuesday, July 27, the day before Landis' meeting with the NTSB, William Vaughn and his assistant Scott Dunham from Warner's law firm of O'Melveny & Myers visited Charlie Hughes at the LA labor commissioner's office downtown. Vaughn personally served Hughes with a limited supply of documents subpoenaed the day before from Warner to determine the studio's involvement in the illegal hiring of the children. The appearance of one of LA's most powerful lawyers at Charlie Hughes' shabby downtown office was not lost on the investigators of the labor commission.

William Vaughn was chief litigator for LA's oldest law firm, which had its entertainment law business headquartered in Century City. O'Melveny & Myers' lasting Hollywood connections began in 1929 with Bing Crosby, including among later clients Mary Pickford, Ingrid Bergman, Jack Benny, Gene Autry, James Stewart, Gary Cooper, William Holden and institutional clients like Paramount, Walt Disney and CBS, whose anchorman, Dan Rather, would be successfully defended by William Vaughn in a 1983 libel suit. The fact that Bill Vaughn, generally recognized as O'Melveny's top trial lawyer, spearheaded the efforts by the studio to escape punishment from the labor commissioner signaled how much Warner feared having its permit to use children revoked. They were up against Charlie Hugh's formidable boss, Colleen Logan.

Aside from heading up the labor commission's LA office, Colleen Logan had drafted the original language of the laws governing the employment of children in the California motion picture industry. In Hollywood she became known after wrangling with high-profile child labor cases such as that involving Brooke Shields, a minor at the time. As the guardian of child film actors she'd been known to override Hollywood mothers willing to do anything to get their kids in pictures. In one of her most notable decisions, she turned down California's former governor Edmund Brown. Brown confronted Logan in her office with four other lawyers and personally lobbied for the studio's efforts to approve a permit for foul language to be used by 12-year-old Jody Foster. As the result of Logan's refusal to grant an exemption, the movie *Taxi Driver* with the under-age Jody Foster was banned from being filmed in California.

But with the involvement of Warner the pressures on the labor commissioner took on an unprecedented form. On July 30, two days following Vaughn's visit to Hughes, Colleen Logan's boss in Sacramento, Patrick Henning, flew down to Los Angeles and during a July 30, press conference called the crash at Indian Dunes an "obscene tragedy." Henning said it "would never have occurred if the child labor laws of the state had been followed." He pointed the finger directly at Warner. "Executives in the motion picture industry know these strict laws well," Henning remarked. He planned to take no actions against the parents. The labor commissioner believed that they had already paid the ultimate price. But he issued a $5,000 citation each, the maximum allowable under the labor code, against the corporation, Warner Bros., Inc. and three individuals, John Landis, George Folsey Jr. and Dan Allingham.

The omission from the list of citations of Frank Marshall's name was conspicuous and perhaps due to a lack of general understanding by investigators of the hierarchy on a Hollywood movie production. Traditionally Marshall, the executive producer who, as Spielberg's man, was present during the shooting of the fatal scene, actually exceeded John Landis in authority on the set. Yet, the only investigating agency to mention Marshall was Cal/OSHA when it cited four companies with nine violations of safety practices during the filming. Included among the Cal/OSHA list of citations was an obscure entity called Twilight Zone Productions and among the names cited, along with George Folsey Jr. and John Landis, was Frank Marshall.

On Tuesday, the day following the first viewing of the crash footage, Don Llorente returned to TBS. The footage was again projected in the screening room before freshly assembled investigators. There was a total of three clips in the NTSB's possession. The first showed the 11:30 rage scene. The second clip was a most innocent looking cut filmed by one camera, no more than a minute in length, which the clapperboard that opens and identifies the scene designated "DOCU," with the time, 2:00, as "DOCU/2:00." The final clip showed the shocking 2:20 final scene. Missing, however, was the first scene recorded that evening, the 9:30 rescue sequence, where the helicopter was off-camera and in the air, its engines and rotors running to create a wind effect. This shot, important in showing the proximity of Vic, the children and explosives early in the evening, would evade every investigator, including the DA's office, until one-and-one-half years later when it accidentally surfaced prior to the trial. Also missing – and never to surface – was the crucial second soundtrack.

Of the clips in the accident footage only the final 2:20 scene was subjected to a minute, frame-by-frame analysis as investigators attempted to determine exactly how the SFX explosives had caused the crash. That same Tuesday when the children were being buried, Llorente spent in the TBS screening room. He went through the blowups of each frame recorded by a half-dozen cameras. As the action unfolded in a series of soundless images, the questions formed themselves in the viewer's mind. How was the scene planned? What preparations were made? How were the scenes coordinated? What was the communication set-up like? What size were the explosives? Who was in charge? How was the helicopter positioned in relation to the explosives? Where were the stuntmen? And the kids?...

Llorente was not satisfied. The NTSB man knew that whatever people saw that night would very quickly become transformed and he wanted to question these people before that happened. For the first few days no one could say with any certainty what brought the gunship down. John Landis himself conjectured that it might have been the lid of a glue pot accidentally hurled into the helicopter by a special-effects explosive. So, in order to find out what had happened, Llorente was to interview subjects from the ranks of the set; from the cameramen, special effects men, grips, electricians and the truck driver who claimed he saw Steven Spielberg on the set at the time of the accident, to the director who insisted he bore no blame in the event.

Yet, despite Llorente's efforts, there were some important omissions from the interviews. Though Elie Cohn, the 1st AD, was questioned, the NTSB failed to interview Andy House, third after Landis and Cohn in authority on the set. Neither did the NTSB record what Dick Vane, the location manager with close ties to the Spielberg organization, knew about the size and placement of the explosives, even though the NTSB was aware that Vane engaged a record number of FSOs for the shooting of the final scene. The absence of Frank Marshall from Llorente's list was to become the pattern throughout the case. The net was passing over the man who as the film's executive producer and Spielberg's righthand man was present when the crash occurred.

When Llorente once tried to get Marshall's cooperation, he was convinced by the film maker's lawyer, Rick Rosen, that Marshall had no knowledge of any of the events, being "just an executive on the set." Neither did Llorente succeed in interviewing Landis' co-producer Steven Spielberg. The NTSB accepted a statement from Spielberg that he was not on the location at the time of the accident. It was the only time that Spielberg was required to address the extent of his involvement in the crash.

16

THE PHALANX

Five days after the crash, at the time the NTSB's afternoon session began, John Landis had not changed in appearance from his first meeting two days earlier with his criminal attorney, Harland Braun. Braun's operative word in describing his new client had been "shaggy" – "shaggy hair, shaggy beard, shaggy clothes." The bohemian air of the *auteur* came from all that hair and once deprived of it, as he would be for his trial four years later, he looked suddenly much younger than his 35 years; with the vanished hair he looked a cross between Jerry Lewis and Alfred E. Neuman, an astonishing transformation; with his cropped head and face he looked like a high school student who might be – for there was a strange resemblance between them – Steven Spielberg's goofy younger brother!

Landis was surrounded by the phalanx of $200-an-hour Century City lawyers. They were like a cabinet with their premier Joel Behr. Behr was assisted by John Diemer who with a prematurely receding hairline still exuded a round-faced collegiate look. Diemer, just two years out of UCLA Law School, had in the *Twilight Zone* his first big Hollywood case. From the very first day, immersed in investigating all the child labor laws that might have been violated by Landis, Folsey and Allingham, Diemer emerged as Behr's righthand man. He was indispensable by the time the grand jury convened a year later. Diemer sat close to Behr during the NTSB interview with Landis. In addition to Diemer and criminal counsel Harland Braun, the Landis legal phalanx, primarily in connection with the expected civil lawsuits, included Martin Rose of Kern & Wooley, the LA law firm that specialized in aircraft accidents.

By adopting the strategy of letting John Landis talk to the NTSB, attorney Harland Braun realized that the defense team took a calculated risk. Even though the strategy cut off the press and subpoenas from other agencies, the interview could turn out to be a Pandora's box.

"The risk could be," Braun explained, "that if he ever got indicted he'd have all these statements that could be used." In that case the DA and other investigators would practically have a volume of testimony not only from John Landis but from all the people who were on the set that night.

No one could anticipate the can of worms that could pose to the defense. There was no way of knowing whether the witnesses called by Llorente would be friendly or hostile to the director.

"We took the position," Braun reasoned, "to be very cooperative on anything dealing with safety on the set. We didn't want to deliver to them a case of conspiracy to hire the kids and then cover up. We weren't sure how far that thing would spread, and we knew we'd probably get charged with it anyway."

In any event, Braun summed up, "I developed a strategy that they're innocent, so let's go forward." And, on Wednesday, July 28, 1982, John Landis sat in his personal attorney Joel Behr's Century City office, facing a panel of quizzical interrogators led by Don Llorente.

"For my own edification," Llorente began, "what are your prime responsibilities for that movie?"

Landis stumbled, Behr quickly intervened; Landis went "off the record," as he did nearly 30 times during the proceeding. The movie director and his lawyer whispered so the tapes would not record the highly delicate question of how to define the director's job. For by defining the actual level of the director's authority serious questions could be raised as to the extent of his actual responsibility for the crash. Thus, in replying to the NTSB man, the film maker witness narrowly defined a director's role on the set as "the placement of cameras and actors." In so doing Landis pointed the finger at others. In his view, the director had to rely on what others did on the set. But as he admitted with aggrieved resignation, citing a Hollywood story, the director ultimately would be held accountable: "Alfred Hitchcock said, 'The director is the one who gets the blame,' so I mean, you know, that's what the director's function is. He's the person who makes the movie."

By vaguely defining his role on the set, Landis tried to distance himself from the event, and since no one as yet knew exactly what had caused the fatal crash, his veiled accusations went unchallenged. He suggested names of other people possibly with knowledge related to the incident: Fred Gallo, Warner's chief of worldwide production; Lucy Fisher, now VP at Warner's; and Terry Semel, Warner president. Landis mentioned that all of them had read the script and approved it. He also mentioned that Steven Spielberg was his co-producer; but Joel Behr was quick to squelch, "Mr. Spielberg had nothing, and has nothing to do with the production of this particular episode at all."

Llorente moved on to Landis' role in the planning. The newspapers had been full of quotes by people claiming they had heard Landis shout "lower, lower" to the helicopter pilot just seconds before the fatal crash.

Understandably, Llorente asked whether he had actually given the command that brought the craft into the "hover" position immediately above the special-effects explosives, a position which Llorente knew was the most dangerous for a helicopter to be in.

The surprisingly simple question seemed to cause Landis to stumble.

"During the filming?" he asked.

"Yes."

"During ... truthfully, I don't know. I – I was.... Shall I describe what happened?"

Landis' personal lawyer gently prodded his client: "Describe what happened."

The listeners hunched over the table with anticipation.

"Please," said Llorente, ever courteous.

"You know how the village's here," Landis began. "There's a river here, and here's an island. I was on the island, and my attention was focused on Vic and the kids. Once I thought where the copter was basically okay, I said okay. Fine. Action. And my cue for Vic was, I had a megaphone, and I go like this for Vic, so Vic can see me. Vic and the kids started across the river. My attention was on Vic and the kids. I was not watching the helicopter. I watched Vic and the kids. The explosions went off. Everything was going off as I assumed it was.

"All of a sudden this helicopter went like that... about 10 feet from me. And I was completely startled. I went, What the fuck is this helicopter doing in my shot!"

The personality broke through the phalanx. One member of the panel recalled he gasped. There was a lady present, too, Marilyn Levine of Cal/ OSHA. But the incident failed to dent the calm, courteous formality of Don Llorente.

"Yeah," Llorente pressed on dryly, going back to his original question, whether Landis had directed the helicopter to fly lower. "Did you have any direct communication with the helicopter pilot?" Avoiding a direct answer, Landis replied that in earlier takes he used a walkie-talkie to communicate with Allingham, who was sitting next to Wingo.

"Yes, sir," Llorente insisted politely. "But on the accident sequence, you did not, at any time then, talk to the pilot via his walkie- talkie?"

Joel Behr qualified cautiously, "If you recall." Llorente repeated, "If you recall."

"Well, two things, Landis answered. "One, I couldn't because there's too much noise, but also, I truly don't – I was asking Joel. I truly don't – I was asking Joel. I truly don't remember. I wasn't told – I don't remember. No, I don't remember that. I don't know. It's the truth. I don't – I was holding on. I was holding a megaphone...

The blue and white "bullhorn" that Landis used to shout orders all night had become identified with his persona. The megaphone was a new electronic type which amplified the voice to a volume that could be heard over the greatest noise. For some time, the investigators regarded it as the symbol of the director's authority on the set. They debated for a long time whether Landis used this instrument to shout "lower, lower," while at the same time waving it, thereby deliberately bringing the helicopter into a lethal special-effects firestorm.

However, since Landis denied having given the order for the helicopter to come lower either through his bullhorn or walkie-talkie, the focus shifted to the person next in the communication chain to the pilot. Seated next to Wingo and operating the spotlight at the time of the crash, perhaps Dan Allingham, Llorente assumed, had communicated the fatal command to the pilot. But when asked to clarify this vital question, Landis' lawyer, now serving as Allingham's counsel too, objected that his client was being asked to speculate. Landis, saying he didn't understand the question, concurred.

Llorente patiently restated the question: "So does anyone else who happened to be standing there! Then I don't know!"

Landis sounded bewildered, repeating after his lawyer, "You are speculating," and continuing, "I do not understand that question. The authority to say no. I mean the authority to say no. I mean I don't understand that question. I don't understand that question."

"Okay," Llorente said calmly, "What you're saying then, when they're shooting the film and when the pilot is in the aircraft, that he has, more or less, the absolute control of that aircraft."

"At any time when you're shooting the film," Landis broke in excitedly, "or when you're not shooting the film the pilot has total control of the aircraft. I've worked with helicopters many, many times in films. In the *Blues Brothers* we did extraordinary helicopter stuff. In fact, I've made some of the biggest stunt movies of all time. When a stunt man says to you, 'This is too dangerous,' or a pilot says, 'I cannot do this,' which happens a lot, you then say, 'Okay, we've got to think of something else.' I'm not God. I can't fucking say well, you know, these visions of Erich Von Stroheim, 'Blow them all up!' I mean, what is that? Of course, the pilot is the only one who has the responsibility where to put the copter. I wasn't flying the helicopter, and neither was Dan."

Landis appeared unable to comprehend.

"I just don't understand that question. When you say, 'Does Dan have the authority?' I don't understand. I'm sorry, I don't understand that question."

"Fine," Llorente said unperturbed. As a pilot himself, the NTSB's chief investigator was aware that ultimately it was up to the pilot to fly or not to fly. "You said the pilot had the authority to either say yea or nay to a shot. Is that correct?"

"Of course," John Landis said.

In determining the director's responsibility in relation to the crash two elements were crucial. One was the positioning of the helicopter, the other concerned the placement and timing of the explosives. At this point John Landis did not appear to think that the disaster at Indian Dunes had anything to do with the timing of the special-effects explosions. Nor did he mention anything about the series of explosives going off in the wrong place or prematurely. There was nothing in his statement to the NTSB investigators to suggest that the two explosions that went off on the shoreline nearest the action, which ultimately were identified as those that brought down the helicopter, were any other than a series that had been planned: "Everything was going off as I assumed it was," he had already indicated.

Llorente passed the questioning to the Cal-OSHA lawyer, Marilyn Levine. She asked if there were any written plans for the sequence with the helicopter flying and the explosions going off. Cavalierly, the director allowed, "There were lots of thumbnail sketches." As for blueprints, he couldn't remember.

At issue was the centrality of the director's authority. Who was responsible on the set? Wingo? Stewart? Allingham? But in a way no one on the panel could have foreseen, John Landis himself settled the question as he turned to Llorente who had just lit a cigarette.

"Could you do me a favor and put out your cigarette?"

The brash manner irked everybody. It only confirmed to Landis' new criminal defense counsel the need to protect John Landis from himself.

"Oh, sure, surely, okay," Llorente said, startled.

In a ghastly effort to be disarming Landis continued, projecting bifocals, beard and hair and the funny smirk, "No smoking on my set."

The lawyers laughed, albeit uncomfortably. But Llorente and his team took it altogether seriously. It settled in their minds who had authority on the set. After persistently toe-dancing around the question of the director's responsibility Landis indicated that the set was wherever he found himself, including his lawyer's office in Century City.

"At first he was saying that he was not the captain of the ship, and then suddenly he was the big boss."

Llorente was indignant.

"No smoking on my set!?"

In wanting to know what brought the craft down, Llorente had a few basic questions. Were adequate precautions taken to ensure that the flight would be safely away from explosives when they were set off? Did John Landis do enough after having been warned of potential trouble following the 11:30, next-to-last shot?

"Did anybody," Llorente asked, "after that particular shot, come to you and say that the pilot voiced any concern, as far as the heat being generated from those shots?"

"Dorcey, the pilot, and Dan Allingham, both came to me and said, we were concerned because, I don't know who, someone voiced a theory that because there was a cliff when the fire – a movie fireball. You've seen them. They just go like this, KABOOM!"

"Yeah," Llorente said dryly.

Quoting Wingo's complaints about the 11:30 shot, Landis made it appear that the pilot was concerned about flying too close to the cliff when, in fact, Wingo had been worried about being too close to the explosives in the village. According to Landis, Wingo had come to him after that shot, and asked, "'When we do the next one, can I be out over the river?' And I said, 'Yes, of course.' And we discussed that, and I decided that the helicopter should be much further over the river."

He told the NTSB that as the result of the complaints at 11:30 he repositioned the helicopter during a 2:00 "rehearsal." This meant that there had actually been four helicopter flights that night, three of which were actual film clips – the 9:30 rescue sequence, the 11:30 rage scene, and the 2:20 final shot. The so-called "rehearsal" flight at 2:00 A.M., in which the craft was allegedly "repositioned," had appeared on the screen at the special screenings. Sandwiched between the footage of the 11:30 rage scene and the 2:20 fatal shot, this "rehearsal" footage showed John Landis waving his bullhorn in an effort to locate the helicopter and its powerful Nite-Sun into the desired position for the big, finale shot. This unusual scene opened with a mysterious clapperboard indication: the viewers read "DOCU/2:00" on the screen. This clip was the only flight of the helicopter that night that was not part of the shooting schedule – it was a "rehearsal," Landis explained to Llorente, which, according to Landis' scenario, came as the direct result of the complaints from the helicopter crew during the 11:30 rage scene. By positioning the helicopter in a new spot "over the river," the director suggested that the "rehearsal" flight showed that the chopper was supposed to be a safe distance away from the explosions.

"We rehearsed it," Landis reiterated. "We rehearsed everything."

Marilyn Levine of Cal/OSHA, however, a lawyer specializing in safety issues, appeared not to be altogether convinced. She voiced her concern that in conversations with other people there was some question as to whether or not the fatal 2:20 shot had been rehearsed at all.

"Just so you know," Landis broke in angry response to her implied skepticism, "It's just a practical reality. You cannot film something unless you know where it's going to be... The cameras had to line up." He seemed to lose his temper.

"I understand," Marilyn replied softly, stunned by the director's brusqueness.

"I'm sorry," Landis backed off, "I apologize, okay?"

The questioning continued.

"At the time that you were actually filming the accident sequence was the helicopter in its position as previously rehearsed?"

"Basically," Landis said. "It wasn't exactly where it was going to be, but I figured that I didn't care."

His answer brought another halt to the proceedings. Without realizing it, his remark was potentially devastating. The most startled person in the room was Harland Braun. He realized the enormity of the job he had taken on by defending John Landis. Throughout the interview the director had striven to portray a well-run set, no smoking allowed. He had mentioned pre-planned positions, safety precautions and a 2:00 o'clock "rehearsal" for the final shot. And suddenly he shattered this placid picture by expressing lack of concern about the most important safety consideration of the shot. As Braun put it, recalling his client's notorious gaffe, "What bothers you on something like that is the emphasis."

Don Llorente was as astonished as anyone.

"Okay," he resumed, "When you say it wasn't exactly–"

But Landis interrupted.

"I thought it was going to be further out over the river, and when it came in and stopped and it was hovering, it was like, well, there, it's hovering, it was like, well, there, it's hovering. Okay – *I'm going to get my shot...*"

17

THE RASHOMON EFFECT

The recollections of what happened that night of the crash in Indian Dunes was like *Rashomon*, the film classic by the Japanese director Kurosawa, in which a crime occurs and as each witness tells what he or she saw the viewer gets a different perspective on what happened. The same theme might have applied to the stories of eyewitnesses to the *Twilight Zone* disaster. Depending on where people were standing at the time of the accident, how close to the set they were, whether they were watching Vic or the helicopter, and numerous other variations, it was understandable that there would be many versions of the actual occurrence.

The *Rashomon* effect came into play each time Llorente compared the above- with the below-the-line version. Above-the-line, the recollections of Landis, Allingham, Cohn and Folsey basically formed a consistent version. Later on, Llorente and his team, treated to the *Rashomon* effect from below-the-line, would see everything take a radical turn.

The day following the Landis interview, Llorente interviewed Dan Allingham. The NTSB investigator had actually been given a thumbnail definition of Allingham's job the previous day by the director, who compared the unit production manager to the plant manager; the "guy on the line responsible for making the deals." At his NTSB session Allingham was flanked by the Landis legal phalanx, including Harland Braun and Joel Behr with his assistant John Diemer. Behr hovered over the struggling witness, frequently assisting to refresh his memory.

At times Allingham's answers to questions seemed to be more specific than Landis, while on others his memory seemed unreliable. Allingham told the panel he didn't know whether he received instructions like "lower, lower" over the radio. He didn't remember "a heck of a lot" of this scene. His further appearance before the panel sent some of Landis' lawyers into near hysteria.

The day before, John Landis had told the NTSB that after the 11:30 scene, in response to complaints from the pilot, he repositioned the helicopter in a new spot "over the river" for the final shot. Though he remembered hearing some complaints, Allingham told the investigators that after the 11:30 near-miss he only heard innocuous comments like, "Boy, that was a little warm," or "Gee, I felt a little hot from that." At first he didn't even recall the 2:00 "rehearsal," which Landis said he had ordered at Wingo's request as a result of the earlier mishap. Not until Behr went off the record to refresh Allingham's memory did the witness return to the subject of the 2:00 "non-filming shot," as the NTSB investigators called the "rehearsal," or DOCU/2:00, as it was marked on the film. With his memory refreshed by Behr, Allingham recalled the rehearsal being "over the water itself" – and he even remembered having been in it!

Allingham, like Landis, did not hesitate to point the finger at the pilot and the explosives chief. The UPM cited his reliance on "professionalism," hiring "what we thought were the best." But once hired, he said, he had little contact with them, basically leaving it up to the pilot and the explosives chief to work out the type of effects that would be used.

The way John Landis described it, movie making was just like any other business in which the set is like a small factory whose product is the shot. Each shot is strung together in the editing room to make the film. John Landis, as director, is the factory owner, the UPM is the key man on the line who makes sure everything is there. The 1st AD, by the same analogy, is the factory foreman, "the guy who makes it run," as Landis put it. The 1st AD makes sure all the departments – costuming, camera, makeup, special effects – are functioning and that everything is ready on the set when, at the cue from the director, he has the privilege to shout, "Roll 'em!" Or as the Hollywood transplant from Israel, Elie Cohn, shouted in thickly accented English, "Turn' em!"

Elie Cohn, whose youthful appearance belied the fact that he had fought in two Israeli wars, gave the impression of a hard, military person. He had met John Landis on the set of the 1981 Costa-Gavras film *Missing*, with Jack Lemmon. The film, for which Lemmon received an Academy Award, was being shot in Mexico for Universal and John Landis came to the set to visit his best friend, Universal's Sean Daniel. The director and Elie Cohn lunched together, and John Landis remembered Cohn when he needed a 1st AD in a pinch for his TZ segment. The addition of Cohn to the production was prompted by Warner's dissatisfaction with Landis' budget cutting techniques. When Warner's Fred Gallo discovered that Allingham was cutting corners by doubling up as a first AD, in addition to his UPM duties, the top Warner executive demanded that Fly By Night comply with the studios' labor agreements and hire a separate individual for the job.

At the time of his testimony, Elie Cohn had professed a deep loyalty to the hyperkinetic director. Central to the first AD's version of what happened that night at Indian Dunes was an effort to show that there was a consensus among the key crew members as to what was expected to happen during the crash scene. Like Landis and Allingham, as would Folsey later, Cohn mentioned the 2:00 "rehearsal" in his NTSB interview. He reiterated that the pilot knew what was happening, affirming that the director had to rely on others. Cohn held to the above-the-line version of the crash. While shooting the crucial crash scene, the 1st AD said he had two walkie-talkies, one to talk to his special assistant and the camera operators; the other to communicate with Dan Allingham in the helicopter who also had two walkie-talkies "just in case," Cohn explained, because one didn't work too well on the prior shot.

By now the NTSB had obtained photographs and some graphics of the set relating to the crash. When being shown a photograph showing a prominent stick that had been planted as a cueing device in the middle of the river, Cohn was asked to point out where in relation to it he saw the helicopter hovering. Cohn pointed to "the stick," indicating that Vic Morrow was to run towards the stick while the helicopter hovered to the north of the village pier with the sampan tied to it. His understanding of the way the scene occurred had Landis positioning the helicopter "over the river," away from the fatal fireballs on the village shoreline. The cue for the fireballs, Cohn indicated, was the machine guns opening fire from the helicopter.

Elie Cohn was a more assured witness than Allingham, more consistent in detail, and in many ways a more arresting witness. Landis' and Allingham's accounts, for example, reflected nothing of the sheer deadly terror which Cohn said everyone on the set felt as the helicopter came down and the entire crew thought it was going to burst into flame and kill every one of them; like Allingham, Cohn believed the helicopter went out of control after the first explosion. "The only thing that came to my mind is that the helicopter would explode, so you know I was standing over here" – he pointed to the spit of sand – "and I went over there..."

Llorente, wondering what happened to the helicopter while Cohn was walking back and forth after the first explosion hit the craft, queried, "It stayed in position?"

"It was really a matter of a very few seconds.... I never lost sight of the helicopter; I mean it was covered with flame. I was a dead man to be honest with you." Cohn repeated, "I was sure I was dead."

"You were sure you were dead because you saw the helicopter..."

But Cohn wouldn't let Llorente finish, "I was dead," the 1st AD repeated stubbornly.

"I was dead, and everybody around us."

The Israeli film man told the NTSB that following the 11:30 rage scene he heard from people who'd flown through the fireballs in the helicopter that they could feel the explosions. He said he could see that they were wet from the water mortar. It was very much on everybody's mind, he noted, that the final shot was going to be bigger.

"You know," Cohn confided, referring to the lunch break following the rage scene, "people were talking at dinner. John was telling about the explosions going to be bigger." Cohn recalled that the director was making the point to the stunt coordinator who had just been in the rocky flight. Cohn remembered the director saying, "We're going to do it again, and explosions are going to be bigger."

Before the start of the final shooting, Cohn told Llorente, "We rehearsed the helicopter, where the helicopter would go, fly to, and the cue again, which everybody was aware of before the explosions." He mentioned that Vic Morrow not only was fully briefed in his "motor home" by John Landis but also participated in the "rehearsal."

An unfamiliarity with the language excused the Israeli film maker from being precise or specific. It gave him the advantage of being obscure or clear-spoken when he chose, or to state two opposite conclusions simultaneously. Thus, there was and was not a bullhorn. Vic's last performance was and was not a stunt. "There was one comment made to me," Cohn recalled, "that everything is fine." At the same time, he admitted, it sounded almost "foolish" not to think that it could be dangerous.

Many on the NTSB panel questioning Landis' 1st AD had already seen the footage of the crash. The Screen Actors Guild representative on the panel was curious about the identity of the man in the bright orange shirt who appeared to be racing across the screen to the bodies. Cohn made it a minor mystery when he said he didn't know. Adding to the mystery were certain additional discrepancies which would be later pounced on at the trial. But where it was consistent with the above-the-line version was in the finger-pointing at Paul Stewart and Dorcey Wingo. Cohn said that the explosives chief knew where the helicopter would be because of the "rehearsal," which was also to have made the pilot aware of the position of the shot.

Elie Cohn had been working for Hollywood directors for about seven years and he defended Landis' conduct in general, seeing nothing inappropriate in the screaming, the obsession with special effects or having the kids on a dangerous set. "He was thinking about the best shot possible without, you know, definitely not injuring anybody; or not even, you know, coming close to it.

"It's done in our business," the 1st AD concluded. "We're working a lot of times. It's a matter of inches. I've seen it a lot of times. It happened. But then, you know, the director would ask for the best thing possible. Ninety-nine percent of the time nothing happened, and unfortunately here there was an accident.

* * *

The NTSB's probe into the *Twilight Zone* disaster was a far from typical job. Obstacles were put in Llorente's way not only by the Hollywood people, but as well by his superiors in Washington. He often found himself shunned and accused of "grandstanding." Several times he received an official reprimand for exceeding his authority. On three occasions following the close of the NTSB portion of the investigation he was passed over for promotion. It was impossible to interview Frank Marshall and Llorente himself confided that if he had attempted to summon Marshall's boss, Steven Spielberg, he would have been "crushed."

Nevertheless, the NTSB's chief investigator chanced the disapproval of higher-ups. Outwardly conforming, he quietly continued digging for answers.

The small crushed lives of the two children haunted him, even though the children were not part of Llorente's jurisdiction. In fact, when the movie director agreed to cooperate with the NTSB it was on the condition that they would not talk about the children. It fell to the labor commissioner's office to answer this question, but all that agency knew was little more than that laws had been violated. The question how the children got to Indian Dunes and who hired them – the true story of their concealment on the set as the "Vietnamese" – would not become public until a year later, and then only because of a lucky break by deputy sheriff Tom Budds in connection with Andy House, the picture's second assistant director, the man in the bright orange shirt that the first AD failed to remember in his testimony a few days after the disaster.

In the chain of command the 2nd AD was technically responsible for the handling of the children on the set the night of the crash. Yet Andy House had been overlooked by the NTSB. It was from House that authorities, incidentally, received their first clues as to how the children had been hired without permits and effectively concealed from the teacher/welfare worker, Jack Tice, the fireman the night of the crash.

Tice had first discovered that kids were in the scene when he found Myca's head in a shallow portion of the water minutes after the disaster. When literally stumbling upon this grim discovery his initial thought was that the production people had obtained the kids from the crowd at the last moment and put them before the cameras. However, with the sheriffs coming on the scene he overheard Andy House give out the children's names, and so Tice realized that House knew something about how the kids had been hired. Subsequently, Charlie Hughes, the labor investigator, obtained Andy House's name from Jack Tice; Hughes recollected with characteristic saltiness, "Andy was as nervous as a whore in a church," when he first spoke to him on the telephone within days of the accident. The second time Charlie Hughes talked to House he told the young film maker, "Look, you've ducked me for two days now." Andy went straight to Warner's lawyers.

Much to his surprise, the labor investigator soon received a telephone call from John Dellaverson, a personal friend of House and a lawyer with a prominent Hollywood entertainment firm, Loeb & Loeb. Dellaverson told Hughes that Andy would tell everything he knew for a grant of immunity and a promise that the labor commissioner would not challenge his client's ability to hire children in the future. But when Hughes took the offer to his boss, Colleen Logan, she turned it down and House declined an interview with the labor commissioner's man.

But even without Andy House, simply by comparing the statements of the three top men running the set that night, Landis, Allingham and Cohn, numerous conflicts were already apparent. Eventually there would be so many that by the time the DA's office began reviewing the case it became inevitable that the grand jury would have to be used in order to place witnesses under oath to get the story straight.

In the meantime, Don Llorente made public for the first time the NTSB findings that the crash had been caused by debris from the explosions striking the copter's tail rotor blade. Other developments in the case were reported on a daily basis by the *Herald Examiner's* Andy Furillo. One development that fixed the newspaper on the story was the fact that the "carrot-top cub" had tracked down an anonymous witness who contradicted the NTSB account given by John Landis as to where the helicopter was supposed to be when the explosives were set off. Quoting his secret source, Furillo reported that the plan for the fatal shot was to place the helicopter directly over the explosions.

"The whole object was to get the helicopter into the flames," the source told the young reporter. "They wanted the blades, the whole bit in there."

Having promised secrecy, Furillo would never reveal the source except to say that it was someone directly involved in the planning and execution of the last flight.

The secret source, it turned out, was the pilot, Dorcey Wingo.

18

NAKED BROKEN BARBIE DOLL

C harlie Hughes and his colleagues were kept a safe distance from the studio people who might, figuratively speaking, be said to have "parented" the children of the Landis segment. In the development of the script, along with Frank Marshall, Steven Spielberg and Warner president Terry Semel, a less known name in the industry, Warner's Lucy Fisher, had played a critical role in rescuing the director's unusable written efforts. A young attractive Harvard graduate, Lucy Fisher was "instrumental," according to one of Warner's internal communications, in incorporating the children into the final Landis script.

Lucy Fisher was an enigmatic figure in the *Twilight Zone* tragedy. Like the fairy tale princess in the tower, she was never seen.

At the time the Spielberg project went into production she had been about a year at Warner, a VP and senior production executive chiefly involved on the creative side in pre-production stages; typically in story development. Before that she helped Francis Ford Coppola run his floundering Zoetrope Studios, becoming at age 32 a production chief and, apart from Sherry Lansing over at Twentieth Century Fox, probably the most powerful woman in Hollywood at the time. An insider eulogizing Zoetrope's 1981 demise suggested that Coppola was only a "figurehead" and that it was really Lucy who had been running the studio. Taking her fourth studio executive job in three years, according to a Warner memo, "Lucy Fisher was hired on a recommendation from Steven Spielberg"; she was put on the TZ movie because of her special rapport with Hollywood's leading director.

Lucy Fisher was one of the first women in Hollywood to break the male-only barrier in the executive suite. Descended of the Fisher Brothers Steel Corporation, she came from East Coast steel and mortgage banking money. She set out for Hollywood with a *Cum Laude* degree from Harvard, eventually joining there the young colony of Harvard alumni, the brightest and the most amusing, who would soon launch the new post-Vietnam humor trend in film making. The chief writer of *National Lampoon's Animal House* was Lucy's closest friend, the tragic Doug Kinney, who committed suicide in 1981. Although best known to the public as "Stork" in *Animal House,* and lesser known as the film's originator, Harvard man Kinney had already pocketed $3 million before joining Lucy Fisher in Hollywood after selling out his share in the *National Lampoon* magazine, whose first issue he had helped publish in 1970.

Lucy Fisher's rise in the motion picture industry was itself a phenomenon. From writing book jacket copy for a stodgy New York publisher, Prentice-Hall, she landed a far more exciting job on the West Coast, reading scripts for United Artists. After a series of breezy promotions in the script and story areas of motion picture production – the creative side – she was appointed vice president at 20th Century Fox by Alan Ladd, "Laddie," Jr., the head of the studio, whose string of serious films about women, including *Julia, An Unmarried Woman* and *Norma Rae,* attracted Fisher, who thought of it as the least sexist studio. She felt that Laddie was "liberated."

Already by the time she had joined Coppola at Zoetrope, Lucy Fisher was hailed by the cognoscenti as an example of the changing Hollywood power elite. Her place in the upper corporate echelons was treated as a society event with her appearance in a photo spread in a *Town and Country* magazine feature article called, "The Lady Moguls of Hollywood." In the spring of '82, Warner harnessed these credentials of power, brains and connections to Spielberg's *Twilight Zone* movie. In a way it was a test. Lucy Fisher's most important assignment was a pressure-cooker – the studio wanted the TZ movie released by Christmas in order to ride the golden wake of *E.T.* and *Poltergeist.* The new female vice president was expected to exert creative supervision over a movie with a release date requiring breakneck production activity.

In a very real sense, it was Lucy Fisher who, along with Spielberg and Warner President Terry Semel, controlled the initial pre-production phase of the Landis segment. The first of the three phases of a movie's development, followed by production, which means the actual shooting of the film itself, and post-production, the editing and mixing of sound for the film, the pre-production phase, because it shapes the film's eventual outcome, is thought by many the most important. In pre-production the film's chief elements are generally established: the stars, the director, locations, setting, costume, budget and, foremost, the script, which tells the film's basic story.

Fisher's involvement as the studio's creative watchdog over the TZ project meant attending numerous meetings with everybody involved in the film, ranging from Jim Miller, Warner's business affairs chief, to Frank Marshall, John Landis and George Folsey Jr. Most of her meetings, however, were with John Landis, Frank Marshall and Warner's new president, Terry Semel, successor to Frank Wells, the Rhodes scholar and Stanford law school graduate who had come to Warner's presidency from Gang, Tyre & Brown (Hollywood attorneys to the stars, eventually to represent Steven Spielberg in the *Twilight Zone* case). In the studio hierarchy, Fisher reported directly to President Semel.

Many of the meetings Lucy attended with the production brass were highly charged and acrimonious, especially those that included both Warner's Fred Gallo and the Landis people, namely George Folsey Jr. and Dan Allingham. Gallo had come to Warner from being one of the most famous and respected 1st ADs in the business on the *Godfather*, as well as on a string of Woody Allen movies. As Warner's world-wide production chief, Gallo held the business reins over the TZ production, working on day-to-day operations. Consequently, the fundamental cause of the conflict between Gallo and Landis was the desire by the studio to control the film's day-to-day production activities, while the director's people sought to be fiercely independent from the studio.

At the earliest of these meetings the format of the film had been worked out and also how all three parties, Landis, Spielberg, and Warner, should work together. For example, although Landis had final cut on his segment, Spielberg had final cut on his own segment, as well as on the two segments other than Landis'. Nevertheless, some details still needed to be worked out and it was in this role that Lucy Fisher dealt most intimately with John Landis – a job complicated by the fact that she dealt not with Landis in his single capacity as director, but also in his auteur character as writer and in his persona as producer. As writer for the other three segments Spielberg had hired Richard Matheson, one of the last survivors of the original nucleus of writers that included Rod Serling who wrote the original *Twilight Zone*, which made its television debut in October 1959.

After reading the first script Landis submitted on April 15, 1982, Lucy Fisher came away feeling that the portrayal of the protagonist as a hateful and coarse drunken character was offensive to the viewers. She recommended that "Bill" be made human by giving him some socially redeeming qualities. Though there were already some children in the Nazi sequence of the script, their antagonistic relationship to Bill in an unedifying apartment scene was hardly calculated to bring the lacking element of human feeling to the story. Their relationship with Bill had nothing in it with which the audience could identify. "Warner Bros.," Folsey remembers, "wanted to soften the character Bill."

The problem with the first script's main character was apparent in the opening sequence in the bar. The character was too violent. Landis' shrill portrayal of Bill as racist and his vitriolic anti-semitic remarks were too much for Fisher, Spielberg and the studio brass. Bill complains that "gas costs so much 'cause some Jew wants more money," and, "Too bad you can't just shoot Goldman." Bill says, "Jew lawyer going to put me in jail," and states that because of the Jews, "This country is doomed." There were also Bill's sexist remarks to the cocktail waitress: at one point, Bill calls her a "sperm bank," and after she serves him a beer he tells his friends Ray and Larry, "I'm so horny the crack of dawn looks good to me."

The studio people found many other defects in this first draft of the unfledged *auteur*. The generous use of racial epithets was not reserved for Jews alone; vicious remarks about blacks and Asians were equally rampant. But apart from the crude portrayal of character, Lucy Fisher was particularly troubled by the story's ending.

In Landis' first draft the Vietnamese sequence was very small. Following similar brushes with Nazis and Ku Klux Klanners, Bill undergoes his final transformation from bigot to victim in a Vietnam jungle swamp amid the "sound of helicopters" and "tremendous explosions." To keep within the low budget, the Vietnamese swamp scene was to be done with the least amount of money possible by using the old-fashioned techniques of Jungle Sam Katzman, the maker of all the *Jungle Jim* movies. By simply using the right camera angles and a few palm trees, Katzman was able to make a confined area look like an elaborate jungle set. In Landis' first draft there was no village and the only reference to a helicopter – "the sound of helicopters" – indicated that sound effects alone were to be used to create the illusion of a real chopper in the scene.

Landis' original draft ended with American GIs opening fire on Bill, mistaking him in the swamp for Charlie. The GIs chase Bill as he runs into the swamp, at which point the film flashes back to the scene with Bill and the Klan. Then, again, still running, Bill escapes to a wooden shed. As he huddles in a corner of the shed, the Klansmen with axes "start chopping down the door" and as the door shatters, in yet another flashback, Nazi soldiers grab Bill and next he's back in a Nazi railroad yard; the German soldiers throw him into a freight car and as the train pulls out Bill sees his drinking buddies, Larry and Ray, smiling as they exit the bar. In scene 29, the segment's last, with his arm reaching through the slots of the departing freight car, Bill screams: "Help me, help me!" and the Landis segment ends.

Shortly after discussing his first draft at a meeting in Lucy Fisher's office at Warner, Landis agreed to rewrite the script with some of Fisher's criticisms in mind. In the second draft Bill was softened in the film's opening bar sequence by eliminating many of the most virulent anti-semitic remarks and completely removing Bill's derogatory references to women. A black patron was thrown into the bar scene for no apparent reason and Landis beefed up the final Vietnam sequence with greater emphasis on special effects, adding to Scene 25 in upper case, TREMENDOUS EXPLOSIONS. For the first time an actual helicopter appears in the story with a "blinding light... tremendous winds"-"Bill looks up in terror as a HUEY HELICOPTER descends on him..." The Vietnam sequence in this draft ends with Bill fleeing while the helicopter "hovers overhead."

After reading Landis' second version Lucy Fisher was still not satisfied. The explosives and the helicopter did not make Bill's character any less offensive to the audience. There were still some distasteful racial epithets in both the bar and the apartment scene, as well as in the Nazi sequence in which the French children shout, "Juif! Juif! Juif! Juif!" at Bill. The second draft also had a new ending that didn't make Bill's character any more sympathetic; instead of closing with the departing train, it ends with Bill's return to the bar scene, showing Ray and Larry helping their freaked buddy to his car" as the CAMERA pans up to see a 747 roar across the sky."

With the deadline near on the weekend of June 12, 1982, another critical script meeting was held at Warner president Terry Semel's home with John Landis and Lucy Fisher attending. Ideas were tossed in the air and Fisher, according to one of Warner's internal memos, feeling that Bill still did not inspire sympathy at any point, suggested the use of children in the final scenes. She felt that the bigot's relationship with the children supplied the missing element, according to Warner's dossier on the case. Landis and Semel agreed that the children solved the problem. In the season of E.T. and Poltergeist, when Spielberg's own film children romped across America's movie screens, Lucy's idea seemed to fit the winning formula.

The next day John Landis sat down to write a third draft. He softened the apartment scene in the Nazi sequence by eliminating the dialogue where the French children scream "Juif!" as Bill flees. The most dramatic change in the script, however, was a series of scenes he added to the Vietnam sequence, considerably enlarging it to include a deserted village with "thatched buildings, maybe nine or ten of them," in which Bill finds himself with two abandoned Vietnamese children and where, following failed attempts to communicate with the boy and girl, an American helicopter "appears from over the cliff and hovers over the village." Mistaking Bill for the enemy the chopper opens fire as "he grabs the kids and runs for cover." At this point he makes the "herculean" effort, carrying a child under each arm while crossing the river with the helicopter hovering over the village as "one after another the buildings blow up in flames." The new exploding village scene even made specific reference – "one of the huts EXPLODES in a spectacular fireball" – to a particular special effect which explodes while the helicopter is "over the village" as it gives chase and "Bill runs as best he can across the river."

The third draft contained nearly all the elements to be staged on the night of the fatal filming, chiefly the exploding village scene. But there were still some small problems. The opening bar scenes still seemed too harsh. The minor incident in the bar which introduces the black patron seemed gratuitous. It made no sense. And even the newly added exploding village scene with Bill and the children did not seem to make the main character any more likable. Neither did the third draft's slightly altered ending seem to help; as in the previous two drafts, Bill was again transported back to the bar scene where, outside the bar, he's hit by a truck and "pinned under its rear tire," while again a 747 roars overhead. Bill then utters the segment's closing lines:

> Help me. Help. I've got to get back.
> The children, I must save the children!

The shooting script used on the set the night of the crash was the fourth and final draft. It was completed on June 22, just weeks before filming commenced. Some disagreement still existed over the coarseness of the bar scenes but, having already compromised in the preceding drafts Landis was able to argue that the main character had to be viewed as despicable by the audience in order to make his redemption "work" in the segment's final rescue scenes. In the final draft Landis prevailed in generally preserving the bar scene the way he had originally conceived it, softening only Bill's reference to the black patron in the bar from "coon" to "black guy."

The only significant change in the script's fourth draft concerned the scene in the village where Bill tries hopelessly to communicate with the kids, as well as a slight modification in the segment's ending. With the apparent object to add some emotion to Bill's relationship with the children, the final script calls for the little girl to hand Bill "a broken and naked Barbie Doll" just before the village explodes and the helicopter chase begins:

> Bill (genuinely touched), responds, "Thank you honey.
> Thank you very much."

With the addition of this new (and inexpensive) prop, Landis was able to give a new twist to the ending. As in the third draft the segment ends with Bill being transported back to the street scene outside the bar. This time, however, he is "clipped by a car and thrown violently to the curb" with the barbie doll in his hand. In an apparent sop to Bill's racial conflicts, the final script has the bar's black patron follow Bill's friends, Ray and Larry, as they rush from the bar to Bill's aid.

> BLACK PATRON: Are you okay man? Can I help?
> Bill looks at Ray and at the Black Patron in wonder.
> He then looks down at the broken Barbie Doll in his hand.
> Following a few more lines of dialogue the Landis segment ends:
> Bill just looks at the doll.

Landis' script revisions were approved by the studio, but Lucy Fisher, apparently, had one more reservation: she specifically asked Frank Marshall and John Landis whether using the children at night would be a "problem." According to a memo generated by Warner's own internal investigation of the crash, both men told her not to worry about it.

* * *

With fresh revisions of the script approved by the studio, Lucy Fisher's official role in the production came to an end. The script's addition of Bill's new scenes raised the Landis budget request, already at $1 million, by approximately $300,000, mainly to pay for the Vietnam village construction. After haggling with Landis over $100,000-or-so, the studio came back with a $200,000 offer, permitting set designer Richard Sawyer to begin building the huts on the river.

By June 25, 1982, one month before the crash, sketches of the proposed village and storyboards showing some of the exploding village scenes had been submitted by Richard Sawyer to the director. With a tight budget that was already bursting at the seams, John Landis had just under four weeks to build a jungle village.

19

THE POWDERMEN

issatisfied with the accounts of the above-the-line witnesses, Llorente and his team next talked to the drivers, camera operators, electricians, stunt people, special effects men – all the hands that had worked to translate the *Twilight Zone* illusion to the screen. A good third of the 100-or-so crew members from the set that night eventually appeared before the NTSB panel and it was largely from these below-the-line versions that Llorente was able to get a clearer picture of what had gone wrong at Indian Dunes.

His most shocking findings concerned the performance of the SFX crew. The powder truck was said to have been a bar on wheels, stocking black powder bombs along with vodka and beer. The powdermen that night on the set presented a scary picture as some with drink in hand conducted the delicate business of setting and firing explosives.

Throughout the filming that night special effects truck driver Carl Pittman, by his own admission, ran the booze-express between the special effects crew and the nearest liquor store. The prop truck also had a cooler with sodas and beer. Special effects chief Paul Stewart was seen holding a drink as he supervised the wiring and firing before the fatal shot. The set hairdresser saw him sip what she thought was vodka and orange juice. Although he was never discovered by deputy sheriff Budds or any of the other investigators, a second witness to the free-flowing alcohol on the set expressed the belief that John Landis knew about the drinking but tolerated it because it made the powder chief more compliant. John Landis' own private investigation turned up a third key witness who claimed he had seen Stewart drunk that night. Just before the crash Stewart and fellow powderman Jerry Williams, according to this account, were reported drinking beer together by the powder truck near the Chapman crane, practically under the director's nose.

A fourth witness said the drinking continued even after the crash while the powdermen frantically loaded the wires, detonators and all the rest of the explosives gear onto a pick-up. From the pick-up they transferred the equipment to the larger powder truck driven by Carl Pittman who was so affected by the alcohol he had consumed on the set that, driving his 10-ton rig back to The Burbank Studios, as a fifth witness described it, he "wigwagged all the way home." A sixth witness who also believed Stewart was drinking on the set told Landis' private eye that he felt Landis knew about the drinking.

Like master shot cameraman Steve Lydecker and associate producer George Folsey Jr., Paul Stewart had Hollywood roots. His father worked for Warner Bros., for much of his life. His brother also had a job in the industry. But Stewart, who was in his early fifties, did not belong to the top rank of Hollywood's SFX establishment. Stewart had SFX credits on movies like *White Mama; Won Ton Ton, The Dog that Saved Hollywood; The Last Hard Man; The Wrecking Crew*, and *Soggy Bottom, USA*. He had only worked on a few up-scale productions like Cimino's $40-million epic disaster *Heaven's Gate*.

Originally, Allingham had considered another man for the job, Cliff Wenger, a special effects veteran whose credits included *Tora Tora Tora, Hooper, Canonball Run*, as well as *Blues Brothers*. Wenger fell through when at the production office Landis recognized in the applicant the person who on the *Blues Brothers* set had been difficult about the safety of one of the movie's big explosion scenes. "You're the son-of-a-bitch that cost me all that money," the bearded young director sneered at Wenger as he completed his interview with Allingham at the Universal bungalow. Allingham never called Wenger back.

Ultimately, Paul Stewart owed his job on the TZ segment through the circumstance that John Landis was a great fan of B-movies. At the time of his meeting with Stewart the director had just been to see *The Exterminator* in a raunchy theatre on Hollywood Boulevard. Landis especially loved the film's special effects. Dan Allingham who, after Wenger's abrupt dismissal, brought Stewart in to see Landis mentioned that Paul Stewart was responsible for the pyrotechnics in that movie. That same day Stewart was hired. Like his helicopter bargain, Allingham got a good deal. Stewart charged a very reasonable $25 an hour and agreed to assemble the rest of the crew at even lower wages.

Stewart had no trouble assembling a crew. He was friends with Jerry Williams, James Camomile and Harry Stewart; Kevin Quibell was new to SFX. They were all rough tough macho types, whiskered and tattooed, in uniform T-shirt and baggy jeans, except for Jimmy Camomile. Trim and clean-cut, he was a former Navy man with a frank, open gaze. Witnesses said he had not been drinking on the set at Indian Dunes.

Along with the stuntmen, the special effects men, who referred to each other as "powdermen," formed a Hollywood sub-caste and were not socially acceptable in the higher circles on the set. Privately, Landis referred to them as "hillbillies." The "hillbillies" formed a small tight-knit world, socially, professionally, even geographically. The powdermen on the Landis segment all lived in the northern San Fernando Valley near the foothills where many of the old Hollywood westerns were once shot.

Although most of Hollywood was experiencing an economic depression in the spring of 1982, these were boom times for the types of film that employed powdermen. In the new Hollywood, box-office success was identified with special effects. A new type of audience, less concerned with drama on the screen, wanted to see movies with spectacular stunts and special effects like *Towering Inferno, Jaws, Close Encounters* and *Poltergeist.* Paul Stewart had worked together on other sets with almost everybody on the crew he assembled for the Landis segment. Harry Stewart and Jerry Williams had also teamed up before, notably on *The Border,* with Jack Nicholson, directed by Tony Richardson; Jim Camomile and Paul Stewart worked together on *Heaven's Gate* and on *Soggy Bottom, USA.* All three had recently worked together on *The Exterminator.*

Of the five-man SFX crew only Paul Stewart, Harry Stewart and Jimmy Camomile held the "A" powder card that allowed them to perform explosive pyrotechnics without direct supervision on Hollywood locations. Jerry Williams with a B-card, and SFX newcomer Kevin Quibell, could only work under Stewart's and Camomile's direct supervision.

Days before the filming of the final scenes at Indian Dunes, Paul Stewart visited the site with Landis, Folsey and Elie Cohn, along with the director of photography (DP) Steve Larner and set designer Richard Sawyer. Sawyer had sketches of the village and with their aid they tried to imagine the scene when Bill goes in among the huts to rescue the children. The film people looked out from the spit of sand in the middle of the river. They talked about camera positions as they reconnoitered and Landis explained how he wanted his shot. Stewart was to gather from the director's indications what kinds of mortars he would need-round or square; 12, 18, or 24-in.; what quantities of gasoline to have on hand; where to dig the holes to position the mortars for each scene, and finally, the size of the explosive charges which he needed to custom-order.

On the Monday of the last shooting week, three days before they were actually needed, the heavy metal pots were brought out to the set by Jerry Williams and Kevin Quibell. The two powdermen dug several holes at the back side of the cliff for the heavy mortars that would launch the fireballs. They left their remaining supplies and equipment near the village where they knew they'd be filming. This left the final placement and planting of the mortars and bombs to the last minute.

The special effects to be used in the final shot was far from the expensive variety favored by movie makers like Spielberg and Lucas in the new box-office blockbusters. The movie set at Indian Dunes that night employed the cheapest methods to satisfy the needs of the tight budget. The stylish movie lab where computers and lasers bloodlessly achieve their visual spectaculars was a world away from the burly powdermen in T-shirts that night with their sloshing buckets of gasoline, the fumes of which engulfed the set, sickening people and adding to the jitters.

To achieve their mighty fireballs in the village, the powdermen filled the various mortars with up to 15 gallons of gasoline, pouring it over the fist-sized black powder bombs that had been taped round with electrical tape and dipped in shellac to enhance their explosive power. Placed at the bottom of each pot, the black powder bombs were then wired to their respective firing boards. These reasonably inexpensive fireballs – costing about $18 each for the 8-oz. black powder bombs plus the cost of gasoline – represented Hollywood's preferred way to create the appearance of battle on movie sets. Combined with sawdust and gasoline, a black powder bomb packed in a heavy steel pot could launch a fireball between 100-200 feet into the air. Unlike "high" explosives such as dynamite, which does not show up well on film, black powder bombs are "low" explosives, burning more slowly on combustion, making them more visually impressive on screen. That night the bombs, which ran 4 and 8-oz., were stored in powder magazines built into the 10-ton SFX truck. The truck used that night was one of the fleet of powder wagons at The Burbank Studios. It was driven to the set by Carl Pittman, the same who ran the shuttle between the SFX crew in Indian Dunes and the nearest liquor store.

With the exception of Dan Allingham, none of the crew on the final night was as busy as the powdermen. After the 11:30 rage scene they were rushed a "little bit of lunch" from the caterers which they gulped down, and though they were paid a little extra for working through the break, they would have rather joined the rest of the crew down the road at the lunch wagons and taken a breather from the hectic pace set by the director. To Paul Stewart, it seemed, John Landis constantly wanted more – more explosives inside the huts, more squibs in the water, more mortar pots, more shots on the shotboard, more fireballs. As a result, the powdermen never left the village and continued rigging right up to the fatal scene while their chief tried, unsuccessfully for the most part, to keep the director from still adding to their job.

Stewart was able only in a few instances to resist the director, notably once when for the final shot John Landis asked him to set up additional electrical squibs to simulate more machine gun fire from the attacking helicopter. Stewart objected that with any more wiring in the river Vic and the kids might not make it across without tripping. This time, heeding Stewart's request, Landis agreed to a rare compromise: instead of planting the river with more squibs, he was persuaded by Stewart to use the powerful air guns that ripped the water like bullet hits, though only shooting marbles.

Stewart's first SFX action on the final night of shooting came at 9:30. There were only a few "effects" and the chief one – the explosion of a hut from which Vic Morrow has just picked up the children to begin the rescue sequence – was cued by the director. The exploding hut in this shot represented a rocket "hit" from the helicopter just as Vic Morrow makes his way out of the hut with the kids under his arms, heading to the shoreline to begin his escape across the river. The hut explosions were set off even while the actor and the children were dangerously close in the scene frame with them, that is, within 10-15 feet of the bursting black powder bombs.

The next shot, the 11:30 rage scene, was more complicated, requiring more special effects and a tricky performance by the helicopter. At 9:30 the helicopter had not been visible in the shot, performing only as a special effects platform with its spotlight illuminating the hut as well as creating a wind effect on the village from its main rotor blade. However, at 11:30 the helicopter was most prominently visible since it was the "establishing shot" to be shown in the actual film immediately preceding the 9:30 rescue shot. It was shot in reverse order at 11:30 because, as the helicopter had to be brought in low, some propwash damage was expected to be done to the set and, in contrast to the earlier 9:30 scene, which was a close-up shot of the village set, at 2:20 it would no longer matter how the set looked since it would be blown up anyway.

With the helicopter hovering over the village, the 11:30 shot required three fireball explosions in the village; the single SFX explosion in the water used a water mortar which instead of a fireball sends up a powerful spume of water. Like the fireballs in the village, the explosion in the water gave the appearance on screen of a rocket hitting near Vic. The scene also called for a shower of bullet hits to be simulated by squibs which, like the mortars, were hooked up to special effects striking boards. The striking boards were primitive contraptions powered by batteries. The charge was achieved by "striking" a strip of brass on them with a nail. The boards had many such strips and each was connected by a wire to an explosive charge.

One of the A-card powdermen, Jimmy Camomile, had set off the two explosions that blew up the hut at 9:30. Again at 11:30 Camomile closely followed the director's instructions as relayed to him by Stewart. For Vic's rage scene three fireball explosions in the village were planted in the back row of huts; they would appear on-screen as rocket hits immediately to the right and left of the hut where Vic Morrow has stashed the kids. This was the opening shot in the sequence in which Vic, the SFX fireballs and the helicopter are all in the same frame, "establishing" the geographical relationship between these elements in the viewer's mind.

Camomile listened attentively to the powder chief as the 11:30 scene approached. Feeling great loyalty to Stewart, who was a few years older, he followed his chief's orders that night, even when he felt he might be doing something that could pose a possible conflict with the principles of Title 19, the California state law which defined the legal obligations of the powderman. On one such occasion, as Camomile prepared the water explosion just before the 11:30 shot, he was already warning Stewart of his concern about potential hazards to the aircraft in the rage scene – "the helicopter might be a little low or get wet, or something like that."

Stewart ignored his warning and went ahead with the water explosion which at 11:30 was to surprise Dorcey Wingo by sending a sheet of blinding mud and water across his windshield. Only by straining out the open window to his right was the pilot able to keep the Huey from crashing into the face of the cliff. James Camomile's account of his early warnings was one of those incriminating admissions made in the aftermath of the crash to which the attorneys for the special effects crew alone were privy; for out of loyalty to his boss, Camomile never repeated this confidence to either the NTSB or at the trial.

Plans concerning the location of most of the mortars had been made days before the crash and conveyed to the chief at the LA fire department's Hollywood wing, DeWitt Morgan. Morgan relied on Paul Stewart to give him accurate information about the placement of the explosives and before issuing the permit for the shoot he had been informed that the mortars and black powder bombs in the final explosive scene would be placed only outside and around the huts. The fire inspector was given specific assurances by Stewart that there would not be any explosives under any structures. The danger from debris would be further minimized, Stewart told Morgan, as the huts would not be involved in the explosion. Based on that information, the fireman granted a permit that allowed giant gasoline explosions to send fireballs 150 feet in the air.

In his last talk on location with Stewart while visiting the set on the night before the crash the fire inspector learned nothing new about the special effects plan. Stewart appeared to be sticking to the original plan, which Morgan had already approved. Once at the location, Morgan didn't even cross the river and look into the village, having no reason to doubt the powder chief's word that no bombs would be put under any of the structures. The fire inspector didn't return the following night to watch the spectacular finale. Had he done so he would have been surprised to see the helicopter hover over the village during the explosions, since he had never been told that was in the plan either.

The supervising fire safety officer the night of the crash was George Hull, a retired LA county fireman like the five other FSOs on the set. Coincidentally, Hull had a background in the department's helicopter unit. He had been supervising sets for 30 years and had witnessed SFX explosives and helicopter stunts on many, many film locations. Having met with Morgan and the show's SFX supervisor on several occasions Hull knew what to expect during the filming that night.

But for all his wealth of experience Hull was effectively removed from his role as a safety supervisor on the set by the time of the 11:30 shot; or, rather, he had removed himself by voluntarily locating himself 90 ft. up on the cliff in order to avoid confronting "the most irrational human being" he had ever been around. The old-timer was intimidated by the long-bearded, shaggy-haired hyper young director whose appearance struck him as "very hippy and greasy that night." Hull was a straight, conservative fireman. He had never met someone who would be "cussing someone out" one moment and "telling jokes" the next.

Hull was proud of his Hollywood duties and though selected by the fire department and not the movie company, he didn't see any point in making waves. He thought it was better to distance himself high up on the cliff far from the "most irrational human being" and ignore the thinly disguised drinking he had seen on the set. Even though the highest visible point of the explosions on the screen would be 40 feet above the village base, the fireballs were expected to cause fire hazards over 100 feet above; up on the cliff Hull joined three FSOs already there, leaving only Jack Tice and Jack Rimmer below.

Initially, following the nearly fatal 11:30 shot there had been some concern among the firemen about the possibility that the helicopter was flying too close to the explosions. But Tice on the ground assured Hull up on the cliff that the pilot was aware of the problem and would adjust his position by flying further away from the village explosions in the next shot. But in actuality, with the firemen, including the top-ranking fire official out of the way, John Landis and Paul Stewart had a virtual free hand in arranging the final exploding village scene the way they wanted.

While the rest of the crew broke for a midnight lunch at the mobile canteen up the road, John Landis remained briefly in the village with Stewart and the other SFX men, walking the set and telling them what he wanted in the shot. It was easy to see that the SFX crew worked furiously during the nearly three hours between the rage scene and the final call. After 11:30 nearly everyone on the set was aware that bigger explosions were yet to come.

At first the director wanted special effects bombs inside both rows of huts, the seven in the back as well as the four in the front row – the huts closest to the action. Stewart explained that because of the way the huts in the back row were constructed against the cliff, placing gasoline mortars inside them would create enormous explosive power due to the concentration of fumes. Stewart declined putting the bombs there.

But the director's objectives with regard to the shoreline huts presented a lesser problem. In Stewart's mind they seemed less dangerous because of their open construction. The director pointed to these huts where eventually, according to later evidence, Stewart's men violated the conditions of their permit by planting mortars inside or underneath three of the four front row structures. For despite all the grumbling, the drama of the 11:30 shot had given the director exciting proof of further cinematic possibilities. So, it was not only in terms of new locations that he changed the plan which Stewart had conveyed to DeWitt Morgan while applying for the permit. Landis was seen by witnesses as never letting up on Stewart that night to make the explosions themselves bigger. Even after the near catastrophe at 11:30, he continued pressing Stewart, screaming at the chief of SFX, related one witness, that for the big finale scene he wanted nothing less than "a wall of fire."

Key legal documents from the powder chief's early defense team indicated that while Landis harangued him to "step up" the size of some of the explosions in several shoreline huts, the lawyers believed that Stewart may have been highly vulnerable to this kind of intimidation because he and his SFX crew were drinking at the time. A similar story, an unusually frank communication, circulated among certain members of the director's own law team. It implied that Landis' pattern of screaming at Stewart after the 11:30 shot prompted the powder chief to grumble to his men that he would show the director a thing or two about big explosions.

"OK. You want it big," Stewart said to Landis, according to one circulated version, "I'll give it to you big."

The powder chief continued to grumble after the director left the village and crossed the river over to where the mobile kitchen was set up. The confidential story went on to say how Stewart griped to his friend Jerry Williams about Landis' "attitude" – he didn't like it, nor did he like "a lot of the things that were happening" – and neither was he "thrilled" with what Landis was looking for in the upcoming shot. To Williams he was reported to have mentioned an incident earlier in the evening when the director had asked him to place a mortar under one of the shoreline huts, and Stewart said that he hadn't wanted to do it.

Outside of the SFX crew, set designer Richard Sawyer was one of the few to actually witness firsthand the interactions among the people who plotted the explosions in the village that night. Sawyer knew Jerry Williams from working with him on the set of *The Border*. Following the 11:30 rage scene he stood next to Williams and watched the rough-tough type with the potbelly and wild hair sort out the electrical lines that traveled far into the river, disappearing into the muddy village shoreline.

The biggest part of setting up the charges was stringing the wires over land and under the river; the mortars were wired in sequence and just before the cameras rolled the lead wires were hooked up to the batteries that were in turn connected to the "striking boards."

As the set designer looked on, Williams told the delicate art school graduate that he could rely on his memory to remember where each of the wires led and that he would fire them off in a memorized pre-arranged sequence. But to Sawyer's amazement and dismay he heard Williams mention just as casually that during the just completed rage scene he hadn't even seen the mammoth fireballs. Keeping his eyes fixed on Vic to ensure that the actor was a safe distance away from the explosions in the scene, Williams said he hadn't been looking up to watch the fireballs' proximity to the helicopter. Although Sawyer made no secret of his dislike for the giant powderman, the set designer never told his full story to authorities.

By the set designer's account, Williams' haphazard procedure showed an unusual departure from conventional film-making practices. Ordinarily, the SFX crew would work from a diagram called the "plot plan." In fact, in the days just before the final night's shooting, Stewart had dispatched his crew to the location with a backhoe tractor to make the holes that were to house the exploding mortars. Sawyer remembered giving Stewart a bare drawing of the village which he assumed Stewart would use as a blueprint to map out the planned locations of the explosives on the set. Director of photography Steve Larner, too, remembered seeing such a blueprint. Typically, however, like most of the artists' renderings and visual representations of the set that night – sketches, drawings, blueprints, notes – a special effects plot plan for the fatal scene was never found.

By the time the final shot was set to go, the five-man special effects crew proved insufficient. Just before the 2:20 crash Paul Stewart was so short-handed that he had Jerry Williams recruit two inexperienced draftees from other jobs; Mike Milgrom, the propman, and Mike Berdrow who drove the special effects water truck, to be marble gunners. While the last of the mortars were being loaded and the squibs were being placed in the water to line the trail traveled by Vic and the kids in their climactic scene, Williams hastily explained to the new recruits to aim the marble guns just in front of Vic and the kids to simulate machine gun fire from the helicopter "during the action." Naturally, as novices, they were told to be careful not to hit Vic with the powerful marbles.

20

HOLLYWOOD FRIENDS

S ometime after the Indian Dunes crash Robert Liddle, a stand-in on the TZ set, received a call from John Silvia, the Warner employee who was also part of the NTSB's investigation team. Liddle, in turn, called John Landis at his office and left a message.

A famous Hollywood director who returns the call from a mere stand-in is highly unusual, but John Landis did, and rather quickly. They had a short conversation. At the end of it, Liddle was asked if he would be willing to talk to Landis' lawyer. "Sure, I'll talk." In the expectation of battles down the road, the movie director's legal phalanx was busy lining up friendly witnesses. Bob Liddle eventually was to receive a call from Landis' private eye.

Though Liddle was still being sent out at meager rates by Central Casting and John Landis was a $1 million-a-movie superstar, the stand-in was remarkably free from envy. He had been an extra player on *Kentucky Fried Movie* and admired Landis as a self-made director who had achieved greatness in the industry. But in the aftermath of the *Twilight Zone* crash, not all his goodwill, admiration and friendly feelings could keep Bob Liddle from feeling disturbed. He had been shocked by the filming of a scene involving Vic Morrow as he dives into the water with pursuing Viet Cong firing into a banana plant nearby; hearing Landis call in real shotguns using live ammo for a better effect, Liddle walked away in a hurry before the bullets flew.

On the fatal night the stand-in witnessed another incident that disturbed him. It occurred during a brief rehearsal just prior to the 9:30 rescue sequence. Liddle watched Vic Morrow grab the kids and, in a short run-by, drop Myca into the water. The little boy got wet and cried. Andy House saw it, too. Later, during the actual shot, Liddle felt that the kids were "shocked at all the noise and stuff." In fact, because of Myca's fall in the earlier run-by, Liddle and House assisted during the actual take a few minutes later: at the water's edge Liddle stood to the actor's left, Andy House stood to the right of Vic, and they took the kids from Vic's arms as he ran out of the frame in the 9:30 take. Liddle briefly held Renee who was crying from sand that had blown in her eye from the propwash before handing her to one of the "oriental" people on the shore.

After the take Andy House went up to Elie Cohn to express the fear that if Vic stumbled in the big exploding village shot later that evening the kids might drown; Cohn assured him that he had already talked to Vic about it – "no problem."

The little girl's mother was also worried after seeing all the commotion caused by the helicopter and the explosions. In her broken English, Mrs. Chen asked Folsey nervously, "Are you sure it's not dangerous?" Putting his arm around her shoulder, Folsey assured her that there was no danger, "only noise." Folsey quickly took her back to the trailer.

Later that night during the so-called 2:00 A.M. "rehearsal," Liddle, who was never interviewed by sheriff's investigators, walked the path in the water which Vic would walk during the actual filming. The helicopter was brought in and its powerful spotlight fixed on Liddle at the same spot Vic would be in 20 minutes later. The stand-in was about the same build as Morrow. He "stood in" so that the lighting crew could get exposure readings for the shooting of Vic's upcoming performance.

The exact reason that, during the 2:00 "rehearsal," the helicopter was brought in over where Vic and the kids would be crossing the river remained a controversy throughout the case. One of the important clues that investigators never realized was that the helicopter was brought in solely to provide a sample of light from the aircraft's powerful spotlight. As Liddle walked the path the lighting men passed their light meters near his face.

During the light check Liddle noticed a problem. The water around him heaved due to the violent wind effect of the low-flying Huey. He had trouble keeping his balance and the thought flashed through his mind, "You could fall down." Since it was nearly impossible for anybody, let alone a stand-in, to get the director's attention, Bob Liddle did not tell Landis that the river bottom was slippery and that Vic might fall. Instead, at the time of the 2:20 shot he positioned himself at the edge of the water near the action, just as he had done at 9:30.

With the promise of thrilling explosions and movie stunt action, Bob Liddle had brought his son to the set. Everybody had heard the rumor, "He's got some big stuff going." Just before the last scene began rolling, Liddle saw John Landis sloshing through the water to the spit of sand. Through the raised bullhorn the director exhorted the crowd that no one was to sit down. The tenseness of the spectators could be sensed from the way they scrambled to their feet and formed a wall in the night. A few terrible minutes later Liddle recalled being alone with Vic Morrow. The actor was lying on his stomach as if drinking the water and when Liddle looked closer, he saw that Morrow had been cut in half. He told the investigators that he was kind of "crazy" and "very upset" by the recollection.

Liddle's earlier walk in the water while the lighting men danced around him with their meters was filmed that night and collected among the film secured by the investigators. In this footage Liddle could be seen in that brief cut identified by the clapperboard as DOCU/2:00 which Llorente and more than a dozen investigators watched in the Warner screening room three days after the crash. John Landis and his close associates identified this episode to the NTSB investigators as the "rehearsal" for the 2:20 final shot. Elie Cohn even told the NTSB that during this "rehearsal" he saw Vic Morrow walk the path in the water, which was walked, in fact, by the stand-in Bob Liddle.

* * *

For almost a year after the crash Don Llorente quietly and patiently interviewed some 35 witnesses. After a while the collection of testimony began to reveal a picture with certain shadings. A few witnesses slammed John Landis for reasons that were subjective. But the personal bias of this sort was offset by witnesses who could not be accused of being hostile to the director. And in the immediate aftermath of the crash, with the details still fresh in their minds, some among Landis' friends on the set contradicted him in many ways. Two of these friendly witnesses with damaging statements, both longtime intimates of the director, were Kathryn "Boots" Wooten, the script supervisor, and Gary McLarty, the stunt coordinator.

Kathryn Wooten's and Gary McLarty's statements to investigators shortly after the crash, while still under the sway of powerful impressions, became a real problem for Landis in the courtroom later. Of these witnesses, no one on the set, apart from George Folsey Jr., had a relationship with the director of as longstanding as Kathryn Wooten's. Not surprisingly, when district attorney prosecutors requested John Landis' personal secretary to provide a list of Landis' close friends, Kathryn Wooten's name was among those that included the godfather, Universal's Sean Daniel, and Colleen Camp, the "bikini-girl" from *Apocalypse Now.*

Kathryn Wooten was a sort of super-secretary on the Landis set. As a script girl, or the current "script supervisor," she stayed close to the director while keeping notes on the filming action for the editor, notes the director himself referred to in order to keep abreast of the shooting. Wooten made note of changes in the script or in dialogue to make sure the actors knew their lines. She also kept production notes, running time and the shot record every day.

A product of 60s radicalism and counterculture like most of Landis' inner circle, "Boots" Wooten began her Hollywood career in the 70s working with Roger Corman's New World Cinema. Known as the "School of Cinema," with the reputation as the most successful low-budget film producer, Corman's company became Hollywood's most prolific training ground for several then unknown young directors throughout the 60s and 70s like Francis Coppola, Martin Scorsese, Peter Bogdanovich and one of the TZ segment directors, Joe Dante. Though at the time of the TZ movie Wooten had retired from feature film work and was doing commercials, she agreed to work on Landis' segment because it was short.

Previously, on a movie called *Heartbeat*, Wooten had worked with a helicopter that came in way low and blew up enough dust that she turned her face away and missed noting what the helicopter did. This experience reminded her that on the final night of shooting for the big exploding village shot she wanted to protect her eyes. Safety glasses were not handed out on the set that night but prop master Milgrom, like Wooten a veteran of *Animal House* and *Blues Brothers*, had a few pair on his truck. Kathryn pulled a knit cap over her ears against the noise of the helicopter. She also wore the high-suspendered waders and at 2:20, with the cap pulled over her ears and peering through the goggles, she watched the helicopter loom out of the dark sky. As part of her job, she had to see which arms Vic had the children under. They had to match the same arms as in the earlier scene to preserve the film's continuity. John Landis put the kids in Vic's arms. Vic started off. The first bomb went off.

Immediately people around her started running, realizing that something was wrong. It looked like the helicopter was in trouble right from the very first bomb. At the 11:30 rage scene Wooten had been worried about the helicopter going any lower; they really "overdid" it, she thought. But the blasts at 2:20 were "outrageous"; they were "like three times the size of the rage scene," she exclaimed to the NTSB investigators.

The whole fiery disaster unfolded within a few seconds. Wooten's memory was incomplete. She heard the explosions and watched the helicopter trying to climb out of the fireballs. She couldn't move. The people around her were running and she just helplessly watched the whole thing. Within a few moments the commotion settled and everyone realized that, indeed, something was terribly wrong. As she left the set she heard the indescribable wail in the night which no one who heard it could ever forget. She went back to Milgrom's prop truck. Hilary Leach, the trainee girl, soon arrived at the truck looking for garbage bags to put the dead bodies in. Wooten heard Andy House yelling, "That's a wrap – everybody go home! Get in your cars, go away!"

In the aftermath of the crash Wooten openly complained to the NTSB of the unsafe conditions on the set, the poor planning, the oversize explosions and the use of live ammo. She mentioned particularly dire disorganization and the lack of pre-production meetings where the director explains what he wants. However, though somewhat forthcoming, she was still friends with Landis. She professed herself unable to tell the investigators very much about Myca and Renee. She never had any contact with the children that night, believing Sue Dugan, the women's wardrobe supervisor who reported directly to Landis' wife, Deborah, the show's costume director, was the person who had talked to the kids. Wooten recalled seeing the children in the 9:30 rescue sequence, assuming they were "pretty much put in at the last minute and taken out right away."

She remembered someone mentioning the little boy and there was something being said about one of the children crying during the shooting of that scene, but she didn't have firsthand knowledge of it. Joining "Boots" Wooten in the first circle on that set, besides George Folsey Jr. and propman Mike Milgrom, was Gary McLarty, the stunt coordinator. Like Vic Morrow, McLarty was getting on close to 50. He was getting older in a business that was for younger men. Over the years Landis had been a dependable employer, but it wasn't easy.

McLarty belonged to the rough-and-tumble world of men who made their living taking spills and getting catapulted, shot at and pushed over cliffs. They flew through fireballs, hurtled in cars and hung from the skids of a helicopter. In the movie set hierarchy, the stuntmen were close to the SFX people, being usually concerned in the same action-type shots: in a familiar example, special effects people put the explosives in the trunk of a car while a stuntman drives the car. McLarty's own specialty was doing breakneck car stunts. He coordinated acts of daring on some 300-400 productions, such as *Cannonball, Baretta, Rooster Cogburn* and *Beverly Hills Cop I & II*. Ironically, when McLarty began his stunt life a quarter century back one of his earliest jobs was on *Combat* with Vic Morrow. Hired as the "stunt coordinator" for Landis' TZ segment, he read the script, made up the budget and brought in a double or doubled himself.

On the night of the crash McLarty, like stand-in Bob Liddle, brought his son to the set with the promise of a huge explosive display as the night's finale. But even the leader of the Hollywood War Babies began to have some doubts just a little after 11:30 upon returning from what he called the "hairiest ride" he'd ever been on. To the NTSB he stated that he told Landis, "We couldn't take anything hotter or bigger," and McLarty said he received the director's assurances that for the upcoming finale the explosions wouldn't be any larger or the craft any lower.

During that final shot McLarty was in the helicopter kneeling on the floor at the machine gun on the right side behind Wingo, facing the cliff. Kenny Endoso, the other stuntman/machine gunner, was on the left behind Allingham with his searchlight, facing the river and most of the film crew. As the chopper rattled into a start position and hovered for about 20 seconds, McLarty from the open door could see Vic holding the kids down below. "It was awful windy on him right then," he recalled, "not enough to blow him down, but I could sure see the effect from the water." Once they received the cue from the ground McLarty was supposed to start firing – Vic's cue to start his action towards the camera. But when McLarty fired, his fully automatic .50- caliber machine gun, like so many things that night, jammed up. By then McLarty, facing the cliff, had lost sight of Vic while, according to his recollection, the helicopter began making a planned 180-degree turn and started back.

In this brief account related shortly after the crash, McLarty contradicted Landis on some key points. Like others before him, the stunt coordinator described the helicopter making the "180-degree turn" which Allingham in his first statement to the NTSB had described as the "U-turn" until corrected by one of his lawyers because it contradicted the director's statement that the plan was for the helicopter to cross the river. On the crucial issue of the bullhorn, McLarty claimed that Vic's cue was the firing of the machine gun, disputing the director who said that Vic's action cue to start his forward motion was his, Landis', waving the bullhorn. If the director wasn't using his bullhorn to cue Vic – that being McLarty's task – the signaling with his bullhorn was more likely to have been a waving motion to bring the helicopter lower, which many witnesses said they had seen.

This issue of why the stunt coordinator was on the helicopter firing a machine gun and not directing the stunt would flare into bitter debate during the trial, for it very clearly showed who was in charge on the set. Being on the helicopter at 2:20 firing one of the machine guns, McLarty stated, was "all that they wanted me to do those last two evenings."

Plainly, John Landis had decided that McLarty didn't need to double for Vic in the 2:20 shot. McLarty told Llorente he didn't object.

"Objections you don't voice to somebody if they're your boss."

The Nazi sequence with the French street scene in which McLarty took the fall two stories down from an apartment building was the first to be filmed of the three episodes chronicling Bill's transformation. Among the onlookers on Universal's backlot were Mr. and Mrs. Wolf Nadoolman. Their daughter had brought her new baby to the set. That night Deborah Nadoolman Landis, with the infant in arms, occasionally shouting and ordering people around, was the pharaoh's wife; and many felt that when she fell into a towering mood it was probably best to somehow get out of the way. She was the film's costumer; and her husband was the Hollywood director who was not deterred by the presence of his in-laws into changing his style. Some crew members could sense the embarrassment of the middle-aged couple as they watched him squeal profanities and abuse prior to the shooting of this scene.

For the Nazi sequence the artists working under Richard Sawyer had been instructed to come up with sketches to create the authenticity of a French street in 1941 occupied France. A short strip of cobblestone street with fake French house fronts, complete with Nazi propaganda posters on the wall and old-fashioned neon lights, was made ready for Bill's *Twilight Zone* encounter with his persecutors. Like every scene in the segment, it was a chase scene shot "night for night"; here Bill, while being pursued, climbs out of a window and runs along a ledge to the next building where he falls from the roof. For the close-up part of the scene Vic Morrow ran along the ledge prodded by the director's barking below. "Faster! Faster!" Landis shouted. Vic did his best. Though the ledge was only eight feet above the ground it was high enough to hurt the aging actor if he fell onto the hard cobblestones below.

Bob Westmoreland, a veteran Hollywood makeup man personally recommended for the segment by Steven Spielberg, cautioned, "Be careful, he might hurt himself."

He received a curt rebuff from the young film maker: "Stay in your own department."

The more dangerous wide-angle part of the shot was to show Bill three stories up on the ledge. A huge air bag was laid down on the street and a young professional stuntman that McLarty had hired tried the dangerous fall twice; each time he failed to satisfy Landis' drive for realism. After the second try and a few profanities from Landis, he was removed and the director gave the nod to McLarty who gathered up his aging bones for another tumble. Knowing from working with the director the kind of fall he really wanted, McLarty ran the ledge and flung himself to the ground.

Landis' cinematic trademark for stunts and action showed a drive for realism which most on the set saw as an infinite capacity for excess. In the last part of a railyard scene the special effects rain was so intense that the cameramen squawked about the volume of water. On Camera A, Arnold Rich stopped filming in order to change into dry clothing afterwards. In this scene Bill, with the yellow felt star of David pinned to his chest, is clubbed and taken to a box car being loaded with 30 people playing Jewish prisoners. Once in the box car, the door was slammed shut and locked. The realism took a threatening turn when shortly after Landis yelled, "That's a cut!" there was a small explosion as the simulated rain shorted out a circuit and an electrical fire broke out on the set near the box car. The makeup man, Bob Westmoreland, noticed it and ran to Landis whom he found deep in gesticulating conversation with Folsey and Cohn. Westmoreland reminded the director that there was a real lock on the door with real people inside the car. They soon found the key and disaster was deferred for another week.

Four years later at the *Twilight Zone* trial it would be argued that McLarty did not stand in for Vic in the final scene solely to satisfy the director's obsession with realism. Gary McLarty recalled that Vic wanted to do the "running stuff," though admitting that he didn't talk to Vic at any time during the last two nights. Perhaps to show the young director that he could be relied upon, Vic Morrow did consent to do the running actions. But the question that arose at the trial was whether the director had used his power to pressure Morrow. Had he intimidated him? Did he urge the susceptible actor to do the scene himself with the promise of increased exposure that would help his comeback?

At least part of the exposure would have been the close-up of Bill by Camera A operated by Arnold Rich. The frame in Rich's lens would show a face made dramatically hard-bitten by the "herculean effort" in the river under blazing fireballs. Originally, the shooting schedule for that night clearly called for Bill and a double. But had that been followed, and McLarty had stood in for Vic, Landis would not have had his "shot," for there couldn't have been a close-up with the real Vic Morrow with real kids.

It had to be real. The attacking helicopter, the exploding village, everything had to be real – the rocket fire and the machine gun fire, Bill and the Vietnamese.

And everything was real … including death.

21

"Oh My God, Cover it Up!"

Making a film requires hundreds of hands but a nucleus consisting of the director, the director of photography, the cameramen and the lighting people is considered essential in making each scene work. Each shot in a film may be covered by as little as one camera with a cameraman and his assistant to as many as 10-15 cameras under the direction of a single director of photography. The DP is one of the highest-paid members of the crew – the better-known can even bargain for top salaries.

For the 2:20 shot John Landis used more cameramen than for any of his previous scenes. Even at the last minute the director of photography, Steve Larner, was drafted into the finale, making it six cameras. In all there were more than a dozen cameramen distributed within a few hundred yards on land, in the river, on the top of the cliff and airborne in the chopper. Michael Scott on Camera E was buckled to a tree overhanging the cliffs edge at a 90-ft. height. Roger Smith, strapped in a harness, balanced with Camera D on the helicopter skids. Steve Lydecker with Camera B, the master shot, leaned out over the intensely lit scene on the delicately calibrated arm of the Chapman crane. Camera A, Arnold Rich, stood with his sensitive machine below the crane. Connor and Larner, the C and F cameramen, stood in their waders in the water behind cameras mounted on tripods looking down the river.

The final shot was in the script. It had an inexorable self- propelled forward motion. Even though five of the six leading cameramen were filming the 2:20 shot against their better judgment, nothing could stop it.

After the close call during the earlier rage scene, the assistant on D camera, Randy Robinson, a recruit from the Spielberg network, had vowed vehemently not to go back up in the helicopter again. Robinson's immediate superior, Roger Smith, had listened intently to warnings from the A camera operator, Arnold Rich, a Hollywood veteran with more than 40 years' experience on movie sets. For the final shot Rich was facing the village across the river, taking close-up shots of Vic and the kids as they came running towards him. Rich had advised Smith of his safety concerns after the earlier close call. Camera D operator Michael Scott was so worried about the 2:20 shot that he had even asked one of the powdermen whether he would be safe on the cliff for the final scene; during the earlier rage scene Scott had been startled to see fireballs streaming over the top of the 90-foot cliff where he was to assume his position during the exploding village scene. C cameraman John Connor discovered that it was useless to remonstrate. When he did, the director screamed, "Are you too scared to do that shot?"

Everybody was scared, yet each cameraman took his place at 2:20: even the B camera, master shot Steve Lydecker, who was deeply disturbed by the way Landis dealt with people. Landis manipulated them, he "treated men like toys."

It didn't look good.

Apart from George Folsey Jr., there was no one on the TZ set whose family and personal life was so deeply rooted in the film capital as that of Steve Lydecker. Lydecker's father Howard and Uncle Theodore, both film pioneers like Folsey Sr., were noted for their contributions to Hollywood cinematography.

Steve Lydecker's father was a special effects man in the old days when this meant not just handling explosives but, like Lydecker Sr., many were "miniaturists"; they built, for instance, a dam so tiny that it took little more than a match to blow it up-the enlarging faculty of the camera did the rest, along with skillful cutting by the editor. Howard Lydecker was a Hall of Fame recipient who had signed the first four pyrotechnic cards in Hollywood. Howard's brother, Uncle Theodore, was an innovative cameraman with a highly respected name in the film industry.

Both Howard and Theodore Lydecker were known in the 30s for the sensationalistic illusions they produced at Republic Pictures. The pictures that won the Lydeckers acclaim were the 1935 *The Phantom Empire*, an early sci-fi film about a fantastic underground city, another 1935 film, *Fighting Marines*, and an early *Rambo* picture. In 1937 Howard Lydecker headed up the special effects department at Republic Pictures, overseeing car wrecks and assorted disasters. The serials the Lydeckers created at Republic won distinction for their exaggerated action-adventure, considered by many the inspiration for the 1981 *Raiders of the Lost Ark*. Film historian George Turner has called this Lucas-Spielberg production featuring Indiana Jones a "tribute to Lydecker."

Steve Lydecker started working on movie sets in his teens. In a quarter-century motion picture career he was a camera operator, special effects man and assistant director. Having logged many hours as a cameraman in a helicopter as well as fixed-wing aircraft, he was thoroughly knowledgeable about explosives, using precise technical language, referring to helicopter parts and maneuvers, the magnitude of explosions and the role of cameras. He filmed "stunt stuff" on *Smokey and the Bandit, Cannonball* and many other films. The ill foreboding he had about the whole TZ production grew stronger in the final days of shooting, when he witnessed one particularly disturbing incident.

During the actual trial several years later, the Landis defense team frivolously dubbed this incident "the banana plant murders." It involved the use of live ammo during the filming of scene 19, the sequence which calls for Bill, while eluding Viet Cong, to dive into some bushes floating in a Vietnamese swamp simulated by the shallow Santa Clara river. There was a platoon of about a dozen soldiers dressed in U.S. Army uniforms carrying M-16s. Vic was to emerge from the swamp and start to run, waving his arms, "I'm an American, I'm an American."

Lydecker operated one of the two cameras at the time. He recalled the SFX men starting in with marble guns to simulate machine gun fire in order to cut down some banana plants about 25 feet distant.

The marbles bounced off the plants and the director cut twice, complaining that the SFX chief didn't give him the shot he wanted. And Lydecker heard Paul Stewart say, "I'm gonna have to hit with explosives, with bullet hits," and the director's anxious reply, "How long's that gonna take?" and Stewart, "Approximately 15 minutes."

"The guys," Lydecker recalled "were standing next to me out in the water with 870 Remington shotguns, pumps, no plugs in the pumps, five shots in each gun. They had extra ammunition sitting out on the battery that I had on the tripod."

Just before the shooting started, Vic Morrow jumped out of the way. He went under the water, then came back up and Kenny Endoso, the stuntman, grabbed the actor and pulled him out of the water onto the bank. While the shotguns blasted away, Vic hid behind some flimsy bushes which promised little protection if one of the wide-pattern pellets strayed. Lydecker put earplugs in his ears. When the shooting was over, he noticed that Vic looked very shaken as he crawled out of the bushes.

Steve Lydecker was tall, balding, somewhat portly around the middle. His approach to problems was deliberate, almost pedantic. He had an expert knowledge of guns. He was a tracker of the wilds, a hunter and outdoorsman who reloaded his own shotgun shells. Reg Parton, the Hollywood stuntman on Llorente's NTSB team, surprised by the report of live ammo on the set, asked if he was mistaken about the live ammo or whether they could possibly have been using blanks?

"They were not blanks, sir, they were sitting on my battery out in the water and I looked." He had actually found an empty ammo box with the marking precisely as he had established it --"12 gauge double ought buck shotgun shells." According to Lydecker, there "was a thousand one, thousand two, Vic jumped out of the way, thousand three, thousand four, and the shotguns started in," giving Vic no more than two seconds to dive into the bushes. As far as Lydecker knew the use of live ammo on a movie set had long been extinct in Hollywood.

Like many on the set, Lydecker was aware of the director's drive to "out-Spielberg Spielberg." They were all engaged in an undertaking, it seemed, to teach Steven Spielberg a lesson in creativity. While filming one of the Vietnam village scenes Lydecker heard Landis bragging to some guests that his film was all original. "It's going to be so much better than Steven's," Lydecker heard the director say while dismissing the efforts of his co-producer, friend and rival.

"His and the rest of them are remakes," the director continued to boast, referring to the other segments directed by Joe Dante and George Miller.

On the final night of shooting Lydecker found Landis supercharged, "like he had his finger in a 220." Lydecker tried to warn him about the ground blasts against the "wall." The wall presented by the face of the cliff would force the blasts upward, there being no other exit.

Landis joked.

"So, we lose a helicopter!"

Positioned aloft some twenty feet above the river looking down into the set, Lydecker's perspective from the finely balanced arm of the Chapman crane permitted his camera a view of the entire village. His wide-angle frame was the master shot for the big scene. The helicopter was not to be in it, so that when the command to roll came Lydecker realized almost at once there was a problem when the skids suddenly appeared in the top of the frame!

Hearing shouts from his left for the helicopter to go lower, Lydecker took his eye out of the eyepiece and looked over the top of the magazine of his camera. At that instant the helicopter had already gone out of control and came spinning straight at him.

Next to him Victor Nakaido, his young assistant, was screaming, "Get me out of here! Get me out of here!"

Especially built for the movie industry, the arm of the Chapman crane was balanced exactly for the weight of the camera and the men on it that included, besides Lydecker and Nakaido, Morgan Renard, the TZ movie's still photographer. Panic-stricken, Nakaido was about to jump off the crane – an action threatening catastrophe worse perhaps than the oncoming helicopter. If someone suddenly departed, as Nakaido threatened to do, the sudden loss of weight would cause the arm to fly up and hurtle everyone in the air.

"Victor, if you jump off the crane you're gonna' kill us all!"

Lydecker yanked his panicked assistant back by the neck.

Meanwhile, the danger of the onrushing gunship passed as the craft, after completing a 360-degree spin, landed at an approximately 70-degree angle in the water, with the nose of the helicopter facing him and the tail facing the set. Lydecker kept his camera running while the grips on the ground "armed" him down through the trees. It would be important to have some type of evidence, Lydecker figured; he told Morgan Renard to keep going with his still camera.

At this point Lydecker still didn't know that Vic Morrow and the kids had been killed, but after dashing the few yards to the tipped-over helicopter he received his first indication of the true scope of the disaster. He saw Randy Robinson standing in a daze next to the scorched, lopsided craft. The engine kept up a hacking noise as Lydecker reached into the crippled craft and helped cut down Roger Smith from his harness. Together with Robinson he helped Smith out the side of the helicopter. The three men splashed through water that ran red with blood, like survivors of a battle.

Awaiting them at the shoreline was an actor gotten up in a Nazi dress uniform, one of the two extras who portrayed Nazi soldiers as called for in scene 34 which continues the chase sequence after the village explodes and Bill escapes from the helicopter. The extra was one of the Germans who recaptures Bill in the wooden shed.

Big and blond, the phantasmagoric figure seemed to be parading on the shoreline with something wrapped in a blanket. On first impression Robinson thought he was carrying some kind of ham shank. It was a child's thigh.

Robinson saw it first and Lydecker heard him cry, "Oh, my God, cover it up. We don't want everybody to see that."

The figure in the Nazi uniform tried to position the blanket.

Two little feet fell out.

A moment later Robinson asked, bewildered, "Who? How many – Who's that?"... A body floated past.

Lydecker said, "That's Vic."

22

THE MAKING OF DOCU/2:00

On the village shoreline the helicopter was located about 100 yards downstream. It was needed for only a few brief bursts of action. For virtually all of its two-day rental the grim-looking Huey sat on the makeshift helipad close to the movie company's constructed dam.

It was that quality of a remote scene dominated by some large brooding presence, the large green hulk in the hot scorched summer dunes, that presented itself to the artist's eye of Tom Southwell. Southwell was first to arrive on that Wednesday, June 22, ostensibly the final day of shooting. As one of the show's illustrators who worked for set designer Sawyer he had done many of the set sketches and storyboards in pre-production, including the sketch of the village that was used as the model to build it from. The job he came out to do that afternoon, to paint the attacking eagle insignia and FLY BY NIGHT legend on the nose of the helicopter, was normally done by a sign painter. Southwell had never done this sort of painting before, but came out to the set in kindness to Sawyer's tight budget.

Tom Southwell's arrival in the hot afternoon the day before the crash was marked by an eerie incident, a portent of the waiting disaster. Southwell met a guard. She was a young woman who stood watch over the helicopter and to his question where the helicopter was, she gave the unsettling reply, "Oh, you mean the one they're going to crash?"

Though the matter was immediately clarified, Southwell was momentarily taken aback. The woman said she had seen the crashed helicopter in a drawing that was literally nailed to the bluff.

"No, no, that's not it!" Southwell interrupted.

He informed her that what she had seen was a "spotting plan" for setting up camera angles and special effects, and that even though it seemed to show a crashed helicopter, the drawing actually showed the helicopter lying on its side with broken rotor blades! It had nothing to do with the planning. He assured her that the helicopter he was looking for was not going to crash that night.

On the helipad by the dam Southwell started painting the nose of the Huey after the sketch he had drawn for the director's approval the week before. A number of ideas for the logo had been considered. One, "Death From Above," was ruled out because it had been used in *Apocalypse Now*. For another, "Grim Reaper," Southwell made some sketches. John Landis rejected some skull designs he drew. Finally, Richard Sawyer told Southwell that the director wanted to use his company name and spelled out exactly the image Landis wanted – an attacking eagle with spread wings and talons extended and over it the bold legend, FLY BY NIGHT.

While Southwell painted, upstream on the other side of the river about 100 yards away, the helicopter pilot arrived. Dorcey Wingo was casually dressed and just as he made his appearance the first person to greet him was Southwell's boss, Richard Sawyer; Sawyer immediately suggested that they go over and see the set. They drove in Sawyer's car to where the Chapman crane would later be positioned. A bunch of people were milling around in shorts, being upbeat and slightly boisterous like people at a party. One woman was drinking beer. Other people were drinking soft drinks from a big barrel. It was Wingo's first time on a big movie set. He shared Sawyer's excitement and everyone else's, it seemed, to be working in a Spielberg production.

Sawyer took off his shoes. The set designer began merrily wading across the river. In between snapping pictures of the village set with his 35 mm. camera, he waved invitingly to Wingo. The pilot didn't like going around barefoot. He had tender feet. The pilot took off his shoes and tested the water. There were pebbles on the bottom. Wingo put his shoes back on and waited on the shore until Sawyer returned.

It was about 6 P.M. when Sawyer drove Wingo to the helipad where Southwell was just finishing up. The eagle glared aggressively in lurid colors from the Huey's freshly painted nose. Tom Southwell wasn't a sign painter, which, he admitted, anyone could tell by looking closely at the uneven quality of the FLY BY NIGHT lettering. Wingo had himself painted insignia in Vietnam and as an amateur cartoonist had offered some suggestions to Allingham for this one. But Allingham had told him it was already decided.

Around that time Dan Allingham showed up. Other people also began to arrive. Although it was already nighttime it was just another Hollywood working day. Allingham soon got word over his radio from the director. Landis wanted to see the helicopter fly a couple of times, no positioning shot but merely a fly-by that would also allow Allingham to test his Nite-Sun and give the pilot the chance to familiarize himself with the terrain, like telephone wires and other possible hazards.

Tom Southwell, invited to climb aboard with the pilot and the UPM, capped his day by whirling aloft. From the air he snapped pictures of John Landis in his waders, capturing the director's grandiose gestures in guiding the helicopter's maneuvers from the ground.

Not long after the evening fly-by, the helicopter's first call to action came and the outpost in the riverbend sprang alive. The first shot employing the helicopter was to establish the aircraft on the screen. It should have been a simple dash; no action, no explosives. But nothing was ever simple during those bedeviled nights at Indian Dunes.

John Landis was all over the place on this twelfth and presumably last night of shooting. The gangling *wunderkind* seemed giddy with happiness as he clowned and bobbed holding his barely two-month-old daughter Rachel in front of "Still-man" Morgan Renard's camera. Though hired on as the show's still photographer for the purpose of gathering publicity shots, Renard was often distracted that night by Landis' constant requests for more baby photos.

It was a very crowded evening in which altogether seven key scenes pertaining to the Vietnam sequence were to be shot. With the production falling behind, the young director began showing flashes of quirky boyish temper. His mood did not improve when he was told by his 1st AD that they wouldn't have time "to do the stunt," meaning the big explosion scenes. At one point, while several crew members looked on, John Landis turned brusquely to his shot list and in a belligerent tone stated that he had carefully planned out the entire shooting schedule and that despite an inept crew it would get done. Throughout the evening he shouted and scowled, and his high-pitched squealing could be heard over the walkie-talkie by Roger Smith's assistant on the E Camera, Randy Robinson, up in the helicopter seated behind Wingo and Allingham.

Because nobody aboard the helicopter could understand what Landis was saying, Robinson finally turned to Allingham. "He screams and it over-modulates." Allingham relayed, "John, don't scream so loud into the microphone because we cannot understand you."

For its first call the chopper had come in clattering over the river from the east, heading west, where John Landis had picked out a bunch of trees that he wanted the helicopter to come in from behind. But a problem with the radios cropped up right away. Distrustful of the set walkie-talkie, Wingo wanted to stick with the special VHF radio. When it was discovered that the VHF didn't work, however, they went back to using the general walkie-talkie. As part of his headset Allingham was wearing a "hot mike" while communicating with Landis on the ground. Being connected to this hot mike system enabled Robinson to hear what Landis was saying to Allingham.

Wingo never spoke directly to the director down below. He only spoke to the ground through his own hot mike via Allingham, who apologized to Landis for the delays as they were still rattling in the dark looking for a tree.

"Look, guys, we don't know what this is," Allingham relayed to the obviously agitated director. "It's awfully dark up here, and he's just checking it out."

"They started this intimidation thing with Dorcey," Robinson later told Llorente. "They kept trying to get us to come to a certain tree, and they said, 'Can't you see this tree?' and they'd yell and scream at us, and then Dan would sort of laugh and say, 'Look, guys, it's not like positioning some Volkswagen up here.' He'd say, 'What tree do you want? Put a tag on it and we'll know which one you're talking about, because there are a hundred trees up here!'"

Wingo poked the bird's nose over and turned and after doing that several times he heard his headset explode:

"Where the fuck are you going?"

Up behind his controls Wingo got flustered. He mentioned to Allingham seated next to him that by using that kind of language they risked losing their FCC license to use radios. "Don't let that bother you. John gets a little excited and talks like that," the UPM reassured him.

When finally they found the trees, they stumbled into an enormous surprise. A powerful arc light on the scaffolding was directed up at the cockpit, nearly blinding everybody.

For the next evening's first shot at 9:30, the helicopter had been used only for special effects: the winds from the propwash and the powerful spotlight from the Nite-Sun.

* * *

Dan Allingham was the busiest man on the set that night. His duties had accumulated by doubling up and more doubling up, so that by the time he climbed aboard the Huey for the final shot he held almost a half-dozen jobs. He was unit production manager, an assistant director, spotlight gaffer, and the 2nd unit coordinator, whose duties actually overlapped with those of the stunt coordinator. But most importantly, he was Landis' envoy to control the helicopter crew. He had a slogan, Randy Robinson recalled, imitating Allingham's voice: "No, no, you're right. Safety first-ta-da-ta-da-ta-da-ta-da..."

Aboard the chopper, by direction of the UPM, Randy Robinson was also doubling up. He was working as camera assistant to Roger Smith, as well as with the two machine-gunner/stuntmen, giving them assistance. Though Robinson could not talk to Allingham and Wingo because of a defective hot mike, his headset enabled him to hear what was being said between the air and ground. Thus, it happened that in the investigation of the crash Robinson managed to complete much of the picture which Allingham so frequently left blank by his repeated claims of, "I don't remember."

Since he would be filming out on the helicopter skids directly exposed to the fireballs, no one was more pleased with Allingham assurances of "safety first" than Roger Smith. He had worked with Allingham before and felt relieved. Having been out on the skids at 11:30 and come close to being consumed by heat blasts, he had nervously masked his deep unease by making light of his fear. "I don't want to get my pants burned off with one of those firebombs underneath," he had nervously joked. Allingham told him that for the final flight they would be over the water away from the explosions, and, pleased, Smith proposed that the pilot turn the chopper around so that it would be like a "camera platform," allowing him to shoot the village exploding in the background. His assistant Randy Robinson recalled clearly Dan Allingham's final words just as the Huey lifted off for the final shot. "Don't worry about any of these explosions 'cause we're going to be out of there before they even go off." With the chopper flying upstream they were moving into position so as to put the village shoreline on the chopper's left side where Allingham sat spotting the light. Allingham's seat was normally that of the pilot who, due to the position of the Nite-Sun, operated the craft from the passenger seat on the right side from where he kept his eyes fixed on the cliff. He measured the dangerously tiny gap between the tip of his overhead main rotor blades and the 90-foot wall of the cliff behind the village. Robinson and Wingo could hear through their headsets the directions Allingham was getting from the ground.

Allingham was nervous and talked incessantly. In the complex radio web, his words literally doubled up. There could be no mistaking them. Wingo and Robinson could hear the order from the ground on their headset and then hear Allingham repeat it in his hot mike. Except for Dan Allingham and the pilot, Randy Robinson was the only one in direct communication with the people on the ground directing the movement of the helicopter during the final flight. Robinson was the only one, in fact, who was able to overhear the communications between three of the five future defendants in the *Twilight Zone* trial, John Landis, Dan Allingham and Dorcey Wingo. Robinson heard the fatal order, from the ground first, then from Allingham – not once but twice.

"They were very clear," Robinson recalled. "They came over kind of excitably. There weren't very many. They were just, 'Get lower, get lower, get down, lower, lower, lower, get over to the cliff.'"

By the time the helicopter was ordered into its final hover, the blades were probably within five feet of touching the cliff. With the chopper in position to start the scene, Allingham relayed the frantic commands from the ground. Robinson tapped the shoulders of the stuntmen, shouting, "Fire! Fire! Fire!" Roger Smith, stepping out onto the skids with his camera, saw Vic Morrow with the kids standing underneath the helicopter, and fairly close.

As this dramatic scene was still unfolding the first explosion went off on the shoreline, occurring at the one o'clock position from the ship. Then a second one beneath it rocked the craft violently to its side "like flying through a bunch of white puffy cumulus clouds, only they were all fire," Robinson remembered, looking out the port door and thinking, "Why don't they stop blasting? Can't they see we're in trouble? Why do they keep blasting us?"

In addition to the airborne cameramen on the chopper, for the last two nights of shooting John Landis hired two additional camera crews headed by John Connor on Camera C and Michael Scott up on the cliff shooting down with Camera D. For the fatal flight the director of photography put Connor in the river with the 75-millimeter on a tripod to film a side view of Vic Morrow and the kids against a backdrop of explosives – "a wall of fire" – downstream at the dam. Landis was so determined on having that shot that he decided at the very last moment to put the DP on a sixth camera, F, as guarantee for Camera C getting his shot. Quite accidentally, Connor's Camera C ended up filming the DOCU/2.00 footage just before the fatal shot that night, as part of a separate pet project of Frank Marshall, the production's executive producer.

John Connor knew Marshall from some films, notably *E.T.*, on which Marshall had also been executive producer. On the night before the final shot, he ran into Marshall again. Connor introduced him to his assistant Lee Redmond. Marshall was with Kathleen Kennedy, his business partner and girlfriend, who was also a business associate and close friend of Spielberg's. Marshall asked Connor to shoot some of the "interesting" side details for one of his Making of ... documentaries. The footage was to be shown to theatre owners, Marshall explained, making them feel they were a part of the film's production.

The most interesting shot Connor picked out for Marshall occurred at 2:00 A.M. on his second and last night of filming. It showed John Landis standing in the water and the helicopter coming in. According to Connor's understanding, the helicopter flight at that time was not a rehearsal but a chance to "establish how the light part of the film's production would be shining down on the actors," and the film he shot depicted the director clearly pointing to the place where he wanted it to shine. This footage, shot incidentally for Frank Marshall's pet project, became the controversial DOCU/2:00 portion which John Landis during his NTSB testimony designated as the "rehearsal," even though all the elements of the rehearsal for this particular flight-the actors, cameras and explosions-were absent.'

For this particular flight was the lighting check in which Landis used the stand-in Bob Liddle. Just prior to the upcoming final flight they had to measure the intensity of the lighting at the precise spot where the kids would later pass through the frame from left to right since Connor was to capture with his camera the silhouettes of the actors against the "wall of fire" downstream behind them. At 2:00 A.M., in order to coordinate the timing with the special-effects men, Connor and the DP, both in waders, consulted with Paul Stewart. That's when it was decided to plant a tall stick in the middle of the river – a "eukie" pole left over from building the huts – so as to mark the point where Stewart would cue the downstream explosions at just the moment when Vic and the kids were lined up with the explosions in perfect position for Connor's camera.

The "stick" became a reference point to help Connor and others line up the shot at an angle where it would record the maximum and most dramatic effect of all those elements the director wanted in the shot. But as Connor turned the camera for the DOCU/2:00 footage, he was, unbeknownst to himself, assisting in the creation of yet another mystery. The "stick" prominent in his shot would join the bullhorn in becoming the subject of much lawyerly contention. In Landis' version of the 2:00 "rehearsal" the stick was explained as the point in the water towards which Vic would run, while Connor knew it only as something that he, Larner and Stewart planted to aid his camera to focus on the background explosions for the big shot.

While the DOCU/2:00 clip was being filmed for Frank Marshall, and the stand-in walked the path to be taken by Vic and the kids some 20 minutes later, the director of photography noted down his light readings. Connor was filming the shot from a considerable distance, 45-feet upstream. He used the positioning of stand-in Bob Liddle to set the proper focus on his camera for the final shot that would require a full frame of Vic, head-to-toe, so you could see that the actor was in the water about knee-deep. In order to achieve this effect, Connor's Camera C needed just the right lighting conditions, showing the reflections of the downstream background explosions on the foreground of the water and just about four feet of the background explosions above Vic's head in the camera.

As director of photography, Steve Larner was key in the 2:00 lighting check. He was responsible for coordinating the camera exposures for the lighting effects required for the exploding village scene. He had to know the direction of the lights shining down from both the helicopter and the scaffolding that had been erected slightly upstream, about 10 feet behind Connor, on which were mounted the powerful arc lamps to illuminate the scene. As far as Larner knew, the third flight of the helicopter at 2:00 A.M. was solely for the purpose of establishing lighting positions with respect to Camera C. It had nothing to do with the complaints of the helicopter's crew following their rocky flight in the near fatal 11:30 shot. Larner specifically stated to the NTSB his understanding that this 2:00 A.M. flight was not a "rehearsal," nor did he recollect anything being mentioned about safety concerns as the reason for that particular flight.

During questioning by the NTSB, in direct contradiction of John Landis, Larner stated that the helicopter's fourth and final flight that evening did not happen as he had expected. It was completely different in its execution from that which had been previously discussed. "The helicopter was much lower than everybody thought it would be," Larner recalled. The helicopter was not planned to be in any of the shots of the six cameras, except from above in Camera D on the cliff. As far as the DP knew from what he had been told by Landis, the craft was to be used in the final scene only to create the lighting effect and propwash on the water. Like Lydecker on Camera B, Larner had been told by Landis that the helicopter should remain above the frame of the Camera B master shot.

The NTSB investigators understood that the actor was passing from left to right in the frames of Camera C and F, and they asked Larner whether Vic showed any hesitation while making his dash with the kids. They were specifically interested in finding out from the director of photography whether it was planned for Vic to stumble in the scene just before the helicopter made its fatal descent.

"No," Larner recalled, suggesting he didn't believe so. "He was told to get out of the frame as fast as he could."

23

SUMMER OF SPIELBERG

The TZ movie would have remained a dull imitation of the charming original, quickly made, quickly profitable and quickly forgotten, had there not been an accident on the set which brought Charlie Hughes into the Warner offices with inquiries into the illegal hiring of two children. His object was to identify, according to the statutes, the employer legally responsible under the provision of the law. It was, therefore, highly surprising that within a month of the crash, on August 24, 1982, the labor commission's Southern California office issued its final report in which the only reference to Warner Bros. Inc. was a copy of a declaration made by a studio vice president, Ed Morey. The commission's report included 20 exhibits, many supplied by Warner attorneys. But notably absent from this nearly 150-page document was any mention of Frank Marshall, Lucy Fisher, Fred Gallo, or any of the other Warner studio brass involved in the Landis segment, including Terry Semel, Warner's president.

If the absence of these names demonstrated anything it was the success of Warner's low-intensity legal barrages aimed at the state and local agencies that targeted it for blame in the affair. In this battle of lawyers Warner would walk a very fine line between having to protect the Spielberg-Landis partnership and the TZ production on the one hand, while at the same time keeping itself out of the scandal created by the crash. Thus, Warner developed a policy of limited cooperation with the investigators which eventually forced the studio to choose between Spielberg and Landis. The studio was compelled into this predicament through the "politics" of the case: the multi-million-dollar lawsuits soon to be filed by the survivors, and, though it was as yet unfocused, the anticipated criminal investigation, which left open the possibility that one of its own executives might become involved criminally.

But the guiding motive behind the "politics," since it had the most far-reaching implications for Warner's bottom-line, was Steven Spielberg. Whenever possible Warner pursued the strategy of coordinating its activities to protect all three entities – Spielberg, Landis, and itself. But as these interests came into conflict it was always Landis who would be sacrificed to the interest the studio had in its precious relationship with Steven Spielberg. With its parent company, Warner Communications, troubled by its Atari video division just then beginning its nosedive crash that summer, Spielberg constituted a bright spot in the corporate effort to remain profitable through its Warner Bros., studio division in Hollywood.

The movie company's leading dilemma in establishing a consistent legal defense in the case arose out of the way the production was set up. It was an extremely complicated and unusual deal by Hollywood standards. There were multi-producers, multi-directors, multi-segments and different crews for different parts of the film. Different payment systems, as well as many different companies were involved: Levitsky, Fly By Night, Stinky Films (Folsey's business entity!), Disc Management, Twilight Zone Productions, to name a few. In this complicated business and legal tangle it was frequently difficult sorting out who was ultimately responsible for controlling the production. From the narrow legal point of view the investigators were interested only in determining the employer as defined by law. And more specifically, which of the different participants involved in the production had knowledge of illegal acts and had the power to override them.

* * *

Although film making is an industry, it is perhaps not surprising that it's not treated like any other. That explains why veteran labor investigator Charlie Hughes couldn't help being a bit impressed with the glamor and prestige of an assignment to a major studio.

His most memorable recent Hollywood hassle involved Dino de Laurentiis Productions which had Tatum O'Neal, when she was still a minor, working until midnight without proper permits or waivers. In Charlie Hughes' experience it was usually the "independents" – the small independent producers – or the smaller production organizations with whom he had most trouble enforcing labor standards in the hiring of kids. Indeed, when the two lawyers from O'Melveny & Myers, William Vaughn and Scott Dunham, informed him that Warner was itself unaware of the illegal child-hiring practices on the Landis set, Hughes laid the question off on the fact that Landis's might be one of those runaway productions notorious for their loose interpretation of the statutes. Awed by the big studio and flattered by the attention paid him by law guns from the famous legal firm hired by Warner, Hughes communicated regularly, and perhaps indiscreetly, with Dunham and Vaughn in connection with the labor commissioner's investigation of the *Twilight Zone* crash.

Charlie Hughes would look back and wonder how he'd let himself be used as an inside source by Warner's lawyers. He was voluble on his most famous assignment, his three weeks on the *Twilight Zone* case with the O'Melveny men, Dunham and Vaughn, who, both tall as beanstalks draped in long flannel well-tailored business suits, made quite a contrast to the rumpled civil servant. Five years later, Charlie confessed in a wheezing voice that, during his stint as child labor investigator on the *Twilight Zone* case, he used to call the two lawyers on a daily basis, sometimes 2-3 times daily, informing them about the labor commission investigation. He even carried their business cards with their home numbers handwritten on the back. Contritely, he referred to himself as a "stoolie" for his disloyalty to the labor commissioner.

The excellent rapport the Warner lawyers established with the salty but impressionable investigator paid off. Of all the potential targets in the investigation, many of whom were interviewed, Warner was able to convince Hughes that its involvement in the violations of law were only of the most limited nature. In fact, the lawyers led Charlie to believe that they could prove Warner's complete innocence in the child labor question.

But the success with Charlie had its downside. Warner's position logically pointed the finger of ultimate legal responsibility to the people directly involved: John Landis, George Folsey Jr. and Dan Allingham. This in itself involved a delicate maneuver, for the Landis group had to be implicated in a subtle way that did not draw attention to Frank Marshall, Spielberg's right-hand man.

Charlie Hughes was vastly overpowered by the sophisticated tactics of the two fast legal guns from "O'Melveny." They successfully deflected his probe from key Warner figures like Marshall, Fisher, Gallo and Steven Spielberg, so that when eventually he brought his boss Colleen Logan a declaration from a Warner Bros. vice president which pointed the finger at the Landis group, he was congratulated. Hughes was actually credited with having scored a coup!

The author of the declaration, Warner Bros. VP Ed Morey, regularly received documentation regarding the various production schedules describing the scenes, their location, cast and stage of production. He also received the call sheets which describe the set, actors and crew to be used on each shooting day, and the "poop sheets," i.e., preliminary reports, as well as the production reports with information prepared after each day of photography. Charlie Hughes was satisfied to receive from Ed Morey a declaration which made it seem that the Landis group alone was responsible for the disaster and that Warner had no knowledge of the illegality of the children on the set.

Issued August 6, 1982, Morey's statement came exactly two weeks after the crash. By that time the Warner lawyers knew far more than what was revealed in the statement, more than Morey revealed in his declaration, more than the studio ever publicly made known over the five years of the TZ case. Specifically, they were aware of the studio's, Spielberg's and Marshall's involvement in the illegal hiring of the children to an extent far greater than the Morey statement disclosed. Even while local police and authorities were still looking for no more than the bare story behind what happened at Indian Dunes, Warner alone had already begun interviewing the most critical witnesses to the crash. At the same time, within days of the disaster, if not hours, Warner had formed a very fragile, and often bitter, alliance with the Landis group. The labor investigator's willingness to accept a written declaration from the famous O'Melveny lawyers spared Warner's Morey at this early stage from any potentially revealing interrogations.

The Morey declaration came to Charlie Hughes on the letterhead paper of O'Melveny & Myers, listing offices in downtown Los Angeles, Newport Beach, Washington and on Place de la Concorde in Paris. It was signed by William Vaughn. The friendly letter stated that the enclosed declaration concerned Morey's "recollection of the events of July 22," the night of the final shoot. It omitted any mention of the preceding days of the production when the kids and their unusual cash payments were actually discussed with Morey at various Warner meetings.

In his narrowly focused declaration, Morey stated that he had been away on vacation from July 2 until July 19 while most of the Landis segment was being filmed. It was upon his return to the office on July 22, while comparing the poop sheets with the shooting schedule, that he discovered under the column "Cast & Atmos" (Cast and Atmosphere) that there was no reference to children or a welfare worker, even though kids were called for in scenes 29 and 31, still to be shot. Since this violated procedure, Morey stated that he called up the UPM to inform him about the discrepancy and that Allingham only said, "he had been in the helicopter most of the previous night" and did not really know anything about it. According to Morey, Allingham explained that "someone else was taking care of that aspect of things." Five days before, Morey, vice-president in charge of production, told Warner lawyers that the day before the final shot he was asked to approve a check "to pay some kids under the table."

"Absolutely not, no way," he claimed he told production people. Following his initial rebuff, a messenger returned later that afternoon and informed him that the Landis people were not going to use kids, apparently convinced, Morey approved the issuance of a cash check to be accounted for as an "advance from petty cash."

Ordinarily it was Morey's job to question every facet of the production. Essentially it was his job to prevent a production from becoming a *Heaven's Gate* or *Blues Brothers* by going head-over-heel into cost overruns. But in overseeing the Landis segment he shared the same dilemma as that faced by his boss, Fred Gallo. They gritted their teeth at the liberties taken by the Landis people. Powerlessly they watched normal production proceedings being flouted. Landis was given power no film maker was given. It exceeded that of most auteur directors. He not only had final cut, but the production executives had given him final say over most budget decisions...

It was the Summer of Spielberg, a very strange time in Hollywood.

24

AUDITION AT FRANKLIN CANYON

On Friday night, July 16, a week before the fatal scene, John Landis shot scene 23, the Ku Klux Klan sequence of his segment, the second of the three episodes following Bill's transformations in the *Twilight Zone*. The production crew of about 60-70 people was set up at Franklin Canyon, a small wooded glade little-known even to native Angelenos, in the middle of the Santa Monica Mountains that separated the San Fernando Valley from Hollywood and the city. With naturally scenic props of thickets and trees and several small ponds, Franklin Canyon was close-by and a cheap location often used to shoot movies.

In scene 23 Bill continues his journey into the "Twilight Zone." After his flight from the Nazis he's captured by Klansmen and led to a burning cross. There a fight breaks out between Bill and one of his hooded captors. The fight required a "flame gag," the term stuntmen use when a stuntman is actually set on fire. The scene ends with Bill shoving the Klansman into the burning cross, igniting his sheets. The Klansman, covered with flames, rolls yelling and screaming over the ground.

The person doing the flame gag was Gary McLarty. Vic Morrow played Bill. There was real action on the set that night. Grips were busy laying the track along which the camera is dollied in a "tracking shot." The sound man angled his boom close to the burning cross to catch the crackling of the flames. There were four Klansmen, their hoods eerily slit with eye-sockets. Two were the director's film friends, doubling up: Mike Milgrom, the propman, and Eddy "Donut" Dunno, the stuntman.

While the cameras rolled, firemen kept watch with hoses and buckets. Earlier, for safety reasons, the firemen had the director substitute the wooden cross for one of asbestos. In another modification to guarantee safety they insisted on changing Landis' original plan to film a chase with flaming torches, restricting it to the open road, away from the dry brush that dotted the canyon. The area was known for fierce summer brush fires that sometimes spread to the opulent homes in the wild-looking canyons.

The pressures of bringing the film in under budget created a feeling of nervousness and tension among crew members. They saw the director leaping and screaming and noted his excitement around the special effects. One soundman heard Landis rave at the powder chief because the flames shooting from the burning cross weren't big enough. During the flame gag some in the crew felt that the director dangerously prolonged the flames leaping from McLarty's sheets. Another incident, involving six bloodhounds used in a "tracking scene," had the dog handlers very upset.

The incident occurred after Landis' 1st assistant, Elie Cohn, was told by one of the handlers, Terry Knapp, that the dogs, being gun-shy, would react badly to any gun fire over their heads. Cohn went over to Landis, it appeared, to convey to the director the handler's concern. He then came back to tell Knapp that she needn't worry. The filming that night climaxed with a chase of Vic by noose-waving Klansmen, barking bloodhounds, flaming torches, blasting shotguns and fiercely brandished clubs. When the shooting started the deafening noise went straight to the animals' heads; the dogs broke into yowling panic and it was some time before their angry handlers managed to get them back under control.

Vic Morrow ran straight for the pond in the blue suit of Bill. His dive would take Bill into the final phase of his *Twilight Zone* journey when, in scenes to be shot at Indian Dunes the following week, he scrambles in scene 24 to the surface of the Santa Clara riverbank … and finds himself in a Vietnamese village…

Bill dove into the water and the director yelled "cut."

On that Friday, while the Klansmen scene was being shot at Franklin Canyon, the collection of huts at the Indian Dunes location was nearing completion. Everything would be ready for the filming of the crucial scenes in five days' time. Only the roles of the two children, which Lucy Fisher and John Landis had introduced into the script to soften Bill, were not yet filled as Fenton & Feinberg, the agency which cast all four segments of the TZ movie, balked at the plan to hire the kids illegally.

The agency came recommended to Landis by Frank Marshall, who had used them on *E.T.* and *Poltergeist*. Some of the roles were easily filled by the director's friends like propman Milgrom, or Sue Dugan, the women's wardrobe supervisor who played the waitress, or Peter Aykroyd, Dan Aykroyd's brother, who played a GI. For the part which eventually went to Vic Morrow, Peter Coyote, who played a leading role in *E.T.*, had initially auditioned, along with Glenn Campbell.

Fenton & Feinberg first learned about the children in the roles called for by the script at a June 16 casting session in Landis' Universal bungalow. Present were John Landis, George Folsey Jr., and from time-to-time

Dan Allingham, along with the two casting agents, Mike Fenton and Marci Liroff. A small vivacious young woman in her early twenties, Marci Liroff would become one of the two or three chief witnesses to testify against John Landis in the trial.

Just three days before this session John Landis had completed his third script that put together for the first time the fatal elements of the helicopter, the explosives and children in one scene, and he asked the two casting agents if they could provide two Vietnamese children 6-7 years old. "Landis was taking great joy and pride in the explosions," Marci Liroff recalled, "how it would be so exciting and wonderful and great." Marci knew that a studio welfare worker was required to be on the set with the children and that no welfare worker in his right mind would allow a child to be put anywhere near explosives.

During lunch with Mike Fenton, she counseled against the scheme.

"This guy is crazy – and I won't have anything to do with it."

Back at the Universal bungalow Mike Fenton politely declined, explaining that because the kids didn't have any lines in the movie, they were technically extras. Fenton & Feinberg regrettably didn't hire extras, only actors with lines.

"Well, the hell with it." Landis reacted fiercely. "I'll just get them off the street. I'll find them. I don't need you guys." Just then Folsey and Allingham walked in. John Landis turned to them. "We won't put them on the production report. We won't really tell anyone."

During the rest of the afternoon Marci continued casting. She saw several people for the Nazi roles; she hired a Vietnam veteran to play a G.I.; she saw a possible bar patron and a KKK. She considered three possible candidates for Bill, writing on her Fenton-Feinberg casting sheet under one, "too young," under the other, "liked," and under the third, "looks great." At 4:30 she saw her last candidate of the day, a woman trying out for waitress; Marci noted, "liked a lot." At the bottom of the casting sheet for June 16, she made her own handwritten note of John Landis' request: *Two Vietnamese kids. Boy!Girl (Chinese or Korean, Thai, two nights).*

Marci Liroff was one of the few people engaged in the TZ production who worked on all of its four segments. Her ultimate supervisor was the film's executive producer Frank Marshall. Sometime after her session with Landis she called Marshall and communicated her concern about the director's dangerous and "crazy" scheme to hire children without a studio/welfare worker.

She received Marshall's assurances that he would take care of it.

George Folsey Jr. first raised the idea of hiring the children illegally to his good friend Donna Schuman after she asked to see Landis' newly revised script. The director's decision not to go through ordinary casting shifted the burden to Folsey who, by his own account, was the "problem-solver and trouble-shooter" in his relationship with the young director.

Folsey explained to Donna the problem with the new script.

"John's written two kids into the Vietnamese section and we're going to have to work them without permits and a welfare worker," Donna recalled Folsey telling her, "and we don't want that information getting out, especially in the light of the explosives and all the stuff that's going on." Folsey told Donna they thought that some insert and reaction shots of a couple of "adorable" kids would do it.

Among the first persons Folsey canvassed was a young gofer in the office with the LA melting-pot name of Carolyn Lee-Epstein. Of Asian extraction, she heard Folsey ask her if she knew of any "oriental children that we can use" while driving him to pick up his Rolls-Royce at a mechanic's garage in the Valley. When she replied in the negative, she was surprised at Folsey's cautious, "Well, we have to be careful about this."

As Folsey soon discovered, going to the streets to cast the children's roles was not as easy as Landis had made it sound. He managed to meet with few Asian families. He had better luck at a grammar school in one of LA's predominantly Asian neighborhoods and with the help of Beverly Mason, principal of the Elysian Heights Elementary School, Folsey was put in touch with Julie Hua, a Vietnamese mother of two.

Mrs. Hua lived across the street from the school where her two children attended. She was a sort of ombudswoman for the Indochinese community in the neighborhood. Her husband, a lieutenant-colonel in the former South Vietnamese army, was still in Vietnam, presumably in a Communist jail. Mrs. Hua had worked for the U.S. Embassy in Saigon as a translator-interpreter until the fall of Saigon. Like Dr. Daniel Le, she used to watch *Combat* on the U.S. Armed Forces Network in Vietnam and was a fan of Vic Morrow.

When Folsey called on the family he found there not only Mrs. Hua's two children but also the four children of her sister. Folsey suggested they all visit the set and meet the director. And so, the following night, July 15, Folsey created a sensation on the rundown street by pulling up in a limo. The children were packed in the limo with Folsey and the Huas, while the rest followed in a car driven by Mrs. Hua's brother-in-law.

Mrs. Hua was not worried. She had Folsey's assurance that there would be no danger other than that the kids might get a little wet. He had promised to have "plenty of hot chocolate and heaters on the set." She told investigators that Folsey had asked her not to talk about the hiring of the kids yet; they were still trying to get the permits, he told her.

In the end her own children, Vinh and Richard, were not chosen; the director picked two of her sister's kids. But three days later, on Sunday, July 18, Mrs. Hua received a call and heard the voice which she remembered because of its distinct high-pitched straining sound. It was George Folsey Jr. breaking the news, "in a very low, sorry voice." The director had found two smaller and lighter children that could be carried more easily by Vic Morrow. Folsey held out the promise that maybe he could get her kids into another set and mentioned that he would come by and drop off some money for her trouble. He reminded Mrs. Hua of the day and the date of the shooting of the scene with the kids, and that they still might need to use her sister's two twin girls if the two smaller children couldn't act.

"So just stand by until 9 o'clock. If you do not hear from us by 9 o'clock let the children go to bed."

In the end it was through his assistant, "flash," Donna Schuman's husband, Dr. Harold Schuman, that Folsey managed to find the right people who wanted to have their kids in a movie. Hal Schuman had done favors for film people before. He once authorized a Vitamin B-12 shot for TV star Brenda Vacarro. He taught Shirley McLaine how to use a yo-yo. More recently he had helped out George Folsey Jr. in getting an R-rating changed on an MGM movie, *Norman, Is That You?*, which dealt explicitly with homosexuality; writing in his capacity as psychiatrist to the Motion Picture Rating Board, Dr. Schuman successfully lobbied for a less restrictive rating. He continued to be helpful in Folsey's latest film. Hollywood was calling. Who could resist?

Dr. Schuman was in charge of a community mental health center which at one time employed eight Asian staff members. On Monday, July 12, barely ten days before the film's scheduled wrap, he made a number of phone calls to his Asian friends, telling them in brief the little he knew about the film. He first called a Korean colleague, but she wasn't in. His last call was to Dr. Peter Chen. Dr. Schuman first thanked him for an earlier favor in which Dr. Chen had referred him to an acupuncturist for his back trouble. He then mentioned that his wife worked for a movie company and that the film they were making called for two "oriental" children.

Chen thereupon contacted his brother Mark who told him that his six-year-old daughter Renee would be interested in the girl's role. He knew another family, the Les, whose son sounded perfect for the male part. Peter Chen told investigators that subsequently he contacted Dr. Daniel Le and his wife Kim. Dr. Le, Myca's father, called Dr. Schuman back to ask if his 7 1/2-year-old son could be in the movie. Dr. Le reminded Dr. Schuman that the psychiatrist had already met Myca one time before at a New Year's party earlier that year.

Three days later, on July 15, Schuman again called Peter Chen, advising him that the producer, John Landis, would like to see the children. And the following morning Folsey personally spoke to Renee's grandfather, Mao Chen, as well as to Dr. Daniel Le. They were informed that a car would come that same evening around 5:30 to take the children and their parents to meet the director on the set. That day Cynthia Nigh gave the addresses of the kids' families to driver Jeff Powell. Later that same day a studio van arrived promptly, first at the home of the Chens in Pasadena and then at the Les in Cerritos. On Friday, July 16, driver Jeff Powell drove the thrilled occupants back to the set at Franklin Canyon where Folsey introduced himself.

Awed by the extraordinary experience of being on a Hollywood set, the Asian families were introduced to Vic Morrow. The adults and the children alike were fascinated by the strange Ku Klux Klan scene with bloodhounds and hooded men. Folsey explained to the parents and children the shot to be filmed the following week. Using pidgin English, he spoke of a "big light" that would go on "making loud noise." The noise, he explained, would be created "by Vic stepping on wood objects under water." There was no mention of explosions or bombs, the helicopter wasn't mentioned, only "lights and sounds." Folsey then took them to meet the longhaired, bearded director.

Landis was in a hurry. He looked at the serious little boy and at the pretty little girl, and seeing they were smaller and lighter than the Hua children for Vic to carry, with his quick decision, "Good, hire them, "the fate of Myca and Renee was sealed. The van would come to their homes on Wednesday, July 21. They were to bring along some warm clothing. Folsey reminded Mrs. Le and Mr. Chen that they would be paid $500 each.

When 2nd assistant director Andy House first hired on with the Landis segment Allingham informed him that they were trying to get as much production value on the screen as possible and that there was a kind of friendly competition between "John and Steve."

"Look, there's a feeling that these guys want to show one another that they can make the biggest best film for the least money," House recalled Allingham telling him. The UPM continued, "You're making a picture that's going to be next to a Steven Spielberg picture – both guys are obviously very competitive." Both Landis after *Blues Brothers* and Spielberg after *1941* had been called "terribly indulgent" following the failure of these big expensive films. Allingham told the 2nd AD that it was kind of a contest to make the best TZ segment as cheaply as they could for around $1.3 million.

What he learned from Allingham somehow failed to reassure the 2nd AD and he never stopped looking for substitutes in place of real children in scene 31. He had just worked under such conditions. During his recent stint on *E.T.*, he had seen "small people" hanging around the set and he told Allingham about them. Further researching the idea of using "small people" for the kids' roles he tried to interest Allingham in using "professional small people," adults small enough to appear as children. House mentioned Little Bobby Porter who had doubled for the little girl in *Annie*. Though Allingham told him not to worry about it, House continued his attempts to find a realistic substitute for the kids. He kept wondering if the children could swim.

But at the time of the Friday night, July 16, shooting of the KKK sequences at Franklin Canyon, House received a clear signal that all his suggestions concerning professional small people, dummies and stunt doubles had fallen on deaf ears. Spotting the "oriental" children on the KKK set, oblivious of their fate as they waited to be interviewed, he was confronted with the absolute reality of the scheme. And in a last-ditch effort Andy House resolved to make a final bold attempt to convince John Landis that the plan should be changed.

He waited all night. Around midnight he saw his chance.

Following the lunch break he found himself walking back to the set with his immediate superior Elie Cohn. John Landis walked slightly ahead of them. Again, House expressed his fears to Cohn that by using children illegally not only could John Landis himself be banned from working with children in the future but also that Warner Brothers, the entire studio, could have its license revoked to work with any children at all in the state of California.

The director spun around.

"What was that?"

House was speechless. Cohn stepped in. He repeated what Andy had just said.

The director said, "Oh," and with that single and singularly mild exclamation he closed the subject.

Andy said nothing. He didn't want to stick his neck out any further.

* * *

On Monday, July 19, at a meeting at Indian Dunes attended by Folsey, Allingham and Elie Cohn, John Landis discussed the plan to have the children on the set without a permit or welfare worker. To avoid detection the children would be brought to Indian Dunes on the last day of shooting and their presence there, the director stressed, would be as short as possible.

25

PETTY CASH

Hiring the children had not been part of Allingham's deal making, but he became a key figure in the aftermath; for with the final decision to shoot Vic and the kids he was faced two days later with the task of coming up with the cash to pay the parents of the children. There was no problem about the petty cash since that was in the custody of his girlfriend, Cynthia Nigh, whom he had himself hired to work in the office. But Folsey and Allingham, after asking her how much petty cash she had on hand for the kids, finally decided not to dip into these reserves and to get the money through the production's ordinary channels.

The person Allingham went to see was Bonnie Radford, the chief accountant on the TZ production. Although she worked for Warner and was paid by Warner, Warner's regular fulltime employees identified her as part of the "Spielberg organization." As paymaster on *E.T.* and *Poltergeist*, she had worked directly with Frank Marshall and she also handled the payroll for *Raiders of the Lost Ark*. Bonnie's sister, Mary Radford, was also part of the Spielberg organization and was Frank Marshall's special assistant. According to one of Warner's internal memos, Bonnie Radford had been assigned by Marshall and Spielberg to work on the Landis segment; she was responsible for all the paperwork to back up checks.

Before funding a request, it was her practice to generate a check and have either the Landis production personnel or Frank Marshall sign it. Once a check was ready for issuance, she prepared the necessary documentation to be sent over to Jim Henderling, Warner's payroll watchdog. Henderling had to co-sign any checks for amounts over $500.

Of all the people on the Landis segment, Radford's most frequent dealings were with Dan Allingham. The UPM sent her bills to be paid or made requests for funds. On July 20, a Tuesday, the day before the scheduled final shooting, Allingham came to Bonnie Radford with a request for $2,000 in cash, and a transaction took place the true details of which have never been unraveled. The often-changing and conflicting statements made since by key Warner people over the five-year period of TZ proceedings have served only to complicate this apparently unsolvable mystery. However, the true story was contained in a confidential internal Warner memo which never came to light during or after the trial. The memo contrasted sharply with what certain Warner people would later testify to under oath. Written immediately after the accident, it revealed that Henderling stated that he was explicitly approached by Bonnie Radford on how to pay the children "under the table."

Jim Henderling, at 75 almost as old as the Hollywood film industry, had grown small and wizened in the more than half century spent working for the studios. Ancient and hard-nosed, a notorious stickler, he was known to return any document if it had initials rather than a full signature. He was a fine-detail man, responsible for monitoring the day-to-day production paperwork – the call sheets, shooting schedules and the daily poop sheet. The studio put him over John Landis whose reputation for keeping within budget had suffered since *Blues Brothers*. For a brief period, in order to be even closer to Landis, Henderling departed from his routine and together with Bonnie Radford occupied a trailer on the Universal lot.

A confidential Warner memo connecting the studio with the child-hiring scandal showed that Henderling had spoken to Bonnie Radford in the final days of shooting about the employment of the children. During that conversation Henderling recalled that he learned from Radford that the Landis people, particularly George Folsey Jr., had some kids that they wanted to use and that they wanted to know how they could pay them "under the table." Leaving Radford's request unresolved, he took it up with his boss Ed Morey. Morey at first opposed the "under the table" plan and sent Henderling back to tell Radford. Radford then spoke with Allingham and Marshall, finally drafting the check as requested.

The confidential memo told of Bonnie Radford's assistant returning later that same day with a check described as a "petty cash advance" made out to George Folsey Jr. It was issued on an account described as "Twilight Zone Productions" with a Warner Brothers Studio, Burbank, address. For Henderling there was no mistaking the purpose of the check. Though Radford informed him it was no longer for the kids but for other purposes, Henderling didn't believe a word of it and so stated when he returned to Ed Morey bearing a $2,000 check payable to Folsey.

In fact, before he took the check to Morey, according to Warner's internal memos, Henderling did not even bother to ask what the petty cash advance was for because he felt he already knew and there was no point in asking. He didn't believe it for a minute when. Bonnie Radford told him they were no longer going to use the kids. According to Warner's memos, Morey directed Henderling to sign the check because the Landis people had every right to take the advance. Henderling did as told and returned the signed check to Radford with the understanding that the exact use of the money would be accounted for at a later time. Two days before the deaths on the set the check was co-signed by Frank Marshall and sent back to Folsey.

There was one last hitch. Folsey was too busy to take the check personally to the bank. But cashing a check made out to his name without personally appearing at the bank to present the required identification was no great problem. John Landis had an excellent banking connection, namely his mother. She was a minor official at the Mitsui Manufacturers Bank in Beverly Hills. Arrangements were made and a messenger promptly took the check from the Universal bungalow to Landis' mother in Beverly Hills. Under her initials, Shirley Levine authorized the cashing of the check to help her moviemaker son. She gave twenty $100 bills in an envelope to Folsey's messenger, becoming herself an innocent part of his dubious scheme.

The next day, studio driver Jeff Powell picked up Folsey at the Universal bungalow in Burbank. They first drove to the densely ethnic neighborhood in Echo Park where Mrs. Julie Hua, the energetic Vietnamese ombudswoman, had her home. Folsey gave her $800 in cash for the children who had auditioned, reminding her of the two who were still on stand-by until 9 o'clock that evening. Folsey waved goodbye to Mrs. Hua and to the children whom fate would spare – because they were too heavy. Then Powell drove to the homes of the Le and Chen families where they picked up Myca and Renee with their parents and transported them to Indian Dunes for what was originally planned to be the final night of shooting.

It was 8 o'clock that evening when Powell arrived on the set. He remained there that night and at about seven the following morning he took the weary Le and Chen families back to their respective homes. They were to return again that same evening because the anticipated wrap had not come off and the shooting was rolled over an extra day. Having paid the two families $500 each, Folsey had obtained their promise to return Myca and Renee for one more night at the same fee.

But because they were held over for another night Folsey had run out of cash. He had to come up with another $1,000 and on Thursday, July 22, he called Bonnie Radford once more. She again came up with the cash.

Folsey sent over the office gofer to pick up the money at Radford's office. Carolyn Lee-Epstein was instructed that no W-2 forms would be filled out for the children. In the days leading up to the shooting she had heard frequent mention of the "oriental children" in conversations between Folsey and Allingham. She had overheard them discussing how to hide the hiring of the kids in the accounting books. She knew from talk in the office that the two kids would earn $1,000 each, and it stuck in her mind as being "an awful lot."

From the Universal bungalow to Bonnie Radford's office at Warner was a ten-minute drive. Donna Schuman was present in Folsey's office at the bungalow around mid-afternoon when the gofer returned from Radford's office with a brown envelope containing the $1,000 in $100 bills. The messenger handed the envelope over to Folsey and again, upon seeing the $1,000, she was impressed with the amount being paid out for such a small part.

Donna, too, saw the cash and watched Folsey count it and put it in his pocket.

As usual, they joked about it.

26

SPIES LIKE US

Just after the Indian Dunes disaster there had been some brief talk
between the Landis group and Warner about not going ahead with
the film. But the talk was never treated seriously. For public relations
reasons the director was reported by his lawyers to be under a doctor's
care; meanwhile, he continued working on his segment.

Despite the funerals, NTSB and legal rap sessions with Harland Braun,
Joel Behr, John Diemer and Marty Rose, the director rushed his segment
to completion in order to move on to new projects. Holed up in his
Universal bungalow editing room with Folsey and film editor Malcolm
Campbell, the reportedly despondent director completed editing the film
within two weeks after the crash. By meeting the deadlines Landis pre-
served his right to have "final cut" on his segment as guaranteed in his
agreement with Spielberg and Warner.

The deaths had very little impact on either the Landis segment's budget or Warner's release date because all of the segment had been shot
by the time the tragedy occurred. Folsey and Landis initially discussed
using some of the footage from the crash scene in the final version but
in the end decided it was the wrong thing to do. Ironically, with the all-
too-real realism of the exploding village necessarily cut, Landis' finished
segment left the script's story line where it had been before Lucy Fisher
intervened and John Landis began his revisions to make Bill more human.
Since Bill never completes his redemption by rescuing the children, he
ends the segment fundamentally "unsoftened," unchanged, unregenerate,
"unredeemed," the same cartoon-like character from the first script. Consequently, the artistic basis on which John Landis in Vic's eulogy tried to
justify the actor's death ended up on the cutting-room floor.

Those who met with him daily, his closest personal friends and his personal secretary, felt he showed no evidence of remorse. While the director
edited the film, Alpha Campbell was disgusted by the business-as-usual
atmosphere in the bungalow. It seemed to her as though everybody in
command acted as if nothing had happened. It bothered her that Landis
behaved as if unaffected by the tragedy

Donna Schuman, too, was revolted to see how quickly everybody forgot their unhallowed part in the event. George Folsey Jr. remained unresponsive to her husband's request to meet with him and give an explanation. Donna herself felt that the basic questions she had concerning the accident had never been answered. She was aware that Folsey's exclamation over lunch at Hampton's a couple of days earlier, "We rehearsed it thirty times!," was a crock.

Donna Schuman grew more and more infuriated, but before her final break with Folsey could take place she needed a last straw. It was shortly forthcoming when Folsey innocently asked her to type up a form. It was an application for admission to the Jonathan Club, one of Los Angeles' most prestigious private clubs, still barred at that time to women, blacks and Jews.

The last straw settled. The nerve gave way. For Folsey to be thinking of his snobby strivings at a time like this did it. Donna threw the application down and after heated words stormed out of the office, never to return.

While publicly the young director gave the impression that buried in movie making he had left behind a painful episode in his life, he was actually very busy privately talking about the case. In an effort to recruit friendly forces immediately following the disaster Landis held highly confidential meetings with several eyewitnesses from the set, including 1st AD Elie Cohn, propman Mike Milgrom and set designer Richard Sawyer. Apart from the many hours spent in planning sessions with his personal lawyer Joel Behr, Landis directed his legal team into gaining an understanding of his role on the set that night so that a defense strategy could be mobilized.

In the first months following the tragedy that strategy was limited by what he himself knew about the causes of the crash. What Landis believed had happened came mostly from his lawyers and newspapers. At first, like the government investigators, he believed that a glue pot lid carelessly left in one of the huts, specifically the drying hut nearest the action, was responsible for knocking out the chopper's tail rotors. His talks with key eyewitnesses had led him to conclude, he informed his legal team, that the burly special effects man standing next to him, Jerry Williams, had fired the fatal shot. During these conferences with his inner circle, Landis showed a cockiness unknown to the public. In confidential discussions within weeks of the crash he told his lawyers that, according to early news accounts, the NTSB investigators had only confiscated five of the six angles being shot that night. They missed the footage from the sixth camera, vital footage still in his possession. Arrogantly, Landis dismissed them as being "stupid" for not knowing the difference.

Landis wanted his team of lawyers to know a little more about John Landis. He led them into the labyrinth of his persona, smugly admitting that he was sometimes viewed on the set as "intimidating," explaining that it was the way a movie director got results. Many of the craftsmen working on his set were prima donnas, he said, "emotionally disturbed." He asserted in his defense how "intimidation" was only one tool and that sometimes, to be effective, it had to be alternated with "seduction." He set himself above Steven Spielberg, his partner and co-producer on the TZ movie, expressing the rivalry and envy he felt for Spielberg that ultimately lay behind his drive for the spectacular which brought disaster on their heads.

To his team of lawyers, he described himself as a "classic liberal Jew." He boasted that in contrast to Spielberg, all of his movies were racially integrated. As he vaunted his advanced liberal views, he berated Steven Spielberg who in *E.T.*, according to Landis, should have had a black kid in the bicycle scene. The director assured his listeners that such a lack of racial sensitivity would never occur to him.

In these sometimes-bizarre defense planning sessions Landis took the position of infallibility. He portrayed himself as a martyr, a "rich boy" hounded by the envious. Strangely, he was able to speak almost casually of the events of that night, even joking about it now and then. On one occasion, pressed by his attorneys as to why he took so much time and trouble to keep smoking off his set by writing it on the call sheets, the implication being that there might have been safety issues on the set in need of equal attention, Landis sarcastically asked his attorneys what they expected. Should he write as a caution, "Don't Kill Anyone, Please?"

Some of his legal advisers appreciated from the start that there were problems with the case. They were especially bothered by Landis' assertion that it was not the director's task on the set to ask if anything was safe. Privately, some of his counsel felt differently. One, in particular, was troubled from the defense standpoint that Landis had never bothered to ensure that the pilot and special effects chief Paul Stewart met to discuss the shot. Landis wasn't even sure if Stewart was actually watching during the so-called "rehearsal" at 2:00 A.M., just twenty minutes before the crash! But perhaps most disturbing was his admission that he knew the fatal shot was "dangerous." He screamed to the crowd through his bullhorn to stand up during the final take. That, if nothing else, showed foreseeability.

While busy consulting with his lawyers and putting the final touches to his TZ segment in the early fall of '82, John Landis experienced the ups and downs of a busy career. The other project he had been committed to during the shooting of his *Twilight Zone* segment, a film project entitled "Whereabouts," collapsed as a result of the disaster at Indian Dunes. But this disappointment was followed by landing a comedy which by the time of its release would become the immensely successful *Trading Places*, a stroke brought about through his connections at Paramount with Jeffrey Katzenberg, then Paramount's second in command to Michael Eisner.

The original name of the comedy was "Black and White" and it was initially scheduled to be directed by someone other than Landis. Katzenberg, according to Landis' closest associates, "slipped" a copy of the script to him as a way of helping out a friend in trouble. Producer Aaron Russo had originally thought of Richard Pryor and Gene Wilder in the lead roles, but Pryor literally couldn't be found, and without Pryor, Wilder wouldn't come in. Russo next thought of pairing Dan Aykroyd and Eddie Murphy. Landis' agent, Mike Marcus, called Russo and said that his client wanted to direct the movie. Russo had produced *The Rose* with Bette Midler; he had been impressed by *Animal House* and shortly after the crash, during lunch at the Paramount commissary with Katzenberg and Landis, the New York producer heard Landis enthusiastically promise that he could deliver Aykroyd: "He's a very dear friend of mine." The female lead in the film was originally going to be a black girl. John Landis, however, wanted Jamie Lee Curtis and so the "classic liberal Jew" who chided Spielberg for not having a little black boy on a bicycle changed the role to a white. It was a break for Jamie Lee Curtis. "It took her from being an exploitation film star," Russo said, "into legitimate movies."

In the following month John Landis moved to New York to begin shooting his second big box-office success, eventually to make even more money than *Animal House* while catapulting the film career of Eddie Murphy to new heights.

* * *

Meanwhile, on a much more prosaic front, far from high-stakes Hollywood wheeling and deal-making, a virtual army of investigators was finished poring over the stricken set in the Newhall desert scrub. Apart from the NTSB's Don Llorente, the most notable investigator was the tall, gangling, sandy-haired sheriff's detective with the brushy tough-guy mustache by the name of Tom Budds.

Between other assignments, Budds plowed away on the case. Speaking to people he could reach, he put their disparate observations in his notebooks. Driver Carl Pittman mentioned that he had smelled marijuana on the set and that a couple of people there "were flying high on cocaine." From soundman Richard Goodman, who was married to script girl Katherine Wooten's sister, Budds learned that some of the crew knew there was a "teacher" on the set, and that the crew members had been urged not to conduct any conversation about the children. Director of photography Steve Larner gave him an indication of the size of the blast by recounting how at the last minute he had to pull his jacket over his head because it got too hot near the village.

But illuminating as these jottings were, they raised many more questions which could be answered only by people from whom Budds found himself effectively debarred. Chief of his sources at this stage were the other investigative agencies, each with its particular area of interest: the labor commissioner with its focus on kids, Cal/OSHA with its focus on safety, and the NTSB with its interest limited to the actual aircraft. After reading some of the original NTSB statements, Budds in his notes revealed his bewilderment: "Did director ask you to have a camera focus on center hut?" "Presentation of Morrow to crew and gallery – why? What was reason." "Any conversation with anyone regarding danger and kids?" "Who put explosives in hut?" "Did Landis tell someone else to plant hut explosive after advisement of danger by Paul Stewart? ..." Budds focused on the SFX crew since they were the only men on the set who knew which wires connected with which explosives and which firing board was manned by which powderman. He was able to establish that Jimmy Camomile and Jerry Williams had been the only two powdermen firing the mortars. But their stories were at odds and did not match the version of the chief powderman, Paul Stewart.

In his very first interview with Stewart one week after the crash the powder chief told the deputy sheriff, "Landis knew where all the charges were placed," though admitting that it was his, Stewart's, idea to place explosives in the vital shoreline drying hut which investigators first suspected in bringing down the Huey. In an interview a week later Jimmy Camomile recalled for Budds that it had been Stewart's idea to put a charge in one of the shoreline huts and that, as a result, Camomile dug in a "round, straight wall mortar ... under a floor of 1" dia (sic) bamboo pieces." Kevin Quibell told Budds, "I thought the one in the hut was square but in talking since I hear it was round." These inconsistencies and contradictions kept Budds in a fog with only here and there a few clear patches.

Budds' notes reflected a clear patch as to who cued the action that lowered the chopper into its fatal proximity with the SFX explosives. He accepted at face value the statements made by three eyewitnesses regarding what was soon to become the most controversial issue in the first phase of the case. Powderman Quibell recalled, "Landis was holding a bullhorn and was waving the chopper lower." Makeup artist Melanie Levitt said she saw Landis "motioning copter down with thumbs down." Cynthia Nigh also told Budds that Landis "was saying bring copter lower and waving his arms in a lowering motion."

But the single issue to elude Budds concerned the children. Who arranged their presence on the set that night? How were they paid?

Though Warner's top men, including Chairman Bob Daly and President Terry Semel, were already briefed on the answers to these questions, Homicide's Budds remained in the fog. The one individual that Budds tried to get hold of to perhaps shed light came from the management end of the set that night, 2nd AD Andy House. Surprisingly, the NTSB had failed to interview him and the labor commission's investigator, Charlie Hughes, had reached a dead end in – his efforts. Concerned about the legal implications of talking to the labor investigator, the 2nd AD went straight to Warner. Warner's lawyers, notably O'Melveny & Myers' top litigator, William Vaughn, debriefed House, and apparently fearing that his evasion from police would create more problems for the embattled studio, surreptitiously helped arrange a highly controlled meeting with Budds.

The meeting between Budds and House took place on August 18, barely a month after the crash, in House's attorney's office, whose fees were paid by Warner. Budds did not know that the 2nd AD had already related to the Warner attorneys the details of the plan to cover-up the presence of the kids on the set and had further agreed, through consultations between his own attorney and the studio's, not to reveal the conspiracy to the sheriffs man from Homicide at this time. For if the account of any one person could be said to have fueled the studio's concerns it would probably be that of the 2nd AD's, Andy House.

Anderson House was the first to tell Warner the shocking story of conspiracy and intrigue a mere 11 days after the crash. Andy House at the time felt he had little choice. Things were closing in. The reckoning in the form of an official interview became inevitable. Charlie Hughes was chasing him. Andy loved the film-making business and feared losing his ability to work with children. Should it ever come to a legal contest he needed the support of his employer. As a 2nd assistant director, according to the DGA basic agreement, the studio was responsible for attorney's fees to defend him against claims stemming from his work on the set. In his predicament Warner provided the only protection he could turn to. The studio assured Anderson House that whatever he said would not go beyond the ears of a few at Warner who needed to know, specifically Terry Semel, the president, and John Daley, the chairman.

Though he told the basic story of the kids on the set, House left out much of the sordid detail. For instance, he mentioned that on the final night of shooting the kids were kept in Landis' trailer until needed; but he made no mention of the elaborate plan to prevent the FSOs, and particularly Jack Tice, from seeing the kids on the set next to explosives. From House, Warner learned something of the role of Jack Tice, the fireman/welfare worker, and how Andy recognized him and warned Folsey, Allingham and Cohn that Tice would do something if he discovered the children. The 2nd AD went on to assure the studio lawyers that he was certain that the fire marshal was never able to spot the kids.

Andy's personal involvement in the scheme was laid out in the account he gave the studio about the way in which the children were kept concealed; in other ways, how Allingham had told him to omit references to the children from film documentation and Andy's admission that he had himself instructed DGA apprentice Hilary Leach to do the same on the production reports for the last two days of shooting. The studio obtained intimate details of conditions on the set that night from the beginning, when Andy House ran into Tice, until the end, when House saw Frank Marshall order everybody to go home. All this it knew before deputy sheriff Budds had ever learned of the importance of House.

His listeners obtained a sense of the emotional impact on House. The 2nd AD recalled the boy crying in the water just before the 9:30 scene. He repeated his personal warnings to Allingham that Morrow's dropping a child could cause a drowning. He told the Warner lawyers of finding Morrow face down, picking him up and dropping him when he realized he was dead. They learned of details such as the bullhorn on which investigators would soon fix their curious attention. And while listening to this bleak recital they probably were somewhat relieved to discover that House knew nothing about the rumor the studio had heard that Spielberg interviewed the children on the TZ set a week before the crash. Though never verified, this rumor was persistent and permutations of it were still current at the time of the trial.

At the end of the meeting with House, Warner's men appeared most concerned about labor investigator Hughes. So far House had been able to rebuff Hughes three times, but under the circumstances the studio advised House to see him. Warner's outside lawyers from O'Melveny and Myers, William Vaughn and Scott Dunham, suggested that House be accompanied by his own attorney rather than one from O'Melveny & Myers. It did not want House to be identified with the movie company.

The meeting with the labor investigator never panned out, and afterwards the lawyer Andy House engaged, John Dellaverson from Loeb & Loeb, worked closely with Warner's attorneys. Jointly they prepared House for his encounter with the two homicide detectives, Budds and Finnigan.

Dellaverson, in discussing with Warner the scope of the interview he anticipated with the two detectives, laid down ground rules for their talk with Andy House. If the police went into certain sensitive areas, Dellaverson pledged, he would end the interview. He would only permit questions pertaining to the cause of the crash. Warner was assured that the interview would be kept short. Dellaverson promised the studio that he would report back to its lawyers following the interview. At this first meeting with the detectives Andy House was not nearly as candid as he had been with Warner. House told Budds and Finnigan nothing about the cover-up regarding the kids. He remained quiet about his fear of danger on the set. While describing his job responsibilities as coordinating things on the set, he omitted mention of his fudging the documents to leave the kids' names off, of the concealment of the children in the trailer, of the code words that were used on the set, nor of his own repeated pleas not to use the kids, virtually begging Landis, Allingham and Cohn to use dummies or stunt doubles. But most poignantly, Andy House never told the police how "upset" he was every time he reviewed the script with its frightening mention of the use of explosives around children.

House told the detectives that he had viewed the final footage. Budds had also seen it at the NTSB screening and now learned that House was the "mystery" man in the orange shirt, the figure Budds had watched on the film footage run to Morrow's headless torso. But on other points, by being vague and unemphatic, House remained a "mystery man." Asked by Budds about the 11:30 scene, he said that he had overheard complaints that it was "hot" – no more. He didn't tell them the explosions frightened him. He did acknowledge having seen live ammo being used and that he had seen Landis and Paul Stewart standing in the river together prior to the final crash scene. However, he said nothing about hearing any conversation between them.

All in all, House told the police very little. He passed over mention of the secret code name, key to the unravelment of much of the frenzied doings on the set that night. Not until nine months had gone by, and only as the result of delicate negotiations between his lawyer and the DA's office, would House finally reveal the outrageous story behind the "Vietnamese."

When just weeks after the crash he entered this meeting with Andy House, Budds had little or no experience in Hollywood affairs. Budds was just another young cop in the sheriff's Homicide division. Faced with the closed world of Hollywood, he was predictably ineffective in establishing the contacts necessary to move the investigation forward. The people who had been on the set that night, like Andy House, were afraid to speak. They wanted to continue working in Hollywood.

Elsewhere Budds found doors closed to him or only opened after difficulty. Though he tried he failed, for instance, to track down the course of the actual film from the time it disappeared from the Indian Dunes set until surfacing at Warner three days later. Of the other evidence that melted away into the night before Budds' arrival at Indian Dunes, one of the two soundtracks that recorded the final shot not only went undiscovered by the young sheriff, it vanished so utterly that he did not even suspect its existence!

Except for a few witnesses at the NTSB who had spoken out to the press like Lydecker, especially informative, Budds found, on the subject of Landis' style of using "intimidation" on the set, making people do things they didn't want to do, not a single person on the set that night came forward to tell police what they had seen. The big breakthrough in the case, in fact, would not come from Budds' frustrating efforts but as the result of the eventual confession of Andy House, long after his first meeting with Budds.

* * *

While Budds floundered in the fog, entertainment attorney Joel Behr was putting in place a far-reaching effort to protect John Landis and his associates, Folsey and Allingham. In anticipation of the lawsuits to be filed shortly by the victims' heirs, Martin Rose of Kern & Wooley, the high-priced Century City insurance lawyers, got extremely busy. Rose became a member of the frequent sessions conducted in the office of Behr, the lynx-eyed general who led the phalanx, coolly weighing every stratagem under his bouffant-like shock of steel-blue hair.

Each of the specialists hired by Behr practiced law in a limited area and each had specific objectives. Braun regularly touched base with his former colleagues in the DA's office, as well as with Budds at Homicide and with Doug Dalton, the outside criminal specialist hired by O'Melveny for the studio's potential criminal involvement in the matter; and with Andy Peterson, the lawyer and labor specialist who monitored the labor commissioner and Cal/OSHA. The first civil lawsuit, filed shortly after the crash by the lawyers for the Chen family, asked for $200 million in damages; those filed on behalf of Vic's two daughters and Myca were soon to follow for what were expected to be equally astronomical amounts. As a result, Martin Rose, Behr's yuppyish aircraft specialist lawyer, in October 1982 hired an insurance investigator by the name of Robert Frasco, best known outside of Hollywood for investigative work designed to help minimize insurance claims. They met at Kern & Wooley, the aircraft law specialists in Century City, where in his office Rose outlined to Frasco the case as it related to their client. By the time of the trial, almost 5 years later, the private investigator compiled a sensational notebook with tape recorded interviews with the most important figures in the case.

Frasco's job, by querying witnesses among the crew and staff that night on the set, was to determine which of them perceived Landis as being responsible for safety there. What Martin Rose hoped to show was that there was a shared responsibility and that John Landis had properly followed the law by relying on experts. The problem, Rose told Frasco, was with why the helicopter was lined up over the explosives on the village shoreline instead of "where it rehearsed at 2 o'clock." Frasco was also asked to find out who among the pool of actual eyewitnesses had heard him say "lower, lower," if, in fact, Landis had given this command.

Rose wanted Frasco to see as many witnesses from the set as possible, particularly Steve Lydecker, who was believed to be the source of all the unfavorable press leaks; Frasco was to "test people to find out what they're going to say" and to discover how many people shared Lydecker's feelings about the disaster. "They were afraid of the same," Frasco surmised.

One of Frasco's most critical assignments dealt with the original design of the Vietnam village scene. Rose wanted to prove that the helicopter was not intended to be over the village when the explosions were detonated. The set designer, Richard Sawyer, was "very friendly to Landis," Rose assured Frasco, who was instructed to contact Sawyer and "keep him friendly," and learn what he had shown Landis in the way of sketches and drawings depicting the village scenes. Richard Sawyer had turned over to Landis' attorneys bundles of artists' renderings produced by his staff. Particularly worrisome to the phalanx were several sketches, Rose told his investigator, "with the helicopter sketched in the air." Frasco was asked to believe Landis' claim never to have seen many of the sketches and never to have approved any sketch that placed a helicopter over the village or its shoreline – "or even over the water." The movie director had already told the NTSB panel that he couldn't remember any blueprints showing the planned final scene, mentioning only to the investigators that he remembered a "few thumbnail sketches."

The sketches produced by Sawyer's staff numbered among them some that were extremely revealing. One strikingly depicted a helicopter descending over the cliff at Indian Dunes and traveling along the village shoreline. A storyboard dated June 25, 1982, showed the main character running in the village, as described in Landis' third draft, scene 32, with huts exploding behind him "one after another." There was also the eerie sketch, the "spotting plan," showing a crashed helicopter wreck in the water. Frasco was instructed to determine if there were witnesses who knew which of the sketches had been seen by Landis, or how many sketches had been drawn which the director had not seen, and most importantly, from the liability standpoint, the extent to which the parents had been informed of what was coming in the final scene. Most emphatically, Rose wanted to know if they had ever been shown a copy of "THE FINAL SKETCH WITH EXPLOSIVES.?" (sic)

By an ironic coincidence, Frasco received this new assignment the same day, September 16, 1982, on which the NTSB requested Landis' attorneys to turn over all of the graphic and visual materials relating to the film's production. Specifically, the NTSB was interested in the same sketches showing the planning of the location of the explosives and the helicopter's flight plan which Landis' new investigator had been briefed about. This request, covering "all notes, or other writings or any scripts, any documents referring or relating to the scripts and all graphic layouts, depictions or representations," was met by stony refusal. Except for three pages of the shooting script that Behr had turned over to Llorente within the first few weeks of the crash, the phalanx did not appear willing to share anything out of the huge cache of visual materials – sketches, storyboards, blueprints, layouts, photos, graphics and other visual tools – that figure largely in a movie's pre-production phase. As a result of Landis' lawyers' uncooperative policy, a federal subpoena was issued which, by executing a rare legal maneuver in federal court, the Landis phalanx also tried to block. Finally, after a federal judge rejected Landis' position and ordered him to comply with the subpoena and supply the NTSB with the requested documents, Marty Rose met with U.S. Attorney James Sullivan and Don Llorente, presumably to produce the documents.

Marty Rose showed up with only a single graphic. Surprisingly, it was the same eerie "spotting plan" seen nailed to the bluff by the female guard that artist Southwell met in the dunes. The federal investigator and the law man looked in puzzlement at the large copy of the set blueprint showing the wrecked helicopter without a tail rotor, uncannily positioned in the river near the village shoreline at the spot almost exactly where the actual crash had occurred. That blueprint, Rose claimed disingenuously, was the only graphic document that fit the subpoena's description. Harland Braun's explanation of this bold defiance was that, with so many people already having seen this striking "wreck" diagram, Behr had decided that by not turning it over to investigators it could have blown up on them at a later time.

Not until John Landis was acquitted did the sketch showing a helicopter hovering over the village shoreline finally turn up. All the while it had been deliberately withheld, along with the remaining visual materials and documents which never surfaced as a part of the on-going cover-up. Three years later, even when the DA's office issued its own subpoenas, Landis' phalanx again denied their existence and refused to produce them. Bundles of sketches that Tom Southwell had completed in Richard Sawyer's garage were dematerialized into the "Twilight Zone."

The tactics of the entertainment lawyers made investigator Frasco feel the effect of a murky and ambiguous reality. It was as if he had come among people who guarded a great secret. They were mysterious, unfathomable, close-mouthed, yet occasionally indiscreet. In this wavering moral twilight, he was asked to perform services that skirted the bounds of what was strictly legal and to countenance practices to which he was unaccustomed.

Typical of his experience with the phalanx was the occasion when Landis' attorneys first learned that during his interview with the NTSB, Elie Cohn had given damaging statements indicating that the director actually shouted "lower, lower" moments before the crash. Marty Rose asked Frasco that he talk to Cohn and "help him (Cohn) out a little bit" by conveying to the 1st AD that, according to those who had already heard it, Landis' voice was not on the film and that, moreover, other witnesses had reported that the "lower, lower" order had occurred in an earlier shot. But despite Cohn's eagerness to cooperate with Frasco, he reiterated during his conversation with the private investigator, to the utter dismay of the director's attorneys, that he had heard Landis "scream" that confounded "lower, lower" order to the helicopter.

Landis' attorneys, particularly Joel Behr, Frasco felt, were overwhelmed by the case and appeared to be suffering from a dangerous garrison mentality. Such an atmosphere was known to breed extreme attitudes, an example of which Frasco personally experienced following one of the series of secret meetings held between Elie Cohn and Landis' legal armada.

Behr and Frasco were chatting casually in the Paramount parking lot on Melrose Ave. when Frasco noted a sudden change in Behr's tone and heard the lawyer ask him if he could get hold of phone records showing a relationship between the NTSB's Don Llorente and Ned Good, one of the civil attorneys representing Myca's parents. It was Behr's belief that Llorente pursued the case so vigorously because he had once worked for Good as an investigator 10 years before he took his job with the NTSB. Frasco felt not only that the job Behr asked him to do was completely "stupid" but that it could easily backfire, not to mention that it might cause him to lose his license.

Frasco reminded Behr that it was illegal to secretly obtain telephone records from Good or a federal employee like Llorente. Frasco did agree, however, to investigate Llorente's background as a pilot and report whether the NTSB man had ever been blamed for any accidents in the air.

27

STUDIO SECRETS

P rivate detective Robert Frasco enjoyed the job of doing something other than routine insurance cases. Like everybody in the city, it seemed, he had been a child actor, a short career highlighted with an appearance next to Bing Crosby in the 1934 *Bells of St. Mary's*. His new role as a private detective for a famous director put him back in Hollywood. This time it was strictly behind the scenes to obtain taped interviews with witnesses in the hope that by securing their early statements they would make less effective prosecution witnesses in the event of a trial. His findings were to assist the phalanx, the lawyers of many stripes – insurance, civil, criminal and labor – engaged in Landis' defense.

But as Frasco began to dig away and his reports via Rose reached Behr and Diemer it became apparent that his results were very far from their liking. His findings reflected a consensus among the crew bitterly critical of the director's behavior on the set that night. In his first interview--which, paradoxically, he considered incredibly successful-the subject was cameraman Steve Lydecker.

In Lydecker's criticism of the director, Frasco believed he had presented Joel Behr with a model of how the prosecution would probably pursue the case in the event of a trial. The private detective noted that Lydecker's most damaging statements pertained to his claim that the helicopter was not even supposed to be in his wide-angle frame for the fatal scene. Lydecker told the investigator that before the last shot Landis had told him not to worry about the position of the aircraft in his Camera B because it was to be above the top of his frame.

In his report to the lawyers, Frasco underscored the significance of this finding as it related to the issue of poor planning: "WOULD NOT THE MASTER SHOT CAMERAMAN BE TOLD OF THIS CHANGE!" Behr, however, after reading the report filled with unrestrained anger and the most pointed criticism of his client, saw only an alarming indictment. Hastily summoned to a meeting in Behr's office attended by the complete phalanx – Behr, Diemer, Braun, Rose and Peterson – Frasco sensed they felt he was a traitor because he brought bad news.

As they went around the table discussing the various legal problems, Frasco could readily see the basic difference between the criminal lawyer, Harland Braun, who like himself wanted to dig up all the facts in order to defuse them, and the entertainment lawyer, Joel Behr, who, in wanting to protect the career of John Landis, judged every fact on how it would impact on his client's reputation. "I could understand their theory," Frasco commented, "but my job was to dig up information, whether prosecution information or defense information."

However, the entertainment lawyer was decisive and Frasco was told by Martin Rose that he should consult Behr before he talked to anybody else. Behr instructed Frasco to interview witnesses friendly to Landis, like Elie Cohn and Richard Sawyer. Behr's assistant Diemer advised the investigator to avoid the "unfriendlies," and instead, to "see a friend like McLarty who likes John."

Martin Rose, too, was frustrated, according to Frasco, by having to deal so closely with Joel Behr. But just when Frasco's role became more difficult because of the restraints put upon him by Behr, the NTSB files opened up and in their pages Frasco discovered a gold mine. He decided to get copies of the statements first and then to go out and see the witnesses. Since photo copies of the material were not allowed to be made, Frasco sat in the NTSB offices and read into his tape recorder from the fascinating documents, transcribing them afterwards in his office.

Frasco dictated verbatim for ten days. He simply couldn't stop. His voice went hoarse. The NTSB Investigation into the *Twilight Zone* Accident answered almost every question an investigator could possibly have. It was all in the annals collected by the amazing Don Llorente. In this-volume Frasco found an answer to the question as to why the chopper lined up over the shoreline when the director had claimed it was supposed to be over the middle of the river. But though voluminous and detailed, the annals of Llorente regrettably contained very little that was not disquieting from the director's point of view. On the whole, Frasco recalled, they gave the impression that the final scene "was a poorly planned and dangerous act."

Again Frasco suffered dismayed reactions in Behr's office over the information he brought back. Again he felt the sting of disapproval. The lawyers were holding him personally responsible for the damning report.

"I remember telling Diemer at lunch," Frasco recalled after one such uncomfortable meeting, "I'm concerned with Landis' defense and that I was going to help him. I felt I had to say this because they thought my earlier characterization of witnesses was my own view."

The most astonishing part of the TZ case was the fact that everything which the sheriff and DA investigators unsuccessfully sought to uncover in years of effort was already known within days of the crash to the top executives at Warner Bros. The top echelon witnessed the crash footage mere hours after it was shot and, shortly thereafter, Warner secretly launched an inquiry that was far more effective than that of either the NTSB or the labor commissioner – and on certain key issues more comprehensive and detailed than even the district attorney's investigation. Warner rapidly unearthed a story that would not emerge – and then only partially – for another five years at the time of the trial.

The inquiry conducted by the studio immediately after the accident revealed its own possible criminal liability on charges that it had condoned the illegal hiring. It learned everything to do with the children – how originally non-existent in Landis' first script they became a prominent part and how after their clandestine engagement they were concealed on the set. The inquiry revealed the size of the explosions and dwelt on the "near miss" during the 11:30 rage scene. The studio discovered Landis' failure to follow standard procedures and other instances of his negligence on the set. In its investigation, Warner had the advantage of ready access to those with direct knowledge of what had actually taken place that night. They included the people who worked regularly for Warner fulltime and were "loaned out" to the Landis segment, as well as the crew hired by the Landis group for the limited purpose of filming his segment. By talking to them, Warner was also able to keep tabs on the other investigations, such as those conducted by the labor commissioner or the DA. By comparison, the labor commissioner and the district attorney investigators, without compulsory process, had very little power to interview witnesses. Those who talked to the authorities did so on a strictly voluntary basis and most declined. Warner had no problem in gaining the cooperation of key people like Elie Cohn, Andy House and Richard Vane. Those on the Spielberg side assigned to the Landis segment, like Frank Marshall and Bonnie Radford, were housed on the Warner lot, and Warner's top executives who worked on the film like Fred Gallo and Lucy Fisher, or lower-level ones like Jim Henderling and Ed Morey, were only a few doors away.

Chiefly what the studio learned as the result of its efforts was the alarming extent of its own direct involvement. Within days of the crash it found out that certain of its personnel had knowledge of the "under the table" payments to the parents of the kids. Yet nothing of this privy information was reflected in Warner executive Ed Morey's August 6 declaration to labor investigator Charlie Hughes. In his declaration aimed at distancing the studio from any knowledge of the illegal hiring, Morey admitted having spoken to Allingham on July 21 about the problem of the kids not being mentioned in the shooting schedule – but said nothing about his dealings in the byzantine scheme the day before to get the check for the illegal cash payments from Warner to the Landis people.

Morey's omission was not surprising as it would have revealed the paper trail spawned by the check with the initials "S.L" of the director's own mother. The check was jointly signed by Jim Henderling and Frank Marshall and the Spielberg organization – through Marshall – should have known what John Landis was doing. Warner's position was further compromised by divisions within its own ranks as to the intended use of the petty cash; Marshall and his handpicked accountant Bonnie Radford had one version, Morey and Henderling had another.

A series of highly confidential internal memos showed how much the studio's top brass really knew about their potential liability. One memo pointedly mentioned that even though director Landis had a near disaster at the 11:30 shot, he did not take any steps to improve safety. To the contrary, the memo lamented, the evidence would show that he actually increased the danger:

> Testimony will indicate that Mr. Landis instructed the special effects people to put more charges in areas not known to the pilot which were in fact closer to the new position of the helicopter than previously indicated. Testimony will also show that this new position of explosives was not related to the pilot.

The memo demonstrated Warner's concern as to the extent of its exposure to liability claims. Clearly, the director's failure in various areas of his responsibility laid Warner open to charges of outright negligence, perhaps even criminal negligence. Some at the entertainment company feared that in Hollywood's pervasive cocaine culture Warner had reason to fear a drug fiasco. One highly confidential memo from Warner's New York office erroneously noted that "although Mr. Landis was not seen as taking drugs during that particular sequence, he had been previously witnessed to snort cocaine at other times." No such evidence of drug use was ever revealed in the TZ investigation.

But a more obvious concern over its exposure, as reflected in these coolly business-like internal documents, was the breakdown in normal production procedures. From its inquiry Warner learned of the often bitter infighting between the Landis group and the studio's veteran production chief Fred Gallo. The Landis people did as they pleased because, as one internal memorandum succinctly stated:

> The normal Warner Brothers Inc. production personnel who requested authority over the Landis sequence were told not to interfere and to give Landis a free hand.

The studio was also aware of the claim made by John Landis before the NTSB-certainly his most controversial – that he was not in charge of the movie set that night. Warner executives appeared skeptical that a disclaimer of this sort could hold up, considering the young director's reputation for behaving in a domineering and intimidating manner on a movie set. A high-level confidential memo showed that at least some people at Warner did not believe this position to be tenable:

> During his testimony, Mr. Landis testified that he did not know who had complete control of the activities during the filming. He stated that because of union problems and union regulations he can not specifically denote who was actually in charge. However, his testimony was refuted by himself or at least weakened by the fact that subsequent to his statement of having no control he turned to one of the people present and asked them to put out his cigarette since he did not allow smoking on his set.

Some at Warner felt that the appropriate government agencies might, according to another confidential memo, "try to use this incident as an example to the industry and may pursue a criminal prosecution Warner Brothers Inc. executive (sic)." It could reach as high as its president Terry Semel, or even the chairman John Daley. That fear was probably strengthened after Warner learned from one of its highest-ranking executives, Lucy Fisher, that Landis and Marshall and herself had jointly discussed the "problem" of using children in the Vietnam village scenes. At the same time, Warner's confidential internal investigation raised additional questions. Had Warner been told the whole truth by the managers of the set that night? For instance, had assistant director Elie Cohn, or the location manager Richard Vane – or even Hilary Leach, the DGA apprentice – told them everything they knew?

Warner's internal investigation was a matter of corporate self-protection. As the film's financier and distributor, the company stood to lose considerably. Besides the possible revocation of its California child labor license, it faced the likelihood – with three segments still remaining to be shot – that bad press might adversely affect the *Twilight Zone* release. The studio hardly wished to see its valuable Spielberg product sacrificed. Apart from the *Twilight Zone* venture, Warner's next deal with the Spielberg organization would soon be brewing with a script for *Gremlins* to be directed by Spielberg protege Joe Dante. The studio could not afford to lose its nascent relationship with Spielberg.

As the final party of responsibility, Warner Bros., knew that ultimately it would be the "deep pocket" in all the lawsuits. The studio was well aware that what it discovered of the conduct of employees on the TZ set was to broaden its exposure in the anticipated lawsuits and criminal investigations. Shuddering to think what effect this would have on the company image, the studio felt compelled to make every effort to keep the famed WB shield untarnished.

For all these reasons John Landis was placed for the time being under the same umbrella the studio held up protectively over Spielberg. There could be little doubt, however, that the studio would let the impetuous young director twist in the wind if it came to choosing between the two.

28

WALL OF FIRE

Nobody worked harder on the *Twilight Zone* case than the junior partner of Silverman, Rosen, Leon & Behr. Colleagues described him as a "typical entertainment lawyer." Joel Behr looked hawkish. He rarely smiled. From a long narrow head rose a wave of hair like a blue Pacific billow. Every item on his person was faultlessly in place except for the billow which seemed slightly askew. It was a wig which towered over his hooded eyes and olive complexion.

In public Behr kept aloof, watchful, silent, stalking. For five years he quietly mounted what appeared to an outsider an impossible defense. He labored indefatigably all these years with one goal in view: to see John Landis acquitted of the charges that were soon to be brought against him.

In every case where an insurance company can be expected to make huge payouts the lawyers swarm like bees. Landis' mounting troubles meant a windfall for any of the lawyers lucky enough to get to the pot. The legal bonanza would ultimately benefit some half-dozen lawyers and cost well over $5 million in fees. Much of this was overseen by Joel Behr who soon after entering the case applied himself full-time to the stupendous job of master-minding the director's defense.

The amount of work was staggering. In the first months following the accident he orchestrated the defense of Landis, Folsey and Allingham. He assembled the phalanx. He monitored the NTSB, appearing at its proceedings with all three of his clients. Behr's single-minded object of protecting his client stopped at nothing. When Llorente asked that Landis' lawyers turn over certain materials, especially visual materials like sketches and photographs used in the planning or depiction of the final scene, Behr's team denied that they even existed. It was the only time that the local federal attorney, Jim Sullivan, could remember a case in which a party did not comply with an NTSB request.

The chief question requiring all of Behr's attention was the business side of the law. It was the fundamental one in cases of the sort where "employer" and "employed" are ill-defined. Who was going to pick up the cost of the anticipated lawsuits? Warner or Landis? Who was going to pay, for instance, for the lawsuit against both already filed by the Chens? This quandary involved Behr at the start in making the pro forma demand for arrangements from Warner and its insurance company, Travelers; and as Behr's demand did not meet with immediate approval, it resulted in the first major conflict to arise between John Landis and the studio.

For, the *Twilight Zone* tragedy involved not only questions of moral responsibility but also of financial responsibility, the latter being preponderant and most pressing. Already as a result of the Chen lawsuit, three weeks after the crash, Landis was being subpoenaed on August 16. As any criminal action would not congeal for some time, the Chen lawsuit highlighted the importance of obtaining legal support to counter the expected civil actions. The Landis defense required two kinds of fees, criminal and civil, and according to the overall liability insurance policy Warner held, individuals would not ordinarily be covered by Travelers in the commission of an unlawful act. This locked both Warner and Travelers as well in an internal dispute, unlike a typical accident case where there would be no question of criminal negligence.

The terms of the Travelers policy clearly guaranteed legal fees for ordinary negligence claims, the so-called civil side. But the issue between the studio and the insurer was over who should pay for the criminal side, Warner, Travelers, or both. This schism reoccurred in various forms throughout the case. The question was hardly academic, for the legal fees were huge. Warner and Travelers together, in the first year alone, poured massive amounts of money into lawyers' accounts. They paid out hundreds of thousands of dollars to Joel Behr, representing Landis, Folsey and Allingham; to Kern & Wooley's Martin Rose; to O'Melveny & Myers' Dunham and Vaughn, representing Warner; to Frank Marshall's firm, Pollock, Bloom and Dekom; and to Howard Swainston of Breidenbach, Swainston, Yokaitis & Crispo, representing the special effects crew.

The clearing house for every facet of Landis' legal effort was the Century City office of Joel Behr. Behr dealt not only with the citations issued by the labor commissioner and Cal/OSHA, or the reports, albeit sketchy, he received concerning the affairs before the NTSB, but he also took control of much of Landis' personal defense by protecting him on other fronts. Immediately after the crash, John Landis had his secretary Alpha Campbell collect for Behr all the *Twilight Zone* scripts and files, including production schedules and other documents, which were picked up and, according to Landis' secretary, taken to Behr's office.

Behr's vital activity was in mounting a criminal defense strategy with his specialist who monitored the DA's office and sheriff's department, Harland Braun. To both lawyers, the NTSB hearings made unambiguously clear the central issue in the case, and after casting for a definition of the movie director's responsibility on the set the phalanx decided on one that limited the director's role, holding that he could not be held responsible for safety matters on the set and had to rely on professionals to ensure that safety was maintained. Nevertheless, John Landis' aggressive and impetuous response to the NTSB questioning alerted Braun to the danger if ever Landis was put on a witness stand.

Behr and Braun were both aware that much work would have to be done with the cocky director. Braun remembers that what struck him was that whenever Landis spoke of his crew, he disparaged them. Braun was also dismayed to hear Landis minimize the expertise involved in many of the *Twilight Zone* stunts which he himself felt to be dangerous. To Braun, precisely this type of shoot-from-the-hip approach proved disquieting from a defense point of view; just as disturbing, he found, was a kind of blind spot in his client; "an obliviousness to certain facts" in that John Landis as director refused to admit *any* responsibility.

Landis, boasting that he could line up "fifty directors" in his defense, told Behr and Braun that he was sure the Director's Guild would support his position. Behr eagerly fell in with this suggestion. As Braun recalled, Behr wanted to talk to Francis Ford Coppola. The idea, Behr enthused to Braun, was to have a parade of directors and film cognoscenti defend Landis' actions. They would explain how movies were really made, Behr strategized, so the defense would not have it appear that Landis was purely trying to justify his own conduct on the set.

Actually, without Behr's prompting, the question was already being hotly argued internally among members of the normally staid and aloof Directors Guild of America. Hollywood's prestigious and most influential "union" found itself stirred by the deaths of children on a Hollywood movie set. With little external fanfare, struggling for the first time with the question of defining the director's responsibility for safety on the set, the DGA soon discovered that it had few guidelines on the subject and no more than a vague sort of safety committee. And so, with the safety issue long overdue, a very private meeting was convened within weeks of the crash. Limited to members of the DGA's governing council, the secret meeting had about a dozen members in attendance, among them noted directors active in DGA politics like Arthur Hiller, Howard Koch,

Norman Jewison, Judd Taylor, William Crane, Jackie Cooper, Jack Shea, and soon-to-be president Gil Cates.

Among the issues aired in connection with the *Twilight Zone* disaster, the discussion inevitably turned to the possibility of drugs on the set. In response to one director who mentioned having heard rumors to the effect that drugs had been in evidence during the filming at Indian Dunes, Robert Aldridge, director of *The Dirty Dozen*, pointed out the virtual impossibility of controlling people on that score without some rather harsh methods.

"When you're talking about sticking stuff up their nose," Aldridge commented, referring to the use of cocaine on the set, "until we get a rule where people are pissing in a jar, we won't be able to say who is and who isn't."

After the meeting broke up there were a number of unexpected repercussions. Their echoes would still be heard two months later when, as a result of the TZ crash, a state legislative committee hearing was held on movie safety. However, according to one member at the DGA meeting, an unusually swift response came the very next morning in a telephone call from Joel Behr to director William Crane, the guild member who had voiced the rumor that Landis was "loaded" on the set the night of the accident. The caller, identifying himself as the lawyer for John Landis, asked Crane if he had accused John Landis at the DGA board meeting. He heard Behr warn him that his statements were "inflammatory" and "unfounded."

Crane was upset; obviously someone had reported to Behr, probably immediately after midnight when the meeting broke.

Against this background, while the studio faced mounting problems from the state legislature, Vic Morrow's heirs, Carrie Morrow and Jennifer Jason Leigh, filed their own wrongful death lawsuits, citing among the defendants Warner Bros., Frank Marshall, and all of the four film directors; Landis, Spielberg, Dante and Miller. Morrow's daughters alleged that some of those named were involved with drugs and alcohol at the time of the crash. The pressure on the studio seemed to be building, for shortly after the Morrow girls filed their lawsuits Don Llorente revealed that he had found three empty beer cans in the helicopter. *Variety*, in a headline story, called it an "ugly new wrinkle."

The drug and alcohol issue wouldn't go away.

29

THE SWITCH THEORY

Meanwhile, deputy sheriff Tom Budds made a solitary inroad into Twilight territory. A conspiracy of silence governed this terrain. With the doors to the fortress-like Hollywood establishment made impassible by lawyers, Budds sought out the three men who worked with the fatal explosives that night. Ironically, because of their marginal status, they were initially ignored by the phalanx; temporarily left without the protection of legal counsel, these three powdermen were the only important participants from the set accessible to Budds.

The NTSB record concerning this trio, Paul Stewart, Jerry Williams and Jimmy Camomile, was filled with inconsistencies. However, tracking down the powdermen whom investigators believed to be evasive, untruthful, "hiding" and coordinating among themselves, was not easy. Of the five SFX men on the set that night the SFX supervisor Paul Stewart remained a somewhat separate case. Budds narrowed the focus down to Jerry Williams and Jimmy Camomile because these two men alone had physically controlled the fatal fireball explosions in the village and river, 14 in all. One of them triggered the explosion responsible for the crash.

In contrast to the shadowy figure of Jerry Williams (Budds first met him skulking on the set the morning of the crash) Jimmy Camomile made a favorable impression on the sheriff's deputy, who was disposed to accept his account that after the crash Paul Stewart and Jerry Williams had cleaned certain mortars and moved them. This was not the sort of diligence Budds would normally expect from people on a death scene, unless they had something to hide. Budds thought he smelled a rat.

Other elements added to his suspicion. There were the SFX vehicles, the ten-ton truck and the pickup which had instantly fled the crash scene, checking in at The Burbank Studios at 4:15 A.M., less than two hours after the crash; and there was the discovery by Cal/OSHA investigators after they located the SFX truck a little later that morning that it had been swept clean of any evidence of alcohol or special effects explosives. And in trying to come up with an explanation of what it was the SFX crew was so anxious to conceal, Budds put everything together. He combined the suspicious behavior and personal friendships of the powdermen with Camomile's candid statements of irregularities on the crash scene and from the sum of these parts developed what became known as the "switched mortar" theory.

With this conclusion, Budds was able to provide an explanation for the suspect diligence shown by Stewart and Williams in fetching and carrying their powder pots and wires under the cover of darkness on the blasted and deserted set. But the theory, while it might have made a dramatic script, was fundamentally flawed and its ready acceptance by higher-ups was unfortunate because, after sending Budds on a wild goose chase and confusing the DA, it was ultimately proven wrong. The "switched mortar" scenario prevented investigators from ever determining the secret of the special-effects men, the only group of people with knowledge of who actually fired the fatal blasts on the set that night.

What led Budds to his unfortunate conclusion stemmed from his appraisal of the film which showed that two particular shoreline huts sitting close together seemed to have been involved in downing the aircraft. In the center stage of the action, was the No. 4 drying hut (No. 4, because sound tests showed that the SFX mortar inside it was the *fourth* to be detonated in the sequence). Screen right of No. 4 showed the hut by the pier with the Vietnamese sampan tied to it, the so-called No. 5 sampan hut (involving the *fifth* mortar, according to the sound tests, to be fired in the same sequence).

Slowed down to a frame-by-frame analysis, the crash film showed that the fireballs from both huts, No. 4 and 5, fully enveloped the chopper's tail section in a thick cloud of smoke and debris. From the early NTSB conclusions, it was already known that the onus for creating the key powerful explosion that ripped through a bamboo floor, hurling spears of rock-hard bamboo into the Huey's highly vulnerable tail rotor, cracking it and thereby causing the helicopter to spin out of control, fell on the mortar under the No. 4 "drying hut."

With this in mind Budds concentrated all of his efforts on that particular hut. Accordingly, during the trial, the No. 4 came in for extraordinary attention as the structure whose debris caused the helicopter to come down. But by focusing on the "square" mortar under the drying hut Budds was misled to ignore the significance of the "round" mortar under No. 5, the sampan hut.

Upon his arrival on the empty set at Indian Dunes, Budds had discovered a square mortar under the No. 4 drying hut along with one other mortar, a round one, standing free on the same muddy shoreline. At the time, Budds happened to know nothing about the role of these odd-looking contraptions and the strange location of the round mortar, set on the ground as if in readiness for a cook-out, had no particular significance for him. Unlike the square-shaped mortar underneath the No. 4 drying hut, the round-shaped pot, unanchored, "free-standing," looked as if it had been moved. To all appearances it seemed to have been taken out from under or near the No. 5 sampan hut; Budds, however, mistakenly determined that it had been dragged from the No. 4 hut. That a switch had occurred.

The assumption seemed plausible to him in the light of powderman Jimmy Camomile's recollection expressed in his first statement that he had fired off the first four devices in the fatal scene; three in the back row and another, his fourth, a round mortar, under one of the shoreline huts in the front row. The "switch" explained to Budds why, when he arrived on the set, the only mortar he found under a hut in the front row was a square mortar. A complete novice in the field of explosives, the lone deputy on the case readily surmised that someone had dragged Camomile's round mortar from the drying hut and, to the end of obscuring the evidence, switched it with the square mortar which he had discovered in that same structure.

Budds never considered, not even much later when sound tests refuted the "switch theory," that anyone else but Camomile controlled the firing of the fourth explosive in the series that night. Budds remained fixated on the "switch" because it alone could explain to him the inconsistencies between what he had first found on his arrival on the set and what he had gleaned from his interviews with the consistently evasive powdermen.

Indeed, Camomile's account of the fourth device he fired on his board matched perfectly the mysterious round mortar fixed on by Budds and snapped by the sheriff's photographer on the morning after the crash. Camomile told Budds that from the photo it appeared that this very SFX device, which he was certain he had placed *inside* one of the shoreline huts, had been moved from its original location by one of the powdermen sometime after the fatal event. Camomile explained to the police that what made the position of the free-standing mortar in the sheriff's photo a mystery was that customarily a mortar is anchored by digging it into the earth so as to point it in the direction required by the shot, as well as for safety reasons. And in fact, when shown the sheriffs photo of the mysterious round mortar, he remarked to Budds, "that looks like the mortar in question," referring to the explosive he said was his fourth, the one he had put inside one of the front row huts.

Budds' original transcript of his taped interview with Camomile shows that the sheriff became confused when Camomile spoke of the location of the fourth round mortar he set off in his series. The transcript shows that the homicide man erroneously concluded that Camomile was referring to the so-called No. 4 hut beneath which Budds had found the square mortar when in actuality Camomile was talking about a different hut altogether – the No. 5 sampan hut!

For Budds to advance the plausibility of his switch theory to his boss, deputy DA Gary Kesselman, was only a matter of pointing out the flagrant suspicions attaching to the special effects people. Furthermore, by discovering what he thought was a "motive" for the switch he completed the symmetry of the theory so as to make of it something weighty and whole in support of his findings: he found that round as opposed to square mortars tend to fire straight up, thereby producing a greater impact on a helicopter's tail rotor. Budds was less successful in cracking other mysteries. He grappled in vain with questions such as how far he should believe Carl Pitman's story, according to which booze had flowed on the set; or the size of explosives used in the final scene and why the special effects people continued to play down the strength of the explosives. However, by mistaking Camomile's initial insistence in describing the so-called No. 4 as round, when Budds with his own eyes had seen it was square, the young detective felt satisfied that he had penetrated to the heart of the powdermen's secrets.

Though Budds' "switch theory" was adopted by the DA's office and later pursued by the grand jury to secure the indictment of Paul Stewart, it was soon invalidated by highly technical sound tests made on the film by the sheriff's department working closely with the FBI. The tests showed the order in which each of the mortars was fired and the approximate location of each at the time of the firing, enabling investigators to number each mortar in the sequence detonated during the final scene. Moreover, these highly sensitive tests were even able to determine the shape of the mortars, round or square.

The result of the tests indicated that no switch was ever made and that when analyzed along with other related evidence they showed two things: 1) the square mortar was under the No. 4 drying hut and had been there all along, demolishing the idea that there had ever been a switch; but it also showed, 2) the square mortar under the drying hut was the fourth one to be fired in the series. Considering Camomile's original statement, that the first three mortars he fired off from his board were in the back row and his fourth on the shoreline was a round mortar, the tests meant that Camomile's fourth round mortar was actually the fifth mortar to be fired in the fatal series – the round one in the sampan hut.

Thus, when six months after Budds had formed his distracting hypothesis the sound studies were finally released and compared against Camomile's original statements they should have cleared up much of the confusion. They showed that in actuality a total of five mortars had been detonated during the fatal scene at the time Camomile had accounted for only four on his board; his fourth being the free-standing round mortar as he had originally described it to Budds. Thus, according to the sound tests, and by the process of elimination, the conclusion became inescapable that somebody else on the set had fired one of the first five mortars in the fatal scene. The only other SFX man with a firing board to control explosions in the village was Jerry Williams. The next question, never answered by the police, was which one of the first five mortars had been fired by Williams?

Although DA investigators never understood their significance, the sheriff's sound tests were invaluable tools that should have helped clear up this mystery. The tests confirmed that in their early interviews with Budds, both Williams and Camomile had been talking about two different mortars at two different locations while the deputy mistakenly thought they were talking about the same location. The results of the sound tests underscored Camomile's original account that the first three mortars he had set off were those in the back row. Camomile's next mortar, according to his original account, was a round one inside a hut on the shoreline. But, according to the tests, the subsequent fireball, the fourth in the fatal series, came from a square mortar located inside the so-called No. 4 drying hut. The mortar that followed – the fifth – was round and perfectly matched Camomile's original account of the firing of his fourth mortar.

Thus, of the first five mortars fired in the fatal sequence, when compared to Camomile's original account, the sound tests showed that Nos. 1, 2, 3 and 5 corresponded to the mortars controlled by his board. Therefore, in-between Camomile's third and fourth shot in his series, the controversial square mortar erupted in the No. 4 drying hut. By the process of elimination investigators could have discovered that this fourth detonation in the series, a square mortar, must have been fired from Williams' board, just as John Landis and set designer Richard Sawyer both had privately concluded in the immediate aftermath of the crash. Robert Frasco, Landis' private investigator, after having read transcripts of confidential interviews with John Landis and consultations with the director's legal phalanx, also identified Williams as "the man who pushed the button."

In the end Jerry Williams always denied that he fired the No. 4 mortar. In other areas Williams' version of events directly countered the physical evidence, notably in his insistence to Budds that the floor in hut No. 4, which he said was the first thing he ran to after the crash, was still intact at that time. Budds, of course, had seen the sheriff's photos, as well as the footage from the cliffside Camera D, both showing that well before Williams had arrived at the No. 4 hut, literally within seconds of the detonation, its floor was utterly gone. However, the investigators never discovered the truth about who fired the key explosives in the scene. Accordingly, the "switched mortar" theory would eventually rank as one of the bigger blunders committed by the sheriff's department and the DA's office in their *Twilight Zone* investigation.

The investigation's early obsession with the "switch theory" had another unfortunate result besides distracting Budds from ever being able to reconstruct what happened at Indian Dunes. It took the heat off other areas where the special effects crew might have been scheming and malfeasant. For example, Budds failed to discover by checking sales receipts and fire department records that the 6-oz. size explosive charges, constantly referred to by the special effects men during questioning in order to minimize the size of the blasts, were non-existent!

The actual sales records, overlooked for over five years by the police and DA's investigators, showed that the smallest-sized explosive charges purchased for the fatal scene were 8-oz. charges. Also overlooked was special permit No. 55926 issued by the fire department to Paul Stewart ten days before the crash. It gave him permission to purchase 200 feet of 100 grain prima cord. This amount of "high" explosive was capable of knocking down as many as 70 telephone poles, "like matchsticks," according to special effects experts. Both of these pieces of evidence ran contrary to all SFX accounts that the highest-powered explosives on the set of the TZ crash were 6-oz. "low" explosives. A "high" explosive far more lethal than the black powder bombs admittedly on the set that night, the prima cord was never mentioned by SFX crew members.

30

NITE-SUN

Paul Stewart's men, resisting every investigative onslaught, hung together. Members of an esoteric trade, the lowest caste on the set, the powdermen formed a tight-knit crew, almost like blood brothers. Even though the sound tests appeared to disprove it, they stuck to Jerry Williams' original story. For to admit that the No. 4 was fired by Williams not only would mean admitting to negligent planning, it would open up the question of how that explosive was cued.

Williams had already told the NTSB that his cue to set off his first fireball explosion in the village was when Vic and the kids reached the "stick," the nearly six-foot-long "eukie pole" planted just minutes before the crash by Paul Stewart himself in a carefully pre-arranged spot in the middle of the river. Stewart had used the stick to coordinate several camera angles for the special effects explosions and the actors. However, at the very same time that Williams was cueing off the stick for his first detonation, according to the director's shot plan, the helicopter with its powerful Nite-Sun spotlight was to pursue Vic as he crossed the river out of the exploding village toward the stick. That meant that Williams' cue to detonate the No. 4, based on Vic's reaching the stick, was timed to go off at precisely the moment the chopper hovered over the village shoreline in the only position that would allow the aircraft to keep the spotlight fixed on the actor. This cueing positioned the chopper's tail rotor directly above the No. 4 drying hut.

It was the failure of the investigators to understand the relationship between the timing of the helicopter's spotlight role and the cueing of the fatal explosives that prevented them from uncovering the risky plan that caused the deadly crash. It proved to be their biggest blunder. Had it been established that Williams had set off the No. 4 fireball at the time Vic was approaching the "stick," as the special effects technician had presumably been instructed, investigators could have pinpointed precisely where the movie director had all along planned the chopper to be at the moment the special effects explosives were cued to go off, especially the fatal fireball from inside the No. 4 hut.

Furthermore, while Budds never understood what occurred in the final seconds, the angle required of the powerful beam from the chopper's spotlight, so as to keep its focus on the actors, explained why it was necessary for Landis to order the helicopter to move closer to the deadly shoreline explosion during the last seconds of the flight. To keep the spotlight on Vic and the kids as they made their way across the river, the director's final order, "lower, lower, closer, closer," as heard by Randy Robinson aboard the helicopter, was given to the pilot. This scenario, in which the cue for the No. 4 explosion was the "stick," thoroughly demolished any claim that the aircraft was ever planned to be out of there before the SFX men set off the village. It also reaffirmed the pilot's private confession to the cub reporter from the *Herald*, "They wanted the blades... the whole bit in there."

Williams' claim that he didn't fire the square No. 4 "drying hut" mortar had the direct consequence of focusing the inquiry on Camomile as the powderman responsible for the fatal explosion. And it turned out surprisingly easy to deflect the issue of responsibility from Williams and ultimately from Paul Stewart, by getting Camomile to profess that he had simply made a mistake. The former Navy man, emotionally affected by the event and unable to remember many details, readily accepted the versions Stewart and Jerry Williams held out to him; by his own admission, he discussed these matters with his two friends and co-workers on several occasions. In fact, confidential interviews between Camomile and some of his own attorneys clearly showed that the most controversial and critical recollections, those in which he took responsibility for loading and firing the No. 4 mortar, came to him strictly as the result of conferences between himself, Paul Stewart, Paul Stewart's lawyer, Arnold Klein, and Jerry Williams. The substance of Camomile's private declarations never surfaced in the investigation; but contrary to what he told investigators, Camomile himself privately admitted to Paul Stewart's attorneys he "had no real recollection" of controlling the No. 4 mortar, and that "one of the other gentlemen could've also loaded it..."

By the time of the grand jury hearings, it appeared that Camomile had been persuaded by Paul Stewart and Jerry Williams to change his story in several key areas. For the first time, for example, contrary to his original statements to the NTSB a year earlier, and this time accompanied by an insurance company lawyer, he told investigators that the "stick" in the middle of the river was designed to help insure safety in the fatal scene. Earlier he had professed to have no idea of the purpose of the stick. Jerry

Williams, in fact, had been the only one among the SFX crew to tell investigators that he was to cue the firing of his SFX explosives in the village once Vic and the kids had reached the stick planted in the stream.

Camomile's newly changed story was accompanied with the SFX crew's apocryphal recollection that only 6-oz. charges were used in or near the shoreline huts. By not checking the receipts and permits, the investigators failed to learn that no 6-oz. charges were ever purchased for the set that night. It was another small oversight but there were many and they added up. And joined to major blunders like the "switched mortar" theory, they went a long way in explaining the investigation's confusion and singular lack of success in accurately reconstructing the events that transpired that night.

Less than a year after the crash, James Camomile privately told Paul Stewart's lawyer that the disaster at Indian Dunes had left him "numb." Whether stricken by grief or leaned upon by desperate friends, by the time the grand jury convened in the summer of 1983 he appeared convinced – even though the physical evidence tended to invalidate his story – that the No. 4 explosion had been on his board. Camomile's acknowledgement that he fired the fatal shot as a result of having made a mistake had the effect of closing down the investigation of Jerry Williams and the other powdermen. This result removed the focus from Williams, the only technician in the immediate proximity to the director, at his side, in the best position to receive a cue to detonate his deadly explosion. Another significant result was that it closed the door on the question of the poor planning and the drinking by the powdermen that night. The consumption of beer and vodka by some of them had been observed by a number of witnesses, including the helicopter pilot's recollection of smelling "beer breath" near the powder wagon. At the exact moment of the fatal No. 4 hut explosion, the director was observed motioning the helicopter over the square mortar that the NTSB identified as the deadly culprit.

The powdermen had good reason to seek the elimination of the issue of Williams' connection with blowing the No. 4 mortar. But perhaps the most compelling motive came from Landis' own private investigation. The propman, Landis' longtime associate Mike Milgrom, gave the director's own investigators a shocking tale of a non-stop drinking party around the SFX truck where Stewart, in Milgrom's words, appeared too intoxicated to handle the firing board in the final scene, therefore assigning Williams to the job.

Milgrom's account presented Landis with a strong card to hold out against the powder chief in any legal proceedings. But in terms of what it might do to implicate himself the card's value was hardly assured, for his own investigation had discovered the disconcerting view held by some crew members that Landis had to have known about the alcohol consumption on the set that night. One particular crew member who knew that Paul Stewart had a history of drinking actually believed that the director had willingly closed his eyes to the drinking by the powder chief in order to make him more compliant. Furthermore, playing this card against Stewart opened the possibility of rousing certain other crew members who had noted among those employed in the TZ filming a number of coke-sniffers from the *Blues Brothers* set. Judiciously, Landis kept his hand. He did not put the card in circulation and Paul Stewart, in turn, did what he could to protect the director. He kept the deputy sheriff in the dark about Landis' drive to create a "wall of fire" in the big scene.

Budds' task in extracting the truth from the pariahs of the set was complicated by the fact that the powdermen contradicted not only each other but also John Landis. Paul Stewart, in a glaring discrepancy with a statement which Landis had made to the NTSB the day before, told Budds that he was never consulted about the location of the helicopter relative to the special-effects charges. In contrast to Landis, who said he had no knowledge that a mortar had been placed inside any hut, Stewart told Budds how he had pointed out to the director where all the explosives were as they walked the set just before the final scene.

Throughout this interrogation by Budds, Stewart insisted on having told the director that he did not want to place bombs under the back row of huts. "He wanted to put mortars inside the huts," Stewart mentioned, referring to the back row, "I said if I put them inside the huts then you might blow something away." In the same police interview, Stewart eventually admitted that he did order his men to place a mortar inside the No. 4 hut, casting his original denial in terms of misunderstanding the sheriff's question about the controversial shoreline structure. He stated that he'd become confused by the questioning because he always had personally referred to this structure as a "lean-to," not a hut!

* * *

It was not until December 1, 1982, some four months after the crash, that a story appearing in LA's *Herald-Examiner* for the first time made public some of the same discrepancies found by the sheriff's homicide man. It was written by Andy Furillo and behind his astonishing report appeared to be the hand of Don Llorente. It could not have been coincidence that Furillo's article appeared at the same time that Llorente's superiors in Washington cut short his NTSB investigation by refusing him permission to reactivate certain suspect witnesses.

The "carrot-top cub" had read all of the 677 sensational pages of the NTSB Investigation into the "*Twilight Zone* Accident," and the immediate result of Furillo's article was to set the stalled investigation back in motion. His article contained the kind of damaging information which Landis' phalanx had sought to keep out of the press by making the initial deal with the NTSB, trading Landis' "testimony" for official silence. Furillo's article noted among the NTSB findings reports that Spielberg had been on the set, that debris from the No. 4 hut brought the helicopter down, and that while Landis denied it, witnesses said that they had watched him order the helicopter directly into the explosions.

For the first time people learned that the TZ filming had been replete with dangerous activities in the days leading up to the fatal crash, including live ammo in a scene involving Vic Morrow, that alcohol and marijuana were used on the set hours before the tragedy, and that some people were "flying high" on cocaine, according to quoted sources. The story revealed that investigators still grappled with uncertainties concerning the deadly mortars. They didn't know how the mortars were placed in the huts or whether a smaller mortar was replaced by a larger one. They even questioned whether someone surreptitiously placed an added charge in the fireball-belching pots.

From Furillo the public first learned of the absolute chaos on the set both before and after the crash. He mentioned Landis' controversial NTSB interview which had never before appeared in the press. "His answers," the cub wrote in a scoop, "were hesitant and stuttering." Furillo pointed out how Landis in the interview had claimed the explosions were different from the ones earlier that evening, and the cub brought up the bullhorn, mentioning that at least six witnesses on the ground at the time of the crash had either heard Landis shouting over the bullhorn to the helicopter or saw him motioning the chopper downward with his bullhorn in hand.

On a related but different front John Landis was experiencing a worsening relationship with Dorcey Wingo. In the very beginning the pilot had tried to contact Dan Allingham in the spirit of cooperation. But incredibly, Wingo never heard from any of the Landis group until almost a year after their indictments when they were being arraigned together. Dorcey felt snubbed; by failing in civility, Landis hurt Dorcey's feelings. Wingo now joined in the finger-pointing fray. Within a week following the accident he appeared for his second lengthy interview with the NTSB, this time with his own insurance lawyer to present a slightly new version of the facts as he saw them that night. In succeeding months, it became very clear to Wingo that he was being singled out as Landis' prime finger pointing target. His attorneys, joining the heirs of the Chens, Les and Morrows, promptly filed suit. Wingo's lawsuit alleged that Landis and Warner had knowingly run a reckless set and exposed the pilot to excess hazard. It further alleged that as a result of the crash, he had personally suffered from the nightmarish scene and was permanently scarred by it.

The differences between Wingo and Landis would not be resolved until the very end of the *Twilight Zone* trial. Their combative relationship of finger-pointing, secret moves and outright threats would continue right up until the moment Wingo took the stand – and, in a dramatic reversal, absolved John Landis, giving the director a favorable account!!

31

Dr. Fantasy

The showdown that forced Warner to reluctantly cast its lot with John Landis took place during the first week of September less than two months after the crash. Its setting was again the Century City office of the entertainment law firm of which Joel Behr was the junior partner. It was a confrontation of high-priced lawyers over a high-stakes game.

The lawyers for each side had gotten to know each other during innumerable powwows by telephone and face-to-face meetings over the preceding month. The polite exchanges between the two groups failed to mask differences which continually flared into acrimony. At the showdown in Behr's office the phalanx: Behr, Diemer, Braun, Peterson, and Behr's law partner, Ronald Rosen, faced the Warner wall of Stan Belkin, Bill Vaughn and Scott Dunham, in addition to the formidable legal gun hired by O'Melveny & Myers, Doug Dalton, one of LA's top criminal lawyers who had represented expatriate director Roman Polanski on rape charges; in another well-known case, that of Norvelle Young, the president of LA's prestigious Pepperdine College who killed two people in a drunk driving accident, Dalton gained great local publicity for managing to get probation for the college president.

A situation existed, according to Harland Braun, where Behr grew to distrust Warner's motives. And it was in a tense atmosphere that Behr laid his strongest cards on the table. During this highly-charged meeting between allies he turned to the formidable Doug Dalton. Landis' lawyer explained that he had called the meeting to relay information gained from his clients, Landis, Folsey and Allingham, that would implicate Warner. Behr specifically mentioned "Spielberg and Warner Bros. people."

With his low-lidded poker gaze and the amazing crest of glossy hair, Behr electrified those present by plunking down trump after trump. They heard again how it came about that the character Bill was "softened." Behr mentioned the script changes Landis made at the direction of Warner higher-ups, adding the exploding village scene with Morrow and the two kids, and receiving an extra $200,000 from the studio to cover the cost of building the village and filming the new scene. Behr mentioned the kids and how they were paid and the role of Frank Marshall. The point he tried to make was that Warner must have known about these matters. It was convincingly done by bringing up Spielberg's man, Frank Marshall, and demonstrating how deeply enmeshed he was in the illegal child-hiring plan.

The studio lawyers heard Behr claim that Marshall actually had a "blind" telephone call made to the labor commissioner, reporting afterwards to the Landis group to forget about getting waivers from that office to film the children in the night scene. Behr informed Belkin and the O'Melveny lawyers that Marshall together with Warner watchdog Henderling signed the check and that Marshall knew that the purpose of this check was to pay the children "under the table." Underscoring Marshall's involvement in the hiring scheme, Behr revealed that Marshall had even been irritated that Bonnie Radford, who drafted the check, was made privy to the secret of the kids. And slamming down his ace in the hole he implicated Warner's top-ranking executive in the film. Exposure of Lucy Fisher's role in writing the children into the Landis segment meant that knowledge of the plan may have reached the studio's highest echelons, perhaps even the pinnacle of the Spielberg organization. It was the last thing the movie company would have wanted.

Lucy Fisher had developed a special "chemistry" with Steven Spielberg, one of the most precious assets to grow out of the TZ movie. The studio hoped that the two elements combined would result in a profitable formula (a few years later, in fact, Lucy Fisher was credited with turning Steven Spielberg on to filming *The Color Purple* which won 11 Academy Award nominations in 1986 and was Warner's most successful film that year, generating over $150 million). The studio lawyers facing the phalanx in Century City heard Behr describe how, upon being told by Landis that the children would be used at night and paid in cash, Fisher had merely responded by saying that she didn't want to know about it and if confronted would say that she had never heard of the matter.

Countering, the studio lawyers zeroed in on matters concerning Behr's own client. Not knowing how much the Warner lawyers already knew, Behr minimized Landis' personal role in the illegal hiring. He admitted that his clients did refer to the children on the set as the "Vietnamese," explaining that the director did not want to alert anyone to their presence. Behr didn't know whether Warner had already learned of the cover-up plot on the set aimed at concealing the kids from the studio welfare teacher Jack Tice. He did not volunteer the information. Myca and Renee were kept out of sight, Behr claimed with a straight face, because they were sleeping in the trailer.

While this high-stakes poker game took place, the studio's own internal investigation had already demonstrated that at least in some areas Landis' attorney was not bluffing. Ordinarily, the fact that a key executive like Lucy Fisher knew about the illegally hired children was disturbing enough. But it was knottier than that. To the studio executives one name was synonymous with Spielberg and implications far more disturbing existed in the person of Frank Marshall, the highest-ranking production official on the set that night. Marshall alone could determine whether knowledge of the illegal hiring had spread to Steven Spielberg. As the meeting ended a tacit understanding of the need for a united front became apparent to all those present.

As it did over Folsey's, the *Twilight Zone* tragedy cast a shadow over the life of Frank Marshall. Young, handsome, tall and lithe, with varsity good looks, boyishly self-absorbed and amiable, Frank Marshall reflected the laid-back style of affluent Newport Beach where he grew up. Marshall had Hollywood connections through his father, Jack Marshall, a civil engineer-turned-musician and composer who provided musical scores for television movies and at one time arranged record albums for vocalists like Judy Garland, Peggy Lee and Vic Damone. At the Marshall home showbiz was always in the air and it entered into the blood of the son who built up a repertoire of magic tricks. At a later stage this repertoire would unfold and transform into "Dr. Fantasy," the magician, showing a Frank Marshall who loved to entertain an audience; Dr. Fantasy became a Spielberg movie wrap-party tradition.

Marshall's career at UCLA reflected an ambivalence. It began with courses in engineering, then a sudden switch to music and drama arts, and finally a lame political science degree and a vague desire to enter law. Like his father, Marshall wanted to have something "to fall back on," and when he fell into film making it was on the business end.

Frank Marshall's formal introduction to the film business came about as a result of meeting Peter Bogdanovich in 1967 at a party, and while still a senior in college he accepted Bogdanovich's invitation to work on his first film, *Targets*. He stayed on as a member of the Bogdanovich production crew that did *The Last Picture Show* and *What's Up, Doc?*, and became associate producer on *Paper Moon*, *Daisy Miller*, *At Long Last Love* and *Nickelodeon*. He had other production credits on Orson Welles' *The Other*

Side of the Wind, and on Martin Scorsese's rock documentary about The Band, *The Last Waltz.* Marshall also served as an associate producer on Walter Hill's *The Driver,* and as executive producer on Hill's *The Warriors.* It was a casually, steadily upward-moving career.

As a trademark, Marshall began making brief cameo appearances in the films he worked on for director Peter Bogdanovich. His best-known spots, however, were in Spielberg productions: he was the flying wing pilot in *Raiders* and the neighbor watering the lawn in *Poltergeist.* Marshall even became a kind of "cameo director," developing a passion for the "Making of..." series, the behind-the-scenes shooting of films like *Raiders of the Lost Ark* or, *Twilight Zone: The Movie.*

Steven Spielberg and Marshall first met in Rome when Marshall was still associated with Bogdanovich. According to Marshall's studio bio, Spielberg was "impressed with Marshall's energy." But it may be supposed that, seeing in the easy self-assurance of Marshall, the perennial preppy, something of the Big-Man-On-Campus, Spielberg was won over by the personality. When the time came to assemble the team for *Raiders of the Lost Ark,* Spielberg and George Lucas chose Marshall to produce the massive project.

Raiders placed first in worldwide box office in 1981, won five Oscars, and catapulted Marshall's career. The following year Marshall produced *Poltergeist,* he was production supervisor on *E.T.,* and at 35 shared a Hollywood phenomenon that comes around infrequently like a comet with a blazing tail of money. With three movies, *Raiders, E.T.* and *Poltergeist* eclipsing all box-office records in motion picture history, Spielberg was the top director of all time and Frank Marshall the top producer.

Marshall's success was in great part the success of the team approach that typified management on the highest-grossing films in history. Like Landis and Folsey, Spielberg and Marshall shared a partnership combining the creative and business side. From a managerial point of view this approach suited the nature of the product, that is, a film, in the new murderously competitive Hollywood where films got yanked straightaway if they were not immediate geysers of profit. With budget considerations paramount, a strong producer often makes the difference as to whether or not a film is profitable by avoiding costly production problems and keeping the filming from going over-budget. The producer who applies the business mind to film making may not be a well-known figure to the public but he is a key person in the Hollywood industry.

Coincidentally, *Raiders* also meant the big break for Kathleen Kennedy, who was to become Frank Marshall's romantic interest. A pretty brunette in her mid-thirties, she had originally wanted to be a ski instructor but took up nursing, also to the common-sensical end that she might have something "to fall back on." In 1972, however, she landed a job with San Diego's NBC-affiliated KSGO, doing primarily camera work and jobs around the newsroom. She graduated from San Diego State University in 1975 in the same year that 26-year-old Steven Spielberg made his first hit movie, *Jaws*. An introduction to Steven Spielberg got her "bits and pieces" of work in *1941*, the movie which Spielberg was then directing.

The dubious significance of Kathleen Kennedy's first job in a Hollywood production was that it turned out to be Spielberg's only lemon. But though it bombed at the box office, *1941* had for Kennedy a practical significance. It introduced her to the often-troublesome realities of making a film. She worked on the set where behind the scenes America's biggest comedy star, John Belushi, was so drugged up that he literally rolled out of the car that delivered him to the set. Tolerating Belushi's habits and watching Spielberg struggle to get the zombified actor to do his scenes taught Kathleen Kennedy the lengths the movie's top people had to go to get it done.

It was during the filming of *Raiders* that Spielberg, impressed by her absolute dedication, broached the astounding news that she was going to be the producer of his next movie. That movie was *E.T.*, on which Kathleen Kennedy was credited as co-producer with Steven Spielberg. Overnight the erstwhile nursing student joined Marshall at the pinnacle of the Spielberg organization.

When Frank Marshall and Kathleen Kennedy began living together there were no headlines. They were not fanzine material. With Spielberg they brought suburbia to Hollywood with no lavishness, dissipation and scandal; jogging, keeping regular hours, Frank and Kathy were workaholics whose total identification with Spielberg grew into a legendary friendship. The trio worked intimately on the world's biggest box-office hits. On *E.T.*, Marshall was production supervisor; on *Poltergeist*, Frank Marshall was Steven's co-producer and Kathleen was production supervisor. "Steven, Frank and I," Kathleen told a reporter, "like to think of ourselves as one little family. We do everything together." In Kathleen Kennedy's case the identification even extended to the $1.5 million piece of equipment that played E.T., whose eyes she proudly described as "my blue."

Hollywood linked them together as "Frank, Kathy and Steve." Their lives intertwined on many levels. Frank, Kathy and Steve would soon launch the Spielberg flagship, Amblin Entertainment, and establish it as Hollywood's most powerful independent "mini-studio" outside the majors.

The TZ movie was Marshall's fourth Spielberg film. The pace on it was hectic. While occupied with the Landis portion he was also working on the other three segments. His hours ran the full day and much of the night. He was busy making the *Making of...* documentary on the *Twilight Zone* filming. At the same time, he was working on *Indiana Jones and the Temple of Doom*, in addition to a made-for-TV movie for NBC and Universal entitled, *A Pennant for the Kremlin*. Marshall had in development for MGM a movie called *The Protector* through his newly formed Frank Marshall Productions which had just completed its first project, a 15-minute documentary its founder produced and directed about the making of *Poltergeist*. Everything Marshall touched in that strange Summer of Spielberg turned to gold. The *Making of Poltergeist* turned out to be a huge success on Pay TV.

As the TZ movie's executive producer Marshall's job had begun before pre-production took place. He made the business arrangements and worked out the complex organizational structure on the four-part film in meetings with Warner's production executive Fred Gallo and with Lucy Fisher. Selected personally by Spielberg to oversee the complete filming operation, he was, specifically, to act as mediator between Landis' Fly By Night operation and Warner.

From the very start the differences between Warner, specifically between Fred Gallo and the Landis group on almost every important issue, required all of Marshall's arbitration skills. In one such instance Gallo objected to giving the young director his own crew, suggesting that one crew be used for all four segments in order to save money and avoid hiring problems, as well complications with film credits. Because Landis insisted on independence in producing his segment, Marshall intervened and arranged it so that Landis would have complete authority with the understanding that he would conform to the rules.

Officially Landis' TZ segment was part of a big studio production directly controlled by Warner. However, by operating like an independent producer, or "indie," the Landis organization was able to exploit cost-saving non-union labor. Even the use of the name Fly By Night in seeking bids from various suppliers disguised the fact that it was a Warner production, so as to give Landis an edge in securing services from outfits known for giving better deals to cash-strapped "indies" as opposed to the baronial majors. This especially applied to the use of low-paid production assistants as drivers in place of the drivers from Hollywood's powerful Teamster Local 395, with whom Warner had a labor agreement. At meetings between the studio and George Folsey Jr. this thorny labor question resulted in tense confrontations. On at least two occasions the studio blocked the cost-cutting measures proposed by Fly By Night, insisting that Landis comply with all Warner Bros.' union agreements.

Frank Marshall, the picture's executive producer, mediated between the studio and Fly By Night right up until the pre-production shooting with Dan Aykroyd and Albert Brooks. The disputed issues always involved saving money. Early on in the film Marshall discovered Allingham doubling up as 1st AD and UPM. By having Allingham double up without obtaining a waiver from the Directors Guild, Fly By Night was potentially in violation of labor agreements between Warner and the DGA. Marshall advised Allingham that it was a bad idea and after completing pre-production work Elie Cohn was brought on board as 1st AD. Marshall found himself constantly caught in internal disputes of this sort on and off the set.

Eventually, relations between the two sides hit a low point. The Landis people, according to one source directly involved in the arguments, hated Warner's Gallo. But the actual source of their resentment was not the exasperating production veteran. It was the rules he represented. He stood for contracts and obligations. He represented soberness as opposed to anarchy. His exasperating quality stemmed from wanting to play it safe rather than fast and loose. In one instance, after learning that Landis planned to shoot Dan Aykroyd and Albert Brooks in the film's prologue without having obtained insurance for them, Gallo quickly intervened to demand that Landis provide the necessary coverage.

Marshall himself at times helplessly watched as snafus piled up due to the economy practiced by the Landis group. An avid Aykroyd fan, he was present at the shooting of the prologue scene on the disastrous first day of filming. When the low-quality camera equipment broke down, Marshall not only didn't get to see the expected entertainment but the production was delayed for a day with the director forced to make a rapid and expensive shift to more reliable Panavision cameras – the same equipment Fred Gallo had suggested Landis use in the first place!

Even to Marshall the Landis organization appeared to want to cut corners more often than was acceptable in his dealings with Warner. An internal memo actually showed that he was not above pointing the finger at the Landis people, calling them "shoddy" and "unprofessional." Yet he could not be entirely unbiased for the reason that his own interest favored saving money. Since he had a piece of the deal, he benefited each time the director doubled or tripled up some position, or shaved off some other money item. The whole deal was structured as an incentive to all those with points in the production to maximize their earnings by keeping the expenses down. That way the studio got its low-budget movie with a big-budget name.

The ambiguity of Marshall's position was nowhere more apparent than in the child-hiring episode. No one had more experience than Frank Marshall concerning the rules that pertained to working with children on the set. That summer Spielberg's *E.T.* and *Poltergeist* were films all about kids in which children were used prominently.

There could be no doubt at the time the Landis segment got underway that Marshall knew about problems involved in using the kids in night shoots. A confidential Warner memo actually describes a meeting held on one occasion in Landis' Universal bungalow at which Marshall admitted that he specifically addressed Landis' desire to use 4- or 5-year olds in the dangerous *Twilight Zone* scenes. Marshall had followed the evolution of the script. He had personally discussed with Lucy Fisher the script revision where the kids are rescued from the attacking helicopter to make Bill more sympathetic in the movie. From his reading of the exploding village scene Marshall, according to the memo, knew that there would be a problem with using the kids at night.

Spielberg's deputy was on the set for the scene in which Bill realizes his transformation on film. Just before the start of the 2:20 scene the kids were being readied to be thrust into the hands of Vic Morrow prior to his perilous dash across the river. Frank Marshall at that time was standing on the river's edge, across from the village where the main action was to take place, with location manager Dick Vane. At the same time, Jack Tice, the target of the concealment plot, remembered that as he set out to move upstream, spotting fireballs, he made his final communication with Landis; at which point, Tice recalls, Dick Vane, standing next to Marshall, shouted at him. For the third time that night, Vane asked Tice where he would be for the final scene. Tice did not catch on that he was being "positioned" until after the crash when he discovered the cover-up of the children.

During the catastrophic final shot Marshall was so frightened he dove under a truck and witnessed the fireballs, the helicopter, the disaster and panic. Spielberg's man seemed to be the only cool head in the chaos that followed. Marshall was one of the first to enter the river, and, though this act was kept a secret throughout the entire five years of the TZ case, he carried the lifeless body of Renee Chen to shore and laid it at the feet of Virginia Kearns, the movie's hairdresser, who held a flashlight while vain attempts were being made to revive the dead girl. Then Marshall ran back to assist John Landis who was observed by Kearns "just running around, saying, "Oh, shit. Oh, Jesus!" When Marshall reached Landis, according to other witnesses, the director was in a state of shock, flailing and scream-ing and beating his hands on the blood-stained water. Marshall helped Landis to the shore and put him next to the small Asian man with the dazed look who was the father of Myca.

The script girl Kathryn Wooten remembered Frank Marshall through the haze and confusion calling "a wrap" and shooing people away. One technician who watched the pandemonium was under the impression that Marshall was trying to get rid of everyone before the police came. He watched Marshall walk up a trail leading away from the scene; other mov-ie execs followed. The special effects people, too, melted into the night, while a lot of the technicians and drivers stuck around to see what help they could give.

When Frank Marshall walked up the trail leading away from the scene he walked for all intents and purposes out of the *Twilight Zone* case. Spiel-berg's man never had to address the many issues raised by the crash. From the very beginning the probers that swarmed over the stricken dunes overlooked him and afterwards any investigator seeking further informa-tion faced the barrier of Pollock, Bloom and Dekom, another high-pow-ered entertainment law firm. Lawyer Tom Pollock, soon to be chosen to head Universal Studios, ran the legal strategy with a small unit consisting chiefly of his assistant Rick Rosen. In spite of its small size the unit was far more effective than the director's own phalanx in keeping their client out of the various investigations.

Tom Pollock was a Kennedy-Democrat liberal and part of the new Hol-lywood establishment. With a handsome Jerry Mahoney mustache, he was one of the rising breed of young ambitious attorneys who moved between Hollywood's influential entertainment law firms and the majors. His law career converged with the youth market phenomenon that consumed Hol-lywood in the early 70s. Pollock was one of the bright young men in the legal profession who helped form the bridge between the traditional studio system approach and the new Hollywood of bearded young auteurs.

At the time Pollock became active as an entertainment lawyer in the motion picture business he was closely identified with Thom Mount. An intellectual-looking former 60s radical, Mount came to symbolize the breed dubbed "baby moguls." Mount rose with breakneck speed through the Universal Studios ranks after having blazed the trail in the teen-action market with *Smokey and the Bandit*. At Universal, Mount was considered a "boy wonder." And with Mount in mind Hollywood rushed to open its doors to the bright, articulate and exceedingly ambitious young men and women from the universities and law firms.

Mount began as reader for Universal's production chief Ned Tanen. Following *Smokey*'s giant box-office success, he rose to head the studio's creative trust, consisting of himself, Tanen and the godfather, Landis' best friend Sean Daniel. Mount was a booster of John Landis, who after *Animal House* was also hailed as a boy wonder. The world of boy wonders and baby moguls was intense and clannish like a small suburb. In the early 70s Mount and Pollock had been involved in the attempt made by Universal to cultivate a relationship with George Lucas, whose *Star Wars* held the number one box-office place until dislodged by Spielberg's *E.T.* By the time Pollock became president of Universal, "Steven" had his base in the Universal lot's Amblin complex with "Frank" and "Kathy." Tom Pollock was one of the most upwardly mobile young lawyers to be found in young Hollywood. But in defending Marshall, Pollock was also lucky. In the finger-pointing that went on between the studio and Landis, pitting O'Melveny against Behr, the finger pointed past the film's executive producer. And the Hollywood lawyers, Pollock and Rosen, had their work cut out by assuring that the finger stayed pointed that way.

The Pollock-Rosen legal unit concentrated its chief effort on a tiny state bureau that dealt with industrial safety matters. Initially, it was the only one of all the investigative agencies to focus on the Marshall/Spielberg connection with the disaster in Indian Dunes. The California Occupational Safety and Health Administration, Cal/OSHA, at a very early stage cited Marshall by name, along with George Folsey Jr. and John Landis in an entity called "Twilight Zone Productions." Among other things this small agency was charged with making the key recommendation to the DA's office as to the actual employer and whether or not to prosecute for criminal violations of work-place safety laws.

In the early days there were frequent meetings and telephone calls between Cal/OSHA and the DA's lawyer in charge of the case, namely, Deputy DA Gary Kesselman. In a September 10, 1982, Cal/OSHA memo, the deputy chief for safety indicated that there were still many unresolved problems with the case and that Cal/OSHA was still "not sure" about the role of Twilight Zone Productions and Frank Marshall as employers in the film. Thus, it was not coincidental that after several meetings between Cal/OSHA and the district attorney, Cal/OSHA's lead investigator, lawyer Marilyn Levin from the Enforcement Division, received a telephone call from lawyer Rick Rosen who introduced himself as representing Twilight Zone Productions and Frank Marshall. Rosen asked to meet with Levin with regard to his client's involvement in the crash. She agreed.

A serious-minded young woman from Chicago, Marilyn Levin, as part of Llorente's team, had earlier questioned John Landis. In her meeting with Frank Marshall's attorneys, Levin heard Pollock and Rosen explain their view of how the film business worked and how it related to Frank Marshall. The movie attorneys joked with the young bureaucrat while discoursing on the arcane customs of Hollywood film making. Levin was given to understand that just because Marshall had the credit for being the film's executive producer it didn't mean that he was top dog; she learned from Pollock that the credit you get is different from the job you do. They practically reduced the role of the executive producer on a film to a figurehead. Although Marshall had actually been on the set for most of the shooting schedule, at least eight out of 12 days, the Hollywood lawyers downplayed his presence and told Levin that their client had only been on the set three or four times. She learned that Spielberg had merely asked Frank Marshall to help him. The attorneys told Levin that there really was no entity called Twilight Zone Productions; that name, they said, was only created so that the production staff could have a name to wear on their stylish Hollywood jackets.

In return, Levin mentioned that Cal/OSHA had decided to "hold back" on prosecuting its civil citations until the DA made the decision regarding criminal action. Levin also advised Pollock that she had talked to people from the district attorney's office and that in these conversations she heard no mention at all of any criminal charges being considered against Marshall.

32

A PLEA FOR ALAN SMITHEE

By the second month following the *Twilight Zone* crash, the district attorney's office became actively involved. On September 9 the DA's office performed the official filing. Initially, the DA handled the case like any other. The filing came within days after the DA Gary Kesselman first viewed the accident footage where the chem machine's frozen frame showed the powerful fireball erupting from "the fourth hut." At the time the chief DA was Democrat John Van de Kamp, soon to become the state's top cop.

Van de Kamp ran the largest DA's office in the country. Numbering over 700 full-time attorneys, with central operations in downtown LA, his office operated 23 branches throughout the monster sprawl of LA County. Newhall, which included the Indian Dunes area, technically fell under the jurisdiction of the local DA's branch manned by a single individual, Joel Hoffman. Hoffman's chief downtown was a tall, crusty, slow-speaking veteran prosecutor known as "Indian" Billy Webb. Webb's office, which supervised the outlying areas like Newhall, was called the Branch and Area Division.

With the DA becoming active, homicide man Tom Budds at the sheriff's department at last could be expected to get a little help; so far, it'd been pretty much just him and Finnigan during the entire month of August. The same went for Joel Hoffman at Newhall. During the first month he was pretty much on his own. He simply oversaw the case until "Indian" Billy Webb made a decision as to which of the 700 attorneys he would pick to handle this unusual movie case.

Webb knew what kind of person he didn't want. His choice couldn't be any one of the lawyers who had acted as technical advisers on Hollywood movies – in the world's movie capital that consideration actually eliminated a good many in the DA's office. The prosecutor had to be resistant to Hollywood. "I wouldn't say you could become corrupted," Webb noted, "but you could be awed by it." Finally, his choice depended on a person's willingness to accept the challenge of a "career case," a case, as it were, that is never-ending, requiring two years to get to trial and a year or two to try it.

The largest DA's office in the US stretched across Los Angeles County from Antelope Valley in the north to Long Beach in the south, from Santa Monica in the west to Pomona in the east; and in the sleepy, sweltering Pomona branch, far from Hollywood, Webb found the individual to prosecute the *Twilight Zone* case. His candidate looked like a 40s movie character; of medium height and sturdy with slicked-down hair and tight-fitting dark suits, a gold chain and jaguar-like movements, Gary Kesselman was a tough New Yorker who had put himself through law school. He impressed Webb as someone who was his own man, not the kind who wanted to be "part of the crowd."

Webb had first met Kesselman sometime previously when he hurriedly needed a Spanish-speaking attorney with ties to the Hispanic community. The case involved a rare instance in which Mexico, which normally doesn't extradite its nationals, agreed to make an exception in one particular situation. But it demanded that Webb at once dispatch someone to pick up this national in Guadalajara. In the nick of time Webb turned up Kesselman, a former Peace Corps member fluent in Spanish who caught a plane that same day. Kesselman again came to Webb's notice in the little-known Danny Young case in Pomona, involving the grisly murder of a young boy by his neighbor. The case was extremely tough. Before Kesselman became its prosecutor, the earlier trial had resulted in a hung jury. Kesselman investigated personally every facet of the murder of little Danny Young; on weekends he spent his own time walking the neighborhood to find out who had seen what. "Kesselman was a bulldog," Webb recalled. After retrying the case and avoiding the errors of his predecessors, Kesselman won Webb's confidence by getting a conviction.

As a fresh appointee to the TZ case in September 1982, Kesselman, with a powerful mandate to bring criminal charges, replaced Llorente as chief investigator. He first contacted Tom Budds in the sheriff's department. Then he asked Don Llorente for a screening of the film. Llorente courteously scheduled a showing in the Warner screening room which Kesselman attended with two lieutenants from the DA's own Bureau of Investigation, William Burnett and Dave Berthiaume. It was the first time anyone from the DA's office saw the film.

In Warner's screening room Gary Kesselman got his dramatic introduction to the case. After seeing it on a big screen he viewed the drama on the chem machine, a smaller machine used in editing which allows the operator to freeze-frame. He studied huts No. 4 and 5 frame-by-frame; inch-by-inch the fireballs unfolded and grew and enveloped the helicopter's tail; the investigators went back over that scene again and again. Don Llorente with never-failing patience answered questions from Kesselman, Burnett and Berthiaume. John Silvia, Warner's safety man, was there as a member of the NTSB team. He also told the select audience about what he had seen at the site and what he knew about the accident.

The fresh screening of the fatal footage gave the studio its first indication that the district attorney was seriously focusing on the accident as a criminal case. The event was important enough for O'Melveny's Bill Vaughn to communicate to Don Llorente on Warner's behalf. Vaughn complained to Llorente that by letting the DA view the film without Warner's prior consent he had come close to violating their agreement not to show the film to outsiders. Though Llorente respectfully apologized, he underscored his intention fully to cooperate with the DA's office. Backing off, Vaughn only requested to be kept informed of further showings of the film.

With the DA's entry the sheer weight of the case now began to be felt by many who'd been involved in the film. Studio employees felt the pressure to keep quiet and not communicate with outsiders. One Warner employee spoke of pressures being placed upon him by the studio's in-house lawyer, Stan Belkin. Other witnesses to the horror on the set were affected on a more personal level. They lived through sleepless nights plagued by nightmares. Some sought the help of psychiatrists. Others couldn't work for weeks afterwards. Eventually cameraman Steve Lydecker was to get out of the movie business altogether.

The DA investigators themselves at this point still knew far less than some of these witnesses. They had no idea of any of the details of the movie makers' plan to use the children illegally. The bodies on the set constituted clear enough evidence that the children had been used without a permit. Yet, despite this incontrovertible fact, investigators faced a wall of silence from several key people who had been not so much instigators of the plan as accomplices; having been dragged into the scheme and stuck with it, right until the terrible end. Ironically, just as Charlie Hughes had problems with Andy House, so did Charlie's partner Bob Chapman with House's assistant, Hilary Leach.

A cherubic, sandy-haired, smiling, casual, co-ed-type in her mid-twenties, Hilary, as part of her DGA training program, had been sent out for an interview with Andy House for a position on the TZ movie. After working on *Tex*, a Disney production starring Matt Dillon, the TZ movie was only her second feature film. Labor investigator Chapman was not at all surprised that during the interview she was "toe-dancing around," but he also felt he couldn't really blame her; as he put it, "You're dealing with people like Spielberg and Landis." She couldn't talk. "Her whole career was here."

One of the young investigators, Dave Berthiaume, moonlighted from the DA's office as a location manager in the film industry and through his Hollywood connections he got word to the TZ's location manager Richard Vane that the district attorney wanted him to submit to an interview. But Vane never responded. Instead, he promptly called Warner's Stan Belkin to warn the studio lawyer of the DA's request. Following the studio's confidential policy against cooperating with the DA's investigation, Belkin advised Vane that he had no obligation to contact the DA's office. He had the final choice to do whatever he thought was "appropriate," Belkin counseled in confidential discussions with the witness.

Vane's course became clear within days of receiving this advice. He didn't break the wall of silence. While avoiding the DA's Berthiaume he secretly met with Warner's own lawyers and denied that either he or Frank Marshall knew about the cover-up of the kids on the set. He told the studio's lawyers much about the behind-the-scenes activities on the night of the crash. But protecting himself and Marshall, he minimized both their roles in the illegal hiring of the children and in the cover-up of what took place in the final scene. Following this highly confidential interview Vane would not figure in the *Twilight Zone* case again until the grand jury hearings some nine months later in June of '83. Not totally forthcoming with Warner's lawyers, he held back his role in the conspiracy to conceal the children from the fireman/welfare studio teacher on the set that night. His role in this scheme would not surface until the Grand Jury hearings nine months later.

Richard Vane first teamed up with the Landis people on an aborted effort to film *Into the Night*. From September '81 until February the following year he worked on the early development of Landis' *film noir* until the financing fell through and the project remained on the shelf for the next two years. He first worked with Frank Marshall on *E.T.*, and got to know him better on another Spielberg movie, *Poltergeist*. According to Allingham, it was Frank Marshall who recommended that he hire Vane as location manager for the TZ movie. The importance of Vane's secret interview with Warner was that he provided an alibi for the film's executive producer and, by extension, for Steven Spielberg.

As a location manager, Vane's duties involved scouting the areas to be filmed and making sure that the film company acted in accordance with the permits he had obtained. Vane privately told the Warner lawyers that neither he nor Marshall knew about the illegal use of the children in the fatal scene. At 2:20, when the cameras began rolling, Vane said that he and Frank Marshall watched the scene from the opposite side of the river and that, because of the conditions on the set and the late hour, they both assumed that dolls were being used instead of kids. According to confidential Warner memos, Vane said he only assumed that Marshall thought they were dolls; he did not recall any specific conversation with Marshall at the time regarding the use of children or dolls in the final scene. The Warner lawyers, after hearing Vane's account, could now be satisfied that Marshall, and presumably Spielberg, the studio's most important asset, did not know about the illegal hiring and the dangerous conditions on the set.

Following Vane, one of the last of the critical witnesses to be debriefed by Warner's counsel was Elie Cohn, who surprised the studio with a startling admission concerning the infamous "lower, lower" quote that haunted the case. In both his interviews with the labor investigators and with Budds and Finnigan, Cohn had stated that he did not recall whether Landis ordered the helicopter to come lower seconds before the crash. But confronted with the high-powered studio lawyers, he repeated the confession he had made only in private to the investigator working for the phalanx. He told the studio lawyers that although he was in general radio contact with Allingham up in the helicopter, he never had time to communicate with him before the helicopter crashed. According to confidential studio memos, Cohn said he saw Landis speaking through a bullhorn to the helicopter and that he heard him calling for the aircraft to come lower.

Other parts of Cohn's recollections tended to implicate some of Warner's people. Cohn told the movie company lawyers that he had seen Lucy Fisher on the set two or three times, referring to her as the "executive in charge from Warner Bros." Like all those from the set that night questioned by Warner, Cohn did not admit to any involvement at all in the hiring and use of the children. In an obvious attempt to protect those involved in the cover-up of the kids on the set he misled Warner's men by telling them that it was only after the crash that he learned about the handling of the children from Andy House.

One result of Cohn's account was that it made Warner's lawyers themselves suspicious. They knew from interviews with others on the set that Cohn must have known more about the illegal hiring.

And so, aware of all the dimensions, Warner continued its public policy of distancing itself from the illegal actions on the set while going ahead with the Spielberg-Landis movie production.

On the legal front Warner followed Frank Marshall's lead in focusing on the young lawyer-investigator from Cal/OSHA, Marilyn Levin. After learning in late October from Marshall's attorneys that the DA's office was not as yet contemplating criminal charges against Frank Marshall, Warner's two top legal advisers set up their own meeting with Marilyn Levin. At this meeting, just as Marshall's counsel had done earlier, Warner, albeit reluctantly, pointed the finger at Landis in order to minimize the studio's involvement as employers.

The O'Melveny lawyers, Vaughn and Dunham, tried to make their point to the Cal/OSHA investigator, just as Marshall's lawyer Pollock had done, by explaining the facts of film making. They pointed out to Levin that Landis had final cut on his segment and that no one at Warner Bros., had seen the film's dailies. The lawyers talked about call sheets and in explaining their importance made the most radical act of distancing Warner from the event at Indian Dunes. They impressed on Levin that these call sheets listing the presence of the children in the scene had not arrived until the day after the crash.

Two days after the meeting with Warner's top legal guns Levin received from them a thoughtful message, thanking her for her cooperation regarding the citations. Shortly after, Cal/OSHA's Levin made her official recommendation to Deputy District Attorney Gary Kesselman. The onslaught by Marshall's and Warner's powerful attorneys on the impressionable bureaucrat from Cal/OSHA had hit the mark. While her investigation recommended that the case was suitable for criminal prosecution, it mainly focused on the Landis group.

At the same time, on another front, Warner vehemently opposed efforts by the NTSB to release the film showing the fatal crash scene to the media for general consumption. Unknown to the media, a relentless campaign was being directed in Los Angeles by O'Melveny's Bill Vaughn. The Washington, D.C., office of O'Melveny & Myers figured largely in this effort. The NTSB's general counsel in Washington was literally bombarded with letters and phone calls attempting to block release of the film. Vaughn based this opposition on the grounds that it could damage Warner's economic interest. Vaughn wrote:

> ... public exhibition of the scene which ends with the accident could substantially diminish public curiosity about the finished motion picture, and create a negative association in the minds of the general public (most of whom are potential moviegoers) with

the finished picture itself. Warner and the other major motion picture studios spend substantial sums each year to prevent copyright infringement.... The only clips which are publicly exhibited are carefully chosen scenes from the finished motion pictures, intended to have a beneficial impact upon the viewing public.

Informing NTSB headquarters that "one or more jury trials can be expected," Vaughn argued that media exploitation of the crash through a televised showing of the film clips could seriously limit the chances of ultimately impaneling a neutral jury or juries.

*　*　*

Three months after the crash the DGA came out of the closet and held a safety symposium. It was requested that because of the *Twilight Zone* crash neither non-members nor the press be present. The members were further asked not to comment to the press representatives outside. Such requests failed, however, to remove Mark Resnick, a recruit to the Landis phalanx from the giant LA law firm, Paul, Hastings, Janofsky and Walker. Resnick, a lawyer and not a DGA member, surreptitiously listened while movie director after movie director held the floor. He took notes which he afterwards sent to Joel Behr so Landis' personal lawyer could see which director was most critical of his client and which would be most suitable as an expert witness for Landis' defense.

Present at this unusual convocation of DGA members were some of Hollywood's most distinguished directors in television and motion pictures, such as Marvin Chomsky (noted for his TV films, *Roots, Holocaust, Inside the Third Reich)*, famed actor and director, Jackie Cooper; Richard Brooks (*Blackboard Jungle, In Cold Blood, Elmer Gantry, Looking for Mr. Goodbar, Cat on a Hot Tin Roof*); Arthur Hiller (*Silver Streak, Man of La Mancha, The Americanization of Emily, Love Story*). Other DGA members in attendance represented sections of the guild involving unit production managers and stunt coordinators, notably Terry Leonard, stunt coordinator on Spielberg's *1941* as well as on Coppola's *Apocalypse Now,* and Max Pleven, stunt coordinator for *Rollerball* and *Silver Streak.* In his report to Behr, Resnick singled out director Richard Brooks;"by far the day's most vocal and temperamental speaker." Over the years Richard Brooks was to become one of John Landis' most strident DGA critics.

In addition to bringing Vic Morrow to Hollywood for his starring role in *Blackboard Jungle,* Richard Brooks had done one of the most famous stunt scenes while making *Elmer Gantry* in 1956. For the scene involving the interior burning of a church Brooks had 40 firemen present and 200 stunt people, as well as 800 extras bussed into the set for the mob scene. Even with all of the elaborate preparations, the director almost had an accident when the heat became so intense that the movie's female star, Jean Simmons, fainted as the fire unexpectedly consumed all of the available oxygen.

Resnick's memo to Joel Behr noted that while Brooks was angry that because of the *Twilight Zone* crash all directors were catching hell, he also criticized the studios for putting time pressures on directors to get the film done. The memo made note of Jackie Cooper, the Hollywood fixture since his child-acting days who was to become active in DGA safety matters. Behr's secret agent described Cooper as having urged members not to make any open references to the incident on the set to outsiders. The meeting ended on the note that self-policing was necessary in order to avoid legislative intervention. Cooper vehemently opposed the idea of safety marshals because he felt it would hurt the creative side of film making. "An omniscient son-of-a-bitch from Sacramento will ruin this business," Jackie Cooper told the gathering. The DGA tried to dissociate itself from the case to "protect the legal process." But even so, intense pressure built within the guild to take action against those who broke DGA rules on hiring the children. Nowhere in the guild was this feeling stronger than in a little-known internal committee, the AD/UPM Council, consisting of assistant directors (AD's) and unit production managers (UPM's). It was within this small unit that the Landis cover-up first came apart as the council dealt with a surprise from a 2nd AD who wanted to talk about his involvement in the illegal hiring. Long before the investigators unearthed the truth, the AD/UPM Council learned from Andy House what had actually happened on the set that fatal night.

Anderson House had become the weak link in the chain which for a year had held firm against cooperating with the authorities. In an unprecedented AD/UPM council session, a small group of DGA members saw House weep and heard his confession and strange plea. His appearance was that of a broken man, nervous, sometimes in tears.

It was not coincidental that the haggard man took his strange plea to the forum of his colleagues just before the TZ movie's '83 summer release. Andy House came to the session to avail himself of a little-used part of the DGA contract with the studios that entitled members to see a copy of the "main" (opening) and the "end" (closing) titles before a film's release. House addressed the council's closed meeting with the unusual request to have his name removed from the credits and replaced with a pseudonym, Alan Smithee, the fictitious name guild members usually reserved for a director who didn't want his real name on a film's credits.

For obvious reasons the DGA was disinclined to grant the name Alan Smithee. As one DGA member who was present at the closed session with Andy House put it, "If you bask in the sunshine of your glories you should also wallow in the mud of your mistakes." In order to obtain the Alan Smithee alias, the film maker really had to prove that his work had been "perverted," and Andy House put himself through a wrenching confession before the small body of his fellows gathered at DGA headquarters on Sunset Boulevard.

"I've been through a lot."

Slumped before his listeners, the 2nd AD made a tearful appeal.

"I knew this was wrong. I told Folsey it was wrong. I told John Landis it was wrong. I feel bad. I don't have the same complicity, but I feel responsibility. I'm having great difficulties because of this incident."

He pleaded, "I beg this council to let me take my name off this film."

The council deliberated and when *Twilight Zone: The Movie* was released that summer the credits included a fictional creation: 2nd AD... Alan Smithee.

* * *

The DA's office had no inkling at that time of the struggles, internal and external, embroiling the phalanx, Warner, the DGA, the Spielberg organization and Twilight Zone Productions. The DA's investigators played outsider to the insider world of Hollywood, excluded even from the rumors always rife within the super-secretive film business.

Without benefit of Andy House's confession to the DGA committee, or the results of Warner's internal debriefings, Tom Budds' investigation remained in the fog. For all intents and purposes the DA's investigation by the spring of '83 had ground to a halt. The new prosecutor Gary Kesselman, still uncertain as to whether or not the DA's office had enough evidence to charge any of the movie people involved with criminal conduct, finally met with the chairman of the grand jury's criminal complaints committee. Kessselman believed that only through sworn testimony before a grand jury could headway be made against the conflicting versions about the crash given by witnesses to investigators from federal, state and local agencies. Meanwhile, the DA's office let it be known that it would offer immunity to key witnesses in return for full disclosure about the events that night. But even with the awesome grand jury powers, the mystery might well have remained forever stalled if it had not been for an accidental meeting between Gary Kesselman and Donna Schuman that broke one portion of the case wide open.

From the labor commissioner's files Kesselman had picked out Dr. Hal Schuman's name and set up an interview for May 11, 1983. Basically, Kesselman knew little from the files about Dr. Schuman other than that the psychiatrist was peripherally involved in the child-hiring scheme in connection with George Folsey Jr. But at Schuman's Hollywood home he met the psychiatrist's wife. For all of the preceding ten months, like others in the case, Donna Schuman had not volunteered information. Perhaps it was the period of moral gestation: responsibility brought to term. In talking to Kesselman, Donna Schuman went even farther than Andy House did before the guild committee when he pleaded for the name Alan Smithee.

That evening Donna Schuman gave the investigation its first inside look into the Landis operation. She supplied Kesselman with names, dates, and addresses of vital witnesses to the disaster. She identified key staffers in the operation who knew about the plan to hire the kids and took part in the cover-up on the set. Primarily, she supplied him with the names of the two witnesses who, besides herself, made the grand jury indictments possible.

From Donna Schuman, Kesselman for the first time learned how Anderson House was involved in the elaborate cover-up to prevent fireman/studio teacher Jack Tice from seeing the kids at night. Schuman also led him to Cynthia Nigh, Dan Allingham's former girlfriend. From Cynthia Nigh the prosecutor learned that Landis and Folsey actually had foreknowledge of the possible legal consequences if they used the kids. Nigh told Kesselman that the director and his business partner had actually discussed the subject of going to jail if their illegal actions became known to authorities.

A week following the partial breakthrough with Donna Schuman on May 19, Kesselman and Tom Budds met with Andy House in the office of House's attorney, John Dellaverson. As the two sides faced each other the situation was unlike Budds' first meeting with House nine months earlier. This time the investigators laid out their knowledge of his deep involvement in the plan and the cover-up.

Essentially, their ultimatum came down to saying that unless he talked, Anderson House, too, might become a target for indictment. At that point

Dellaverson and Kesselman agreed on a sort of "informal immunity" for the 2nd AD, that is, if he cooperated with the grand jury and told all he knew he would not be a target. Dellaverson made the same arrangement for House's assistant the night of the crash; unlike her meeting with labor investigator Bob Chapman, nine months earlier, Hilary Leach would now tell her part of the story to the investigators and repeat it a week later to the newly-convened grand jury.

33

FRIENDLY WITNESSES

On the eve of their indictment, Landis, Folsey and Allingham were unaware that the links in the chain of silence had already irreparably weakened. The new developments on the prosecution side involving Donna Schuman were out of range of the phalanx. In Century City, Joel Behr and his criminal advisor Harland Braun still focused on the bullhorn because of its connection with the "lower, lower" issue. The strategy they formulated included cooperating with the grand jury. Landis, Folsey and Allingham would testify in the hope that they could avoid indictment and at the same time have a grandstand, as it were, from which to point the finger at others, namely, the helicopter pilot and the special effects crew, particularly Paul Stewart. In line with this strategy the phalanx sought out people who could bring testimony before the grand jury that would support Landis' side of the story. It meant finding "friendly" witnesses willing to go to bat for the director before the extraordinary body of 21 no-nonsense citizens.

At Behr's suggestion Harland Braun met with two of these friendly witnesses. One was the veteran propman from many Landis movies who would help corroborate that the director was not screaming "lower, lower" through his bullhorn at the time of the crash. His duties included handling the bullhorn and the director's chair; moreover, he had definitely pointed the finger of responsibility at the powdermen, secretly informing Landis' private investigators that he saw both Paul Stewart and Jerry Williams at impromptu parties on the special effects truck when beer was being consumed just before the crash ("They didn't go to the lunch line and have a meal with the rest of us. They stayed back, hung in their truck and drank beer.") He also accused Paul Stewart of using crude equipment and of appearing intoxicated with "bloodshot eyes" during the filming of the final shot. This friendly witness, Mike Milgrom, was willing to swear that Landis did not even have a bullhorn. He'd already talked with representatives of the phalanx and was thought to make a creditable appearance.

The other friendly witness who was thought to be valuable in shoring up Landis' case before the grand jury was a Vietnam War veteran with casual good looks named Paul Hensler. Hensler had worked as technical adviser on several Vietnam War scenes in films that included *Apocalypse Now* and *The Deer Hunter*, as well as *The Exterminator* on which Paul Stewart had been chief special effects coordinator. Reading about Paul Stewart's involvement in the *Twilight Zone* crash, Hensler contacted Landis' attorneys and informed them that he was not surprised that an accident had occurred.

Disregarding the fact that, ironically, the special effects in *The Exterminator* was what had originally recommended Stewart to Landis, a meeting was arranged with Hensler. It took place at the Moustache Cafe in Westwood. Hensler elaborated to Harland Braun and Joel Behr's assistant, John Diemer, on some dangerous incidents during *The Exterminator* filming for which he blamed Paul Stewart. In the shooting of one SFX scene, Hensler said, he was up in the helicopter while Stewart set off a land mortar directly underneath the aircraft, causing it to lose substantial altitude so that it came close to crashing. Hensler also mentioned three actors in *The Exterminator* who received minor burns when Stewart set off an explosion in their close proximity. In yet another incident Hensler blamed Stewart for exploding a water mortar while a stuntman stood directly over it. Stating his belief that Stewart drank while working, the Vietnam vet with the strong antipathy against Stewart would make an altogether favorable grand jury witness. Dividing their time, Behr and his assistant Diemer interviewed potentially friendly witnesses like Robert Liddle, the stand-in, who was willing to state under oath that Landis had nothing to do with ordering the helicopter to come lower. Another possible consideration as a friendly witness, James Glickenhaus, the director of *The Exterminator*, was assigned to Landis' private investigator Robert Frasco. Frasco returned from this interview again with bad news. The confidential account Glickenhaus gave of the detailed planning that went into *The Exterminator*, particularly into the dramatic helicopter and fire sequence, made sharp contrast with the haphazard and uncontrolled conditions on the TZ set: Glickenhaus was not asked to help out.

As the result of the grand jury proceedings Behr, on Braun's advice, hired separate criminal counsel for Folsey and Allingham, respectively. For Folsey it was Roger Rosen, another Century City criminal attorney; and for Allingham it was Leonard Levine who would remain Allingham's attorney throughout the trial. The attorneys could have kept their clients from testifying by letting them take the Fifth Amendment, except that it would have guaranteed an indictment – precisely what everyone wished to avoid. The best alternative seemed to be that John Landis, briefed, pre-pared, behaviorally modified, in conjunction with "friendly" witnesses, could perhaps defuse the criminal character of the case and thus get him-self and the others off the hook.

The grand jury proceedings that opened nearly a year after the crash, on May 31, 1983, were held in the grand jury room on the 13th floor of the Criminal Court building in downtown LA. In the two-week sitting more than two-score witnesses, apart from Landis, Folsey and Allingham, were interrogated by Gary Kesselman, who conducted the proceedings.

On the first day of the grand jury the most damaging witnesses in the entire case appeared: Donna Schuman and Andy House, the Le and Chen parents, fireman/studio teacher Jack Tice, and the driver of the Chapman crane who on the final night of shooting had heard himself yelled at by John Landis for being a "fucking idiot." Unknown to either Landis or his phalanx, the Chapman driver brought to the grand jury room a series of slides of photographs he had taken the night of the crash, one of which would wreak havoc with a pet premise of the defense planned by Landis' attorneys.

The grand jurors heard from Donna Schuman about the script prob-lems, how Folsey told her "John" had written some kids into the script and how, ultimately, they had managed to find the kids. She related conversa-tions she heard about hiring the kids illegally and how she helped in the scheme without realizing that the kids, copter and explosives would all be used together. Donna Schuman's account was amplified by Andy House.

The 2nd AD described his fruitless attempts to warn Allingham and even the director himself after learning that children would be used in connection with explosives and a helicopter and that the shooting would be – he explained the term – "night for night." He stated how he urged Allingham in vain to get the director to look at professional small people, or else use dolls or dummies. He mentioned his discovery of Jack Tice at Indian Dunes, and did not spare his own role in widening the conspiracy by going to others on the set and warning them of Tice. House related an incident he had witnessed just before the final scene when, while stand-ing in the river, he heard the director ask Stewart to place a mortar under one of the shoreline huts closest to the action. House told the grand ju-rors that after Stewart declined, saying it was too close to the helicopter, "Landis became very upset" but then "immediately cooled down."

The grand jury heard testimony in Mandarin from Shyan-Hei Chen, Renee's mother. An interpreter translated that Renee was "frightened" at

9:30 and that when she cried John Landis picked up the little girl to comfort her. George Folsey Jr. put his arm around Mrs. Chen, according to the interpreter, assuring her that it wasn't dangerous. Renee's mother told of Hilary Leach escorting them from the director's trailer to the set. The interpreter translated Folsey's strange warning to Mrs. Chen. "If a fireman questions you, just say that you are helping, you are a friend of mine and you are helping out. Don't say anything about the money or the children being paid money." Shyan-Hei Chen identified photos of Landis and Folsey in People's Exhibit 4 and 5.

Next, Jack Tice came before the grand jury with impressive credentials of having been a studio teacher on over 250 films and having done extensive work with helicopters, especially in their most dangerous hovering position. He recalled his discovery of the boy's decapitated head bobbing in the shallow water near the nose of the fallen craft and how he had held it between his feet until somebody came with a black garbage bag. He said he later discovered the girl, Renee, lying dead on the bank 30 feet from the helicopter. Tice mentioned the suspicions that afterwards dawned on him, saying he "thought it was quite unusual" that of the six firemen present on the set, the location manager, Dick Vane, would ask only him, as many as three times in one evening, where he would be at the 2:20 filming: "It was quite unusual for him to insist on knowing where I was going to be." The witness remarked on the crude figure Landis cut on the set and described how the director "got physical in gesticulating widely (sic) with his arms," dispensing vulgarities like, "When the fuck can we start!"

The grand jury heard from Colleen Logan, chief of the Labor Commission's Standards and Enforcement Division; after ruefully stating that when younger and thinner she had worked in television and had some small parts in movies, she cited from "Rules and Regulations Governing Employment of Minors in the Entertainment Industry." As the author of this document she explained the paperwork involved to get a permit that guarantees the child's safety, health and moral welfare on a set. She informed the grand jurors of the California labor code which made both under-16 employment after 10 P.M. as well as hazardous or dangerous employment conditions illegal.

Colleen Logan was followed by another thirty-or-so witnesses. Grim-faced, serious, Warner's VP Edward Morey focused the blame on Landis; describing the Landis operation as independent of Warner Bros., he informed the grand jurors that Frank Marshall simply lent his name to the production, doing nothing more than representing Steven Spielberg. Cynthia Nigh said damning stuff about getting the cash to pay the kids, the meetings behind closed doors, Folsey's joke ("We'll probably be thrown in jail after this, just because of the kids"), and how she heard Folsey tell Renee's mother over the phone "that it was just like fireworks" and she needn't be afraid. Kathryn Wooten complained about the lack of pre-production meetings with crew, director and producer. The grand jurors heard Hilary Leach corroborate Andy House about wanting to use small professional people for the "stunt" in the explosion scene. Even the so-called friendly witnesses that had been prepared under Joel Behr's supervision couldn't avoid damaging the director's image in front of the grand jurors. Elie Cohn stated to the panel that Landis told him they had to be careful not to be caught once the studio teacher had been recognized on the set. Set designer Richard Sawyer recalled that the odor of gasoline on the set at the time was "overpowering, beyond belief."

Neither were the special effects men helpful in their appearances. Before the citizens in the secret grand jury room passed the parade of powdermen. All except the chief, Paul Stewart, had been given immunity. Paul Stewart did not testify; instead, his NTSB statement was read into the grand jury record. In addition, the grand jury heard indirect testimony on Stewart from Deputy Sheriff Budds, who repeated statements Stewart made to him in two police interviews.

One of the powdermen made frank acknowledgement to the panel that special effects men drank on the set in certain situations, stating it was not uncommon "to have a bottle and go sit in a corner."

And so it went before the impassive panel of 21 silent citizens. Witness after witness dealt blow upon blow to the carefully laid defense of bouffant-crested Behr, acerbic Braun and eager Diemer. Makeup artist Melanie Levitt and master shot Steve Lydecker told of the live ammo on the set and hearing Landis' "lower, lower" screamed through a megaphone.

One of the most damaging exchanges took place between Kesselman and Roland Chiniquy, an SFX hand for forty years, five of which as head of special effects at Universal Studios. Although he was not involved in the TZ production, Chiniquy was a veteran noted for SFX on such films as *Airport, Jaws* and *Earthquake,* for which he won one Academy Award, and for *Hindenburg,* for which he won another. He elaborated in detail on all the standard preparations that had to be made for a scene of the kind that brought down the helicopter that night. Kesselman asked Chiniquy what he would have done if a director had ordered him to be involved with a helicopter hovering in general proximity to the children, knowing that explosives were going to be detonated in their general area. "I proba- bly would have been fired," Chiniquy said, "because I wouldn't do it."

Of all those who came before the grand jury the appearance of location manager Richard Vane was the most crucial. His testimony dramatically fixed the course for the rest of the case. It allowed the two top-people on board to bail out, leaving Landis as the sole helmsman.

Following advice from Warner's counsel, Vane had maintained the wall of silence by not cooperating with the DA. In subsequent private talks with Warner, the film studio had been relieved to learn from him that neither he nor Frank Marshall knew about the kids on the set. The studio memo which recorded this interview noted at the time that Vane had assumed that Marshall thought they were going to use dolls, since he was unable to recall any specific exchanges with Marshall on the subject of kids and dolls in the final scene. But under the grand jury subpoena, Vane was able to recollect that when the action for the final shot began Marshall had concretely verbalized to him his belief that there were actu- ally dolls under Vic's arms.

Up till this point, nothing in the case so explicitly severed Spielberg's executive producer from any connection with the deaths of the kids than the alibi Vane stated before the grand jury. It cut loose not only Marshall but also Spielberg and pointed the finger directly at John Landis.

As the secret hearings proceeded, Joel Behr directed Harland Braun and John Diemer to attend an important meeting with John Landis on June 12, a Sunday, two days before Landis' grand jury testimony. They met at the director's home on Lloyd Crest in Beverly Hills. His wife Deb- orah was there with his daughter Rachel.

The Landis home was inwardly dominated by a primate motif. Braun and Diemer, while briefing the director in the living room, faced a huge stuffed gorilla standing guard at the door. It was so lifelike it was eerie. In the den library were stacks of movie books, a lot of them about goril- las. The den was loaded with electronic gizmos and videos; a huge TV faced another giant portrait of a gorilla that hung on the wall. Pictures and books on werewolves abounded. A few weeks before, after attending a 50th anniversary screening of *King Kong* at Mann's Chinese, Landis paid $8,500 for special effects expert Harry Hansen's giant Kong statue to add to his collection. The stuffed gorilla at the door was a wedding gift from Academy Award winner and close friend Rick Baker.

The home reflected the Landis personality. While Behr and Diemer passed around memos and newspaper articles or tried to engage Landis' attention for his upcoming testimony there were digressions to admire the bearded director's huge collection of miniature toys, especially his collection of old-fashioned lead cars displayed on shelves in the den.

In spite of his troubles during that spring of '83 John Landis was preoccupied with film projects. "Landis is up and happy," reported Dan Aykroyd who had gone on after the TZ movie to star with Eddie Murphy in *Trading Places*, which was about to open. Like Spielberg, Landis was making movies for all the major studios: *Trading Places* for Paramount, *Twilight Zone* for Warner, and for Universal's Pay TV and Home Video Division he put together his first video, a compilation of classic and modern horror movie trailers, *Coming Soon*, hosted by Jamie Lee Curtis.

By the time of the meeting in his home, the limits on Landis' testimony had already been agreed upon in discussions Braun had earlier with Gary Kesselman. Through his attorney Landis had already agreed that he would testify on all matters pertaining to the accident on the set that night except to questions specifically related to the hiring of the children, based on the Fifth Amendment principle against self-incrimination.

One day following the top-level Sunday meeting at Landis' home on Lloyd Crest, Folsey and Allingham appeared in the secret sanctum on the 13th floor of the Criminal Court building. It was the next-to-last day of proceedings; the only other witness yet to appear, John Landis, was scheduled for the next morning.

In Allingham's afternoon appearance the grand jurors met for the first time the smallest wheel of the troika on the set that night. But by the time he presented his incredible story to the grand jury the panel had already obtained from Donna Schuman, Andy House and Cynthia Nigh the portrait of an obedient UPM who without hesitation, with some bullying, in fact, labored to implement the illegal hiring plan, dismissing the numerous pleas from Andy House and setting in motion the cover-up to avoid detection.

Allingham casually told the jury that after the near-fatal 11:30 rage scene he never attempted to communicate the danger to John Landis: at the time he felt the explosions were not dangerous and that all he had heard from the crew was, "It's a little warm up here." He couldn't recall whether he ever discussed with Landis the use of alternatives for the children. "It's been over a year," he said, but even if it had been discussed he knew that such a proposal was unfeasible because of the type of photography they were doing and the box-office aspect. "There was just no way," he explained, "that you could put a midget in there that would, I guess, sell."

Deputy DA Gary Kesselman focused on his part in hiring the helicopter pilot. Had Allingham looked into the qualifications of the pilot? Had he simply hired him because he was cheapest? Or because he would be the most compliant in cooperating with the director's dangerous climactic scene? Why had he hired Dorcey Wingo who had no experience with fireballs when also interviewed for the job were hugely experienced people like John Gamble and Hollywood professionals like Clay Wright, both of whom had already appeared as grand jury witnesses? Clay Wright, Allingham said, was "too flakey." Of Gamble, who'd met with him at the Universal bungalow, Allingham simply said, "the name doesn't ring a bell with me."

When George Folsey Jr. took the stand Kesselman informed the grand jurors, as he previously had done with regard to Allingham, that the interrogation could not touch on the hiring of the children, nor on the topic of the licenses or permits related to their employment. During the interrogation George Folsey made his presence on the set that night appear to be a casual visit. In the fateful scene, Folsey testified, his chief concern was that the rough river bottom might cause trouble for Vic's crossing while carrying the children. He told the grand jurors that he hadn't heard anyone suggest it might be unsafe to have the children near explosives. But as in Allingham's case, the grand jury already knew in detail the extent of Folsey's role through earlier testimony it had heard.

Folsey told the grand jurors that he had gone to the set because it was the last night of shooting and wanted to see "if everything was all right," minimizing his role as "just an extra pair of eyes and ears" in case anybody had a question to ask him. He denied having expressed fright at the 11:30 shot, in contrast to Cynthia Nigh's testimony of his remark to her during the stupendous blasts about being relieved that his wife and children had not come to the set. Folsey could not be questioned about Myca and Renee; the grand jurors, however, had already heard from Cynthia Nigh of his joking, "We could all go to jail for this," and that around the office it was common knowledge that the children would be employed unlawfully.

Wingo, like Paul Stewart, did not appear before the grand jury but instead had his NTSB testimony put into the record. Allingham and Folsey testified for two hours that Monday afternoon. When they were done the grand jury adjourned and bussed over to the Academy of Motion Picture Arts and Science building in Beverly Hills. In one of the darkened screening rooms in which Academy members meet to appraise candidates for the Oscar the jurors watched rough cuts of three sequences; the rage sequence at 11:30, the "rehearsal" at 2:00, and the fatal scene at 2:20. The failure of the DA to discover the fourth sequence that would become prominent in the trial nearly three years later, the rescue sequence at 9:30, had less to do with the wall of silence they faced and more with the ineptitude of the investigators. The grand jury saw the crash scene from six different camera angles and at the end the foreman asked whether they wanted to see the sequence again. The silence of the panel of men and women indicated that they had seen enough.

34

THE PROPMAN

The legal practice which allowed the phalanx to "proffer" the grand jury witnesses friendly to John Landis stemmed from a 1978 California Supreme Court decision, *Johnson vs. Superior Court*. This made it obligatory for the DA to present to the grand jury any evidence which a potential defendant felt might be exculpatory. Thus Behr "proffered" Paul Hensler, the war movie expert, and Mike Milgrom, Landis' propman, to appear among the 40-odd witnesses who were called before the grand jury.

The purpose of these two special witnesses was to support the Landis defense on two key points. Hensler's negative feelings about Paul Stewart from his experience with the explosives chief on *The Exterminator*, Behr hoped, would back up Landis' contention that the director had no responsibility and, by stressing reliance on others, point the finger at the powdermen. Milgrom would say that John Landis never even had a bullhorn in the fatal scene and thus silence the haunting infamy, "lower, lower, lower."

As is customary, the DA's prosecutor, Gary Kesselman, had been provided Hensler's name by Landis' attorneys. Kesselman realized that Hensler's appearance before the grand jury was designed to place the blame on the powdermen. But he was also aware that in the chain of command the special effects chief took orders from the director and that he would not do anything with explosives without the director's close involvement. And so, in a telephone conversation with Hensler, the prosecutor used a clever ploy and outflanked Landis' costly phalanx. He devised a "hypothetical" question that was actually a description of the Landis set at Indian Dunes in the final scene.

Kesselman mentioned specific conditions on this "hypothetical" set, the late hour and darkness, the explosives and children, the helicopter, the cliff, and got Hensler to respond, "Anyone who does that would be insane."

This telephone conversation took place a week prior to the time Hensler was sworn in as a grand jury witness. In the grand jury room Kesselman, continuing to probe in the "hypothetical" vein, described a set on which there was a lack of coordination between the pilot and the SFX chief, and the grand jurors heard Hensler react strongly that under these conditions he would not let the children onto the set.

With these statements Hensler nullified anything exculpatory he had to say about John Landis, and made it seem even worse for the director since he was supposed to be friendly. And what was true of Hensler was true to an even more devastating degree in the fiasco of propman Mike Milgrom. Milgrom's testimony completely shattered Landis' credibility.

In accordance with the custom, Harland Braun had provided the prosecutor with a list of questions that Landis wished to be asked of the friendly witness. Since the phalanx "proffered" Milgrom to deny the bullhorn, Braun included in the list of questions many references to this instrument and its connection with the "lower, lower" issue. But by the time Milgrom appeared before the silent grand jurors and Kesselman read him the questions, the propman's position was already undermined by previous witnesses, a total of six, who had testified that they witnessed the director yell "lower, lower" through the bullhorn. To a bewildered grand jury Milgrom alone protested, "Absolutely not!" Milgrom testified that Landis couldn't have been yelling through the bullhorn. He swore he saw the bullhorn on the director's chair.

Kesselman had in his list of exhibits a photograph obtained from a series taken just before the crash. The photograph came from Kenny Williams, the Chapman crane operator that night who had been sworn at by Landis for being a "fucking idiot." Williams had brought his camera to the set to capture the sensational fireballs promised in the final shooting. One of Williams' slides was taken just seconds before the helicopter plunged. Marked Exhibit No. 35, the photograph showed a scene that was not captured by any of the six cameras filming the shot. It showed John Landis on the spit of land, with Milgrom standing next to him on one side and SFX man Jerry Williams on the other.

"Who is this person I'm pointing to here?" Kesselman asked, holding up the photograph.

Milgrom said, "John Landis."

"What does he have in his hand?"

Lamely Milgrom replied, "A bullhorn."

In the end the Milgrom fiasco was for the grand jurors not so much a determining factor of Landis' guilt or innocence as much as a test of his credibility. The 40-or-so witnesses preceding the director to the stand had pretty well demolished any chance he had of being believed. The director's voice, even when raised to the shrillest denial, could not refute this ava-lanche of testimony to chaos, bad planning and mad whim. Consequently, Landis' personal appearance was important not for what he might say in his own defense but in determining whether he would take personal re-sponsibility for all the conditions the jurors had heard described.

As previously he had done with the friendly witnesses, Braun gave Kes-selman a list of questions to ask John Landis – about 25 in all. Their twin thrust was to lend support to the defense argument that the *Twilight Zone* crash was an industrial accident and to establish the point that the direc-tor relies on others. Though well-rehearsed by his high-priced attorneys, Landis faced a bulldog who with "hypothetical" questioning snapped at the witness, then lunged for the kill. Kesselman listened to the director give an example of his reliance on experts with a smug analogy. "When you get into a taxi," he heard Landis assert, "you assume the driver is not going to drive you off a bridge. It's just assumptions, the guy is a licensed taxi driver. These are experts."

Frequently Landis contradicted the testimony already on record of not one but two or three and even more witnesses. When asked specifically what preparations he had made after the 11:30 scene, Landis replied, "At the 11:30 shooting I was not surprised. I was watching Vic. And the ex-plosions in the water were what I expected. However, Dorcey and Alling-ham came up to me, and said, 'My God, these explosions were big. And we could feel the heat in the helicopter.' And then I said, 'Fine. Well, then let's get away from them and put the helicopter over the water!'" Here he contradicted not only Allingham, who had already testified that he never communicated to Landis about this particular incident, (only "It's a lit-tle warm up here"), but also Wingo, whose NTSB statements, already in the grand jury record, included Wingo's report of Landis' response to his complaints about the just-completed rage scene. "Don't be squeamish," and "You ain't seen nothing yet."

Landis tried to avoid saying that he wasn't involved in the fatal shot's planning. At the same time, he wanted to get across the idea that he, as director, had no responsibility. But keeping these two strands separate proved impossible and drew attention to his strange confusion. He re-called nothing definite about what he had told the powder chief about the placement of the bombs. "The explosions on the shore, I honestly don't know how specific – if I was saying, 'Put one there.'" Nor could he recall if before the 2:20 crash he had set up a meeting between the SFX coordi-nator and the pilot in order to discuss their tasks in the upcoming crucial scene. Smugly he countered, referring to the pilot, "Did I take him by the hand to Paul?" No, he couldn't say whether the three of them together had discussed that, admitting that there was never a meeting with the entire crew, "only department heads."

One of the most heated exchanges between Landis and Kesselman took place over the issue of final authority on the set. After much wrangling Kesselman asked, "The final authority in terms of camera, actor, positions, helicopter, or whatsoever, on that set—" But before he could finish, Landis interrupted, "is not mine, sir, because if I ask an actor, 'Would you please take your hand and stick it in this garbage disposal?' the actor is going to say, 'Of course not.'" He denied having had a discussion that night with Paul Stewart in which he requested explosives be placed inside the huts. Addressing the "lower, lower" controversy, he denied that he even saw the helicopter near the end; he was signaling to Vic and not for the helicopter to come lower. He denied that the village was to be blown up at 2:20. When Kesselman asked whether anyone told him at any time prior to the filming that it was unsafe to have children in proximity to explosives, the answer was a vehement, "Absolutely not!" And when Kesselman persisted whether anyone suggested that stunt doubles be used, Landis bristled.

"For the children? No, sir, and – I'm sorry. Vic Morrow is...was, a professional who had made hundreds of television shows and films and would not place himself in danger."

After Landis' morning appearance the session broke for lunch. The 21 panelists returned at 1:00 P.M. for Kesselman's closing statement.

"After reviewing the entire testimony," Kesselman began, "and the notes that I have, on behalf of the district attorney's office at this time, I am requesting that this grand jury bring back indictments against five individuals for involuntary manslaughter. And those five individuals are John Landis, George Folsey Jr., Dan Allingham, Dorcey Wingo, and Paul Stewart."

Kesselman explained that involuntary manslaughter can be based upon one of two legal principles. "The first is a death which occurs as a result of the commission of an unlawful act, not amounting to a felony: i.e., a misdemeanor, which is inherently dangerous." He mentioned in this connection the violation of another penal code section, child endangerment, meant, Kesselman said, "basically is a person who has care, custody, or control of a minor, who permits that minor to be placed in a situation where the person or health of the minor is endangered." Apart from the commission of the unlawful act, the child-hiring and endangering of a minor, Kesselman mentioned the second legal basis for involuntary manslaughter, "and that is the commission of a lawful act, but an act which involves a high degree of risk of death or great bodily injury which is done without due caution and circumspection."

The prosecutor asked the grand jurors to bring back an indictment against Landis on all five counts, two counts each for the children and on one count for Morrow. Kesselman sought indictments for Stewart and Wingo on three counts each, based on the lawful act "without due caution and circumspection." Folsey and Allingham were asked to be indicted on counts 2 and 4, the unlawful act of hiring Myca and Renee and placing them in danger that resulted in their deaths.

Kesselman in closing dwelt on two points, the children and the responsibility of the director. "Now, maybe Vic Morrow had a choice," he argued, "if he knew what was coming. But those children didn't. Those children didn't by choice, by informed choice, choose to be there. And, I submit to you, neither did their parents." And as to the question of who had the final authority, Kesselman ended dramatically:

"Do you have any doubt in seeing John Landis ... seeing his performance here today, when I'm sure he was trying to restrain himself as much as he could, as to who was in charge of that set, who was making the decisions on that set?

"You heard the testimony. There was no question. It was John Landis.

"Don't let him come in here now and tell you that, 'That was not my job to be concerned with coordination. That was Cohn. That was Stewart. That was the pilot. That was someone else.'

"There has to be responsibility.

"That man was responsible.

"He was on notice after 11:30 ..."

The grand jurors deliberated for two hours. The case was unique. They went home and came back the next morning and handed in the involuntary manslaughter indictments for the five men. It was the first time a director was to be put on trial for deaths on a movie set.

Bench warrants were issued – and bail was put at $5,000 for each.

35

"The Son of a Bitch is crazy"

The next morning Gary Kesselman called to inform Harland Braun of the grand jury decision. Braun took it badly, as he did every defeat, but it also stimulated his combativeness. He immediately informed Joel Behr. They agreed to meet and together take the long drive from Century City to Universal Studios. As they drove, Braun sensed in Behr a fear of telling Landis the bad news and, after shuffling into their client's office, the two lawyers, for once, had little to say. They were themselves unnerved, still uncertain as to the cause of the debacle and highly interested in looking at the secret grand jury transcripts which were not due out for several weeks. The director called Folsey into the office. Behr related the bad news. Landis said, "Oh, shit!" Braun recalls.

John Landis' thick beard had been erased for a trimmer, much neater version. His hair, though still longish, was sleekly cut. The massive bifocals no longer seemed surrounded by shaggy growths. He dressed in suit and tie for rendezvous with the authorities. Society forced its rules. He had to make adjustments, exert self-control and learn compliance. As the result of the criminal indictments the criminal specialist, Harland Braun, became more prominent in the case. Joel Behr was a Hollywood lawyer in the classic deal-making tradition but out of his element in the arcane world of the criminal court. Although he remained the master-mind, tactician of the bulldozer defense, much of the work was now shifted to Braun who explained the tedious legal process: Landis, Folsey, Allingham, Stewart and Wingo were scheduled to appear in a week's time for arraignment. They would be booked and have their mug shots taken. By agreement with the DA's office, they were to be released on their own recognizance.

That third week of June 1983 must have been a strange week for John Landis. The *Los Angeles Times* carried a banner headline, "*Twilight Zone* Indictments, Director, Two Others Charged in Film Deaths." At the same time, it was also a week of wild success. The arraignment of the *Twilight Zone* defendants on June 24, 1983, ironically took place on the same day Warner released the TZ movie in theaters across the country. *Trading Places* was not only drawing crowds but received respectable praise from

Vincent Canby, the *New York Times* film critic, who called it "the funniest American comedy of the year to date." Canby wrote that in contrast to *Animal House* and *Blues Brothers* it showed that John Landis was capable of directing a comedy "of precise style as well as those that are accumulations of gargantuan often messy effects."

That morning the five defendants accompanied by their lawyers, struggled through a crush of reporters in the Criminal Court building. Ordinarily, booking is done in a police station, but the Hollywood party went up to an area on the 16th floor set aside for VIPs. After being finger-printed and having their mug shots taken, they made their way to Department 100 where a near riot broke out when reporters tried to get close to the director. *Trading Places* stars Ralph Bellamy and Don Ameche, the movie's "Duke brothers," present at the request of Landis' attorneys, helped make the arraignment a Hollywood event.

The mob streamed into the courtroom where they heard Judge Ronald M. George inform the defendants that as a result of the grand jury finding a "true bill," Landis, Folsey, Allingham, Wingo and Stewart were indicted on multiple counts and would be booked under Case A391583. It was the first time Dorcey Wingo had seen or heard from the other film makers since the morning of the crash. After pleading not guilty the defendants were released on their own recognizance and scheduled to go to trial within 60 days. On August 5 they appeared before Judge George again to inform the court that all five elected to have a preliminary hearing and that they would appear in the courtroom on a selected date later in the year. Soon thereafter John Landis flew to London to vacation and resume work on a script by Ron Koslow, *Into the Night*, a project he'd started just before the TZ movie, his first serious departure from comedy.

The decision by the authorities not to draw attention to Landis' partners meant that Warner Bros. and Spielberg got off with very little in the proceedings. Spielberg only sent a one-line letter to the NTSB. Dick Vane's grand jury alibi on the dolls let off Marshall. Warner got off by its executives' portrayal of Landis as an independent. Their impunity, however, was not to be total. Marshall and Warner, though spared indictment, were still deeply enmeshed in the tragedy. Though the investigators accepted Marshall's alibi, they wanted him as a witness against John Landis, while Warner Bros. found itself still very much part, if not the essential part, of the disastrous business at Indian Dunes.

Along with Landis and the others, the studio was still a defendant in the civil cases and liable for millions of dollars. Again, the issue as to who should pay for the criminal cases put Warner in conflict with both its insurer and the Landis group. The wrangling and the eventual agreement between the two corporations – Warner and Travelers – were classic examples of the way in which insurance companies and their big clients work together to minimize their exposure when confronted by giant damage claims.

The studio's insurance covered the civil case costs and the actual damages which might arise from the claims of the three victims' families. However, the criminal case costs and possible "punitive damages" were not covered by the policy Warner held with the Travelers insurance company or the coverage that was provided by another carrier. In a straightforward way Warner wanted Travelers to pay for the criminal case costs of the Landis group. Warner argued that in the long run it might cost the insurance companies more if Landis lost the criminal case. In that event, his conviction on involuntary manslaughter would undoubtedly increase the value of the claims made by the Le, Chen and Morrow families against the studio.

Everything depended on what investigators in the case could turn up. If the prosecutor wanted to make the involuntary manslaughter charge stick, he had to nail down the question of whether the director foresaw the potential for danger on the set either before he hired the kids or while he worked them during the film's shooting. Kesselman sought to prove "foreseeability," a burden of proof greater than that required in civil cases in which the victims only had to show "liability" in order to get a judgment in their favor. "Foreseeability" formed the legal basis of criminal negligence. As opposed to general liability, a guilty verdict in a criminal case concerns the situation where someone has knowledge by which he is able to foresee the possibility that his conduct might result in death or loss of limb.

Immediately following the indictments, Bill Vaughn of O'Melveny met with top claims officials from Travelers to discuss the fees of four of the five defendants, not including the pilot; Wingo's employer, Western Helicopter, was covered by a different insurer, Houston Casualty. Vaughn felt that under California law the conviction of a defendant in a criminal case could be used to establish the facts against the defendant in a later civil action. For this reason, Vaughn was able to justify his request that Travelers pay for the criminal defense.

The insurance company was reluctant. It had paid fees to Harland Braun up until the indictment. Vaughn argued that following the indictments both his client Warner and its insurer Travelers had even more compelling reasons to continue supporting a vigorous defense on the criminal charges. It was Vaughn's belief that Travelers' willingness to continue paying the criminal fees, which were, it should be remembered, not covered by the insurance policy, would help maintain the fragile united front. Vaughn noted how in the eleven months since the accident the four defendants whose lawyers had been paid by Travelers had formed a "loose but effective alliance."

Concerned about the criminal case being lost to the possibility of one or more of the defendants going to the DA (there was already a serious rift with Dorcey Wingo), Vaughn made it clear that money for the criminal defense was the only way to prevent this from happening. Vaughn maintained that without Travelers or Warner it was probable that only John Landis would be able to hire a first-rate criminal attorney. He doubted that Folsey, Allingham and Stewart could do the same; in fact, Allingham and Stewart were said to be short of funds. As to the necessity for Warner's behind-the-scenes posture, Vaughn explained to Travelers that the studio was in a bind: if it didn't pay, Warner would be criticized throughout the industry for not standing behind those it had retained to make the TZ movie; if the studio openly paid for the criminal defense it might be seen as embracing the conduct of the defendants.

It was not lost on either Warner or Travelers that sensational publicity surrounding the criminal case could result in disastrously high judgments later at the time of the civil trials. The amount of Travelers' exposure, however, was limited by the $1 million ceiling on its policy with Warner. The New England based insurers knew that any huge monetary judgments won in a civil trial by the families of the three victims could be directly assessed against Warner. It was widely believed among insurance executives that the studio was directly vulnerable to potential punitive damages because of its involvement in the handling of the children.

Many financial questions between the insurer and the movie company remained unresolved. However, a far-reaching united front consisting of the criminal defendants, the studio and the insurance companies congealed less than a month following the 1983 indictments. At a remarkable meeting of the lawyers representing the defendants in the civil actions, the Landis legal phalanx successfully secured a formal alliance to combat its criminal and civil adversaries.

Present at the meeting in the offices of O'Melveny & Myers were Bill Vaughn; Stan Belkin, Warner's in-house lawyer; Landis' civil attorneys,

251

Eugene Wooley and Marty Rose; Landis' personal attorney John Diemer; Frank Marshall's attorney Richard Rosen, and representatives of the insurance carriers, Travelers, and for Western Helicopter, as Wingo's employer, Houston Casualty. Of all the key movie people named as defendants in the civil lawsuits only Steven Spielberg's attorneys, Gang, Tyre and Brown, communicated directly with Warner and were not present.

A surprising degree of unanimity prevailed at this meeting. Formal discovery among the co-defendants that might produce unfavorable evidence in the case, like depositions and interrogatories, was forbidden. A gentleman's agreement was secretly hammered out in O'Melveny's office. It assured that the attorneys for the Morrow, Chen and Le families, as well as the district attorney's office, would not become aware of any of the differences that existed among Landis, Marshall, Spielberg and the studio. To the same end the lawyers agreed to hold off all cross-complaints against each other and that those already on file would be placed on the back burner.

The civil cases had sensationalistic value and there was a consensus among the lawyers that they should be settled as soon as possible. O'Melveny's Bill Vaughn, representing the studio, took the hard line, arguing that even though sensationalistic, the cases of the three victims ultimately were ordinary death claims. Landis' civil expert Eugene Wooley stressed the aggravating factors arising from the *Dillon v. Legg* precedent; the "emotional distress" case which established the legal principle that because of the fact that the parents of Myca and Renee actually witnessed their children die in front of their eyes they were entitled to a larger recovery than was ordinarily recommended as part of the typical wrongful death claim.

A number of money figures were thrown about. One of the dozen-or-so attorneys conjectured that the Morrow daughters' case might be worth as little as $250,000. There was general agreement that the Chen and Le cases were worth about $1 million each. Though large, these figures were anticipated. But what the insurance carriers, and especially Warner, feared far more was the potential for punitive damages. The main difference between punitive and actual damages lay in that the former was usually not determined by the conventional loss-of-earnings formulas or economic facts of the case, but rather by the purely emotional impact the children's deaths would have on a jury. Unlike the actual damages that a jury might award the parents, which all defendants' lawyers agreed were in the low 1 millions, there was no telling how much a jury might award in punitive damages. A jury might decide to "punish" the studio, Landis and Spielberg and teach them a lesson.

After months of haggling among the attorneys, on the eve of the preliminary hearing in late 1983, Landis and Warner came to a final understanding with the studio's compromise to participate in funding the continuing criminal defense costs. The studio insisted, however, that its role remain confidential.

Intense negotiations had developed between the film director and the studio as the result of the real threat that if the studio refused to pay for his criminal defense Landis would sue. Vaughn's lieutenant, Scott Dunham, urged Behr not to pursue the litigious road because the "publicity would be unfavorable." Behr did not want publicity either, and in a memo he welcomed Warner's decision to pay the ongoing criminal defense fees as a "turning point." But Warner cautioned Behr that it was not prepared to write a blank check for the director and his co-defendants.

The one defendant not covered under the various arrangements between Warner, Travelers and the Landis group was Dorcey Wingo. Bitter, seemingly irreconcilable differences divided them. Angry at the attempts to blame him, Wingo had filed a lawsuit against Warner and Twilight Zone Productions. Wingo's insurance company, Houston Casualty, further aggravated the situation between the pilot and the film makers by hiring Eugene Trope from a prominent Westside legal firm best known for its divorce cases. Trope lent a sharp contrast to the dapper Century City and Hollywood lawyers on the case. With his rotund figure, baroque head and trim pointed goatee, Trope was distinct for bringing to the courtroom the flavor of turn-of-the-century Vienna. Trope was portly, graying, vested, collared, studded, fully suited with fob and chain. For reasons none of the other criminal lawyers could explain, he was apparently chosen as Wingo's attorney for being a noted civil attorney with a prestigious name and experience in the aviation field. However, he had little experience in criminal law and, as a result, Eugene Trope would become a byword for bumbling, the stock figure in a *Twilight Zone* comedy of errors.

In what appeared to be a direct collision course with John Landis, the civil attorneys hired to represent Wingo planned to prove that the director bore full responsibility for the crash. Their search for witnesses most critical of Landis' behavior quickly led to Steve Lydecker's North Hollywood home. One of Wingo's civil attorneys noted in a memo having obtained information which "may be helpful in showing that Landis is guilty of involuntary manslaughter." With the preliminary hearing fast approaching,

Wingo's attorneys felt they had a good case, for they discovered a witness, overlooked by Kesselman's grand jury, even more damaging to Landis than Lydecker.

A matronly lady, Virginia Kearns like Alpha Campbell was one of the few people connected with the production with whom Vic Morrow had developed a friendship. As his hairdresser she kept close to Morrow; she had to keep his hair looking the same from scene to scene. She was angry because she felt Morrow had been pressured by the young director into doing the hazardous stunt rather than letting stunt coordinator Gary Mc-Larty take his place. She believed the rumor on the set that John Landis had talked Vic into doing the job himself as the chance to make his big comeback. She had spent a year and three months trying to forget the accident. "I had very bad nightmares; I was very close to the accident," she told the pilot's attorneys when they contacted her.

She had been one of the last to have spoken with the actor before he died. The next day she recorded notes of her recollections. She told Wingo's attorneys that in her final conversation with Vic he had been extremely nervous. Suspecting that people on the set were high on cocaine, he kept going around and looking into people's eyes. He first went up to Wingo and looked into the pilot's eyes. "I think he's straight," he reported to Virginia. She then asked if he had checked Landis' eyes, "Did you see them?" Vic said, "Yes. They're pinpointed. The son-of-a-bitch is crazy."

Kearns said she had the opportunity to observe Landis and substantiate that his eyes were pinpoints.

That evening she had firsthand experience with the supercharged director when he sat down for a haircut. After trimming his hair – "I declined doing the beard" – she turned the frenetic personality over to her friend, Melanie Levitt, the makeup artist. "I let Melanie do it and it took almost 45 minutes because he couldn't sit still long enough in the chair for her to do a really good job." When Wingo's attorney wondered whether perhaps all the pressure had simply made the director nervous, Virginia countered brusquely. "There's a difference between nervousness and craziness. I thought Landis was crazy. I am sorry." She recalled that he was extremely "hyper," with arms flying at all times. "I would have to say he was totally psyched out," smiling one second and screaming the next, she recalled, Landis couldn't sit still for a second.

Kearns characterized the Landis set as having been for her a place where everything was "overdone." She said Vic told her that he thought Landis was re-enacting Vietnam "for real."

Vic had mentioned to her one particularly frightening scene in the Vietnam jungle sequence when he shared the make-believe Santa Clara swamp with a live python while hiding from the Viet Cong. Even John Landis, who maintained that he was fearless throughout the explosions in the final scenes, admitted in a highly confidential moment to his attorneys that, frankly, being next to the big python in the water had him rattled. "It was the only time I feared for my own safety," he said, "when the snake got away and came toward us, we went, Whoaa." But Vic was terrified, then angry. He complained to friends that he had a skin allergy that was aggravated by being in water, but that John Landis made him stand in the river until the snake was ready.

Everything was "overdone." Virginia gave other examples when the super-realism turned frightening: the gun fire in the water ("He used real bullets"); the Ku Klux Klan flame gag ("Gary McLarty almost got burned because they wanted a couple of seconds longer"); the Nazi sequence in which a fire broke out while people were locked in the railroad car ("If somebody hadn't screamed, 'Get 'em out of there!' they could all have died").

But there was one element pertaining to that last night in the desert dunes which was difficult for Kearns to convey to the pilot's attorneys. No one who hadn't been there that night could have a sense of the atmosphere of eeriness and foreboding on the *Twilight Zone* set, of a reality that threatened to dissolve at any moment under some horrific freak of man or nature. "Everybody felt uncomfortable about the whole situation," the matronly lady recalled. She thought of the "Dodge girl" that was decapitated by a movie crane during the shooting of a TV commercial. Vic kept ruminating about his experience on the Combat series, remarking each time that there had never been an accident.

He was nervous, Kearns remembered. "This didn't feel right to him."

Virginia Kearns' stinging account supported the pilot in his lawsuit which held the director responsible for the crash. After all of Landis' finger-pointing at Wingo it redressed the balance for him. Nonetheless it still did not erase the conclusion that Wingo had been so eager to fly in a Spielberg movie that he had himself skimped certain cautions normally taken by a pilot. Strictly from the FAA standpoint, he should have gotten a waiver for the explosives scenes, since, in accordance with regulations, every pilot at the time was required to prepare an operation plan for any stunt-type movie performance in which he was involved.

Prior to his first flight Wingo never had a detailed meeting with the special effects crew. He admitted to NTSB investigators that he had talked with Paul Stewart only the week before the Indian Dunes filming. He had no flight manual with him as required by FAA regulations; there were no proper seat belts and the chopper's torque meter was not functioning. Most importantly, Wingo could not deny that as a pilot he had been put on notice after the evening's second flight, the rage scene. He even told the NTSB, "It was a risky thing to film." Yet he took no steps to ensure greater safety. His attorneys could only explain the pilot's damaging compromises as the result of chaos on the set and intimidation by the director.

Curiously, Wingo's lawyers found that everybody had heard the story of Vic's big comeback. Even the pilot was led to believe that the final scene was designed to help Vic Morrow's career. Wingo was told by Dan Allingham that in the exploding village scene, "John was going to recuperate Vic Morrow (sic), that his career had been sagging a little bit and that he had always sort of been a bad guy." Wingo was told that Vic would still be a "bad guy" throughout the movie "until the very end when these two children showed up at the village.

"He was going to save them and give him redeeming social value," was the way Dorcey Wingo explained it, "And it would help his career and it would make a great movie."

But even Wingo could see after meeting Vic for the first time on the set that the actor appeared far from pleased. Morrow was cold and wrapped in a blanket and to Wingo "he looked tired and unhappy." The pilot's last encounter with Morrow was part of that eeriness Virginia Kearns felt so vividly that last night of shooting. It occurred during one of the many last-minute adjustments Landis made to intensify the excitement in the final scene. The director surprised Wingo by appearing with the show's star to make one last request of the pilot who'd already been shaken during the near fatal rage scene.

It was around 1 A.M., after "lunch." Vic himself came to Wingo with a big bamboo stick in his hands and said, "You know, it would really work for the scene if I could throw this stick at the helicopter as part of my rage."

Wingo saw John Landis standing not too far away with a script in his hand, "riveted on what Vic was telling me," the pilot recalled.

Dorcey Wingo was flattered by the attention from the star and tried to be diplomatic.

"Well, Vic, you know, if you were to hit the rotor system of this aircraft it would work its way into the tail rotor … it would bring the helicopter right down on your head."

The pilot heard a loud outcry expressing scorn from the bearded director. "Fuck it! Fuck it! Forget it. We won't do it." And he saw Landis turn around and walk off.

"And Vic smiled," Wingo remembered, "turned around and walked off."

36

A Green Card for Trudy

Others besides Virginia Kearns acknowledged that feeling of the unexpected. It was in the air, it seemed, mixed with the gas vapors. A soundman on the set named Roger Pietschmann, put a wireless microphone on Morrow for the 11:30 scene. The soundman said he thought he heard the tired actor mutter to himself.

"He would not stand still. He was pacing back and forth. It was like he thought something was wrong."

Among the very last of the crew to see Vic before he died was the show's makeup artist, Melanie Levitt. Just before the final shot, while standing in the fume-laden village, she had admonished Elie Cohn for smoking on the set because of the gasoline. She saw Vic pick up the children to test their weight. Her last words to the actor were jokingly, "I'll send flowers." The makeup lady, like the hairdresser, had observed his nervousness and concern about drug use on the set. "Please send flowers," Vic answered enigmatically.

Morgan Renard, the still photographer whom Vic had befriended on the set, was shocked to see Morrow's fatalism before the final scene.

"The man was completely physically, emotionally exhausted. He looked like he'd been through a goddamn war." Working for the young director had drained the old actor. Moments before the final scene he shrugged to Morgan, "He can't do anything else but kill me."

Morgan Renard had been close witness to the python incident. The photographer had felt sorry for Vic standing in the river behind some bushes, concealing himself from Viet Cong, irritated, for Renard heard him shout to the director, "Come on, let's get it, it's cold in here. Let's roll."

Trudy, Vic's English girlfriend, writing Alpha Campbell from England after Morrow's death, indignantly related the python incident: "He (Vic) thought something was very wrong on the set. But he couldn't put his finger on it. The stunts bothered him. Especially with the shotguns. Did you know Alpha, they had real bullets? That made him very angry... Then when Landis said to Vic, did he mind waiting, while he finished filming with the snake, because it was getting cold and stiff? Never mind Vic being in water a couple of hours and then having to wait another two hours to do a shot that took five minutes. So you see Alpha, Vic was not happy. He really thought something was going on."

Before his death Vic Morrow was planning to direct a movie in which Trudy would star. It was a low-budget film called Chained Heat. His old pal Billy Fine, who was going to try to get Trudy a green card, put it together. Movie packager/promoter and aging Hollywood enfant terrible, Billy Fine was well-known about town. His packaging credits included *Hedda Gabler*, which got its star Glenda Jackson a 1974 Academy Award nomination for Best Actress, and Charles Bronson's *Death Wish II*, among many others.

Fine had scheduled dinner with Vic and Trudy after that final Thursday night filming. Speaking with Vic earlier that evening he heard the actor grumble, "pissed" that the production was delayed another day, Fine remembered, because "his gums were in bad shape."

Afterwards, the shameless eulogies at Vic's funeral which tried to portray his friend's final hours as having been happy only reinforced Fine's suspicions of the circumstances which led Vic to do the final scene himself. "At his age Vic didn't like doing his own stunts." Fine believed that Morrow thought there was going to be a stunt double.

Vic also told his business manager and attorney Alvin Green about his fears during the *Twilight Zone* filming. "Between the drinking and the coke on the set it was pretty bad," Green remembered. I wanted to pull him off the set as late as that Thursday. But Vic said, 'I've only got one more day to go, and then it's over.'" Green explained that under his contract Vic had just cause to walk off. However, it was an important picture for Vic because it was a "Spielberg" picture, and Vic didn't walk off.

Like Billy Fine, Al Green also suspected that there was considerable evidence to show that Landis had pressured Vic to do the final scene without a stuntman. The film's official shooting schedule clearly showed that the exploding village scene called for a stuntman in the column "Cast and Atmosphere" marked:

DBL

Bill

This meant that a double would be used for Morrow. It supported the view held by many that at the last moment, even though he always denied it, John Landis pressured Vic to lend his own person to the director's drive for superrealism – the hard-bitten close-up of Bill framed against the background of thrilling explosions, the "wall of fire."

The most damaging evidence to show that the aging actor didn't really know until the end what was planned by the director in the final scene was contained in a key conversation overheard the day before the fatal shot. Like so much about the five-year case that never surfaced, only the movie director's private investigators, and not the authorities, discovered the existence of this revealing vignette. Witnessed by the set greensman, Jerry Cutten, it concerned a discussion between the 1st AD and Landis in which the greensman overheard Elie Cohn propose, "Let's not tell Vic that we're going to have explosions." According to highly-confidential notes circulated among the phalanx, Cutten felt that John Landis objected to the suggestion only because, in the greensman's words, many times actors "just freak out when something happens if they don't know about if, '

That, obviously, would ruin the shot.

Just as in the *Twilight Zone* movie, the *Twilight Zone* case was filled with special effects. Not, however, meant for visual presentation on screen these special effects were coded in legal clauses. The special effects were not deafening fireballs but contracts of silence.

While settlement discussions with the Chens and Les quickly reached a stalemate, talks with the Morrow girls, Carrie Morrow and Jennifer Jason Leigh, moved fast. Aware that sensationalism and publicity gave the girls' case a higher visibility, the movie attorneys were especially eager to work out an agreement. John Landis' civil lawyers, Kern & Wooley, underscoring the publicity value of the Morrow heirs, encouraged settlement sooner rather than later. One memo circulated among the phalanx warning that a history of mental instability of one of the Morrow heirs might interfere with a smooth settlement.

So, with the approach of the preliminary hearing at the end of '83 the issue became urgent. Landis' civil lawyers felt that if the judge held over the defendants at the prelim to go to trial the Morrow girls' claims would actually increase in value. Landis' main civil attorney wrote Behr, after reviewing the films of the crash, "I'm concerned that the cases might have a higher value than initially evaluated if the films are shown to the trier of fact." Behr went along with the recommendation provided the settlement discussions were kept secret from the public.

As the actual settlement with the actor's daughters neared, Al Green, Vic's long-time lawyer and manager, faded out of the picture. Green still followed the case as an interested party; he had written Vic's final will. Vic left everything to his eldest daughter Carrie, while leaving a symbolic $100 to Jennifer, his estranged daughter. Green had taken care of Carrie during difficult periods in her adolescence and had been first to inform her of her father's death. Originally, he assumed that he would represent her in Vic's death. But following the weekend of Vic's funeral Carrie changed her mind and told Green, one of her father's pallbearers, "Jennifer wants me to go to Barbara's lawyer" (Barbara Turner, Vic's ex-wife, and the girls' mother).

The new lawyer was Sydney Irmas. Within three months after proposing it to the movie lawyers Irmas shrank down his original $2.75 million settlement demand to a mere $840,000 for both girls, the amount to be deposited in a Merrill-Lynch account that would bear interest and pay the girls accordingly. The movie makers jumped at this relatively mild settlement. They even attached to it extraordinary conditions which by going far beyond the normal terms in assuring confidentiality of the negotiations revealed more than the usual Hollywood paranoia over bad publicity. When considered alongside the payment schedule, the secrecy provisions of the settlement bought the silence of Vic Morrow's two daughters well into the next century.

Although the financial figures favored Carrie, the real beneficiary was the younger Jennifer who would have been cut off with $100 if it had gone according to Vic's will. Now, under the hastily worked-out terms, each immediately received $81,000, in addition to a $2,000 monthly payment for the rest of their lives. In 1994 they would each receive another $50,000 and in the year 2004 Carrie would receive $275,000 and Jennifer $75,000. But in exchange the girls agreed to harsh provisions designed, it seemed, to make it appear that Vic Morrow never existed; the Morrow girls agreed not to "in any way participate in or contribute to any public discussion about the accident." Perhaps even more Draconian was the condition which practically compelled them to efface their father from their own lives by not talking in public, "nor contribute to other publicity concerning or in any way relating to the personal relationship between and among plaintiffs and their father, Vic Morrow."

In marked contrast to the censorship provisions of the actual settlement with Morrow's heirs, the public release was a watered-down statement. Landis and Spielberg, even though they were parties to the settlement, were not mentioned by name:

> The settlement was made without any admission of liability or wrong-doing by any of the defendants. Carrie Morrow and Jennifer Jason Leigh as well as the defendants wish to avoid the time, expense, lengthy delay and emotional trauma involved in a trial.

Unlike the Morrow girls, Sydney Irmas, their lawyer who put together this deal, did not wait until the next century. He took his fee, $175,000, right away. When Vic's lawyer Al Green heard about the settlement he was shocked and amazed. He assessed Carrie's case at least "worth a minimum of $4 million and as much as up to $5 million."

37

MRS. BEASLY'S COOKIES

The indictments of Landis, Folsey and Allingham had no adverse effect on the continued upward mobility of their careers. Just as the grand jury had earlier played against the giant box-office success of *Trading Places,* the arraignment was set against the background of Landis' fresh success, a film project with Michael Jackson, the million-dollar music-video blockbuster *Thriller,* as it turned out, to become part of the biggest-selling record and video package in the industry's young history. *Thriller,* which has Jackson turning into a werewolf with corpses and ghouls rising from their graves, was inspired by Landis' 1981 *An American Werewolf in London,* featuring Rick Baker's Academy Award winning work. Landis and Folsey produced it with Jackson. It was released a few months after the arraignment in November 1983.

Michael Jackson first approached Landis about the *Thriller* project because of his relationship with makeup wizard Rick Baker whose intimate relationship with John Landis since the days of *Schlock!* was well-known throughout the industry. In making the deal with Jackson, Baker's loyalty to Landis was an important bargaining chip. Landis' lawyer, who also represented Baker, made a deal whereby Landis and Baker came as a package. Landis demanded that he share the credits and part of the profits with Jackson. The high-profile project could not have come at a better time for Folsey either, and for the little wheel on the troika, Dan Allingham, who worked on *Thriller,* again as UPM. The set on which *Thriller* was shot was visited by a steady stream of Jackson's friends, such as Jackie Onassis, making it acceptable to shake hands with Hollywood's only director ever to be charged with manslaughter.

In a strategy worked out at Jackson's Encino home, Landis and Jackson decided to open *Thriller* in a double bill with Walt Disney's classic *Fantasia.* Though it might have seemed a clever idea to ride on the Disney name and put John Landis' new release in the company of Hollywood legend, the strategy was a bust. The family-oriented *Fantasia* clashed with the brutal imagery of *Thriller.* It not only created bad publicity for the director but again cast serious doubts on his judgment. When Rick Baker's big-screen *Thriller* werewolf transformation scene first began showing in Westwood just after Thanksgiving 1983, Folsey and Landis were shocked to see screaming children followed by angry parents flee into the lobby. On Folsey's suggestion the theatre manager posted a warning, alerting parents to the possible danger of the short subject *Thriller* to children. In addition, each screening was preceded by an unusual personal message from the theatre manager speaking from the front of the auditorium:

"*Thriller* is not suitable and is very scary for children and they should be taken to the lobby for the duration of the movie to eat popcorn."

The *Hollywood Reporter* quipped that the booking of *Thriller* with the Disney classic had all the wisdom of booking the *Texas Chainsaw Massacre* with *Bambi*.

While Landis worked on *Thriller*, Tom Budds ran down one of his more intriguing new witnesses. Prosecutor Gary Kesselman had impressed on Budds that Landis' former personal secretary had firsthand knowledge of Landis' involvement in the cover-up. When Budds first contacted Alpha Campbell she no longer worked for Landis. He had fired her just before the grand jury while he was in New York filming *Trading Places*.

Since the days of the crash Alpha had been witness to many strange occurrences in Landis' Universal bungalow. Three weeks after the crash, Alpha confronted one of the early mysteries. Someone had entered the bungalow over the weekend and removed the phone messages from the director's daily log covering the period of the crash for the entire month of July and the first two weeks of August. She noted in the daily phone log: *July 1 to August 13, 1982 all messages gone (disappeared) over weekend.* She told Landis and he casually promised he would take care of it.

The director's first attempts to dispose of Alpha had met with failure. Landis couldn't easily fire her because she was protected by her union at Universal. At last, he called from New York and vowed to Universal executive Sean Daniel and his assistant Bruce Berman that he would not come back from New York until they got rid of Alpha. Shortly thereafter, Alpha's supervisor told her that Landis wanted her off the job and that if she decided to fight, the supervisor added ominously, it would become "very dirty." Bowing under pressure, the secretary who once regaled Landis with stories about working with Alfred Hitchcock, finally sought transfer to another position. From her supervisor she learned that the reason for all the ruckus was the upcoming "trial," referring to the grand jury.

It was not until more than a year after the crash that Tom Budds first called Alpha at Universal Studios. He asked if she would answer a few questions. At first reluctant, Alpha cited the pressures of a new assignment and the fact that she would be going on vacation soon. Moments later, uncertain and frightened, she called Universal executive Bruce Berman. Since it was her understanding that Berman had taken her off the job in Landis' office, she informed him about the call from the homicide man. Berman wasted no time. He told her that he would get back to her. But Berman did not call back. Instead, one of Landis' lawyers did. Speaking on behalf of Joel Behr, lawyer John Diemer dissuaded her from cooperating with the police, telling her that the sheriff's department couldn't force her to be interviewed. Diemer urged Alpha not to be afraid and that Leonard Levine, a criminal lawyer, would call her and further explain the situation.

Levine called a half hour later. He advised her on how to deal with Budds. In her neat secretarial way, she recorded the lawyer's instructions in her notes: "You do not want to speak to him before you go on vacation... I should call the Sheriffs Department on Monday, as promised and tell him THAT I CANNOT MEET WITH HIM. I AM TOO PRESSURED WITH TIME. I DO NOT WISH TO SPEAK TO HIM AT THIS TIME IN THE CASE. OR, SORRY, I APPRECIATE YOUR DESIRE TO TALK TO ME ABOUT MR. LANDIS, BUT I DO NOT WISH TO TALK TO YOU ABOUT THIS CASE. OF COURSE, IF YOU WANT TO SUBPOENA ME, IT IS YOUR RIGHT DO SO AND I'LL OBEY." (sic)

Alpha went on vacation and at first did not cooperate with the authorities.

Alpha Campbell's real name was Del Monte. At the time she joined Landis she was in her mid-fifties. She had come to America from Germany after World War II while still a teenager with a career already behind her, begun at 16 when she published her first novel, as a French-German authoress. She frequented Hollywood literary circles that included Aldous Huxley and members of the expatriate film colony. Before he fired her, John Landis had originally been anxious to have her as his secretary because she had typed scripts for Alfred Hitchcock. She had not been amused by her cocky young boss who referred to her as a "Nazi."

Alpha's cooperation with investigators did not come about smoothly. In his customary style Sheriff Budds initially nearly botched the breakthrough. A personal visit from the deputy district attorney brought Landis' former secretary around, and Kesselman was amazed to find a wealth of information. For the first time many vital production documents fell into the hands of the investigators. Alpha Campbell told Kesselman about suspicious activities in the office after the accident, boxes moving between Warner and the Universal lot and Century City, the destruction and concealment of scripts, and the disappearance of Landis' phone records. She supplied Kesselman with copies of important documents, including all four drafts of the script. Kesselman decided to put Alpha on as a witness at the prelim and announced his choice as was required of him to Landis' attorney.

Just a month before the prelim was scheduled to begin a colorful package arrived at Alpha's desk at Universal. It was a fancy box of Mrs. Beasly's Cookies from a Malibu bakery patronized by the status-conscious Hollywood crowd. Alpha asked the messenger who delivered it to wait. She opened the envelope and read the card: "Merry Xmas, With Much Love," signed John, Rachel and Deborah.

"It was an insult to my intelligence. First he throws me out and then he sends me cookies." Alpha fumed. She returned the gift with a note to the director: "I have accepted our differences, Why don't you?"

Four years later, at the time of the trial, Alpha caustically observed that she hadn't had an executive position at Universal Studios since.

Following the indictments, one key witness, Spielberg's closest associate, the most senior production official on the set that night-remained obdurate in his refusal to cooperate with Budds. Budds first realized he'd have trouble with Frank Marshall when in late 1983 he went to The Burbank Studios to serve him with a subpoena.

At Marshall's office he was met by Bonnie Radford's sister, Mary Radford, at the time Frank Marshall's assistant. When Budds asked to see Bonnie or Frank, Mary Radford told him they weren't in. After many similar failures to serve Marshall the subpoena, Budds at last arranged for sheriff's investigators to stake out Marshall's house in Santa Monica. When that failed, he called Marshall's attorney Rick Rosen. Budds learned that Marshall was off in England working on a film. The attorney promised that as soon as his client returned, he would notify Budds.

Just before the prelim Budds received a tip from an inside source at Universal: Marshall had returned. Angrily he called Rosen and reminded him of his promise. Rosen reneged.

"There's little question in my mind that Marshall didn't want to be interviewed," Budds concluded. "We went to his place of business, we went to his home. We spoke to his attorney several months back, and we waited for his return from England." When the controversy reached the pages of *Variety* – "*Twilight Zone* Witness Still Missing" – Rosen commented to the Hollywood journal, "Frank isn't running from anybody. He's busy working out of town."

This began Budds' three-year hunt for Spielberg's partner and elusive friend.

Joel Behr, the Hollywood lawyer, while remaining grand strategist, yielded to Harland Braun in the criminal court. This was indisputably Braun's territory and the preliminary hearing turned out to be his finest hour. He had been on the case for 1 1/2 years while Joel Behr called the shots. At the prelim he finally got to do what he was paid for – to defend his client in open court.

Harland Braun was a legal hard-charger. He was not meant for soft-footed counselor behind-the-scenes. His rapier wit required a courtroom setting. He was known for aggressive cross-examining. Like a relentless hammer he humiliated and embarrassed witnesses and beat them into inconsistencies. Judge Brian Crahan, the prelim's presiding judge, had once before ruled in Braun's favor. This time Braun actually succeeded in getting some of the counts dismissed. The prelim was also where Braun first aired his ingenious new theory to explain the crash, an alternative to the debris theory cited by the NTSB that would become very big in the trial. As always he was generous to the media. They received ample quotes and plenty of barbs of mockery and ridicule of his opponent, prosecutor Gary Kesselman.

Granted at the behest of the defense, preliminary hearings in California determine whether the charges merit a trial. Even if the hearing were to fail the TZ defendants by not dropping the charges against them, Braun favored the "prelim." Unlike the grand jury, the prelim allows the defendants' lawyers to cross-examine witnesses while the judge decides whether or not to hold over the defendants for the actual trial. At the prelim the prosecutor has to show his hand. Besides defining the issues in the case and the evidence against Landis, the prelim would serve Braun, in addition, as a way of testing the impact of new facts to be used in the *Twilight Zone* defense, notably the "delamination theory." Joel Behr in his Century City office prepared for the prelim on two fronts. The first had to do with the new delamination theory.

Technical experts, brought in by the phalanx to try and explain the factors that had brought the helicopter down, intended to show that the director could not possibly have anticipated that the illusion-creating special effects could be so powerful as to blast a helicopter out of the sky. Off-the-record talks between the phalanx and NTSB investigators had pretty much established that the soon-to-be-published NTSB findings would indicate that debris from the No. 4 shoreline hut had damaged the tail rotor and caused the crash. As debris was a known and foreseeable hazard for a low-flying helicopter, and there was ample evidence that the helicopter pilot issued several warnings to the director about debris hazards, the anticipated NTSB findings did not bode well for a Landis defense based on unforseeability. However, with "delamination" Braun came up with the perfect alternative theory; a strange and unfamiliar word that would puzzle jurors and spectators in the trial, and prove very effective in the preliminary hearing.

While the new theory also held that the helicopter crash was caused by damage to the tail rotor, it did not blame debris, as the NTSB's Llorente had concluded; instead, the metal skin of the tail rotor had "delaminated," detached and separated from the blade because the adhesive which bonds the skin to the blade failed when exposed to the heat of the SFX explosives. As never in the annals of aviation history had there been a helicopter crash caused by delamination, not even during combat involving intense exposure to napalm, the theory "proved" that the accident was unforeseeable and not due to negligence. "Delamination" dominated the prelim and resurfaced during the trial as one of the main buoys of the defense.

On the second front the phalanx aimed to use the prelim to show how Landis' use of stunts and special effects did not depart from the custom and practice of Hollywood film making. George Folsey Jr. went to De Forest Research, a Hollywood company specializing in script research, looking for a list of motion pictures for possible use as evidence in a film montage. Braun worked with Folsey on this cinematic presentation designed to demonstrate how other film makers used screen illusion in scenes with explosions.

On the eve of the prelim, in a small editing room in North Hollywood, Folsey and Braun spent hours looking through reels of motion picture footage for scenes resembling that of the crash in Indian Dunes. They searched for the ideal clip from another movie that combined all three elements – a helicopter, explosives and kids. Unable to find the right combination, they settled on a montage with just the combination of helicopter and special effects alone. A 30-minute montage was assembled from four films: *Apocalypse Now*, *The Deerhunter*, *The Exterminator*, and *V*. This was eventually shown to Judge Crahan.

As Harland Braun mapped out other lines of defense, Joel Behr approved some and turned down others. Behr himself continued to be enthralled by having a famous director testify at the prelim on special effects and their role in creating film illusion. He arranged a meeting between Harland Braun and John Huston through one of his clients, producer Michael Fitzgerald, then producing the film adaption of Malcolm Lowry's *Under the Volcano*; Huston, in town cutting the film, though he had never met the young Landis, with characteristic feistiness declared himself willing to defend a fellow-director who had some problems with the authorities. Back in the 30s, Huston had himself had a run-in with the LA district attorney over the mysterious death of a young girl. Huston was never tried but the experience left him so shaken that he was unable to work for a year. It also left him a generous, if indiscriminate sympathy for a director in a similar plight.

John Huston and Harland Braun met at the Beverly Hills Hotel. America's grand old director was hooked up to an oxygen machine for his emphysema. He coughed at one point in the conversation and joked with a painful grin, "It's worse than it sounds."

John Huston had a rough-and-tumble way of talking about special effects. He bantered with Braun about the scene in the *African Queen* where Humphrey Bogart and Katherine Hepburn come out of the swamp covered with leeches. Huston insisted on the inevitability of danger on a movie set. Braun specifically remembered Huston's alarming description of an accident on his own set while filming in Japan when a series of boats broke loose, nearly killing the director and the crew. Huston as a witness, Braun noted, "was scary, too dangerous."

John Huston was Behr's only Hollywood choice. There were other witnesses that Braun wanted but Behr did not: Spielberg people and studio people; Warner president Terry Semel and Warner production chief Lucy Fisher; Frank Marshall, Fred Gallo and Bonnie Radford.

In California the prelim is usually no more than a quick formality, over and done within 10 or 20 minutes. But with the *Twilight Zone* case this pre-trial judicial proceeding entered a new dimension in which time stretched. It lasted a month and produced a fresh mountain of testimony, adding 20 volumes to the already staggering documentation concerning this extraordinary disaster on a movie set.

The prelim was memorable for the surprising introduction as evidence by the defense of a fourth clip of film footage which, like the fatal 2:20 shot, showed the combination of kids and explosives. Until this show-

269

ing John Landis had made a point of highlighting his own cleverness by ridiculing in private to his attorney the investigators' incompetence due to their failure to identify and impound the 9:30 shot; the first scene to be filmed the night of the crash, it was necessary from the standpoint of continuity to an understanding of the conclusion of the escape from the exploding village at 2:20. Raising it at the prelim was designed to cast doubt on the parents of the children who claimed that they were never told about the explosives in the fatal scene. If the parents were present for the explosion scene at 9:30, Behr reasoned, they must have had knowledge that their kids would be in a scene with explosives at 2:20.

But more poignantly, the prelim was marked by a series of exchanges between the cocky director and the "bulldog" prosecutor, by some very damaging testimony from one of Landis' own inner circle, as well as for the light it threw on the growing rift between Dorcey Wingo and John Landis.

Unexpectedly, some of the most damaging testimony came from Landis' close, longtime friend, script supervisor Kathryn Wooten. She testified to an incident, the existence of which, though already well-established, yet still had much mystery surrounding it; the fact that in the final seconds before the fatal scene Landis screamed through a bullhorn that people on the set stand up for the upcoming fireball display. Every investigator had made note of it, as it pointed to foreseeability, saying in effect that the director had to have known that the shot was dangerous.

The 1st AD Elie Cohn had minimized the significance of Landis' final communication with the spectators by telling investigators the director had told him it was done so that people could take the shock waves from the blast better. But much to Landis' dismay, under direct examination at the prelim, Kathryn Wooten recalled Landis' summons to spectators to be on their feet, "which he often said on films I've worked with him before, anything that had potential danger (sic)." Since there had been no similar warning to the spectators from the director at 11:30, the inference was that in his own mind the final shot was dangerous. Wooten at the end of her testimony seemed to indicate as much, saying that because 11:30 was a much smaller shot. "There: would really be no reason to tell anybody to move or stand up."

Braun asked for a brief recess before he began his cross-examination of the script girl who'd worked with Landis on *Kentucky Fried Movie, Animal House* and *Blues Brothers*. In the hallway, outside the presence of the judge and spectators, he was surprised to see his client fly at Wooten, enraged, cursing the script girl and shouting profanities at her because of her testimony. Some minutes later, back in the courtroom under Braun's cross-examination, Landis' last-minute warning to the crowd on the TZ set no longer signaled any particular danger to her. She now said that the director routinely made requests for people to stand up "whenever there is any action on the set like explosions or cars." After the hallway castigation from the director who was also her friend, she mentioned having heard such warnings spoken to her "many times before and by other directors."

Nevertheless, Braun did not escape his client's anger. In the cafeteria at lunch Landis humiliated his chief criminal counsel publicly, blaming him for not having "prepared" Wooten. Braun felt embarrassed.

Along with some of Landis' powerful studio friends like Universal's Sean Daniel and Paramount's Jeffrey Katzenberg, the preliminary hearing was attended in part by another personal friend, Berkeley psychologist Daniel Goldstine, who had a long-standing friendship with the director's closest confidant, Sean Daniel. As an expert in behavior, Goldstine used the prelim to observe Landis and make suggestions as to how his public persona might be modified.

The events at the prelim rattled Landis considerably and he became particularly offensive to prosecutor Kesselman. The contrast between a young, hip, high-living Hollywood director faced with a squarish-built dresser in flashy clothes, stacked heels and slicked hair, could not be more striking. Dressing style, like ethnic types, was one of the things upon which Landis invariably felt obliged to comment out loud. In the hallway Landis was heard joking with the bailiff that he should check Kesselman's high-heeled shoes for cocaine. The bailiff bantered back that he had to have "probable cause," to which Landis quipped, "Well, look at his tie. He must be stoned on cocaine." One time, hearing Landis taunt him as "the guy with the Cuban heels," Kesselman protested to one of the lawyers. "I wear Florsheim boots. You better get that guy under control."

When the prelim concluded, Judge Crahan, in his final decision, dropped counts 2 and 4. His decision let out Landis, Folsey and Allingham on the two manslaughter counts which were based on the principle that at the time the children were illegally hired by the threesome the danger was foreseeable. After a parade of witnesses and technical experts testified that debris alone had probably not caused the crash and that heat delamination was at least partly responsible, Braun's oratorical and legal skills carried the day for "delamination." Judge Crahan, however, bound over Landis and the two other defendants on counts 1, 3 and 5, the manslaughter counts based on criminal negligence on the set. The judge concluded:

> Finally, Mr. Landis with his quest for cinema verite directed the actors, as it were, including other principals, to demonstrate an effective conclusion to this film segment, which would be both noteworthy and memorable. In achieving such absolutism he appears to have gone beyond the realm of simple mechanical direction, but in fact set up, among other things, the combination of circumstances which in the final seconds of filming, caused death and destruction. There were ample warnings to these individuals prior to the 2:20 filming episode, which made their conduct from the time of such warnings, calculating, and unreasonable and therefore criminal in nature.

* * *

Right after the prelim, Harland Braun convinced Landis to get hold of Steven Spielberg. From his office at the Universal bungalow, with Braun standing by, Landis called up Spielberg and urged him to use his influence to have Frank Marshall come forward.

Spielberg told Landis that he would see what he could do.

38

A BASIC TRUTH OF FILMMAKING

For 2 1/2 years following the prelim the *Twilight Zone* trial was delayed by a series of legal maneuvers. A lengthy series of writs and appeals from both sides eventually took the case to the California Supreme Court. Meanwhile, a series of "continuances" granted by the court enabled John Landis to continue making movies. As a million-dollar-fee director his earnings climbed phenomenally. Just on *Twilight Zone: The Movie,* he split with Spielberg a little under a million from the first three months' revenues alone. The period between the prelim and trial brought John Landis nearly $5 million in director's fees.

After *Trading Places* and Michael Jackson's *Thriller* video, the following year was again a very busy one. A strong "personal" relationship with Paramount's young production executive, Dawn Steel, helped Landis and Folsey produce a movie for Paramount adapted from the famous Parker Brothers board game, *Clue,* directed by British film maker Jonathan Lynn, best-known in Britain for his popular television series, *Mr. Minister.* Starring Martin Mull and the woman whose name appeared on Alpha Campbell's list of the director's most frequently-called people, Colleen Camp, the seductive bikini-girl from *Apocalypse Now, Clue* failed to make any money.

Following the partially successful results at the prelim, even more legal funding was required. The cost of all these efforts was now being fully shouldered by Warner Bros., even though its spokesmen continued to decline to comment whether the studio paid for Landis' defense. The Travelers insurance company had paid half the defense costs up to the prelim and, according to their agreement with the studio, dropped out of the 50-50 deal. Although the officers at the insurance company admitted being impressed by the new findings, they noted dryly to Warner that as a result of the prelim the settlement values stemming from the deaths of Renee and Myca had increased. Warner's decision to continue disbursing money to the legal firms was set forth in communications between the lawyers. The studio desired not to have it appear within the industry that it was willing to abandon Landis, and as it perceived the results of the criminal trial to be binding on the civil cases, Warner became the single source from which the criminal lawyers received their fees.

More money from the studio allowed Behr to make fresh preparations. He enlarged the ranks by hiring new lawyers to formulate writs. Immediately after the prelim he appealed a portion of Judge Crahan's decision, filing a 995 motion to dismiss, on insufficiency of evidence, the three remaining counts, arguing that since delamination made the accident unforeseeable there should be no trial. At Behr's suggestion the famous Harvard lawyer and media figure, known to millions for rapid-fire legal opinions on ABC-TV, Alan Dershowitz, was brought aboard to help formulate the writs. Dershowitz had just won a great victory with the acquittal of Claus Von Bulow in a sensational New York society murder trial.

On the civil front O'Melveny's Bill Vaughn conducted hard-nosed negotiations on behalf of the studio with the redoubtable aircraft recovery specialist Ned Good, who represented Myca's parents. Any offer of less than a million would be seen as an insult to his clients and a declaration of war, Good forewarned. At the same time that Vaughn coordinated the efforts on behalf of Warner Bros., he made money offers to the Le and Chen families. The figure was deliberately low. It was hoped that any giant damage awards could be controlled by partially blaming the parents for being willing participants who understood the risk to their children. Vaughn's offer was for $500,000 to each family. Ned Good declared war.

As part of developing a successful strategy for the criminal trial the phalanx quietly argued its case among industry opinion-makers. At major studios John Landis had close supporters like Dawn Steel at Paramount, Jeffrey Katzenberg at Disney and Lucy Fisher at Warner, all of whom would hopefully echo Universal's Sean Daniel's message that Landis was unfairly put on trial for what was "obviously" a human catastrophe, "not a criminal act." Braun tried to establish in the mind of the public that Hollywood itself was being put on trial. The press quoted Braun that Landis was being persecuted solely because he was a successful director. Braun implied a shared fate by calling Hollywood "the biggest moving target in town."

Behind the scenes, Behr and Braun made this case vigorously to the Directors Guild of America. Braun had been told by Folsey and Landis that DGA president Gil Cates was sympathetic. For some time, the DGA had been struggling in its Sunset headquarters with a growing runaway production crisis and the gist of Braun's lobbying was that the *Twilight Zone* case additionally threatened to drive directors out of California.

Braun argued that what was happening to Landis jeopardized every director. Braun used a memorably pious phrase, "There but for the grace of God go I," in reminding guild members that what had happened to his client could happen to any director.

Joel Behr, meanwhile, advised Michael Franklin, national executive secretary of the DGA, that it was in the guild's best interest to support John Landis' efforts to have the NTSB drop from its final report the language it borrowed from the DGA statement on safety on the set. Specifically, Landis' point man sought to have both the NTSB and the DGA leadership retract its official position that "safety on the set is the director's responsibility." While not altogether successful at the DGA's executive level, Behr succeeded in convincing some of Hollywood's top directors that their fate depended on the outcome of the case. The names of these directors surfaced in a letter called "A basic truth of filmmaking," composed by Folsey and publicist Saul Kahan, and published in *Rolling Stone* magazine and the *Los Angeles Times*.

The letter was signed by 16 of the DGA's most prominent members, including Francis Ford Coppola, George Lucas, John Huston, Sidney Lumet, Billy Wilder, Fred Zinneman and Ron Howard. With the letter in hand Behr urged the DGA to issue an official guild statement for the purpose of convincing the NTSB that the substance of its approach to the director's responsibility for safety was misguided. He backed it up by the strong testimonial of the 16 top directors, among whom, hardly noticed at the time, the name of Steven Spielberg was missing.

The existence of blue-ribbon Landis support within the DGA and elsewhere merely reflected what had long been painfully apparent; to the extent that Hollywood was still unaware of the actual circumstances at Indian Dunes the night of the crash, the cover-up was a success. The DGA's own safety committee put off discussing the subject until after the trial. With the flow of information carefully controlled by Landis' legal phalanx, it was doubtful that any of the directors cast for cameos in Landis' films or signatory to Folsey's "basic truth" knew about the near miss at 11:30, or about the inexperienced helicopter pilot selected for budgetary considerations; about the special effects crew and alcohol, the intimidation by the director, or the full extent of the concealment of the kids. Like John Huston most directors accepted the tragedy as an industrial accident; not one of them had seen the fatal footage.

The decision to bind Landis over for trial had no effect on the filming or on the post-production work of *Into the Night*. Far from persecuting him, top city officials even stepped in so that Into the Night might have the LAX airport for location shooting of certain chase sequences. City commissioners had first rebuffed Landis, saying they didn't want the airport used for the shooting of terrorist scenes. But George Folsey Jr. pulled off a coup.

"I got Bradley to swing the deal," he recalled, referring to Los Angeles Mayor Tom Bradley. "Universal got me into Bradley's office."

The city reversed itself, giving over a portion of LAX to the making of John Landis' strange filmic statement.

39

MOCK JURORS

In early November 1984, two very different kinds of events occurred. Each was to have a far-reaching effect on two of the protagonists in the *Twilight Zone* case, defense attorney Harland Braun and his opponent, prosecutor Gary Kesselman.

The optimism that had followed Braun's success at the prelim was short-lived. Braun suffered a severe setback when the new judge, Gordon Ringer, after hearing arguments, rejected the 995 motion filed by Braun earlier to dismiss the remaining three manslaughter counts on insufficiency of evidence. The judge agreed, "This isn't nickelodeon time anymore"; the case should go to trial. The defeat of the new motion was in sharp contrast to the prelim where the judge kicked two of the five counts. In fact, the new judge reversed Judge Crahan's earlier ruling, restoring the two counts. The phalanx was back on square one. Delamination was apparently dead. All five counts again loomed at the trial.

Braun's prestige in the case never recovered. In the view of many, this blow in Judge Ringer's court foreshadowed his eventual fall from being the lead criminal counsel on the case and his final replacement by a new attorney. The days of his personal friendship with the director were over – no more invitations to be in Landis' movies; no more exchanges of gifts, like the game of Hollywood Trivial Pursuit the lawyer had given his client earlier that year; and no more yucking-it-up over Joel Behr's exaggerated hair-piece, the imposing blue bouffant which until then had always been good for a chortle between the lawyer and his famous client.

While for Braun this late LA autumn with its mild weather was a frustrating period nagged by professional defeat, for Gary Kesselman this same period spelled a more deeply felt personal humiliation.

In a seemingly unrelated event, on Saturday night, November 3, 1984, the LAPD raided in LA's Hispanic downtown a taxi-dance place, Club El Gaucho, where customers paid 25 cents a minute to dance with hostesses to live music. El Gaucho, one of ten licensed hostess dance clubs in the city, served no alcohol. In an earlier raid that year police had taken in hostesses for lewd conduct. In the latest raid, on the eve of Judge Ringer's important hearing, police arrested ten people, one for lewd conduct in one of the back rooms. All of them illegal aliens from Mexico and Central America, they were turned over to the Immigration & Naturalization Service. The name of one of the partners in the club was Abraham Mohammed-Issa. The other was Gary Kesselman.

Someone tipped the *Los Angeles Times* about the raid and the morning newspaper gave it headline billing. The police commissioner warned Kesselman that El Gaucho was a potential location for prostitution. (A bilingual agent dispatched by Landis' own investigator to look into the El Gaucho scandal wrote a report for the phalanx dispelling the idea that the taxi-dance place was a house of prostitution, epitomizing the girls, "In a word, they're dogs.") According to the police commissioner, the *Times* reported, the *Twilight Zone* prosecutor pledged to avoid lewd conduct and increase lighting in the dance hall, to remove curtained areas, and reconsider whether it was necessary for the club to have three television-viewing rooms at the back of the hall.

The effect of the raid on Kesselman's personal standing was devastating. The exposure of his connection with taxi-dancing destroyed his moral stature. But as his authority in court fell to zero, his predicament made for much merriment in the DA's office. Commonly heard in the hallways on the 16th floor of the Criminal Court building at the time was the joke, "Have you heard, Gary got a job dancing at the El Cid Club." Suddenly everyone felt entitled to be disrespectful and witty at his expense. Gary Kesselman felt humiliated.

He had no doubt that this attempt at character assassination was connected with his being prosecutor in the *Twilight Zone* case.

It was no secret that Kesselman had many reservations as to the commonly accepted version of certain elements in the case. He differed, for instance, in his version of what had happened to the film immediately following the crash. He told lawyers in the DA's office that, contrary to the story that the film had been exclusively in Warner's possession, he believed it was possible that Landis had gotten hold of it and altered it. Even before the El Gaucho fiasco his colleagues noted that he seemed "paranoid." Kesselman suspected that witnesses had been bought out from under him and that the specter of blacklisting had affected many of the potential witnesses. He complained that it was hard to get experts to testify because they were afraid. He was particularly upset about an "accident reconstruction expert" who suddenly withdrew from the investigation after receiving a telephone call from one of Landis' attorneys. He dropped dark hints of pressures, even suggesting that Landis had somehow influenced his superiors in the DA's office. After his latest humiliation in the case Kesselman confidentially voiced his belief to Tom Budds that Harland Braun was behind the raid.

Although it offered little comfort to the embarrassed prosecutor, Kesselman's bitter adversary, ironically, began to feel a similar insecurity about his position. There had been many disappointments with Braun's promises that the case would never go to trial. His victory at the prelim had lifted everybody's spirits, especially Folsey's and Allingham's, since on the dismissed counts 2 and 4 they were being let out of the case. But Judge Ringer's decision reversing the dismissal was a turning point. Braun's irrepressible optimism had gradually become a source of annoyance to Landis and Behr. They decided they needed a second opinion.

It was the first time Braun had the feeling that John Landis was dissatisfied with his handling of the case. Perhaps not coincidentally, he received the news on the day of the Ringer hearing, while driving back with Joel Behr from the court to the Universal studio lot to inform Landis of losing the motion.

Behr muttered while driving that John Landis was willing to go all over the country looking for another lawyer. As they got closer to Universal and the burden of bad news weighed proportionately heavier, Behr kept saying, "Landis is going to go crazy."

* * *

The year before the trial saw a lot of action on the *Twilight Zone* case but much of it was within the walls of Century City. The legal process created a small industry built on formulating writs and appeals. But by the end of 1985 the exhaustion of all trial delay tactics on the part of the defense was apparent and a strategy was developed for finally taking the case to trial. During that same period John Landis made another film, a $23 million production called *Spies Like Us* for Warner, proving that the differences between the studio and director were minor when it came to doing business. The film starred Dan Aykroyd and Chevy Chase; Aykroyd's wife, Donna Dixon, and Steve Forrest of *Dallas* fame. It was a comedy of which Aykroyd had written the first draft while John Belushi was still alive.

The script originally had a Belushi-Aykroyd theme in mind. Using an old Hollywood formula, the Crosby-Hope "road" movies, Chase and Aykroyd, cast as two espionage agents, are chosen for their spy mission because of their ineptitude. But apart from this ho-hum story of Chevy Chase and Dan

Aykroyd averting nuclear war, the film showed Landis' continued recruiting drive for potential friendly witnesses to help him out in his legal troubles. With the trial coming up, his effort to win Hollywood hearts and minds was reflected in a fresh line-up of directors in cameo roles, including Michael Apted, Martin Brest, Costa-Gavras, Joel Coen, Bob Swain, and Frank Oz. (George Folsey Jr. even got Bob Hope to make a cameo appearance through the help of his ninety-year-old father who knew Hope from the wartime USO shows). *For Spies Like Us*, John Landis received his standard $1 million directing fee. The film was released for the '85 Christmas season and received a terrible drubbing from the critics.

While his legal defense was able to delay his day in court, elsewhere, on and off the set, Landis encountered constant reminders of his notoriety. In his movie and business life it showed most noticeably in a more cautious attitude among some Hollywood stars and producers. Before making *Spies*, Folsey and Landis were very far into an arrangement with rock record producer David Geffen to do a remake of Roger Corman's famed *Little Shop of Horrors* that had featured a young Jack Nicholson. They had developed a budget and were close to making the final deal, but they could never make the terms with Geffen who refused to give in to Landis' demand for final cut. When in the end Geffen decided on another client of Joel Behr's, Frank Oz, to do the remake of the Corman classic, Landis' friends in the industry interpreted it as Geffen turning his back on the director. The rub between them became clear sometime later at a party where Geffen in an exchange with Landis responded sharply, "Yea, John, but I didn't kill three people." It caused a feud between the two men, and a similar incident embroiled Landis with the co-star of *Spies*, Chevy Chase.

Relations between the director and the boyish comedy star were already strained, dating back to the success of *Animal House*. Chase at the time had a feud with Belushi stemming from ego clashes on *Saturday Night Live*. Universal had wanted Chase to play the part in *Animal House* of a character called Otter but he missed getting the role. On the set of *Spies* Chase's relationship with Landis was further irritated by the film's shooting conditions in the frozen wilds of Norway, holed up with the *Spies* crew in a remote town named Songdahl. Chase had just become a father, and he had just finished making *Fletch* with director Michael Richie. He hadn't wished to start shooting that early but, because of the missed U.S. winter weather and the Christmas release date for the film that year, the set was moved to Norway, which still offered snow scenes.

Aside from some esthetic differences Chevy had with the director during the filming, an accident he witnessed on the set really shook him up. It involved a scene with gunfire and non-Hollywood horses. Unused to gunfire, the local Norwegian horses spooked and, charging into a camera platform, knocked over equipment, nearly causing a fatality among the cameramen. The incident was reminiscent of the night on the TZ set during the filming of the Klan sequence when the dogs went wild due to guns being fired over their heads. Even Folsey recalled, "It was like 'holy shit' for a while. It was scary. The cameraman was knocked down and Chevy said something about it." In what everyone present took as an obvious reference to the *Twilight Zone* crash, Chase quipped, "I guess it's another John Landis film."

According to Folsey, the director took offense. "He doesn't like people implying he did something wrong."

Chevy Chase and John Landis would again work together, on *Three Amigos* the following year, but they never got the friendship back.

With Braun's influence on the wane, Joel Behr actively sought a new attorney to help in filing the appeals to Landis' setback at the 995 hearing. He brought in the media-wise professor from Harvard, Alan Dershowitz, to assist in the formulation of the appeal and as consultant on projecting Landis' best image to the public. At the same time Dershowitz was trying to sell the screenplay rights to his book on the Von Bulow case in Hollywood and asked Landis for his opinion. Landis, after reading the book, criticized the professor for repeatedly praising himself in his work.

As for Harland Braun, in retrospect, he realized that Dershowitz's involvement in the case should have alerted him that his days as chief counsel were already numbered. Braun began to increasingly feel that he was being left out.

The first hint indicating that John Landis was really serious about bringing in a new lead lawyer came when Behr told him they wanted a "gray-haired eminence" to soften Landis' image. Braun actually bought the idea of a co-counsel and was interested to hear the big-name trial attorneys Landis had been seeing around the country, among them Washington, D.C.'s Edward Bennett Williams, San Francisco's Melvin Belli, and less known nationally by name but better known for the notoriety of his cases (Jimmy Hoffa, Watergate, Ford Pinto, Elvis' doctor James F. Neal), from the firm of Neal & Harwell in Nashville, Tennessee.

The co-counsel approach for the trial as yet did not seem threatening to Braun's position. Dershowitz himself, already a consultant on the case, told Braun that he wanted to come out to Hollywood and assist in doing research while Braun handled the courtroom staging. Dershowitz said he had a semester coming at Harvard when he would be off.

Meanwhile, Behr only kept Braun informed of a limited number of the legal maneuvers on the case. But while gradually easing out his chief criminal counsel, Behr did, however, keep him informed of one unique group of public opinion experts he had consulted to help project a better image of their client. They were three psychologists, Dr. Robert Buckout, Dr. Eli Baker, and Dr. Allen Lichtenstein. Analyzing Landis' potential image before a jury, they consulted about issues such as the impact on a jury of conflicting testimony, a jury's possible view of the contradictory theories concerning the cause of the crash, and "the myths which have been perpetrated in the news media concerning very damaging statements and evidence."

Informed by Behr that Landis planned to argue a defense based mainly on the issue of "unforeseeability," one of the psychologists responded by proposing the legal tactic of questioning the memory of hostile witnesses concerning events that had occurred nearly five years before. On the subject of Landis' public image, the psychologists stressed that in order to have the greatest impact on public opinion it was necessary to bring out "positive information" in the media, presenting Landis as an individual and not "a representative of the Hollywood director profession." All of the opinion experts believed that Landis had been hurt by earlier statements attributed to him in the press, resulting in the "impression that Mr. Landis is somehow immature." However, Dr. Buckout made it clear that the jury would decide on Landis' motives on the basis of his own testimony on how "he can account for his own personal human feelings about this event."

After reviewing the findings of the opinion experts, Behr decided that the phalanx needed an even more detailed blueprint for developing a winning trial strategy. He next turned to another unorthodox legal group run by professional jury experts to help determine beforehand the eventual outcome of the trial. This expensive new legal service involved the use of highly successful simulated trial techniques to learn the strengths and weaknesses of the case and how to measure potential jurors' attitudes. Billing themselves as specialists in picking a winning jury, they helped give their customers a better understanding of how jurors perceived cases and made decisions. Of this controversial approach Braun was not informed. All he heard every so often were cryptic reports that the "juries" liked the "plan." The organization Joel Behr hired consisted of high-tech law consultants from Northern California called the National Jury Project (NJP). The jury experts used "social science methods" in juror research and their glossy advertising brochures promised winning results for the defendant. According to the sales hype, they could even identify the "juror most likely to take over in deliberation and press other jurors for a verdict in your favor or against." Braun was told the National Jury Project charged the Landis group $80,000 for the "mock trials" and "focus groups," the most modern social science techniques in winning with juries.

In the mock trials conducted by the NJP both sides of the case were argued in a courtroom atmosphere to a carefully screened panel of "mock jurors." The arguments were presented by actors who played roles portraying the parties, the witnesses, opposing counsel and the judge. While the mock jurors deliberated the issues candidly, they were video-taped from behind one-way mirrors so that the lawyers could watch how the "jurors" analyzed the case. For more detailed information the project used "focus groups," small groups of mock jurors that focused on the weak and strong elements of a case. They were to evaluate which argument would have most influence on real jurors.

Understandably, not all of the results were positive, some were even disturbing. The focus groups identified the issue of the children as the paramount problem for the defense. It was found that when the mock jurors made their analysis from a strictly legal stand-point, they leaned toward letting Landis off on counts 1, 3 and 5, the reckless manslaughter charges. But they had a less easy time, it was found, with the child endangerment charges based on counts 2 and 4. On that issue the mock jurors were not disposed to forgive the director.

The consensus of the mock jurors' attitudes on the child endangerment was, "This guy did something wrong. We've got to get him for something." The jury experts found, however, that the focus groups were prepared to absolve the film makers provided they could show that the final scene was "rehearsed and well-planned." Once the mock jurors heard about a "plan" they would acquit. The plan would prove that the film makers had taken the necessary caution and abided by the standards that prevailed in the industry.

And so, on the eve of the trial, the phalanx stood in need of a "plan."

CITY OF ANGELS

40

A SOUTHERNER IN HOLLYWOOD

The setback dealt Braun by Judge Ringer's restoration of all five counts left open one last legal remedy. In order to have the charges dismissed before going to trial Braun tried to get the California Supreme Court to hear the argument. Harvard's Alan Dershowitz was put to work on the petitions going up to the state's highest legal body. A few months later the court voted by a narrow margin not to review the petitions. The legal system offered no further recourse; the phalanx had exhausted it; even with Dershowitz's name the effort failed. John Landis would have to face trial on all five counts.

During this period in the spring of '85, while Landis was busy with post-production work on *Spies Like Us,* his rift with Wingo grew wider. Despite a recent agreement between the two sides to "avoid any cross-fire" and refrain from attacking one another, Wingo's attorney, Eugene Trope, filed a brief that was tantamount to a declaration of war with Landis. Essentially it boiled down to holding Landis alone responsible for the accident. The thrust of Trope's argument was that the helicopter pilot never intended to be on the set at the time the fatal special effects were being detonated. Trope argued in his brief that Wingo had understood there was a "safety plan" in which the helicopter was to be used in an "off screen" role positioned at the far side of the river away from the village at the same time the special effects were activated.

Trope's brief caused a furor in the offices of the other defense lawyers. Harland Braun fired off a copy to Dershowitz's Harvard Law School office. Branding the arguments "dishonest," he sought to counteract Trope's allegations, recommending to Dershowitz that a supplement be filed to the Supreme Court. This surprise development boded ill for the hope of Landis' lawyers to maintain, at least to the outside world, a semblance of unity among the defendants.

The phalanx responded to Trope's tactics in an internal memo. Written by Dan Allingham's lawyer Leonard Levine, it attacked Wingo's version, that he was to be away from the village when the SFX explosives were detonated, as "cinematically impossible":

The simple reason for this was that the scene was to be of the helicopter firing down upon the village and the actors as they made their escape across the river. In addition, there was a spotlight shining down from the helicopter which was to create the appearance of the enemy helicopter searching out the fleeing actors as they made their escape. Such a scene would have been impossible if, as claimed by Mr. Trope, the helicopter was to be stationed far across the river at the time the scene was being filmed.

In the end, believing it would only highlight Wingo's contradictions to Landis, the lawyers decided against filing anything in response to Trope's brief.

For their own satisfaction, however, they rejected the pilot's insistence that the blowing-up of the village was not to occur until his helicopter was a safe distance away, citing one of Wingo's NTSB statements as proof of his knowledge that the helicopter was to be near the village shoreline when the special effects were set off. The memo quoted Wingo insofar as he had admitted using the third explosion as a cue to begin his left-hand turn away from the riverbank ["I would begin a left-hand turn... so he (Allingham) could keep the light shining on them as they made their escape, and then the final set of explosions would take place."] This the phalanx indignantly memorialized as showing that the pilot knew that the helicopter would be in the special-effects flames (the "final set of explosions") and not on the "other side of the river."

Landis' lawyers simply *had* to oppose Trope. During Landis' NTSB appearance three years before, the director had said nothing of the "other side of the river." When the final set of explosions went off, according to Landis' earliest account, the helicopter was not on the other side. "Everything was going as I assumed it would," Landis had told Llorente.

* * *

The summer of '85 was again a busy season for the Landis-Folsey team. Landis was huddling with Orion Pictures in a joint HBO venture for his next film, *Three Amigos*, which like *Animal House*, was a resurrection of the old *Saturday Night Live* gang of a decade ago. Landis' director's fee was just under $2 million. The picture, overburdened with above-the-line expenses, was typical of the brand name "star" syndrome, with Chevy Chase getting $4 million, Steve Martin $3 million, and Hollywood newcomer also from *Saturday Night Live*, Martin Short, just under $.5 million.

In the third summer since the *Twilight Zone* incident, as pretrial pressure built, John Landis began to expand his active role in the defense. His lawyers had to make some critical decisions following the State Supreme Court's vote not to hear his petition. They had to finalize a trial strategy and decide who would finally represent Landis and try the case before the jury. The young director's new activist role began with the summoning of private investigator Robert Frasco. When Frasco arrived at the Universal bungalow the bearded director and Folsey were in the cutting room with Elmer Bernstein, putting the last musical touches to the soon-to-be released *Spies Like Us.*

Landis' active new role was evident in the ambitious selection process for a new criminal attorney that had gone on without Braun's knowledge. John Landis personally consulted with Harvard's Dershowitz. It was like an old-fashioned talent search except infinitely more difficult. There were very few criminal lawyers who combined the ability to be persuasive in front of a jury while also able to do their homework on a case that was highly complicated, technically intricate, and massively voluminous. "It required an ability to turn a very technical case into something that was understandable and presentable to a jury," Dershowitz noted. The list of prospects Landis eventually came up with was predictably short. "By the time the list came to me Jim Neal was the leading candidate," recalled Dershowitz. "He was the perfect choice."

James Neal was in his robust mid-fifties. Compact like a bantam boxer, short but with a great deal of aplomb, he spoke with a musical Southern lilt. He looked like a successful preacher, perfectly tailored, with silvery grey hair and a disarming "aw-shucks" way of speaking. He was known not so much by name but as a high hitter who won acquittals in famous cases. In the courtroom he combined these charms with an outsized cigar that remained unlit and a way of strutting while twirling a pair of glasses. Neal had been involved in two of the most controversial cases during the past two decades, as a prosecutor at Watergate and as the famous criminal defense lawyer in the Pinto proceedings, in which Ford Motor Company executives were acquitted of charges stemming from the deaths of several victims in exploding Pintos.

Neal rose to prominence as a lawyer during the Kennedy years. He was one of the few Southern Democrats who became close to the Kennedys. He first came to national attention in the early 60s after being handpicked by Bobby Kennedy to prosecute Jimmy Hoffa (who called Neal the "most vicious prosecutor" he'd ever seen.) In 1968 James Neal worked with Bobby Kennedy as a "law and order Democrat" to secure Bobby's position as presidential candidate. Neal's reputation as a tough prosecutor in the Hoffa case earned him his Watergate appointment, and after his return to private practice with the Nashville firm of Neal & Harwell he soon ranked as the leading criminal lawyer in the South, if not the country, with clients ranging from bankers and businessmen to those high in political office, as well as in his own backyard of the Nashville entertainment world. Among his clients were Elvis' Dr. Nichopoulos, country and western singers Johnny Cash, Waylon Jennings and Barbara Mandrell, and a governor, Edward Edwards of Louisiana (charged with a scheme of making $10 million on a hospital development business).

One thing was very obvious about James Neal: as a lawyer he could not co-exist on equal footing with another lawyer on the same team. There could be only one "star." He could never be co-counsel, much less with someone with a strong ego like Harland Braun.

Landis and Behr were faced with the task of breaking the news to Harland Braun very gracefully so as not to damage the case. When because of personal problems with Folsey's lawyer at the time, it became Folsey's turn to obtain a new lawyer, Braun was enlisted to look for possible candidates. At one point, Braun suggested, "Let me take over for Folsey," but Behr insisted that he remain co-counsel for Landis. "That's when I knew it was over," Braun realized. "It didn't make any sense."

The talk about the co-counsel role abruptly ceased following a cool exchange that took place when Braun and Neal met for the first time at Behr's office in the summer of '85. Braun did most of the talking, repeating that it didn't make any sense. "You're not going to handle my briefcase. I'm not going to handle yours. One of us has got to be clearly superior to the other. Who's going to do the closing argument?" The antagonism and suspicion of that first exchange never completely disappeared. Braun said he told Neal that if he took the case Braun would not be co-counsel; he'd rather switch to representing Folsey. Not long after that meeting Braun learned that, while he would be taking over Folsey's defense, he would for an interim period continue to represent Landis in order to finish up the on-going discussions with the DA before the trial. Braun decided to make a last grandstand play with the DA's office to dispose of the case.

It was a bold move and had it succeeded it would have eliminated the need for the Tennessee lawyer or for any counsel whatsoever, for the case would not have been brought to trial. With the Supreme Court decision having given clear proof that every legal technicality was exhausted, Braun fixed his sights on a second plea-bargain attempt.

In a strange coincidence a development paralleling Braun's removal from lead lawyer on the Landis team was in progress in the DA's office, with results for the case that would be even more far-reaching. The central figure in this bureaucratic drama was the prosecutor, Gary Kesselman, who since his El Gaucho fiasco had not been very active on the case. Because of the Supreme Court writs, the case had been in a dormancy stage and Kesselman had not really locked horns with Braun since Judge Ringer's decision. When Kesselman next met Braun it was in the summer of '85 at a pretrial status conference in front of Judge Arturio Munoz. Kesselman learned from Braun two remarkable items. The first was that Braun would be coming off the case representing Landis, the other that as a last move on his client's part he brought a plea-bargain proposal.

Braun laid his proposal before Judge Munoz to "dispo" the case without wasting valuable court time in a lengthy trial. He roughed out the idea that his client would be willing to plead guilty to lesser felonies. At this point Judge Munoz suggested they "conference" on that. Kesselman immediately took it up with his superiors who, suspecting that Braun might have a trick up his sleeve, reacted cautiously. The prosecutor was directed by the office's top brass not to negotiate with Braun. He was only to listen to his proposal and then bring it back to them.

Kesselman returned with these instructions to his office on the 16th floor of the Criminal Court building. Tom Budds was present along with Harland Braun and a couple of other defense lawyers. They dragged in extra chairs and formed a ring around Kesselman's crowded desk. To utter silence Braun offered to plead Landis et alia guilty on felony counts of hiring the children. He argued to Kesselman that the defendants were not ordinary criminals and that even if found guilty on the more extreme manslaughter charges they would probably not be sentenced to any more jail time than would arise out of a lesser felony.

In Kesselman's mind the meeting represented a breakthrough. The first plea arrangement he himself had tried to work out a year earlier had been rejected by Joel Behr. Under Braun's renewed proposal, the guilty plea again would have limited impact on the civil lawsuits. Like the earlier "dispo" talks between Kesselman and Joel Behr, the charges that would form the basis of the guilty plea would specifically avoid the negligence issue, leaving that question open to argument in the civil cases of the Chens and Les.

In conveying Braun's offer Kesselman met with Gil Garcetti, next in command to LA District Attorney Ira Reiner, the third DA to wrangle with the case since its filing in 1982. After hearing Kesselman repeat that the *Twilight Zone* defendants wished to plead guilty to felonies, Garcetti excitedly urged Kesselman to draft a memo to Ira Reiner himself, outlining the legal issues and explaining the facts.

Not long afterwards, in the latter part of the summer of '85, on the eve of the trial, Kesselman was summoned to a high-level meeting with chief DA Ira Reiner, his deputy Garcetti and other ranking deputies to present Braun's plea-bargain proposal. The meeting was held in Reiner's office. Before it began Garcetti announced to the gathering that Ira Reiner "is not present at this meeting," a clear sign to Kesselman that the district attorney wished to distance himself publicly from the case.

Taking the floor, Kesselman explained why he personally supported Braun's proposal. He tried to convince Reiner that if Braun's very technical "delamination theory" should be challenged by the prosecution, a jury would get caught up in the argument, even though it was not imperative to prove the specific cause of the accident for the manslaughter conviction. A jury would want to know why the helicopter crashed, he reasoned, and delamination would help the defense in showing that the crash was caused by a unique occurrence, creating the appearance of an act of God rather than an act of negligence – in other words, it was unforeseeable. Kesselman pointed out that the prosecutor's "debris" theory, in the face of delamination, would have hard going before a jury; if it could not be backed up it would taint the rest of the prosecution case; debris meant it was foreseeable. In such an event it would be easier for Braun to prove "unforeseeability" because a crash caused by delamination had never before happened in helicopter history.

At the end of his presentation Kesselman remembers Reiner materializing with a speech and with eyes rolling in his massive face, thundering, "What the hell, does anyone care whether it is delamination or debris? You've got two dead kids. You've got a helicopter. You've got explosives. What more do you need?"

And in a final remark, Reiner addressed Kesselman's other argument that even with a guilty verdict no judge in the building would ever sentence the director to very much jail time in any event.

Kesselman remembers Reiner saying, "Landis is going to go to the state prison on this!"

* * *

Despite an adversarial relationship, Gary Kesselman had developed an admiration for Harland Braun. It did not stop Kesselman from suspecting Braun's hand behind the El Gaucho raid. Kesselman judged him on professional grounds. Harland's gift was a dynamism of speech, an enormous belief in himself that was infectious. Juries had never seen anything like Harland Braun. He raised the voltage in the courtroom. Kesselman was able to see Braun at his best at a follow-up meeting on the plea-bargain offer that took place on September 23, 1985, in the office of the chief district attorney. Braun's meeting with Reiner was the last time the DA's office showed an interest in "dispo"-ing the case short of a trial.

Kesselman's stature in the case was by then at its lowest ebb. The El Gaucho affair darkened all his official relations. His support for a plea-bargain expressed at the secret meeting with Reiner and Garcetti turned out to be unforgivable in the eyes of his superiors. He experienced a rapidly deteriorating relationship with his immediate superior, Richard Hecht. In one such encounter Kesselman told Hecht he had received a call from Harland Braun in which Braun gave astonishing details about the secret meeting where Reiner was not even supposed to be present. Kesselman accused Hecht of leaking the information to Braun. Shortly afterwards, Braun went over Kesselman's head and arranged his own meeting with Reiner. At this very rare occurrence, when the chief district attorney meets with the lawyer for a criminal defendant, Kesselman attended merely to observe; he was again humiliated with the emphatic instruction not to make any remarks.

District Attorney Ira Reiner, burly as a boxer with a boxer's combative head, fidgeted as Braun delivered himself of a monologue that soon had the room spellbound.

Braun zeroed in on the defects of the DA's case. He hammered away on how the state had botched the investigation. His dazzling performance did not omit an appeal to Reiner's liberal reputation.

Braun and Reiner, equal in age, were also political colleagues active in the same local Democratic Party circles. Braun described the Landis segment of the film as being concerned with racism and social injustice. But he saved the most telling hammer blows for last. Squaring off before Reiner, he proclaimed that the case was bigger than John Landis. He charged Reiner with missing the big fish. Braun pointed out dramatically what it was really about. "Where are they?" he demanded, referring to Steven Spielberg and Frank Marshall. "Where the hell are they? Why hasn't the DA's office interviewed these people? Steven Spielberg was co-producer, Marshall was executive producer. Marshall participated in meetings in which the hiring of the children was discussed. Your office says he was never questioned." Braun ridiculed the idea that the district attorney's office was unable to find Marshall. "It must be assumed," Braun declared, "that Spielberg had full and complete knowledge of all that had taken place that night."

As Braun continued, Kesselman for the first time heard Kathleen Kennedy mentioned by name. He learned that Kennedy was herself an associate producer on the Spielberg segment of the film. According to Braun, she had been deeply involved in the decision to employ the children without permits and had been present on the set the night of the crash, yet she was never interviewed. Braun argued that the breadth of the participation of so many people destroyed the credibility of the DA's charge that there was a foreseeable danger.

The meeting ended with Reiner telling Braun that his office would consider the proposal further. But after Braun left, the chief DA turned to Kesselman and asked him to prepare a response to Braun's arguments and, in addition, to draft a letter asking Harland Braun to identify those areas in the case where he thought the DA was deficient.

Kesselman replied incredulously, "You've got to be kidding. You want me to send a letter to Harland asking what we missed in the case?" He told Reiner that it would only create undesirable publicity. "That's going to appear tomorrow on the front page of the *LA Times*," he promised, "and give Braun a chance to shove it up your nose." Reiner insisted, and after brooding for days Kesselman at last composed the draft, which was later sent to Braun's office and, just as he had forecast, eventually resulted in a media coup for Braun.

Kesselman's growing lack of enthusiasm was interpreted by his superiors in the DA's office as a lack of conviction for the case. His openness to settlement and tendency to "dispo" finally made him the wrong man in Reiner's eyes. He wasn't hardnosed enough. There was El Gaucho. Kesselman had earlier raised it with Reiner's assistant, Garcetti, as possibly being an obstacle to his job as prosecutor. Kesselman never hid the fact that he continued to own an interest in El Gaucho. He had even suggested the possibility of being removed, as the embarrassing taxi-dance business could trip him up again. For some time, he was spared any direct reference to it from his chiefs until one day Garcetti mentioned that his continuing involvement in the dance club might taint the *Twilight Zone* case.

"We have a director who thinks that he's fighting for his life. We have off-the-wall criminal attorneys like Harland who will do anything. Whoever tries this case will have to be whiter than white and cleaner than clean. They could come after Ira or me," he closed, referring to Landis' phalanx.

Garcetti informed Kesselman, "Maybe it's time we review this."

41

THE DRAGON LADY

On the eve of the trial the most recent LA court drama to gain national notoriety in LA had been the DeLorean cocaine trial. The case against DeLorean seemed watertight. There was even film recording the defendant in the criminal act. DeLorean's acquittal, however, taught the DA's office that there were two juries, in effect, one in the courtroom and the other in the hallway outside where the prosecutor and the defense lawyers talk to the press. It was in the latter forum that Howard Weitzman, DeLorean's defense counsel, had won his case, in contrast to the federal prosecutors who had adopted the strategy of not responding to the media.

The *Twilight Zone* trial, like the DeLorean, was a high-profile event that promised national attention to be focused on the DA's office. After taking a first step, the decision to remove Gary Kesselman, the district attorney began looking for someone who was a sharp trial lawyer capable of preventing another "DeLorean," where the case was lost in the press.

Ira Reiner's chief deputy, Gil Garcetti, was responsible for the search. But as he tried his luck in the downtown office he encountered unexpected resistance. One experienced prosecutor turned him down because Garcetti wouldn't tell him why Kesselman was being taken off the case. Garcetti had to extend his search to the DA's 23 outlying offices, in one of which he found Lea D'Agostino. Garcetti didn't have to ask her twice. She jumped at the chance.

A prosecutor for 4 1/2 years in the San Fernando Valley's suburban Van Nuys office, Lea Purwin D'Agostino had the impeccable record of never having lost a case. She was 48 years old and worked in the Career Criminal Division as a prosecutor in the sexual assault program, dealing with rapes, incest, child molestation and sexual abuse in children. By comparison to other women in the DA's office she had reached a very high level – grade IV – in a very short time. She was known as a hard-working and high-energy person. She was also known to have Hollywood connections. The story circulating in the DA's office was that Peter Sellers had once asked her to marry him.

Lea D'Agostino's personnel file showed Gil Garcetti that she had come relatively late to the legal profession. She was 31 when she enrolled at the University of West Los Angeles School of Law. But more interestingly, perhaps, the file showed that she had worked as a top-level executive secretary and administrative assistant for many big Hollywood names, such as David O. Selznick, the producer of *Gone with the Wind*, and Freddie Fields, the famous theatrical agent and for a period the president of MGM, who represented Judy Garland and Paul Newman as well as Peter Sellers, with whom Lea's name would become romantically linked. She had also been a secretary to David Begelman, the future 20th Century Fox chief to be tried by the DA's office on charges of embezzlement. Her file further showed that she had already won considerable local fame by prosecuting the fanatical Croatian terrorist known as the "Alphabet Bomber" who in 1980 carried out a bombing attack on LA International Airport, resulting in several deaths. In the courtroom she was known for a fiery style and as someone who couldn't be pushed around.

The Alphabet Bomber bestowed on Lea D'Agostino the epithet of the "Dragon Lady." Yet she was pint-sized, barely 5 ft., a mere 90 pounds, frail and angular as a bird with a high delicate forehead accentuated by a towering black upswept beehive. Lea D'Agostino was not Italian, as her name and appearance might imply, but actually a Sabra, born in Tel Aviv, the only child of a Lithuanian mother and Polish father who left Europe on the eve of World War II, in which members of both sides of the family eventually perished. Her father died in Tel Aviv when she was five. A year later she moved to Birmingham, England, after her mother married a British soldier (acquiring the "Purwin" featured in the full name). Six years later her mother divorced and took her daughter to Chicago. Vague residues remained of these early wandering years, strengthening the impression that Lea Purwin D'Agostino was someone from another place, and perhaps from another time.

In Chicago, attending an all-girl high school, she showed a strong interest in drama. Her idol was Ingrid Bergman. Because of her deep voice, at school she always played men's parts. She lost out on a possible career, getting turned down when trying out for a radio advertisement because she sounded "too much like Lauren Bacall." She briefly attended Northwestern University in Chicago and then moved with her mother to Los Angeles where she found work as a secretary in an investment banking firm. Hard work as a secretary eventually opened the doors to the entertainment world. She found employment in the industry as an administrative assistant of high-powered efficiency and marvelous organizational skills. She was a whizz at shorthand, a fury at dictation, a paramount system maker; all of which became valuable later in mastering the complexity of the *Twilight Zone* case.

The secretarial-administrative route led to several other jobs where she rubbed shoulders with Hollywood people. She was manager of a trendy night club visited by high-rollers like Frank Sinatra; known as The Factory, it was owned by eight of Hollywood's most prominent high-lifers, including Pierre Salinger, Sammy Davis Jr., Paul Newman and film director Richard Dormer. At this hot spot she was known for her Halloween parties, once winning a prize as Marie Antoinette. At The Factory she also met her husband, Joseph D'Agostino, who was in food services; they were married in 1975. For a while she worked as a social director at LA's Marina City Club. One day, while thumbing through career ads in *TV Guide*, she simply made up her mind to go to law school.

Lea Purwin D'Agostino was regarded as an oddity in the DA system. She was an amalgam of realist and dreamer, the pragmatist who could still lose herself in the fantasy of Hollywood. She had superstitions and observed certain rituals. She kept off freeways, driving everywhere by surface roads. She pinned golden good luck bees to her right shoulder when giving opening statements or receiving verdicts. During trials she always carried six felt-tip blue pens, a habit retained from her first law school exam when the six pens helped her do extraordinarily well. She had another superstition about not wearing the same outfit twice during a trial. Consequently, her wardrobe never ceased to amaze the courtroom with its inexhaustible variety. She brought to the judicial sessions a dash of flamboyance with sometimes expensive, high-fashion clothing.

When she first received the telephone call from Garcetti inviting her downtown for a meeting she thought that because of her work in the sexual assault program she might be made head of the unit. In Garcetti's office she met Richard Hecht, the head of special trials, and after the two men explained the *Twilight Zone* case they discussed her Hollywood background and how the case would have to be handled in the media. They didn't want another DeLorean situation. They asked her whether she had any health or vacation problems that might interfere with a lengthy trial. Hecht, a dour-looking bureaucrat, made a point of querying whether her high-fashion style could become an issue with the jury. Lea assured the towering 6 ft. 5 figure of Hecht, to her own scant 5 ft., that jurors liked the way she dressed. Hecht asked her whether she wanted an assistant. Lea declined, saying that all she wanted was someone from the DA's Appellate Division to be available to do legal research. It was then that she learned that a mysterious high-powered legal talent from the east would shortly arrive and take over Landis' defense.

The DA's two top men instructed Lea on the official policy regarding Gary Kesselman. His removal had nothing to do with the merits of the case, Lea remembered Garcetti telling her, and that if asked about Kesselman being replaced she would say he was being relieved for personal reasons. She was not told the reason for his removal, but she was soon given a hint of the true story of Kesselman's backdoor treatment in a telephone call she received from him personally just after she got the news of her exciting new assignment.

At first, she thought Kesselman merely called to confirm that she had taken over the case. He spoke in a strange tone, however, and the way he asked her about the assignment, using Tom Budds as a pretext, sounded fishy. She decided to hold her discussions with Garcetti about her new assignment confidential and stonewalled.

Then she threw herself into the case. It was both a professional challenge and a long-last dramatic fulfilment, *almost like being Lauren Bacall in a Hollywood movie!*

42

THE SPIELBERG LETTER

Not fully aware of Kesselman's removal, Harland Braun continued his race against time to preempt James Neal by keeping the case from going to trial.

In response to the DA's unorthodox request that he identify the prosecutor's weak points, Landis' criminal lawyer drafted a seven-page letter outlining 16 areas where the DA's case fell short. Predictably, it made for shattering reading but what made it sensational was Braun's charge that Steven Spielberg, Frank Marshall, Kathleen Kennedy and the executives of Warner Bros., had been able to escape a "consciously truncated investigation."

When leaked to the press, the "Spielberg letter" injected the world's most famous director publicly into the controversy for the first time since the earliest days of the crash. The media had a field day depicting a DA fumbling with a case that had 16 glaring holes in it, the largest of which concerned Hollywood's top director and one of Hollywood's top studios.

News that the Spielberg letter with its highly volatile legal name-calling had been sent to the DA's office sent shock waves through a number of offices in Century City. The immediate response came in Folsey's voice nearly breaking as he called Harland Braun from a restaurant where he was dining with John Landis and Joel Behr, whimpering, "I have to fire you because of the letter." The day following the letter's release, James Neal's assistant, attorney James Sanders from the Nashville firm, dispatched a letter speaking for John Landis to the district attorney, repudiating Braun's broadside as objectionable, Sanders informed the DA that a formal substitution request would soon be made to replace Braun as Landis' counsel.

In the end Braun was not fired. He remained Folsey's lawyer, even though the letter that dragged Warner and Spielberg into the fray remained unforgivable. For a while it lingered as a sore spot between Braun and his new client. Braun was puzzled by Folsey's criticism and maintained that he had cleared the Spielberg letter. "Obviously," Braun reasoned, "they'd gotten to him," referring to Folsey's panic-stricken telephone call from the restaurant. "Behr must have gone to him and told him, 'You're gonna be ruined in Hollywood.'"

Although Braun was kept on the case for continuity's sake, he had no illusion as to the real reason any lawyer who's been on a case for over four years is kept on.

Such a lawyer, knowing where all the bodies are buried, need not fear getting fired.

* * *

With a new attorney appearing in the case for John Landis, the trial was granted a continuance for another six months in order to give Neal time to prepare himself. Reviewing the volumes of statements and testimony, James Neal remained in the Neal & Harwell offices in one of the more prestigious of the downtown Nashville bank buildings. He had only recently married a former Miss Tennessee, a stunning belle twenty years his junior. Except for brief jaunts to the *Three Amigos* set in California to talk strategy, Neal sent his assistant, short, affable, diligent Jim Sanders, to smoggy Los Angeles in the early part of 1986 to do most of the background work for the trial.

From Nashville, Neal established phone contact with Landis' private eye Robert Frasco and, assisted by Behr's John Diemer on the California side, he outlined the new legal strategy to defend the director. In a departure from Braun's emphasis on the highly technical "delamination" defense, Frasco was briefed about the findings by the focus groups of the National Jury Project and the problems with the case. Neal laid out a program of working with witnesses in which Frasco would function, in Frasco's own words, as a "hostility reducer." Neal explained that he and Frasco would divide up which witnesses each would see. Neal had the "priority list" with the more important names he considered key to the defense: Elie Cohn, Anderson House, Gary McLarty, Kathryn Wooten and Jerry Williams. Frasco was to interview other key witnesses, like Steve Lydecker, many the same as those he had interviewed three years before.

Through discussions with Behr and with his own righthand man Jim Sanders, Neal narrowed the issues to problem areas raised by witnesses. Apart from flushing out issues like live ammunition and alcohol on the set, Frasco was told to talk to witnesses who said Landis "disappeared" immediately after the accident. The detective was asked to identify crew members who'd witnessed certain damaging statements made by the director just before the crash. "Anybody you can get who can put a better light on 'You haven't seen anything yet, … anything that *softens* that," Neal instructed.

Neal's approach to the case was evident in his instructions to the "hostility reducer" in Los Angeles. He explained to Frasco how a body he called "jury pickers," the National Jury Project's focus groups, had shown that they had to prove to a jury that the fatal scene was well-rehearsed and well-planned. Frasco was instructed to look for people who were around during the 2:00 A.M. copter flight and who could testify to the "seriousness of that rehearsal." These witnesses would have to testify that the flight was really a planning session, or in Neal's own words, that "it wasn't a frivolous thing." They would have to be able to state that the entire fatal scene was planned in this so-called rehearsal; that it "was a real run-through," Neal stressed.

"What we need to do," the Nashville attorney summed up, "is to show better planning and soften these statements."

Frasco was further instructed to look for suitable people who had talked to the parents of the children or had assisted them. Neal told the private eye to identify witnesses who should be able to say of the parents in court, "They are very sophisticated people. They spoke good English. They weren't intimidated." As to this particular witness category, Frasco was told to enroll the name of the women's wardrobe supervisor, Sue Dugan, a friend of Deborah Landis and her subordinate on the set that night who had spent time with the children while they were being kept hidden from Tice.

James Neal blew into town on the eve of the trial in the late spring of 1986. He set up headquarters at the Beverly Comstock on Wilshire Blvd in Westwood, about a mile from Behr's office in Century City. There Frasco met John Landis' "gray-haired eminence" for the first time, face-to-face. Neal reiterated to Frasco to help communicate to witnesses the defense argument that there was a plan for the fatal scene but that it was not followed correctly.

Frasco was surprised at this latest twist. He recalled of his own participation in the early stages, "In the beginning no one wanted to hear about a plan because it meant that if you had a plan something went wrong." Nonetheless, by the first weeks of the summer of 1986 he had helped set the stage for Neal's master strategy. Shortly after his next meeting with Neal in Joel Behr's office, the detective informed Neal that he'd confronted many of the key "unfriendlies" and had done his best to soften up the most "hardened."

At this point Neal's chief role was that of the elder statesman who persuades his wrangling cohort to get behind "the plan." The most difficult was Eugene Trope; Wingo's lawyer criticized Landis' choice of a Southern lawyer. ("You go to Nashville when you want a banjo player," Trope huffed, loathe to acknowledge Neal's "Watergate" credentials). Harland

Braun was also reluctant to fall in behind the strategy. Braun claimed he had never heard of a so-called "plan." Of the other four lawyers in the case, Neal singled out Braun as key to holding the team together.

Braun, by virtue of his skills and reputation, had tremendous influence on the lawyers for two of Landis' co-defendants, Leonard Levine representing Dan Allingham, and Arnold Klein representing Paul Stewart. Levine and Klein actually officed together in the same Century City tower down the hall from Braun and they all shared the same secretary. Jim Neal and his assistant Jim Sanders together visited Braun in his office to convince him of the necessity of arguing "the plan." As Neal sketched it, the plan involved a scenario in which the helicopter was not supposed to be near or over the village when the special effects were detonated in the fatal scene. At that point the aircraft was supposed to leave the main action above Vic and the kids and go all the way across the river and become a camera platform in order to film the final set of explosions as the village went up. That plan was interrupted, according to Neal, only because of the premature ignition by special effects man James Camomile.

Neal's scenario was largely adapted from the statements recorded in the NTSB record four years earlier from 'E' cameraman Roger Smith. They were statements related to what Smith believed the helicopter's position would be during the scene at the time the village went up. After hearing Dan Allingham give assurances to the mutinous airborne camera crew that the helicopter would move away from the village before it exploded, Smith had told the NTSB that it was then, just before they boarded the fatal flight, that *he*, Smith, suggested that after photographing the first set of explosions in the village the helicopter could become a "camera platform" to film the final explosions.

Harland Braun told Neal he had never heard of this scenario in all his four years on the case, pointing out that besides Roger Smith, neither Landis, Folsey nor Allingham had ever mentioned to investigators the existence of a plan to have a camera platform. He argued that the idea was both unnecessary and unnecessarily complex. In Braun's view it could already be shown that there was adequate planning. Besides, no one ever thought you could down a helicopter with special effects. Braun also argued against placing the whole strategy on the impression by one witness of the helicopter's intended position in the final shot.

Braun left the meeting with the feeling that Neal's plan was full of holes.

* * *

In the latter part of '85, Lea D'Agostino moved from the Career Criminal Division in Van Nuys to a new office set aside for the prosecutor of the *Twilight Zone* case in the downtown Criminal Court building. Though windowless, it was on the 18th floor with the top brass. The office of Richard Hecht, who would act as her liaison with Chief Ira Reiner, was just down the hall; Reiner's office was on the same floor. Upon turning over the case, Kesselman had agreed to bring the new prosecutor "up to speed," and for the next three months, until the early part of '86, the Dragon Lady consulted on a daily basis with her predecessor whose office was two floors down.

Kesselman could never be completely rid of some resentment against his replacement. Nevertheless, he did his professional best to fill her in on the myriad facts and facets of the case, the movie terms, the variety of witnesses. He advised his successor to concentrate on Donna Schuman. He described her as the best witness because of her former friendship with George Folsey Jr. and her knowledge of intimate details of the *Twilight Zone* production.

In sharp contrast to Kesselman, the new prosecutor, fired up with gusto, did not see obstacles. Adopting the DA's view, she didn't buy Braun's arguments about delamination or Spielberg. With all of her dramatic, coiffed, high-fashion, bird-like 90 pounds she came on like a gunslinger. She pooh-poohed Kesselman's tales of mysterious pressures, relegating them to the realm of paranoia. From Tom Budds she learned that Kesselman believed there were leaks in the DA's office to Harland Braun and that someone in the Landis camp had set up the El Gaucho raid. The new prosecutor felt Kesselman was too frightened of Braun. She also sensed a deep concern in Kesselman about whether she knew why he'd been taken off the case – she had never been told.

Prosecutor D'Agostino believed she had figured out Braun's strategy. From Braun's previous meetings with the DA, she concluded that it was his style to distract the prosecution from defining the issues.

She guessed that Braun was still going to focus on both delamination – the "unforeseeable" – and the "botched investigation," claiming that other important people like Spielberg, Marshall and Kathleen Kennedy, as well as a big studio, Warner Bros., knew about the illegal hiring of the children. Her game plan was to outfox the fox, that is, give the impression that she was going to meet Braun head-on in those issues while in actuality her real strategy was to ignore them. She planned a wholly original and unexpected attack.

Meanwhile, by the beginning of '86 she got fresh support in the form of Jerry Loeb. Pleasant and well-spoken, Loeb looked more like a young executive than an investigator with the DA's office. Loeb got assigned to the case due to his experience with the "Hollywood crowd," as he called it. A member of the special Crime Task Force into movieland corruption, he had investigated the *Charlie's Angels* case in which the show's two top executives, Leonard Goldberg and Aaron Spelling, were the subject of a probe as to whether they diverted profits away from their partners in the show, Natalie Wood and Robert Wagner. Jerry Loeb had worked once before with Lea D'Agostino in a case involving the successful prosecution of one of Mickey Rooney's lawyers. Loeb's most notorious case was the 1980 Begelman affair, the investigation into the petty pilfering by a major studio chief that shook up Hollywood.

With Jerry Loeb and Tom Budds, two tall good-looking males for escort, the tiny prosecutor became fully acquainted with the *Twilight Zone* terrain. Here Tom Budds was indispensable; in an investigation that doggedly ran into its fourth year he had amassed a bundle of four spiral-bound notebooks jammed with notations and descriptions. Neatly and patiently, Budds had recorded in hundreds of crowded pages his interviews with witnesses of every stripe, from film experts to stunt people.

With the trial six months away, the new prosecutor had to master four years of investigations. Frequently she arrived at her office at 5 A.M. and did not finish work till midnight. She studied not only the Budds' notebooks, the six volumes of grand jury testimony, over 1,000 pages of single-lined NTSB statements, 20 volumes of preliminary hearings, besides familiarizing herself with the statements of over 100 witnesses, as well as sheaves of technical reports submitted by the NTSB and FBI; she also tried to talk to motion picture insiders.

She went to Hollywood, visiting sets in person. On the set of *Hill Street Blues*, Tom Budds photographed her sitting in the lap of star Daniel Travanti. She visited the *Love Boat* set. She met with famous directors. She went to Warner Bros. studios and faced down supercilious company lawyers, teaching them that if they thought they had merely to deal with a "civil servant" they had quite another think coming.

Over the phone she debated Burt Reynold's best friend, director/stuntman Hal Needham, who himself was caught up in a controversial lawsuit from a crippled stunt woman. She tried to get movie actor Cliff Robertson to talk about industry blacklisting, and Clint Eastwood to be interviewed as an expert witness about safety standards on the set. The windowless 18th floor office began to resemble a movie production office. At times it was like a remake of the Landis segment. Lea D'Agostino actually wanted to build a Vietnamese village, hire an SFX crew and blow it up for the jury.

In practical terms, the new prosecutor's first official duty was to address the Spielberg letter. Early in '86 at a meeting with Ira Reiner's top deputy, Gil Garcetti, she was directed to locate Frank Marshall in order to rebut Braun's charge that the office hadn't lifted a finger to find the highest-ranking executive on the set. In taking over the case from two earlier administrations the DA's top men were themselves unaware as to why Frank Marshall had not been interviewed. They thought it was a good question, especially since they might have to account for a possible oversight committed by their predecessors.

The secret mission to find Marshall brought the new prosecutor her first taste of defeat. Her more experienced investigator, Jerry Loeb, ran into the same wall of silence that earlier had forced Tom Budds' withdrawal from the chase.

Like Tom Budds, Loeb staked out Marshall's house in Santa Monica to no avail. But he made an interesting discovery. From the security company guarding the house he learned that it listed another address for Frank Marshall in the name of Kathleen Kennedy. Loeb saw the chance to refute the accusation made by Braun in his Spielberg letter that the DA's office had deliberately omitted questioning Kathleen Kennedy. So, he drove over to the Studio City condo listed as her address. There he found out that all her mail was being forwarded to Spielberg's Amblin Entertainment at Universal; people in the neighborhood told him that she had not been seen in the area for some time.

Following up the lead, Loeb found himself rebuffed at Spielberg's newly risen mini-studio on the Universal lot. Neither Steven Spielberg nor Kathleen Kennedy, purportedly busy with Joe Dante's new movie, *Innerspace*, was available. Bonnie Radford, the TZ production's accountant who had drafted the "under-the-table" check, was in England working on an Amblin assignment. Finally, after trying normal Amblin channels and being constantly referred to Marshall's lawyer, Rick Rosen, Loeb decided to cash in a chip from an inside studio contact who still owed him a favor from his Crime Task Force days. As a result, Loeb came back to his boss with the news that Frank Marshall was working on a film named *Who Framed Roger Rabbit?* at the Elstree Studios in London. The film was being directed by Robert Zemeckis who had just finished directing *Back To The Future* on which Frank Marshall had also been the executive producer.

Scheduled to commence on July 17, the upcoming *Twilight Zone* trial rippled to London in the latter part of June. The mass-circulation *Sun* ran a banner headline and a photograph of the bee-ornamented Hollywood prosecutor in a story about her near-betrothal to Peter Sellers. The tabloid's local stringer who did this story was contacted and enlisted in the search for the vanished witness. At the same time, through official channels, Marshall's name was also put on the Interpol list.

The *Sun* reporter quickly confirmed through his movie contacts that Frank Marshall was staying at "Number Seven Park Place," the highly exclusive St. James Club with a largely Hollywood clientele, including Michael Jackson and Steven Spielberg. The newsman reported that Marshall's stay was *very, very* quiet. Marshall usually stayed at the Atheneum in Picadilly, the man from the *Sun* said; but most curiously, he didn't this time.

The prosecutor immediately made arrangements with Scotland Yard and a few days later, armed with no more than an international subpoena, Tom Budds was aboard a plane to London. Again, as he had been earlier in being sent up against the Spielberg organization, Budds was vastly outmanned.

Perhaps Jerry Loeb, a keen history buff, would have felt more at home in the land of tradition. Tom Budds was chilled by the foreignness. In a cool reception from the Scotland Yard inspector, Budds was cautioned not to pull any "Mission Impossible stuff," which did little to make him feel more at ease. In London the LA cop was a fish out of water. In his quandary Budds ended up at the U.S. embassy where he managed to enlist the assistance of the legal attaché. She was a brisk American lady. Together they went to the exclusive hotel on Park Place where the attaché rang up Frank Marshall in his room. The brisk lady stated that she had a legal document which she wished to serve. Marshall replied that he would be down in a half hour. Budds and the embassy employee waited in the lobby for an unconscionable time. Frank Marshall never came down.

Tom Budds later found out from Scotland Yard that Spielberg's friend and business partner had packed his bags and left by limousine for the airport and taken a plane to Paris. Interpol reported that he met in Paris with Steven Spielberg and Richard Benjamin to promote a new Benjamin movie. There was a question as to whether the plane that took Marshall away belonged to Steven Spielberg.

Again, it made a big splash in the *Sun*.

* * *

Budds' failure in London to bring Marshall to heel, though it deprived the pint-sized prosecutor of a possibly sensational coup, did not affect her basic strategy. She privately feared that on the witness stand Marshall might well have ended up supporting John Landis. She realized that Braun's charge of the "botched investigation" was designed to draw a wider circle, including Hollywood's biggest director and a major studio in an effort to divert the attention from Landis. It was this paradox that formed the basis of her strategy – to respond to all of Braun's challenges on the public relations front while in actuality keeping her focus solely on John Landis and the issue of his personal responsibility as director on the set.

As the trial drew near, despite the Hollywood rumor mill and the fear of witnesses about losing their jobs, that focus had become increasingly sharp. Many of her best witnesses were not unlike those she had dealt with on previous assignments, only here drawn from the workaday reality of the movie set: hairdressers, fire safety officers, cameramen, electricians and truck drivers. In their comments she detected a common note of revulsion.

Four years after the accident the hostility and anger in those the prosecutor interviewed remained undiminished. She heard repeatedly of the "screamer" and from the descriptions by witnesses became acquainted with an erratic, waving, whining, leaping and cursing tyrant of the set. One witness said the director was "always irrational"; yet another commented that Landis "went apeshit that night." She heard about the director's obsession that night to "outdo *Apocalypse Now*" and "out-Spielberg Spielberg." In the prosecutor all her maternal instincts rebelled. In her mind the director became a mythical monster who devoured children for the sake of the "shot." The strong personal attachment she developed with key witnesses like Steve Lydecker, Randy Robinson, Alpha Campbell and the makeup artist Bob Westmoreland, were cited by the Landis defense as proof of female instability. During the trial her unorthodox relationship with Donna Schuman, who also identified emotionally with the children, would be pounced on by Harland Braun and become a dominating issue. As a woman among the all-male defense she was called "over-emotional" and brutally blamed for being herself childless.

Lea D'Agostino never denied that she identified closely with the deaths of Myca and Renee. She kept photographs of the children. One day in the hallway, after seeing off Dr. Le, she wept, and she wept for the Chens who had lost Renee. Like Llorente she recognized the real crime that had been committed at Indian Dunes.

Two children were dead because of the lies by adults.

43

A PIGEON FOR "THE PLAN."

For nearly a year, from mid-July 1986, till the late spring of 1987, the trial preoccupied the film capital and company town. Lea D'Agostino's list of 151 potential witnesses, in one form or another, touched the lives of many of the 60,000 men and women who made their living in Hollywood. It affected Spielberg and his righthand man and studio executives and directors, down to crews, craftsmen, cameramen, union reps and stunt people. It was talked about in the exclusive Colony at Malibu, in the high suites above Sunset, and in the modest homes of the film workers in the Valley.

In her representations to the press Lea D'Agostino portrayed this community as unanimously standing behind her, though nothing was further from the truth. Few in Hollywood liked this trial. Many high-level movie people saw the criminal indictments of the five men as an encroachment on artistic freedom. The rank-and-file, conscious of the blacklist, predicted trouble for witnesses who made damaging statements about John Landis and his co-defendants.

No eyebrows were raised by the refusal of some of the chief witnesses to be cooperative: that the highest-ranking person on the set fled the country; that the stunt coordinator dodged the prosecutor; that even the accountant stayed out of the country until the end of the trial were in the main, thought of as actions justified by the undue rigor of a legal process aimed at Hollywood as a whole.

The prosecutor encountered resistance along more subtle lines from the Newhall Land & Fanning Company; the owner of Landis' Indian Dunes filming site, at first resisting the court's request for a jury view of the place where the helicopter had crashed, prompted the judge to consider calling in marshals to secure the location by force. In the case of Universal Studios, which initially denied access to DA investigators, it took a call from the head DA's assistant Gil Garcetti threatening Universal Chairman Sid Sheinberg with a search warrant. The studio finally allowed investigator Jerry Loeb on the lot to take a photograph of the European street set where the Nazi sequence was shot and Vic Morrow tottered dangerously on a ledge.

While Universal made mild resistance to the DA's office, it was different with respect to Warner Bros., which stood to lose a lot more than Universal.

The chief defendant was a Warner agent. Any damaging information that surfaced in the criminal trial could be used in the still unsettled Le and Chen cases where the studio remained a defendant; and in its efforts to keep distant from the criminal trial, Warner openly resisted key requests from the prosecutor, refusing, for instance, to supply payment records which would clarify its role in bankrolling the legal expenses for John Landis and his co-defendants. Similarly, Morgan Renard's still photographs of the crash scene, which he said he had turned over to Warner the morning of the crash, required a subpoena before the studio responded by yielding a partial group of photos, omitting the critical ones.

But in the Hollywood of guilds, agents and producers, Warner Bros. went uncriticized.

Among Hollywood's top movie people support for what was merely seen as a beleaguered movie director was strong. No one challenged the issue of the auteur capable of sparking a kind of madness on the set. They simply couldn't have known, and perhaps wouldn't have believed it, for not until the trial was underway did a partial picture first begin to emerge of what had transpired at Indian Dunes the night the children and Vic Morrow died. And if the brave, bird-like prosecutor achieved one objective during the judicial proceedings it was that of shocking Hollywood into taking a fresh look at its brilliant *wunderkind*.

Though he had four co-defendants, the trial was ultimately about John Landis – his personality, his reputation, and his responsibility. Before the trial began James Neal filed a series of motions called "limiting," that is, the limiting of the evidence that can be presented to the jury; and since John Landis faced five counts, Neal filed more such motions for his client than any of the other co-defendants' lawyers did for theirs. Neal sought to limit evidence of the use of alcohol and live ammo on the set, any photographs of the children or their death scene, as well as any reference to Landis' conduct on previous movies.

The court granted most motions on the basis that they tended to create undue prejudice. Lea D'Agostino did not oppose some of them for motives that were strategic. Thus, she allowed Neal to keep the overwhelming testimony to drinking on the set out of the trial. An admission that alcohol had been used during the filming by the low-echelon SFX crew, she reasoned, would lessen Landis' share of the blame for the accident.

But not to bring before the jury the incredible story of people drinking beer and vodka while firing explosives near children was to omit a devastating portion of the totality of chaos during the final shoot. The problem with a strategy based simply on getting a conviction by proving the director's responsibility was obvious. It blinkered the prosecutor, forcing her to paint the issues in unrelieved black and white. The failure of this strategy became clear in the trial's crucial phase when during the jury selection her choice, ironically, turned out identical to that which the "jury pickers" had recommended to Joel Behr.

Just days before jury selection began a representative from the National Jury Project visited Los Angeles and addressed the defense lawyers. A late-thirtyish lawyer-like woman by the name of Beth Benaro was introduced to the group that included Braun, Klein and Levine, but excluded Eugene Trope. In light of the consensus arrived at by the "focus groups," Benaro opted for older people who had more experience with misfortune in life and would be less judgmental, warning the defense lawyers especially against choosing young women jurors. Like Beth Benaro, the prosecutor sought to exclude better educated, upper-middle-class candidates from the selection process, though in the belief that a blue collar-type jury largely comprised of older and minority members, being less sympathetic to the rich and famous aspect of the defense, would not get "hung up" on what she considered technicalities like delamination.

Of the final jury selection, eight were minority – one Hispanic, two Philippines and five blacks; the four white jurors, two women and two men, were all near 60. They had answered to the satisfaction of both the prosecutor and the defense a confidential questionnaire about their movie tastes, what movies they had seen, and in a specific question posed by D'Agostino they had accounted as to their reaction if Hollywood stars showed up in court.

The relations between the two sides were by now fixed. All of the suspicion and belittling of purpose, meanness and pettiness, the blackening of character and motive – above all the spectacle of the barking of seven male attorneys and the desperate clawing of one frail, female prosecutor – all the elements were fixed even before the trial began and the succeeding ten months would only repeat the pattern. It was a contest, a kind of psychological warfare, in which the onus was on the tiny Dragon Lady. She had to prove equal to a $5,000-a-day Watergate prosecutor. She had to stand up to the razor-sharp legal mind of Harland Braun. The DA's office exerted constant pressure to prevent a "DeLorean," and she showed nerviness very early in the proceedings by firing off a resounding newsmaker. In a daring lunge for the headlines, she served notice on Braun that he had met his media match by telling the press that should she originally have filed the charges against the movie director, it would have been not for manslaughter but 2nd degree murder.

The result was not only an eruption of wrath among the phalanx; Kesselman was dealt yet another sharp cut by the implication that he had done a poor job of evaluating the conduct of the defendants.

By the time the trial began Lea D'Agostino had gotten to know Harland Braun, James Neal and the other defense lawyers. With none, however, had she established a cordial note except Eugene Trope. The prosecutor knew about the lawsuit filed by Wingo against Landis and this split in the defense made possible her rapport with the elderly Westside lawyer representing the pilot.

At 69, the oldest attorney on the defense side, and also, as heir to a prosperous law firm possibly the richest, Trope was avuncular and kind to the new prosecutor. During the early weeks of cordial relations, he informed her of his defense strategy in numerous telephone talks. Now and then he mentioned tidbits about what the Nashville attorney was up to. He was also helpful in other ways. When Trope found out that the prosecutor had not seen certain portions of the film, he invited her to a screening showing footage shot the night before the helicopter crash; D'Agostino watched the children flub their lines, doing and redoing their takes with that pathetic resolve each time to do better.

Then suddenly, in the third week of jury selection, the prosecutor broke with Trope. Two events led to her taking this step. The first occurred during Neal's limiting motions when Trope told her that he was not going to support Neal on excluding the live ammo issue from the evidence, citing as his reason for doing so that he felt such evidence would help Wingo in showing a pattern of Landis' recklessness. A few weeks later Trope's inexplicable reversal on this question, ending up supporting Neal, raised the prosecutor's hackles. She alleged that Trope had told her of having received a call from Neal asking him to get together "and agree upon a story." She became convinced that Dorcey Wingo was being denied an adequate defense because of his own attorney's conduct.

When the break came it was dramatic. The prosecutor said she "agonized" at having to confront the elderly law figure with the baroque head. But on August 19, 1986, she nerved herself to make the highly unusual request for a secret meeting with the judge and Trope without the knowledge of the other lawyers. At this hush-hush confrontation in the judge's chamber Eugene Trope vehemently denied the allegations, maintaining that he changed his position on the live ammo issue independent of Neal's limiting motion and that he had never discussed coordinating Wingo's defense strategy with that of John Landis. The secret proceedings ended awkwardly for the prosecutor with the judge doing nothing. On that same day, however, Trope took part in a second meeting. It began informally in his Rolls- Royce while driving to a gathering called by James Neal at Harland Braun's office. Also in the car was Trope's assistant, Bill Anderson, who could not remember when the head of the firm had been more upset.

Lea D'Agostino had assailed Trope's legal integrity and wounded his self-esteem. She had imputed to him not only incompetence in representing Dorcey Wingo, in effect, she had called for his removal. The judge, puzzled as to what to do, had ended up sealing the record of the secret meeting. But it was far from sealed for the baroque Westside figure fuming behind the wheel of the Rolls. Anderson recalled that by the time they got to Neal's meeting, "if the devil himself had walked into the room and proposed a deal against Lea, Gene would have bought." And so, at that very critical time when the jury selection process was nearing completion, the meeting saw the pilot heal his four-year rift with John Landis. Trope's earlier explosive encounter with the prosecutor in the judge's chamber would not become known to the other attorneys present until the end of the trial. Irrepressibly, Lea D'Agostino, six months hence, would make a dramatic attempt at once again trying to pry Wingo away, and though she nearly succeeded, Trope and his client stayed on the Landis side for the remainder of the proceedings.

The August 19th conclave in Braun's office, originally called by James Neal to coordinate the defense among the attorneys and their clients, became with the eleventh-hour accession of the pilot, represented by Eugene Trope, the key strategy session of the entire ten-month-long trial. Except for the sessions in open court, it marked the first time all of the attorneys and defendants were together. Taking the chairman's role, patiently, with statesman-like cajoleries and craft, Neal forged a loose confederacy based on the importance of having the jury understand that there was a plan. He then proposed that each of the defendants give their recollections of that night.

For Wingo, the first speaker, it was also the first time he discussed the case with his co-defendants. And, remarkably, as Wingo gave his version the four other defendants sprang alive with spontaneous interruptions like, "Oh, yeah, I remember that." Or, "I'm glad you brought that up because I hadn't." Particularly when the pilot talked about the 2:00 A.M. flight, the so-called "rehearsal," he received encouragement as John Landis filled in the gaps. Assuming that Dorcey might not have known it up in his craft, he clarified that the 2:00 A.M. "rehearsal" was complete. The director told Wingo about Bob Liddle, Vic's stand-in, and how later, after the "rehearsal," Vic Morrow himself had walked the path in the water.

Neal's plan had mainly to do with Landis' three counts of manslaughter related to the negligence issues which affected only Landis, Wingo and Stewart. Predictably, each had a different recollection. Thus, it became the first order to iron out major inconsistencies such as when, according to "the plan," the various SFX explosions were set to go off.

At first Wingo gave his recollection of a plan in which his helicopter was to make a 45-degree turn, circle around and exit the scene on that angle after the shooting had started. James Neal's plan, in contrast, had the helicopter making a 90-degree turn and moving across the river, thus positioning the aircraft farther away when the village was to be blasted. Nevertheless, a conflict between the pilot and the movie director was instantly averted. "Neal switched the plan at that moment to 45 degrees," Braun recalled. The new plan was sketched out on a piece of scratch paper and Braun recalled Neal's prompt, "If you say 45, our plan is 45, too. We can go along with that."

Arnold Klein alone found fault with the crucial part of Neal's plan according to which the helicopter was to become a camera platform across the river from the village to film the explosions located on the village shoreline. The attorney for Paul Stewart flatly asserted, "It can't fly," citing that in all of the various interviews over the previous four years his powdermen had not once mentioned it. But Klein offered that, as opposed to "across the river," he could live with a plan that put the location of the helicopter at a "safe distance away" when the village was to go up. Both Eugene Trope and James Neal concurred that they could go along with that, Bill Anderson, Trope's assistant, remembers.

Neal then passed out a seven-page document, afterwards referred to by some of the attorneys present as "the plan." A compilation of brief excerpts, it combined Neal's personal interviews with some of the key eyewitnesses with evidence combed from the statements made by others. It contained one important note: "The only witness we have found to conflict with the plan is Camomile." While admitting having fired what was generally thought to be the fatal explosive, the "pigeon" had never mentioned that his actions were due to a departure from any plan. If anything, his earlier statements indicated that he had not the least inkling of any plan – a point Arnie Klein duly underscored in his notes.

Simply stated, Neal's "plan" proved that the helicopter crash was a pure accident and that John Landis never intended to put a helicopter over an exploding village. Ironically, just a year before, writing on behalf of the phalanx, Leonard Levine had demonstrated in a memo that the helicopter's position in such a plan, away from the village when the explosions hit, was "cinematically impossible." Now, as Neal's document had it, except for the accidental misfiring by Jimmy Camomile, the helicopter would have been elsewhere.

After the meeting Dorcey Wingo went to dinner with Trope and Anderson. The pilot remarked his relief at hearing from Landis that there had been a complete 2:00 A.M. rehearsal. Bill Anderson observed that the new information appeared to bring comfort to the pilot. Wingo had been "fuzzy" on the purpose of that flight at the time.

"It made him think," Anderson noted, " that it really was an accident, and not the case of a madman running around."

* * *

The *Twilight Zone* trial opened on July 17, 1986, on the 15th floor, Department 132, of the Criminal Court building in downtown Los Angeles' Civic Center. With four courtrooms facing a long broad hallway extending in a T-shape from the bank of elevators, the 15th floor was known for high-profile media cases. It was always packed like a bazaar. The door to Department 132 was covered with a number of court orders to regulate people as to how far they had to stand away from the door and where they could sit in the courtroom, as well as a warning against eavesdropping on the conversations between lawyers and clients.

The courtroom was divided in three sections. On a platform under the great seal of the state of California sat the judge in his black robe. In the second section facing him stood a long table that included from left to right Lea D'Agostino with her assistant Tom Budds; Eugene Trope and Dorcey Wingo; John Landis with James Neal and Neal's assistant Jim Sanders; Folsey's lawyer, Harland Braun and Allingham's lawyer, Lenny Levine. Powder chief Paul Stewart sat with his attorney Arnie Klein at a small table to the right of this line-up, separated from the desk of a uniformed LA county sheriff known to the trial regulars as Larry the Bailiff.

In the course of the trial Larry the Bailiff was to become a great favorite of the embattled movie director.

Presiding over the trial, Los Angeles Superior Court Judge Roger Boren was known as a low-key, no-nonsense judge. Cherubic, balding, on the portly side, he was a Mormon, a Republican and a Vietnam veteran. No stranger to bizarre and protracted trials, before his judicial appointment, while a deputy district attorney with the state's attorney general's office, he was co-prosecutor of LA's two-year-long Hillside Strangler case. Two stenographers, providing a daily transcript, sat in the well before him. Directly to the right of the judge near the door through which he exited sat the clerk who administered the oath to witnesses, kept the court papers and managed the exhibits.

The seating arrangement was important to the parties since they played their adversarial role not so much before the judge as to the 12 jurors who sat day after day in a raised box, a gallery with theatre-style seats on the left side of the room. Lea D'Agostino sat nearest them separated by an aisle.

Everybody in the courtroom got to know the jurors' faces. For nearly a year they lived in almost daily contact with the rich and famous, and though the prosecutor had carefully screened them for susceptibility to Hollywood razzle-dazzle, the reality proved too much. However, the jury was hardly alone in being vulnerable to the heightened drama provided by a Hollywood trial. Even James Neal managed to get in a bit of movie-acting, playing a lawyer in an Andy Griffith TV movie while appearing as a real-life lawyer in the *Twilight Zone* proceedings. Only Judge Boren appeared immune to the Hollywood bug. He endured like a stone effigy the antics of the freewheeling legal body before his bench. Venturing a cautious comment only near the trial's end, he compared it to a "three-ring circus" in which he identified the "ring master" as Harland Braun.

* * *

Up until the last moment the lawyers bickered over payment of fees. But on the eve of the opening arguments James Neal hammered into place the final plank to keep the structure together. By settling the financial question, he removed the last obstacle to the internal cohesion of the team.

In his own fee arrangement with John Landis, James Neal was to be paid directly from Landis' pocket, with the understanding that the director would be compensated by Warner at a future date. At this time John Landis received $2 million in director's fees for *Three Amigos*, a figure said to be close to his $1.7 million in legal expenses. Wingo's attorney Eugene Trope had his fees paid directly by Houston Casualty. The fees for the attorneys representing Folsey, Allingham and Stewart, respectively Braun, Levine and Klein, had been paid for in combination between Warner and Travelers until the insurance company backed out of the criminal fee payments following the prelim in January 1984. But despite numerous requests by the attorneys that Warner advance them enough to pay the anticipated 4-5 month-long trial, they were still waiting for the studio to pay the money. Joel Behr, since he also represented Folsey and Allingham besides Landis, had agreed with their attorneys, Braun and Levine, to negotiate on their behalf to secure the trial fees. But for reasons that Braun termed "unbelievable" Behr alienated Arnie Klein by refusing in his negotiations with Warner Bros. to include the attorney for the powder chief.

Like Trope, Arnie Klein was not party to the nucleus of the defense but became key to "the plan," just as for different reasons Trope would. For "the plan" to work the inclusion of favorable testimony from the special effects crew was crucial, and only Arnie Klein could deliver them. Paul Stewart, Arnie's client, was the link to the two key powdermen, Jerry Williams and Jimmy Camomile. Neal had already singled out Camomile as the key witness whose recollections of events that night could make or break "the plan." Arnie Klein was a small person, as were all the lawyers except Harland Braun, a six-footer. Klein had curly hair and wore black-rimmed glasses and dressed in the odd-matching California style. His young proud wife brought cookies to the trial. Klein had a hip problem that caused him to drag one foot slightly and in other ways he might be said to limp slightly behind the hot-shot lawyers on the team. At this point, however, Neal approached Klein and after a series of discussions about fees assured him that he'd go to Warner's head counsel, John Schulman. The Nashville attorney gave Klein his personal guarantee that he'd get him the $100,000 he requested.

Shortly afterward, Neal's assistant Jim Sanders accompanied Harland Braun to a meeting with Schulman and O'Melveny's Scott Dunham at Warner's offices over at TBS. Braun put it in no uncertain terms. If the studio failed to come up with Klein's $100,000, "we'll lose the powdermen and we'll all go down the tubes." The argument was persuasive, and Warner fell into line and agreed to pay.

Warner's strategy was consistent with the overall case strategy conducted by Neal. The outcome of the criminal trial would determine the extent of Warner's liability in the still unresolved Le and Chen civil lawsuits. Once the trial opened the studio kept close tabs on the courtroom developments, having the daily transcript messengered over to Scott Dunham at the O'Melveny firm in Century City. From Warner Bros. Inc., Braun got paid ($150,000) and Levine ($100,000), and before the special-effects men took the stand Arnie Klein had been given $110,000.

James Neal always honored his personal guarantee.

James Neal made his entrance in the trial in the opening argument. The drama would not peak again until six months later when John Landis took the stand. A trial, especially a long one, is only interesting in snippets, and professional trial-watchers like the media people who sit through endlessly boring sessions, welcome a "personality." They were not disappointed in the Southern lawyer with the deceptive aw-shucks manner famous for winning the biggest cases. His opening appearance was the high point of the proceeding.

Among the media throng were two veterans who had followed the case since that first eerie excursion to Indian Dunes in the already faded Summer of Spielberg. Andy Furillo, no longer a cub, spoke like a seasoned newsman but he was still the same "carrot-top," honesty and freckles shining from his face. The other time-traveler from that strange distant summer dominated by *E.T.*, Sandy Kenyon of CNN, still blond and boyish and zestful for the newsman's chase, had also changed very little. Also among the crowd of television newsmen was Paul Dandridge, the local ABC station reporter and Robert Redford lookalike who would cover the case for the entire ten months. Dandridge became a Landis intimate, though wryly acknowledging even at the height of his favor that he had every expectation that after the trial he would be unceremoniously dropped.

Neal's prepared speech promised the jury his intent to prove that the disaster at Indian Dunes was an accident, a tragic accident, but one that was, in what would become his signature phrase, "unforeseen and unforeseeable." The jury was told there had been a "complete rehearsal" and "a plan," and that they would meet two witnesses whose testimony would bear out that had it not been for "unforeseeability," the "plan" would have come off successfully. Neal did not fail to describe the Landis production as a "Steven Spielberg film," and, perhaps with an eye to Warner, the "deep pocket," he brought up the name of Lucy Fisher as a person at Warner who worked with John.

If the defense case was like a movie with a financial backer, Warner Bros., a producer, Joel Behr, and a director, John Landis, it had in Neal found the star. From the opening argument until the closing session, he dominated the trial. His speech overshadowed the addresses made by the other lawyers on the team, and although the prosecutor's response was a model of succinctness and her presentation had great drama, the powerful impression left by James Neal made those who followed him seem anti-climactic.

Considering the prosecutor's lack of experience in a high-notoriety case of the *Twilight Zone* caliber, she made a very strong opening argument. She focused on the personality of John Landis and on the common-sense notion that no one would put kids near explosions at night under a low-flying helicopter. To prove the director's share of blame for the accident she informed the jurors that not only would she demonstrate the power of the explosives and the low position of the helicopter but also the role played by the screaming and tyrannical director. She promised to produce witnesses who would testify that Landis' erratic behavior on the set had created complete chaos and that despite repeated warnings from Andy House and Marci Liroff, Landis, Folsey and Allingham had gone ahead, even though they must have foreseen the possibility of exposing Myca and Renee to unsafe conditions.

The prosecutor's strategy was to start out with either Donna Schuman or Alpha Campbell as the lead witness. Although neither had been on the set that night, and though inadmissible as evidence, they had painted a shocking background in their discussions with the prosecutor. From Alpha Campbell, D'Agostino had heard of the director's closed-door meetings with a disheveled, drugged John Belushi. Alpha had mentioned to her the silver "snuffer" used to snort cocaine which she found on her desk one day and that when asked, according to Alpha, Landis said he didn't know what it was and told her to throw it away. The director's personal secretary told the prosecutor about Landis' order to destroy all copies of the script's third draft and his instructions to her on the morning of the crash to say nothing to anyone and not to send anything over to Warner.

But like Kesselman before her, the new prosecutor relied for the most devastating information from Donna Schuman. In recounting the constant joking about the explosives by Landis and Folsey in the Universal bungalow, Donna Schuman gave Lea D'Agostino her strong suit that could prove "foreseeability." Donna Schuman made a powerful emotional impression on the prosecutor and on September 3, 1986, she appeared in court as the prosecution's lead witness.

44

THE SECRET OF THE BABY DUMMIES

The prosecution had developed a kind of shorthand for the case. The bullhorn stood for the whole "lower, lower" business; similarly, the joking in the Universal bungalow by the two principal defendants about "going to jail" stood for "foreseeability." But while in the one instance six witnesses stated they saw John Landis use the bullhorn to give the fatal command, only one witness, Cynthia Nigh, had been reported as the source of the incriminating banter about going to jail. By putting on Donna Schuman as the prosecution's star witness, however, Lea D'Agostino had someone for the first time to corroborate Cynthia Nigh and help her in the trial's opening testimony fix a shattering impression on the minds of the jurors.

"If they find out we're using the children," on the stand Mrs. Schuman quoted Folsey, "it'll be a slap on the wrist, but if they find out about the explosives, they'll throw our butts in jail." She described the director at the time as standing down at the other end of the hallway where she observed him throw his arms up and heard him shout, "I want it big! I want it big!"

Though the testimony did not fail in impact, an important difference between the statements by the star witness and Cynthia Nigh's became immediately apparent. Nigh's depiction of Folsey joking about going to jail existed in transcripts of earlier proceedings and in investigators' notes. But in contrast, nothing like it had been recorded anywhere from Donna Schuman. And when the defense on cross-examination asked her why, in all of the previous four years, she had never brought up hearing such statements that were both dramatic and incriminating, her reply made the courtroom gasp. Astonishment ran through the galleries. In the press section pens dashed to paper as the media men and women scratched out notes that would produce a headline-making story the following day. According to the witness, the prosecutor at the time, four years earlier, had persuaded her to keep it as a surprise for the trial. Deputy DA Gary Kesselman, she testified, warned her not to mention it either at the grand jury or prelim because, in a flat affectless voice she quoted the ex-prosecutor of the case telling her Landis' lawyers "would kick the crap out of her."

In a sense the prosecutor's strange experience with the star witness was her real introduction to the *Twilight Zone* case. It led D'Agostino into the realm of the irrational and conundrum that was its characteristic. The star witness backfired. For if Donna Schuman told the truth, then the DA's office was at fault for having clearly committed a procedural violation by not informing the defendants earlier; and if Donna Schuman did not tell the truth, the prosecutor was putting on a liar. Here was Hobson's choice, the dilemma of having no choice at all, complicated by the fact that the most important witnesses to Schuman's statement were those who had interviewed her; that is, Gary Kesselman and Lea D'Agostino. And like a true tale of the unexpected, the episode climaxed with the unprecedented phenomenon whereby both prosecutors ended up taking the stand as witness against each other! Their appearances were brief, with Kesselman's limited at first, speaking as he did without benefit of his investigator's notes. But it was enough for the defense to cry foul and demand a mistrial on the basis of impropriety in the handling of the case by the DA's office.

All of this took place within the first weeks of the trial. While in the end the matter remained unresolved, the event briefly proved a media bonanza. Most of the excitement remained veiled from the jury. But more important than either the facts and statements or the witnesses was the damage the jurors saw inflicted on the prosecution. At the very start of the trial, they received powerful impressions of a high-fashion prosecutor tripping over a mine field and a pretty blond witness who had kept a sensational disclosure secret for four years. By putting on Donna Schuman first the prosecutor had sought to place an unredeemable light on the director's behavior; instead, the jury got lost in peripheral issues as D'Agostino ended up calling witnesses to corroborate Donna Schuman.

The irrational backfiring continued when a gossipy elderly chatterbox and occasional Hollywood writer named Kendis Rochlen took the stand ostensibly to help D'Agostino. In corroboration of her friend Donna Schuman, she told the court that Schuman had told her three years before about the "going to jail" banter by the two chief defendants. But as a witness Kendis Rochlen continued to chatter while being cross-examined by James Neal with results that were mortifying to the prosecution. Her admiration for Neal brought to the jury's attention the fact that Landis' chief defense counsel was a famous person, allowing Neal to seize one of the very few occasions the trial offered to impress the jury with his celebrity status. He was constantly interrupted by cries of praise from the admiring chatterbox.

"I watched you during Watergate. I know you're good," exclaimed Rochlen, the prosecution witness, in one such paean.

Neal was aw-shucks.

"There are a lot of people at Watergate that wouldn't agree with you."

* * *

The entire opening episode with Donna Schuman consumed two weeks of the actual trial. It provided the Gothic mold from which poured the rest of the lengthy, sprawling proceeding. A pattern was contained in the backfiring of witnesses like Schuman and Kendis Rochlen, or in the bizarre twist where two prosecutors turned witness in their own case. The reintroduction of Gary Kesselman was the ghost of El Gaucho come back to haunt the DA's office. Kesselman brought the excitable woman prosecutor to the edge of hysteria when six months later he returned to the stand to accuse both D'Agostino and Schuman of conspiracy to commit perjury!

Meanwhile, the prosecutor established at this early stage the pattern of unorthodoxy to which she remained faithful till the end of the trial. To counter the tactics of Landis' phalanx she conducted her own "disinformation campaign." In one instance, she peppered her office with phony technical material bearing the names of non-existent experts. She simply made them up, like Col. Nagaer (Reagan spelled backwards) in the hope of catching Harland Braun in his well-worn rounds of the DA's office late at night, thus spreading the erroneous impression that she would focus on his own pet delamination theory (and, in fact, one of the attorneys actually sent her a discovery request asking her to turn over all the information, including Col. Nagaer!) To the end of fomenting disarray in the Landis marriage she considered subpoenaing Jacqueline Compton, an acting student at UCLA who, as Landis' driver during the 1982 TZ production, had been rumored to have had a "relationship" with the director. Another tactic was a psychological shocker aimed at defeating Landis' portrayal of the deaths on the set as merely an "industrial accident." She erected in her office a gruesome picture board with photos from the coroner's and sheriff's departments showing the dead children and Morrow's decapitated head with his completely unidentifiable face. Occasionally she brought witnesses to look at it and until the end of the trial Harland Braun would get the best of the prosecutor by periodically inquiring in the hallway whether she still decorated her office with pictures of cutoff heads.

At the same time, the defense lawyers worked on Neal's "priority list" of witnesses. Neal had plenty of time to perfect the plan for it took the prosecutor six months to work through the more than 71 people she would call out of the 151 potential witnesses on her list. Assisted by his aide Jim Sanders, Neal met with the prime witnesses potentially key to "the plan" – stunt coordinator Gary McLarty, director of photography Steve Larner, script supervisor Kathryn Wooten and 1st AD, Elie Cohn. Paul Stewart's attorney was responsible for bringing in the powdermen, especially the man on whom the whole plan hinged, Jimmy Camomile. To Braun fell a delamination expert by the name of Gary Fowler, as well as Folsey's onetime gopher, Cynthia Nigh. Andy House, though on the priority witness list, refused to be interviewed by James Neal, but Leonard Levine, operating as a legal link between Nashville and LA, managed to set up what was to become an extremely critical meeting with him. To the chummy southerners Levine was "Lennybob," whose own client, Dan Allingham, would never testify. Allingham sat quietly and rather forlorn through the entire ten months next to Folsey, who would not testily either.

One of the witnesses in whom the prosecutor put great hopes was Jack Tice. But whether through bad luck or bad planning, the uncanny "back-firing" continued. The problem was the order of Tice's appearance. He followed the five other fire marshals to the witness stand. Among them they had worked on thousands of Hollywood movies over the past twenty years; and although they satisfied the prosecutor by stating in court that they had never observed the magnitude of special effects in conjunction with a low-flying helicopter as they had seen it done on the Landis set, their overall impression was of a group of ragtag retirees; a drab parade that went on for days, ending in unseemly finger-pointing capped by a bombshell that deepened D'Agostino's credibility crisis with the 12 citizens in the box. Fire marshal Richard Ebentheuer jolted everyone as he testified for the first time in the case that he had given an early warning that the helicopter would crash and that his warning had been ignored by fire officers on the set.

The defense again rose to cry foul. Implicitly, in front of the jury and explicitly in the hallway before the thronged media, Neal asked how John Landis could be held responsible for not knowing the scene was dangerous if the fire marshals didn't think it was? Neal queried into the whirring tapes and blinking cameras, "Wasn't it their job to prevent fire dangers on the set?" And when it was further revealed that Ebentheuer had issued a post-crash memo related to his early warning that had since disappeared from the files, Neal pulled thoughtfully on his Encanto cigar, "Now I know I really am in the 'Twilight Zone.'"

The whole episode reflected poorly on the prosecution. Even though the fire marshals were able to explain how they handled Ebentheuer's warning, the doubt persisted that they sought to blame Landis for their own shortcomings. The defense did all it could to spread this feeling to the jury and it was largely due to this background of lingering suspicion that Jack Tice turned out not nearly as effective as the prosecution had hoped he would be.

Since much of what had been done on the set that night appeared to have had the object of deceiving Tice, his testimony could have been devastating. He testified to the concealment of the children. He claimed that he was not shown mortars under any structures or huts. He asserted that the helicopter departed from its flight path in the final scene, moving far closer to the explosions than expected. He also mentioned that no one had ever asked him as persistently as the location manager Dick Vane did that night where he would be located for the fatal shot.

The defense prudently waived cross-examining him, the only time it did so for all of the 71 prosecution witnesses in the trial; as Jim Sanders put it, "You don't fix something unless it's broke." The purpose of cross-examination is to discredit but this time they preferred to get the volatile witness off the stand rather than give him the opportunity to express anything that might be any more damaging.

The trial's most important group of witnesses were the people who had been closest to Landis on the set and had witnessed the final explosion and the crash: Kathryn Wooten, Elie Cohn, Andy House, Gary McLarty and Cynthia Nigh. Before appearing in court, they had met often with John Landis' lawyers. In the process, some had been "softened," others stiffened or bolstered, and one, at least, the second in command on the set that night, had been carefully groomed: by the time 1st AD Elie Cohn came face to face with the Dragon Lady he had met a number of times with the director's private investigator Robert Frasco, as well as with Landis' personal attorneys Joel Behr and John Diemer. On the eve of the trial, he conferred with James Neal and Neal's aide, Jim Sanders.

Though nominally witnesses for the prosecution, the testimony of this group tended to support Neal's "plan." For the prosecutor its members sounded a steady drumbeat of frustration. Her hopes of getting them to reiterate earlier accounts containing much that was damaging to the director went down in the "softened" versions they delivered on the stand. Their mild responses to the prosecutor's questioning waxed even more tender of the director's case under cross-examination by Neal. Their stories not only got changed and amplified but in buttressing "the plan" were decked out with fresh detail never heard before.

Typical was Kathryn Wooten's explanation of her own handwritten notations in the shooting script. Her original notes appeared to indicate that the exploding hut "spectacular" was scheduled for 2:20. Under oath she told the prosecutor that the reference applied to the explosions for the 9:30 take; by claiming that her actual 2:20 notation was a mistake, she helped defuse the characterization of a director driven to achieve "bigger" fireballs. Similarly, she backed off from the comment made four years before that the fatal fireballs were "three times" the size of those at 11:30; she explained that she had referred to them numerically and not by magnitude, bigger because "there were more of them." In defiance of logic, she clung to positions that forced her into contradictions. When asked about the director's last-minute warning to the spectators and crew to stand up for the final shot, Wooten testified that Landis customarily prefaced all action scenes with this summons. Unlike the occasion once before during the prelim, this time Landis' one-time script girl did not mention danger as the reason.

Elie Cohn's gyrations in support of "the plan" were even more tortuous.

Throughout the proceedings Landis' 1st AD had never failed to evince a willingness to change his recollections, notably those dealing with the cues to be used in the final shot. To Warner studio's own in-house probe, as well as to private eye Frasco, he accounted himself as being "ninety-five per cent sure" that John Landis was the person who had screamed the fatal command. At the same time, he confided in the phalanx, giving them details which he never transmitted to the authorities or even to the studio. The trial heard him offer a new statement. This time he was "ninety-five per cent sure" that it was not John Landis but himself who issued the "lower, lower" order!!! Previously he had described to the phalanx the mysterious "stick" in the middle of the river as being an important cue for what he referred to as the "big one" – a particularly large village explosion in the final scene which he said was controlled from the firing board in the hands of Jerry Williams. At the trial Cohn never mentioned the "big one."

This time the stick was described as the cue for explosions on the dam while the purpose of its being planted in the river, he explained, was to give direction to Vic Morrow's path.

Cohn supported the director on key issues even when, like Wooten, it forced him into double talk. On the stand, under prosecution questioning he had been unable to specifically remember a single session either before the 11:30 or 2:20 takes; nonetheless, he gave a ringing affirmative when asked by Neal whether in his opinion it was a complete and well-rehearsed plan. Cohn confirmed "the plan" by stating that it was the helicopter's mission to turn and go across the river and film the exploding village. Once more he revised the account he gave to Warner Bros., as well as his NTSB version from five years before when he never mentioned such a plan, instead stating that the helicopter was to "go back the same way we came.... turn and go back."

As far as the defense was concerned it mattered little that its own priority witnesses in sworn trial testimony contradicted statements they had made earlier. It would matter very much, however, if on the stand they contradicted each other. And with no one was this concern more apparent than with the troubled "Alan Smithee" of the movie's screen credits. Remorseful over his participation in a venture which he knew to be dangerous, Andy House could deal a mortal blow to a plan which sought to characterize the tragedy in Indian Dunes as "unforeseen and unforeseeable." He might well contradict Elie Cohn who was on record as telling the jury that his 2nd AD had never raised safety matters with him, let alone approached him time and again with requests to use dummies.

The intervening years had failed to erase the event from House's mind. Despite the Alan Smithee substitution, he had been unable to sever himself from the deaths on the set. The pressures had mounted. During his terribly damaging testimony at the prelim Harland Braun had attacked him in the press. While House was working as a 2nd AD over at Walt Disney Studios in Burbank, John Landis had personally enlisted one of House's superiors there, a senior VP of TV and motion picture production, to exert influence on him to meet with Landis or his lawyers. But even though House feared for his future prospects at the studio where Landis' close friend Jeff Katzenberg held power, he continued to save his story for the witness stand, refusing to meet with James Neal.

In his late thirties with three kids, including one new baby, he worried about the blacklist. Ultimately House was vulnerable to pressure. Nevertheless, he remained unwilling to get involved directly with the Landis defense – and if he did in the end it was because he felt certain sympathies with Dan Allingham. Both were little wheels within big wheels and there was probably tremendous pressure on Allingham as well, he felt. Andy

House finally did agree to a meeting with Allingham's lawyer Leonard Levine on the condition, rather naively, that "Lennybob," the LA nexus to Nashville, promise not to share the information with James Neal.

The meeting took away much of House's former militancy. As a result, the trial saw the "softened" form of House who gave a watered-down version of his almost constant danger warnings. Under the careful cross-examination of defense lawyer Levine, House testified that, although safety was a concern during the filming, his chief worry had been the "illegality" of the act of hiring the children.

For Andy House the case remained a continuing ordeal.

* * *

Gary McLarty was a taciturn stuntman with a rugged profile who kept his emotions bottled deep inside. Around the time of the trial, he suddenly moved out of his home in the suburban San Fernando Valley to a remote part of the county. Up in Angeles Crest Forest, hidden in the brush and sage, he lived in a trailer invisible from the narrow mountain road, up which he would roar on his motorcycle to the empty spread he called his "ranch."

As the trial opened a mystery arose in the sheriff's department; in the DA's special investigative division people asked where was Gary McLarty? The Dragon Lady breathed fire. She threatened to have him arrested if he didn't respond to a subpoena. The elusive stuntman was finally served the summons before the trial as he was working on a movie set, but to investigators his mountain hideaway high up in Angeles Crest Forest remained unknown.

The trial of John Landis came at an especially vulnerable point in McLarty's life. While being chased by subpoenas from the DA, he was in the midst of an acrimonious marital breakup. At age 50, after nearly 35 years of flipping over in cars and spilling from buildings in over 400 movies, McLarty was ready to make room in the business for younger people. McLarty was Vic's age, but unlike the actor who hoped to make a comeback, the stuntman dreamed of retirement and turning his ranch into a small location setting where movies could be shot.

In reviewing his career, Gary McLarty liked to make a point of mentioning that when he first began stunting for Landis in *Animal House* his fee was just about that of the young director's. Ever since, for over a decade, he had been Landis' loyal stuntman with a working relationship that had always been intimate. The various action sequences in the Landis segment had involved the stunt coordinator from the earliest stage, when he accompanied John Landis to Morrow's Sherman Oaks home, to the final night of shooting when he climbed aboard the helicopter with a combat-blackened face while Morrow in the blue suit of Bill got ready to make his dash with the children in the shallow river. McLarty had been the only one with direct knowledge of what Landis really wanted from Vic Morrow in the final shot. Understandably, he was not eager to get involved in a controversy in which, as far as he was concerned, he had only been following orders from the director.

Keeping his mountain hideaway secret as the trial wound on, it was not until after McLarty testified that, following a tip from a reporter, Tom Budds was finally able to locate and interview the stuntman outside the courtroom – and experience the same "difficult" behavior that had angered Lea D'Agostino. McLarty was more forthcoming in his dealings with the phalanx. On the eve of the trial, he met with James Neal in Behr's Century City offices. On another occasion he welcomed Eugene Trope to the "ranch." Trope joined the stuntman in downing a bottle of whiskey, holding his own by pretending to keep up with his host while surreptitiously pouring out his tumblers.

McLarty's interest to the DA's office was obvious from his prior testimony and the many questions it raised. Why was he up in the chopper during the final take and not on the ground with the director coordinating the stunt? Especially, why wasn't he doubling for Vic and carrying two dummies instead of the 100-pound weight represented by two children that made the river-crossing so precarious?

The account he gave in court failed to answer these questions. Some contradictions to this version could be found in the NTSB record, but the stuntman's real story emerged only in private remarks confided to intimates. According to a number of these confidants, McLarty's actual experiences on the set were far different from the way he described them under oath in the courtroom. But all that the prosecutor was able to learn concerning the doubtfulness of the stuntman's courtroom story came during makeup-man Bob Westmoreland's pre-trial interview with her. Westmoreland related having listened to McLarty complain during the shooting of the Nazi sequence that he was ready to be the stunt double in the scene with the helicopter and explosives, but that Landis wanted Vic to do it himself. Away from the trial setting, in fact, McLarty elaborated, "Landis definitely wanted Vic Morrow in his shot, he was the one he was shooting the movie about."

By the time Gary McLarty was called as a witness he was working as stunt coordinator on *Beverly Hills Cop II*. On the stand he denied the makeup artist's recollections during several hours of grueling questioning by the prosecutor. The exchanges between the taciturn stuntman and the sharp gadfly marked the most unabashed hostility to be seen in the entire trial. McLarty with his emotions precariously bottled up inside looked menacing. He snarled at the prosecutor, who showed her emotions perhaps too plainly, for at times she could be seen visibly recoiling. Afterwards she dramatically recalled her fear that the witness would step down and sock her one.

McLarty could later be seen seething in the hallway. Up in his trailer in Angeles Crest Forest he unburdened himself to Helen English, a close friend and neighbor. He discussed with Helen his fears of potential blacklisting as a result of his testifying a certain way and not in another. There was little encouragement for him as to his own predicament in his neighbor's reminiscence of an incident that had involved her husband, a Hollywood cameraman over at RKO studios in the old days, who once witnessed an accident on a set. The moral of the story appeared to be that her husband had suffered as a result of telling the truth.

But despite or because of his official reticence, McLarty seemed eager to let the truth be known. Perhaps in the belief that only stuntmen could understand his feelings, he chose for his confidants other members of his profession. One of these, an aspiring young stunt player who sought the veteran stuntman's help in breaking into Hollywood, heard him grumble enigmatically, "Had they listened to me nobody would have been killed." Only McLarty's innermost circle was familiar with the allusion, for they heard him tell the true story of what took place between himself and the bearded director in the final moments before the fatal shot.

What was remarkable about the story, and lent it credence, was that it supported the accounts given by others: from the greensman Jerry Cutten, Vic's friend Billy Fine and Vic's attorney Al Green to the set hairdresser Virginia Kearns, makeup-man Bob Westmoreland and the shooting schedule notation DBL/Bill, each supplied separate confirmation of the stuntman's highly confidential account that the director pushed Vic into performances which the actor neither wished nor was equipped to do. In a recollection that contrasted sharply to his sworn testimony before the jury, McLarty gave this astonishing account at a party in the home of another well-known stunt coordinator:

On that night in Indian Dunes just before the cameras rolled the rugged stuntman had in his arms two baby dummies wrapped in blankets. Ready to step in for Vic with the dummies he asked Landis to let him go on and run across the river. McLarty related to his small circle of friends how in the last minutes he had tried to convince Landis that his run across the river with the dummies wouldn't make any difference on the screen. Reportedly, he told the director there was no sense in getting Vic wet in the middle of the night. McLarty ended his story by saying that he got "talked out of it" by Landis who told him that the actor actually wanted to do the stunt himself...

As it did for Andy House, the disaster never ceased being an ordeal for Gary McLarty. The complications of his life in the latter part of '86, beset by a bitter marital breakup, the prospect of becoming a key witness in a criminal trial and his secret of the baby dummies, seemed to come to a head one day as he was returning home on his motorcycle from the shooting of *Beverly Hills Cop II*. Perhaps when he heard the police siren, he saw only further complications. In a real-life action scene that might have been an outtake from the cop movie he was just then working on he attempted to evade arrest, leading a high-speed police chase as he fled for the haven of sanity in the sage and brush of the clean, high Angeles forest. In a strange turn, a helicopter joined the pursuit, and it was as if the silent stuntman in his escape from the law was himself reenacting Vic's chase by the Huey. The chase led up the narrow mountain road to the ranch where the helicopter roared and clattered as it stood over the trailer... as once the Huey had stood over the hut.

The penalty for McLarty's attempted evasion of arrest would certainly have complicated his life by putting him in jail. But it was Hollywood; and the complicated business was to have a happy ending. Just before his court appearance in his own case, discovering that the judge was an "an old movie buff," McLarty invited the magistrate to the set of *Beverly Hills Cop II* where, as a special favor to the stuntman, the star, Eddie Murphy, allowed himself to be photographed with McLarty's special guest, later signing the photos and presenting them to the judge.

Though he was fined the mandatory $5,000, McLarty boasted to friends of the power of Hollywood connections. Even a stuntman could get off without doing his ten days in jail.

* * *

The press, like the jury and the public, saw nothing of the battle for the souls of the key witnesses. The maneuvering of big law firms and big Hollywood studios, the restless movement of interests, the constant calculating of clever minds, the clandestine meetings and *sub rosa* signals were beyond the capacity of the press. The TZ press corps divided its time between the courtroom where decorum prevailed, more or less, and the hallway which, with its cameras, gossip and commotion, was like a movie set. Like any Hollywood trial, the personalities overshadowed the issues. The triad featured a famous Hollywood director and a leading man from Watergate. The press discovered in Lea D'Agostino a surprisingly feisty supporting role as the prosecutor who gave as good as she got. In the hallway the media people watched her hold her own with Harland Braun. She would come right up to the six-footer with all her little height and on tiptoe inform him that he was good-looking and reminded her of Spencer Tracy, while cautioning him to put his "mind in gear before it got going"; another time the press heard her tweak Braun's countenance – if he was Pinocchio his nose would already be in Brooklyn.

The hallway served the prosecutor as the arena to settle scores with the defense lawyers. In the middle of the corridor just outside the courtroom she dealt with those witnesses who on the stand backed off in favor of Landis. She accused them of out-and-out lying to protect their friend and employer. She blamed the blacklist for making witnesses hesitant to testify. During these hallway dramas the defense called her everything from being "star-struck" and wanting to be a movie star herself to being "strange-looking" and having the "brain of a radish." Neal's assistant Jim Sanders would ask, "How do you tell someone to have class?" But with her feisty repartee she stemmed in part the flow of Braun's media quotes and with her confrontational stance she prevented the hallway from becoming completely a Joel Behr-John Landis production. She worked herself to exhaustion in order to satisfy her superiors in the DA's office, who had bet on her that she could keep the trial from turning into a "DeLorean."

In the hubbub of the hallway, Landis, talking cautiously to a select few friendly reporters, showed he was now much better versed in press handling. "Neal trained him not to argue;" Braun explained. In the Criminal Court building, and oftentimes out, John Landis was never far from James Neal.

Landis' restrained appearance demonstrated the success of Neal's modification of his personal behavior, at least for the duration of the trial. Judge Ben Landis had died the year before and it seemed as if James Neal replaced the father figure in the director's life. Asserting parental supervision in the form of client control, perhaps only a man of Neal's moral stature, prominence and authority, a "gray-haired eminence," could keep John Landis in line. On numerous occasions during the trial when Judge Boren felt compelled to warn Landis or members of his party not to disturb the proceedings by making strange faces or communicating in esoteric signals, it was the calm paternal assurance of James Neal of Neal & Harwell which satisfied the judge that such incidents would not reoccur.

Like much of the vital testimony, like "Bill" in the script, the Landis personality had been softened. For his daily courtroom wear Neal had changed his client's glasses from hornrims to a softer wire frame. On occasion, when he arrived at the courthouse still wearing the dark black glasses that were his trademark, Landis' costume designer wife could be seen shuffling through her purse and handing her husband the less striking wire spectacles that marked his ten-month courtroom appearance. Landis' face was softened by removing much of the hair. On top the raven locks were shrunk down and the once rabbinically disordered beard was neatly trimmed. He looked gangling, like a Rick Baker creation in ill-fitting suits. In the hallway he was inseparable from his wife who tottered and towered over the small-statured flock of lawyers and even over her husband's own six-foot frame. They held hands like a honeymoon couple and across the barrier in the courtroom continued to steal glances and pass messages. Mrs. Landis played down the look of a Hollywood wife. She appeared at the sessions looking like a middleclass homemaker in drab grays and browns, without jewelry, her hair long and free-flowing, without apparent benefit of a Hollywood stylist.

The press quickly discovered, however, that the young Landises were not the stars of the trial but that the dominating personality was James Neal. Vintage southern in gesture and phrase, he intrigued and enthralled the media people. They clustered around him in the hallway and never grew tired of hearing his crackling observations for all of the ten months.

At the beginning of the trial, in order not to create jealousy among the defense team, Neal kept himself aloof from the hallway forum, leaving to Braun the role of axe-man and ring master of the antics. But as the trial dragged on (Neal said he tried Jimmy Hoffa twice and it never took this long) he could no longer pass up the opportunity to tell marvelous tales of Watergate and the times of Bobby Kennedy. He had been prosecutor in the Kennedy battle with the mob and related the chilling experience of seeing Jimmy Hoffa in court raise a hand at him, giving the unmistakable sign of "the finger." To the younger cubs among his listeners the name Alexander Butterfield had little meaning but the older reporters in the hallway heard Neal add a footnote to the century's biggest political scandal when he identified Butterfield, the former Air Force secretary in the Nixon cabinet, as the man he believed was Watergate's mysterious "Deep Throat."

Neal came across to the jury as a good ol' boy. During Elie Cohn's testimony he reminded the jurors that he came from the Bible Belt. He brought a country note to LA law, a Nashville sound in which a ride to the courthouse in Trope's Rolls was pronounced to be "high-cotton." His approach to womanhood was respectful and gracious. "Oh, it's not this pretty lady here, is it?" he cried out one day when Larry the Bailiff escorted Neal to meet his wife. "Ah always keep mah ize out for a pu- retty woman." His southern courtesy failed only with respect to the lady he insisted on calling "Mizz De Owgustino." At the height of the flap caused by Donna Schuman's appearance he quipped to Braun, referring to the salad days of Watergate, "Remember the days of the truth squad, Harland? Do you have a truth squad to follow Mizz De Owgustino?"

On the prosecutor's birthday Neal proposed to make a cake. "I wouldn't make an ordinary cake," he noted, "I'd make a cake in the form of a chocolate Oscar." On another day the hallway was entertained by his suggestion that a psychiatrist who was asked to testify about Dorcey Wingo's memory also analyze "Mizz De Owgustino." There were other moments when the court adjourned with the lawyers packing their briefcases and the lagging spectator in the visitors' gallery was treated to seeing the man from Watergate steal up impishly behind the bird-like prosecutor to swat in mock panic at the golden bee on her shoulder. Occasionally in her presence he would whistle a few bars from Dixie, or mull out loud with Dan Allingham's lawyer, announcing to the hallway at large the future of the prosecutor in politics:

"Lennie Levine ... Mr. Chairman ... the delegation from the great state of Tennessee casts its one vote for ... Lay-ah De Owgustino."

45

THE ARNIE KLEIN SHOW

The hallway with its party-like atmosphere showed the Landis defense team in a harmony that was for the most part superficial. The banter with the press and by the lawyers amongst their own, masked serious tensions which at any time threatened to break the ranks.

Tearing at the unity of the lawyers was the same social division of the set between the above-the-line-Neal, Braun and Levine-and the below-the-line, Eugene Trope and Arnie Klein, representing, respectively, Dorcey Wingo and Paul Stewart. The differences between the two sides had been bridged by the consensus over "the plan" which laid the entire accident to the misfiring by one man. Accordingly, Arnie Klein, though rank-wise lowest among Landis' lawyers, for a brief time came to hold leverage over the defense team. It was up to Klein to deliver Jimmy Camomile since, for the plan to succeed, Camomile had to say for the first time that he fired early.

For the sake of a plan whose viability rested on the testimony of the special effects crew, Neal continued courting Arnie Klein. As for Stewart, since he was a defendant, he had the right not to testify and like Folsey and Allingham he would follow Neal's strategy by keeping off the stand the mass of contradictions which would become admissible if he testified. However, Neal was unable to prevent the prosecutor from subpoenaing under a grant of immunity the other powdermen, Jerry Williams, Jimmy Camomile, Harry Stewart and Kevin Quibell. Like Paul Stewart they had already in the past testified to many particulars that could undermine the "plan." From Neal's standpoint their appearance marked Klein's moment of truth. It was his baptism of fire, the test whether he could deliver.

The first powderman to take the stand was one of the youngest, Kevin Quibell, who at the time of the crash had been relatively new to SFX. For much of Quibell's testimony Neal sat white-fisted behind his table as he watched a near-disaster unfold for his client. It could have been avoided, Neal felt, if Klein had handled it better. Quibell presented a picture of powdermen who did not pay much attention to the safety aspects of their trade. Quibell didn't remember a 2:00 A.M. "rehearsal" and stated that he had been firing squibs in the water from the shore opposite the village, stopping just before the helicopter crashed as he saw Vic Morrow stumble with the kids; he believed Vic was in trouble since the stumble had not been planned. Neal was upset because until Quibell the stumble hadn't been an issue, not even when the prosecutor had asked the 1st AD about it once before. Klein's test was doubtful. Neal had reason to fear whether Klein would come through.

More important than Quibell were the next two witnesses, Jerry Williams and Jimmy Camomile, both, according to their earlier testimony, responsible for the fireball explosions in the village and river that were in the helicopter's flight path. Jerry Williams was questioned first, and this time Neal did not ball his hands so the blood drained from the knuckles. Bearded and burly, Jerry Williams showed hostility to the prosecutor second only to that of Gary McLarty, who would follow him to the stand a week later. Well-prepared by Klein on the Sunday before he took the stand, frequently glowering at the prosecutor, he told a story that was largely a repetition of past statements. But with the DA's investigation already hopelessly bungled it hardly seemed to matter. The fact that during the crash Williams had been standing right next to John Landis and that he was the probable triggerman whose firing board connected to the fatal No. 4 mortar was not even an issue in the trial.

Jerry Williams presented an extremely confusing account involving mortars, square and round, fireballs and the mechanics of black powder explosions. He was very clear, however, in a startling statement never heard before from him but which lent crucial support to "the plan." Williams testified to attending a meeting with Stewart and Camomile just before the fatal shot where he said he was admonished by Stewart, "Whatever you do, don't set off any explosions under the helicopter." Asked by the prosecutor why in all of five years he had never throughout his various statements and interviews mentioned this meeting with the powder chief, Williams merely shrugged and said he had forgotten.

The prosecutor, with a deep sense of his deliberate obfuscations, tried to make the most of the poor figure the burly witness cut in his testimony. But she was playing with a lot of loose ends and her goal of convincing the jurors eluded her. The rambling "hillbilly" scattered the threads or pulled at them with a brazen force so that they ravelled in her hands. To tie the knots she would have required answers to basic questions – answers which investigators or other parties never provided her. She had no clear idea as to who among the powdermen fired the fatal No. 4 "humdinger" or how explosives got spirited from the set; the picture of powdermen boozing on the set was never laid before the jurors; other support in the form of cooperation from Warner studios which had all the evidence of a "shoddy" operation was equally lacking. These vast lacunae in an already bewildering picture had the effect on the jurors of making the issues presented by Jerry Williams even more intricate and confusing.

Deprived of a pattern capable of delineating the role of each powderman, the prosecutor could only use Williams to cast doubt on the SFX crew's credibility as a whole. Among other things, she demonstrated that Williams himself, contrary to his testimony, was not watching the helicopter during the final flight. By furnishing as proof the sound studies done by the sheriff's department, she showed that Williams was still firing his explosions long after the helicopter had been hit. This strongly suggested he was not looking. Even if Williams had been told by his chief to look up and not set off any explosions under the craft, which he'd never mentioned before, the sound studies indicated that he violated Stewart's instruction by not looking up.

The strangest story of a witness was that of Jimmy Camomile, the "pigeon" singled out by Neal because some of his previous statements were completely out of sync with "the plan." Unlike the confused and ambiguous expressions from the other powdermen on record, Camomile in his very early interviews with investigators had made explicit denials of having been told anything about the flight path or where the chopper would be, or of any discussions in which he was instructed not to fire any bombs until the helicopter left the area. Of all the powdermen, Camomile was alone insofar as his prior statements and testimony ran absolutely contrary to the defense version Neal wished to present to the jury.

Camomile's eventual adherence to the "plan" came about largely as the result of forceful promptings from his friends. At the time of the prelim Paul Stewart and Jerry Williams had succeeded in convincing him that he was the "triggerman," despite the fact that almost all the original evidence showed that it was Jerry Williams who, from his firing board, blew up hut No. 4. But for the trial Paul Stewart asked Camomile to take one further step and corroborate Jerry Williams' novel testimony. Camomile was asked to say that just before the last shot Stewart had conveyed to them a "safe plan" not to fire any bombs under or near the helicopter. Camomile agreed in principle to corroborate Stewart's last-minute instructions: Arnie Klein, however, was not satisfied until he took the unusual step to obtain a signed statement to that effect just before Camomile took the stand.

Klein was the only defense lawyer able to develop a rapport with the powdermen, who were still Paul Stewart's close friends. Through a discreet network Klein was able to keep in touch with the SFX crew without directly involving his client. Just how loyal they remained to Stewart became evident when Frasco, Landis' detective, informed Neal that Jerry Williams would not meet with the Nashville attorney without Arnie Klein being present. Klein's counsel had helped the SFX crew deal with seeming inconsistencies by subtly shading their testimony. But the task of bringing round Camomile was an operation delicately borderline to soliciting perjury. At a crucial meeting in Klein's Century City office on the eve of Camomile's appearance before the prosecutor, Camomile listened as Klein explained that, if convicted, Paul Stewart might end up in San Quentin. Camomile came to realize how important it was for him to testify that just before the fatal shot Paul Stewart had instructed him not to fire any SFX explosives under or near the helicopter.

"You understand," Klein reiterated solemnly with reference to Paul Stewart, "she's trying to send him to state prison."

Camomile burst into tears. He hugged Klein. Klein hugged him. Camomile promised, "Don't worry, Arnie. I won't let her send him to state prison." And still streaming tears, Camomile signed the statement which Klein had ready lying on his desk.

By the time Camomile took the stand just before Christmas of 1986, the jury had heard his name mentioned many times as the triggerman who allegedly fired the fatal explosion. In the hallway the press, at least the male portion, had heard Neal refer on many occasions to what he termed facetiously Camomile's "premature ejaculation." Klein all the while feared that his story about Stewart being sent to state prison might inadvertently slip from the tongue of the witness, and with the prosecutor asking, "Is that why you're changing your testimony?" send the plan, and perhaps his law career, crashing to the ground. But Camomile's trial appearance turned out to be Klein's finest hour.

Just before the crucial session commenced, Klein basked in the attention of the Landis legal squad, was nervous and excited. "Get ready for the Arie Klein show," he announced with bravura just before he entered the courtroom; and afterwards in the hallway during the break it was like being a star during the intermission of a successful performance.

Klein had delivered!

He was warmly embraced by Neal, slapped on the back and, on the only occasion during the entire trial, offered congratulations by the famous lawyer from Nashville.

On the stand Camomile had stuck to the new version supporting the "safe plan" which proved the tragedy at Indian Dunes to have been an unforeseeable accident. The youthful-looking ex-Navy man with his frank gaze and refreshing sobriety kept his promise. He testified that he had been warned by Paul Stewart just before the crash not to fire off his mortar near or underneath the helicopter. He stated that Stewart told him to look up before firing…

Jimmy Camomile, the loyal powderman, the poor "pigeon," carried the load – for Stewart and Wingo, for Folsey and Allingham, for John Landis – and ultimately for Spielberg and Warner.

46

"MALATROPISMS"

O
utside the presence of the jury, D'Agostino persistently raised the issue of blacklisting and tried to have the judge admit as evidence examples of industry pressure on witnesses. In most instances the judge either banned such testimony or in a few cases limited it to very narrow areas. In the hallway James Neal argued before the press that the prosecutor had no basis for her allegations. The national hero of Watergate blunted the critiques even of witnesses who at the trial confessed to fear, or who had actual experience of being deprived of jobs in Hollywood for political reasons. Nevertheless, despite these hindrances, the prosecutor did manage to get before the jury some highly effective witnesses drawn from the industry itself.

Years after the *Twilight Zone* crash, news spread that cameramen Steve Lydecker and Roger Smith still had difficulty getting work. But in other cases, like Andy House at Disney, subtler examples of work-place pressure on witnesses never reached the press. Alpha Campbell complained that a particular secretary had been planted next to her in the office at Universal studios to keep an eye on her at the time of the trial. And Marci Liroff, the casting agent who once cast for *E.T.* and *Poltergeist*, felt that she had suffered professionally as the result of having testified that she warned Landis about the danger of using the kids in the scene.

Due to certain rulings by the judge, the prosecution had to focus its case exclusively on the fatal scene. To show criminal negligence it had to prove to the jury what the Hollywood customs and practices were in the shooting of similar action scenes involving dangerous special effects. A fine line separated simple negligence due to error or oversight from a reckless act in which the dangers are explicitly known. At the same time hardly any California law dealt with standards regulating Hollywood's use of explosives and aircraft as they related to special effects. To help show the wanton recklessness and implied malice of the act with which Landis was criminally charged, Hollywood's foremost motion picture helicopter pilot, James Gavin, made an impressive appearance. Ironically, Landis had three years before attempted to recruit Gavin for *Blues Brothers*, but the famous stunt pilot had been busy at the time.

Ramrod straight, salt-and-pepper Hollywood handsome, Gavin had performed as a precision pilot in over 500 motion pictures in his 27 years in the industry, from John Huston's 1959 *The Misfits* to his recent *Blue Thunder*. Besides being a stunt pilot and stunt coordinator, he was also a 2nd unit director and member of the Director's Guild and well-known for his activism in the DGA to upgrade the professional standards for air stunts. He had been trained in the military. Moreover, he had not only flown through many explosions and fireballs but also had extensive experience flying in scenes with SFX explosions shot at Indian Dunes. Gavin had been involved, along with another famed Hollywood pilot, Ross Reynolds, as adviser to NTSB investigators immediately following the 1982 *Twilight Zone* crash. He had even been the recipient of a leaden letter from Harland Braun at the time of the crash because he openly criticized Landis in a *People* magazine article. His declaration that he would not have piloted the helicopter under the conditions that existed that night contained a stinging rebuke of both Landis and Wingo.

Well up on the case, having actually read key documents, Gavin described the whole operation that night in the dunes as a catastrophe. His most damaging criticism was leveled at the pilot for not having followed the customs and standards of the profession. At 11:30, after near disaster in the rage scene, Gavin maintained, Wingo should have removed himself and his helicopter from the set. After being surprised by the location of the uncommonly powerful fire and water mortar that buffeted his craft, he should have realized that the director had either failed to inform him or had altered the plan without telling him – sufficient reason either way to refuse further participation in the filming of the scene.

A different problem for D'Agostino was finding a peer of John Landis in the industry itself. She wanted a professional film maker to explain to the jurors in simple terms film as the art of illusion, making it clear how John Landis could have achieved his cinematic effects without exposing cast and crew to danger. But no director came forward. Stumped in her search, for D'Agostino, despite her rumored liaison with Peter Sellers, was not at all well-connected in Hollywood, she was forced to concentrate on directors whose comments in response to the crash had been quoted in the press. The DGA had gone on record with the promise to take some action once the trial was over, and a review of the 1982 state senate hearings enabled the prosecutor to identify certain key people involved in guild safety issues, notably, Harry Evans, DGA executive vice president, and directors Jackie Cooper and Richard Brooks.

Accompanied by her DA investigator, Jerry Loeb, the prosecutor held the first exploratory meeting with Jackie Cooper and Harry Evans at DGA headquarters on June 14, 1986, a month before the start of the trial. Harry Evans had known Vic Morrow personally. Jackie Cooper at 64, whose film career beginning at age three almost spanned the entire history of Hollywood, regaled the prosecutor with stories of the film capital's fascinating past. On a more serious note, however, he felt uncomfortable about committing himself to an appearance as a prosecution witness since the DGA itself still adhered to a non-aligned stand until the trial's conclusion. As head of the DGA safety committee, Jackie Cooper declared himself firmly behind statements he made at the senate hearings in October 1982. He voiced the same strong belief that the director's role included "an obligation for the safety of those on the set," mentioning proudly the guild's new safety standards prepared as a result of the crash. The prosecutor, in turn, urged him to see the fatal *Twilight Zone* footage. At last, she pulled out of an envelope a series of photographs of the decapitated heads of Vic Morrow and Myca, as well as a photo of the shoulder and arm separated from the boy. Loeb could see that Cooper was shaken by the presentation.

Ten days after the meeting with Jackie Cooper, D'Agostino met with Richard Brooks. The noted guild director, who 30 years earlier had actually brought Vic Morrow to Hollywood from New York to do *Blackboard Jungle*, recounted to D'Agostino the famous fire scene in *Elmer Gantry*. He readily acknowledged that the director and the stunt coordinator had to be prepared for every eventuality when doing a hazardous scene. In Brooks, too, the prosecutor felt a willingness to depart from the guild's neutral position on the *Twilight Zone* tragedy.

Both directors were in their sixties and two days after the meeting with Brooks she met with John Milius, a director from the brash young world of John Landis. Jerry Loeb had arranged the meeting by using one of his studio contacts. Milius was identified with the youthful mainstream, Coppola and the University of Southern California film school group. He'd written the screenplay for *Apocalypse Now* and belonged with Hollywood's money-making movie makers that filled screens with action movies like his own *Conan the Barbarian* and *Red Dawn*.

The prosecutor knew that she had left behind the mellow generation of Jackie Cooper and Richard Brooks and entered the strange world of the new young Hollywood in Milius' office on the 20th Century Fox lot. Facing down from one wall was a giant portrait of Marine Corps General "Chesty" Bowles. The director was surrounded by swords and rifles functioning as decorations. His girlfriend was there, a Hollywood starlet, and together the director, the Dragon Lady, the starlet and the investigator went to lunch. The prosecutor again carried her grim bundle of photos. She displayed them during lunch. The pictures succeeded in riveting Milius' attention. He agreed with much of what she said about her belief that Landis had caused a needless accident by being disorganized and reckless on the set. He even made specific mention of his disagreement with Landis about putting the kids beneath the helicopter. But in the end, he showed weakness as a potential prosecution witness since he didn't believe, as a director, that someone could be held responsible for something that was what he called unforeseeable.

Unable to find a witness for her case from among Landis' own generation of directors, the prosecutor concentrated on Jackie Cooper. One week before the trial officially opened, she returned to the DGA screening room with Loeb and Budds for a showing to Cooper and Brooks of the scenes depicting the crash. Both men were appalled. Brooks in astonishment shouted out during the showing, "These kids are next to gas and explosives! He shouldn't be doing that!" As he watched the scene unfold with the kids waiting in the hut, he shook his head. "It was unbelievably stupid." Loeb heard Brooks curse when the screen erupted with explosions next to the helicopter. Afterwards, Jackie Cooper expressed being "very disappointed in Landis' techniques." The scene should have been shot with a long-range camera. The kids never should have been placed near the explosives in the first place due to the possibility of an accidental detonation.

After seeing the film neither man any longer objected to appearing as trial witness, though on the stipulation that they would not comment on how or whether Landis handled his responsibilities poorly; they would only testify that, given the circumstances, they would have done it differently.

Jackie Cooper was one of the last witnesses for the prosecution and his appearance on February 9 and 10, 1987, created a considerable stir. After six months of trial proceedings the prosecutor finally had a real star to help her case. Entering film acting at age 3, Cooper was the first child actor ever to receive an Oscar nomination, at age 9. After that a steady series of appearances on screen and TV made Cooper's cherubic face a recognizable icon to a generation of viewers with more in common with John Landis' mother than her demographically distant son. Even Judge Boren's wife came to see the famous witness. Harvard's legal pundit Alan Dershowitz showed up, as well as director Dan Petrie. Petrie had done a

cameo in Landis' *Into the Night*. A member of the DGA executive committee like Jackie Cooper, Petrie was deeply opposed to Cooper's cooperation with the prosecutor.

Jackie Cooper was something of an institution in Hollywood. On the
stand he proudly mentioned his honorary Navy flying wings. In his testimony he described the film the jurors had also seen, and going through
the takes, 9:30, 11:30 and 2:20, he opined that each of these scenes posed
danger to either Vic or the children. As a director he could easily spot the
lack of safety precautions by just looking at the film. Even at 9:30, he said,
the kids were sitting right next to the explosives in the hut and he could
see them again at 2:20 placed near live explosives before the crash occurred. Like the Hollywood stunt pilot before him, he believed that after
the near miss at 11:30 the set should have been shut down and everybody
sent home.

Jackie Cooper's courage in breaking with the ranks of Hollywood di-
rectors provided a high point in the trial but for him personally the after-
math was a letdown. The virulent reactions to his testimony surprised him.
Death threats were actually phoned to the unlisted number at his home in
Beverly Hills. At the same time the DGA's official leadership rebuffed him.
Following one DGA meeting, director Dan Petrie was seen confronting
Cooper, "How could you rat on a fellow director?" DGA president Gil
Cates went so far as to depart from the guild's five-year policy of silence.
He issued a statement in the Hollywood trade papers, without approval
from the guild body or counsel, that Cooper, the chairman of the DGA
safety committee, did not speak for the guild in his appearance at the trial.
To Cooper personally, Cates lamely explained that he had received a lot
of phone calls and had gone public in the belief that it would be best for
the guild. Jackie Cooper realized the DGA didn't want to make waves. In
his disappointment he prepared to resign from the safety committee. He
didn't understand it.

"The station-wagon liberals I've known for 30 years, they just said,
'Don't meddle!'"

* * *

As D'Agostino came to the end of her witness list and the trial entered
its sixth month, the position of Dorcey Wingo vis-a-vis his co-defendants
still remained that of outsider. The fact that at this late hour the pilot still
had lawsuits against his co-defendants indicated just how anomalous his
position was. In fact, both the prosecution and defense recognized Win-

go as the pivotal defendant whose testimony ultimately might help either side. He was still up for grabs.

The lawyers for Landis and Wingo were never more distrustful of each other. The two men were of contrasting styles. The goateed Trope, a figure from a Victorian picture book, wore suits of an unfashionable cut and bold in color. Neal always wore subdued Wall Street suits. Trope, at 69 the oldest member of the defense team, sensed from Landis a lack of deference and felt that Neal snubbed him. He felt ignored and hurt and unwelcome in the circle that had Neal at the center. Despite Wingo's readiness to fall in with "the plan," Neal had never revealed to Trope the latest Landis' defense strategy.

Both Neal and Trope feared being outwitted or surprised by the other. The trial on several occasions saw their conflict spill from the courtroom into the hallway. Better versed in business than criminal law, Trope's legal tactics at times baffled everyone. His gaffes quickly earned the sobriquet "malatropisms" and his blunders injected into the proceedings an unexpected dose of humor. He and Neal collided strikingly on the different approaches to handling certain key witnesses.

Neal's Olympian demeanor often sustained severe jolts from his portly colleague. One such occasion presented itself when on the witness stand fireman/studio teacher Jack Tice displayed such hostility to Landis that, rather than cross-examining him, the defense lawyers wanted him to vamoose as quickly as possible – all except Trope, whom Neal only in the last minute succeeded in turning the angry witness away from further questioning and creating a possible catastrophe.

A far more serious clash between the two lawyers occurred in connection with the testimony of Jimmy Camomile. Neal practically begged Trope not to question the key SFX man about his involvement in a separate helicopter accident during the filming of *Blue Thunder*. Bringing to the jury's attention another incident with a chopper, Neal feared, would damage the defense argument of "unforeseeability." According to the dossier that the phalanx kept on Jim Hensler, the safety conditions under Paul Stewart's control on *Blue Thunder* were appalling. But Trope's mind was made up: he was going to ask Camomile about *Blue Thunder*. In the hallway Neal practically went down on his knees. "I beg you, Gene. Please, I beg you…" Neal continued imploring in the courtroom. In full view of the spectators, he reached behind John Landis' chair and tugged beseechingly at Trope's jacket. When Trope passed up questioning Camomile, Neal could be seen breathing with visible relief.

All in all, however, Trope was less leery of Neal than he was of John Landis, and of neither man more so than he was of Joel Behr with whom he had warred for four years. Just before Landis was scheduled to take the stand in mid-February, Trope became alarmed when a sudden thaw entered the relations between the movie director and his client. He suspected Behr had something brewing.

Normally Trope and Wingo ate lunch separately in the courthouse cafeteria and were never invited over to the table of the Landis crowd. But suddenly John Landis and Wingo together began walking up to the 15th floor courtroom after lunch break rather than take the elevator. Ostensibly, both liked the exercise. About the same time John and Deborah Landis accompanied Wingo and his wife to the drag races. The warmth between them grew. Mrs. Landis shared baby photos and exchanged spicy recipes with Mrs. Wingo, who was born in Mexico. Trope became more and more irritated. Suspecting that Landis tried to influence his client he called out to Wingo one day, "Hey, Dorcey, you keep listening to John Landis, and you'll be wearing those striped pajamas!" In the hallway Trope on occasion would return from visiting the men's room or making a phone call and find Wingo conversing with Neal. Trope learned later from Wingo that Neal had been trying to get the pilot to change his version of the facts. These latest indignities, coupled to his personal dislike of Landis and Behr, had the combined effect of making Trope no longer reluctant to consider a deal from the prosecution.

Approaching Trope with such an offer was Lea D'Agostino's idea. From her early dealings with Trope, she had continued to perceive Wingo as the weak link in the defense. She knew that Trope felt that Landis had been reckless and that Wingo basically got dragged into sharing the charges with his co-defendants. To district attorney Ira Reiner she explained the opportunity Wingo offered to fragment the defense. They could show there was no plan. Reiner fell in enthusiastically. But because of her alienation from Trope following the secret meeting in Judge Boren's chamber, she was thought not to be the best person to initiate the delicate contact.

At this late point in the trial Reiner was eager to make good the series of snafus that had made him grow impatient with a case where Kesselman, Donna Schuman and Ebentheuer were names for disasters which he associated with D'Agostino's conduct of the proceedings. The deal with Dorcey Wingo also looked good to Reiner's high command, provided they could first hear the pilot's story. DA investigator Loeb was charged with secretly establishing contact with Trope in order to feel him out. Loeb made the contact and set the condition. "You'd have to initiate the deal," he told Trope. "It could not come from us." Trope was surprisingly receptive to the idea of lining up with the prosecution against John Landis. In a meeting between Trope and Reiner in the DA's office, Reiner officially blessed the deal and guaranteed that if Wingo's cooperation proved acceptable the DA would offer dismissal of the charges against him.

The key meeting of the DA's men with Wingo took place in the office of the Trope law firm on February 4, exactly two weeks before Landis would surprise the courtroom and take the stand. Reiner and *his top advisers* had agreed that Lea D'Agostino should not attend the session because Trope was too "intimidated" by her. That left the highly sensitive debriefing of the pilot to investigators Budds and Loeb, neither of whom had the prosecutor's breadth of understanding of the case. In addition to the investigators, the session was attended by two attorneys, Dick Hecht, of the triumvirate with Reiner and Garcetti, and the DA's chief expert on appellate matters, Harry Sonnheim.

In a three-hour recorded interview Wingo gave a much more personal impression of his two nights at Indian Dunes. He described for the first time his own observations of the director's erratic actions; charming one moment, abusive, foul-mouthed and tyrannical the next. Although Wingo said that he had never heard Landis refer to him abusively, he mentioned numerous instances when he had heard the director yell, "fuck you," and other four-letter words. He recalled Landis' outburst at the best boy, "chickenshit," for refusing to climb a tottering scaffolding on the set. He remarked on Landis at times behaving "just like somebody who asked for a pie in the face." He spoke in terms that frequently contradicted the idea of a plan, especially in a key phrase where he stated that he had been "blown out of the sky."

Unexpectedly, like so many of the contretemps in which the case abounded, the meeting was marked by a potentially spectacular encounter in the hallway of Trope's Westside legal suite. Taking Hecht aside during a break in Wingo's interview, Trope told the highest ranking DA lawyer in attendance that, during the trial, the former Watergate prosecutor had made attempts to get Wingo to change his story – in Hecht's words, "to suborn perjury." Trope advised Hecht that when the interview resumed, he should ask Wingo about it on the record. Hecht returned to the room and, before the pilot had the chance to confer with his lawyer, Hecht questioned him and heard Wingo confirm under oath that one of the defense lawyers had attempted to persuade him to alter his version of the facts.

Astonished by the allegations made by another officer of the court, and corroborated by a defendant in the case, that James Neal would try to suborn perjury, Hecht was nonplussed by the way in which it had supposedly been done. He wondered if Trope's shocking revelation might be a trick by the defense to cause a mistrial. He faced the unsettling element of surprise which others in the case had experienced before him. Confounded, Hecht explained to himself that he was not there for the purpose of opening up perjury charges; he quietly let the matter rest.

Loeb and Hecht, both excited about the transcript from their three hours with Wingo in Trope's office, the next day played a 30- minute portion of the tape for Ira Reiner. The DA was pleased. He particularly liked the key sections where Wingo talked about how he was blasted out of the sky, with which the DA hoped to show that Landis had no safety plan. With the single reservation that Wingo needed more work, Hecht joined Loeb in communicating the sense of a breakthrough in the case. They all agreed it was a "go," and Reiner proposed a press conference with himself in attendance. There was tremendous excitement, even talk of further debriefing the pilot and using the nearby New Otani Hotel as a safe house to keep Wingo out of Landis' clutches.

The trouble began, however, when Loeb and Budds brought the tapes of Wingo's interrogation to be played for the prosecutor in her office. She went into a fury and threw a temper tantrum of the sort familiar to her inner circle, to which both Loeb and Budds unhappily at that moment, belonged. When informed of Reiner's plan for a press conference the prosecutor raged that her boss had evaluated the issue without her even seeing the transcript. She resented Reiner for taking all the credit. Earlier, when it first appeared that the recruitment of Wingo might succeed, there had already been ego battles between the prosecutor and the DA about who was going to preside over the headline-making press conference to announce the deal.

In the end the prosecutor rejected Wingo's story. Despite its far more critical view of Landis, and for all the raw personal detail, she felt dissatisfied that he still hedged and held to the position that there were meetings, that there was planning, and that the director was not entirely responsible for the crash.

She listened to the tape. Budds and Loeb quietly hung back following their dressing-down. She interjected relentlessly as the tape whirred:

"*This is wrong… This is wrong… This is wrong…*"

47

"Frank Knew What the Money Was For"

Apart from John Landis' role in the fatal scene, the question for Hollywood was not whether the director was guilty but why Landis was the only high-ranking production member being tried. The obvious question was whether Steven Spielberg, through Frank Marshall and Kathleen Kennedy, had known that children were being employed illegally on the set, and if so, why wasn't he or someone from his organization on trial? Why weren't Spielberg, Marshall and Marshall's girl-friend, Kathleen Kennedy, ever questioned? And what did the big studio know of the illegal hiring?

But from Paris to India to Spain and even China, the global travels of Frank Marshall kept him far from the LA Criminal Court. In the five years since the crash Marshall studiously avoided every opportunity to provide authorities with the Spielberg organization's side of the story.

His absence was perfectly consistent with the gentleman's agreement that had been hammered out three years earlier among all the defense lawyers. At one of the most important strategy meetings in the offices of O'Melveny & Myers the gentlemen had, in effect, pledged to prevent their adversaries from becoming aware of the differences that existed among them. According to the people at Spielberg's Amblin Entertainment at Universal City, Marshall's absence was due to his work on two new Spielberg productions, *Empire of the Sun* and Roger Zemeckis' *Who Framed Roger Rabbit?* Spielberg's closest associate was kept away from the entire judicial proceedings, sparing the trial what would have certainly become a sensational face-off. For there could be little doubt that, if called to testify, Marshall would give damaging testimony against Landis.

An open confrontation between the two men would have also drawn Warner Bros., unavoidably, into a public exposure in the criminal case – clearly not in the interest of either. Even should Marshall comply with Landis' earlier request and admit at the trial that he, and by implication Spielberg, knew about the illegal hiring of Myca and Renee, it would not necessarily guarantee that the jury would go any lighter on the director and the other defendants. At best it might encourage sympathy for the director as being the lone fall guy. On the other hand, the prosecutor could always argue that the act of just knowing about the illegal hiring was far different from actually exposing the children to hazardous conditions. She could argue that Spielberg and Marshall had little to do with the actual event relating to the deaths on the set. At the same time, an open denial by Marshall that he, the studio, or anyone else associated with the Spielberg side of the production knew about the illegal scheme to employ the children would pit Spielberg squarely against Landis, both of whom along with Warner Bros., were still co-defendants in the multi-million-dollar civil suits of the Le and Chen families.

Aside from Spielberg and Marshall, only the executives at Warner realized the havoc a confrontation between the two movie partners would bring in its wake. Marshall and his lawyers had made it clear to Warner executives that Spielberg's man knew nothing about the illegal hiring. At the same time Warner had been warned by the phalanx at the "showdown" meeting four years before that the young director, if pushed, was prepared to point the finger at Frank Marshall, Kathleen Kennedy, Warner's Lucy Fisher and Spielberg himself. It would have been easy for Landis' lawyers to show that throughout the affair Marshall acted like someone who had something to hide. Had it surfaced through a court confrontation, the image of Spielberg's close associate carrying the crushed body of little Renee Chen from the river to her wailing mother and then dashing from the scene before the police arrived would have made a very poor impression on both the jury and the public.

Apart from confiding in his lawyers and Steven Spielberg, the only account Marshall gave of his role in the seamy affair was to Warner's own high-level investigators shortly after the Indian Dunes disaster. Through close consultations with Marshall's own lawyer, Tom Pollock, the men from Warner heard his assertion that at the time of the fatal shot he had been standing with Dick Vane across the river, watching the scene in the belief that Vic was carrying dummies. Vane was the only person on the set who supported Marshall's version of the story, even though the location manager had admitted that he knew the kids were still on the set illegally at 2:20 A.M.

Just how destructive an open confrontation between Marshall and Landis would be was revealed in a highly confidential Warner memo in which Spielberg's man maintained that he had been deceived by the Landis people. Marshall claimed that he was told nothing by Folsey about

349

the use of the kids in the fatal scene. About the $2,000 check used to get the cash to pay the kids with his signature on it, Marshall confided to Warner that Folsey had told him it was a "salary advance." According to Marshall's version, when his own accountant, Bonnie Radford, brought him the check, neither he nor Radford knew its actual purpose. Indeed, Marshall depicted an M.O. involving deception as having been rampant on the Landis segment. Marshall's accountant had reported having already once before blocked an attempt by Allingham to pay electricians "under the table." Characterizing the Landis operation as "shoddy," Marshall insisted to Warner that he had let Allingham know his concern about making the right arrangements for the kids and getting the right permits.

But while impugning Landis in his highly colored account to the studio investigators, the attempt to extricate himself knotted Marshall into numerous inconsistencies. Even as he admitted to having discussed the children's scenes, he maintained that neither Landis, Folsey, nor Allingham ever told him anything about the illegal hiring plan. At the one meeting where the subject of the two explosion scenes involving the kids came up, Marshall said he had warned Allingham that Landis' idea of using four- and five-year-olds at night would pose a problem if the scenes were to be shot after 6:30 P.M. He suggested, in the version he gave Warner, that for one of the village shots Folsey and Allingham consider using young-looking 12-year-olds as he and Spielberg had done in *E.T.*, explaining that with 12-year-olds waivers could be obtained until 12:00 or 12:30 A.M. – an assertion the implication of which could not have failed to be noted by the sharp studio lawyers. It simply meant that Landis' motive for breaking the law had not been the late hour! A waiver could have been obtained, as Marshall pointed out. The inference was inescapable that Landis had not chosen to obtain a waiver because it would have included a studio teacher to see to the safety of the kids in a shot whose super-realism demanded that they be placed near explosives!!!

When the meeting's agenda turned to the final exploding village scene, Marshall claimed Allingham had assured him that there wouldn't be any problem with real kids because it would be a "long shot" – doubles or dolls would be used with cameras back far enough from the set so the difference wouldn't be apparent on screen. Having contended with a similar problem in a scene in *Poltergeist* in which a woman appears to be running with her child, while in actuality, a lighter and less cumbersome doll, Marshall said his experience with the doll made Allingham's explanation sound reasonable.

The studio heard Marshall indicate that until the night of the crash the issue of the kids never came up again. As he had done on most of the 12 days of Landis' night shooting schedule, Marshall came for the wrap and this time brought his girlfriend and business partner Kathleen Kennedy with him. Together they watched the filming of the 9:30 scene in which they saw the kids with the explosions going off behind them. It was his belief at the time, so Marshall stated to his listeners from the studio echelons, that Allingham and Folsey had taken up his suggestion of using 12-year-olds with waivers to film past 6:30 since in his eyes the kids looked "big." With Kathleen Kennedy he next watched the 11:30 rage scene; his listeners were informed that he didn't think it was dangerous. After they had dinner together with Dick Vane around midnight, Marshall's girl-friend went home, leaving Marshall and Vane to watch the final shot.

When the final action began, Marshall told the Warner brass that he was standing next to Vane and was dumbfounded to see live children in Morrow's arms as the actor crossed the river. Marshall said he expressed disbelief to Vane who replied that he, too, thought that dolls were to be used. Marshall noted that even the film's paperwork and documents backed him up in showing that he could not have known about the use of real children in the final scene. He maintained that the notations in Landis' actual shooting schedule were consistent with Allingham's explanation that dolls or dummies would be used in that scene. Specifically, the notation in the shooting schedule "DBL/Bill," indicating that a double would be used for Vic, conveyed to him the assurance that cameras would be shooting from a distance.

Landis' shooting schedule listed no children under the "Cast & Atmosphere" column; that would not have been the case, Marshall suggested, if live children had been planned for the final scene.

The story in which Spielberg's man pointed the finger directly at Landis remained known only to a select group of powerful executives at Universal and Warner. Marshall's attorney, Rick Rosen, confidentially let it be known that he and his client believed that Landis had created an "incredibly dangerous situation putting the kids below the chopper with bombs going." To only a select few Rosen circulated the story that Marshall never knew about the kids and had he known he never would have let it happen.

Marshall's account never received a public airing in a court of law or otherwise and so the fundamental differences between Spielberg and Landis did not turn into a messy credibility contest before the public or the jury. But in the hallway of the Criminal Court building the feeling among many of the defendants was that they had been abandoned by Spielberg and Marshall. Their anger was expressed in accusations of betrayal, dishonesty and weakness. Only the most trusted insiders were privy to this resentment felt by the Landis people against the Spielberg organization. To the contrary, in the courtroom and elsewhere, James Neal tried to convey the impression that everything was harmonious between Landis and Spielberg.

Folsey and Allingham were the most resentful. Their position, never expressed publicly or directly, ran counter to every single tenet in Marshall's account. They blasted with bitter sarcasm Marshall's claim of how he first thought that Vic was carrying dummies in the final shot. They derided Spielberg's man as having been the only one on the set that night who didn't see the children over on the village shore with Vic Morrow just seconds before the shot started. Recalling the background differently from Marshall, they had him attending two meetings and not one; at one of which, after being specifically informed of Landis' wish to use real children with explosions and a low-flying helicopter at night, Marshall even had his girlfriend, Kathleen Kennedy, place a blind call to the labor commissioner to see if they could use the kids legally. It was the labor commissioner's reply that it would be too late at night to permit the use of children, Folsey and Allingham asserted, that set the stage for the illegal hiring. At the second meeting in Landis' Universal bungalow, they maintained, Marshall told them to "forget it," with reference to getting proper approval from the labor commissioner's office to use the kids legally. It was then agreed that the children would have to be hired without permits outside ordinary channels.

Because Marshall stayed far out of reach during the trial proceedings, and Spielberg was never even summoned during the entire five-year affair, both sides were spared having the truth of their respective versions put to the test. It served all the wrangling parties concerned in the defense. Any victory could only be "Pyrrhic"; neither side could escape an open confrontation unscathed. Even had Marshall defended his claim that he'd been told doubles or dummies would be used, his argument would only pit his word against Landis'. Marshall's incriminating connection to the hiring scheme was dramatically corroborated when Marci Liroff, the casting director, testified that upon learning of the illegal plan she had phoned Marshall who "said he would take care of it." Also, the studio had knowledge that its own Lucy Fisher had specifically mentioned to Marshall her concern about problems with filming the kids this way. In her debriefing by the man from O'Melveny, Scott Dunham, only days after the accident, she stated that she asked Landis and Marshall on two separate occasions about casting the children's roles.

With regard to Marshall's explanation of the $2,000 check prepared by Bonnie Radford and signed by Marshall himself, Folsey labeled it plainly false. "Frank knew what the money was for." Folsey pointed out that even if Marshall's and Bonnie Radford's claim about not knowing the true purpose of the first check was correct, how could they explain the $1,000 in cash in a sealed envelope that went to the second series of illegal payments? – part of the complex scheme of concealing the illegal cash payments supplied by Warner, a scheme which even the prosecutor failed to understand and was never revealed during the entire five year-long case!

What made Folsey angriest was Marshall's alibi supplied by Dick Vane. Vane knew all along about the concealment plan, Folsey maintained. As location manager, Vane was actually the first on the set to alert him to the presence of Jack Tice. Vane helped keep tabs on the location of the firemen and, according to Folsey, it was impossible for him not to have known about the children for the 2:20 shot.

At the time he was called as a witness at the trial, Dick Vane had testified only once before on Marshall's role in the fatal shot. His account given three years earlier at the grand jury, in fact, was the only time authorities would ever raise the subject of Frank Marshall's involvement in the illegal hiring. Under oath Vane had testified to the grand jurors that as the cameras began rolling for the 2:20 shot both he and Marshall believed that Vic was carrying dummies. Vane's sworn testimony was sufficient to keep the investigation away from Marshall.

More importantly, it kept the DA's indictment efforts focused solely on Landis and his group. Along with the NTSB's Steven Spielberg affidavit, consisting of a one-line statement in which Spielberg indicated he was not on the set the night of the accident, Dick Vane's story was key in keeping public awareness of Spielberg's and Marshall's involvement in the incident to a bare minimum. At the trial Vane never mentioned Marshall's role.

George Folsey Jr. cynically remarked on the meteoric Hollywood career in the Spielberg organization of the only person to corroborate Marshall's story of being surprised at seeing the live children instead of dummies. During the trial Dick Vane worked on another Spielberg/Marshall picture, *Harry and the Hendersons*, an '87 Amblin release listing him as executive producer. Folsey pointed out that Dick Vane was employed by

Spielberg all the way through the five-year legal proceeding, rising from a comparatively lowly location manager at the time of the crash to an executive producer title with regular contacts with the Amblin troika; whom Vane now familiarly referred to as "Frank, Kathy and Steve."

48

Schande for the Goyim...

Following an opening torrent, the trial soon settled into a sluggish pace. After a few months the courtroom activity was reduced to a deadening routine that threatened to drag on endlessly in time. Repetition was inevitable among the many witnesses but what bogged the proceedings down were two common legal conventions, the "sidebar" and the 402 hearing, which constantly interrupted the normal course of testimony. Although both maneuvers were originally designed to keep a jury free from prejudicial information, in the TZ case they became the twin tactics used by the defense to take the wind out of many of the most damaging statements witnesses were prepared to offer concerning John Landis.

Nothing symbolized the proceedings like the breaks in testimony – the "sidebars" – than the sight of Lea D'Agostino as Mother Goose, indefatigably leading the brood of a half-dozen short-statured defense lawyers towered over by six-footer Braun back and forth to the judge's side bar. The "sidebars" resulted from the judge's ruling barring "speaking" objections, that is, those objections in which the lawyer stands up and objects, and then speaks his reasons behind the objection. Under the judge's ruling all objections in the trial had to be first announced in open court with the actual objection heard privately in whispers to the judge at his "side bar," so the jury could not hear what was being said.

The "402" was another dilatory tactic. It allows the defense to request that the jury be kept in the jury room while in the courtroom a witness is being examined and cross-examined; a kind of prescreening, it permits the judge to determine whether the witness might say something about the defendant which could be prejudicial and irrelevant to the specific facts of the case. The logic behind the 402 was that once a witness testifies, you can't unring the bell. At the TZ trial the defense in particular benefited from 402's since it gave an angry witness the chance to get things off his chest, so that with his emotion spent, his subsequent testimony before the jury tended to be flattened.

As the trial slowly wound on those in the courtroom saw John Landis mostly bent down over a yellow legal pad furiously scrawling. Everybody wanted to know what he was writing, and the curious would perhaps have been disappointed to learn that the sheets he filled day after day for ten months were letters to his wife, each headed with the date and "Dear Deborah." Between daily sessions, the "Dear Deborah" letters were secured inside the desk of the court bailiff, the LA sheriff who in a rare rapprochement became the director's best friend in the courtroom.

Larry the Bailiff performed little odd services for the famous director and Landis, in return, surreptitiously slipped him small gifts like a *National Geographic* videotape or an autographed photo of Dan Aykroyd. And when Aykroyd appeared at the trial from the set of *Dragnet*, which he was then filming, the director introduced them, "Dan, this is Larry." At other times John Landis' wife exchanged her freshest baby pics with the beaming bailiff who also had small children. Larry was in turn very helpful in making special seating arrangements for the director's friends and supporters. Perhaps it was not lost on the director that Larry the Bailiff would stay with the jury during final deliberations as they came to their verdict, guarding them and acting as their sole liaison to the judge and the outside world.

While in the courtroom, with a few exceptions, John Landis' behavior remained under control, his Aunt Gloria, Uncle Ben's widow, caused concern in Judge Boren's mind after he spotted her one day emerging from the private chambers behind the courtroom. Aunt Gloria could usually be found in the hallway doling out pieces of hard candy. Her husband had passed away the year before, but as a judge's wife she continued to use his key to enter areas that were off-limits to the public, including the judge's elevator and the private parking lot. Following this discovery, Judge Boren hastily called a conference with the defense lawyers to point out the inappropriateness and request that Aunt Gloria return the judge's key!

On rare occasions John Landis emerged in the hallway from his courtroom shell and showed more of his true personal style. In general, he kept the morale up by tirelessly joking and beaming a lopsided smirk. He lost control once when, physically seizing and shaking a frail, studious-looking young photographer, he denounced this individual as the "most obnoxious paparazzi" he'd ever seen. His behavior often strikingly exemplified the "seduction/intimidation" method he had once expounded to his phalanx. Still photographer Morgan Renard on the day he testified got the intimidation treatment. "He used a lot of body language," Renard recalled. "He sort of moved in front of me, kind of blocking my entrance to the courtroom, so I would have to brush shoulders with him to pass by. And his wife was right behind him. She's even bigger than he is."

With the person who represented the greatest potential danger of any witness, Landis alternated intimidation with seduction when they met in the hallway; at the time of the trial, Andy House, pressured at Disney over the case, had just lost another job there. "I understand you're mad at me," the director said it friendly enough just outside the courtroom – but House felt intimidated; and when next on the witness stand he saw Universal's Sean Daniel seated in the gallery the thought ran through his mind, "I'll never work on a feature film at Universal."

The chill felt by Andy House was felt by Alpha Campbell even before the trial. Within minutes after prosecutor D'Agostino paid a visit to her Universal Studios office, Landis' former secretary suddenly received a series of phone calls from the director she hadn't heard from since he sent her the box of fancy cookies. She never returned the calls. But the coincidence began to make sense when at the trial on the day she was called to testify she heard Deborah Landis in the hallway refer pointedly loud in her presence to a secretary who sat next to her at her Universal office; "Let's get Ahuva to come in and say how Alpha is out to get John." Shocked and angry at what she considered a clear attempt at intimidation by the director's wife, she nevertheless entered the courtroom and related from the stand how Landis told her to destroy certain copies of the script.

Upon her return to her office the following day, Alpha confronted the woman with the Israeli name who sat at the desk behind her. Ahuva didn't deny being the office leak to Landis. In fact, she warned Alpha that John Landis had friends in high places at the studio and mentioned Sean Daniel. When Alpha reported this brazen example of office surveillance to her superiors, she encountered mixed results; Ahuva was immediately transferred but at the same time Alpha was informed that, mysteriously, her entire seventeen-year personnel file had disappeared.

A different type of intimidation was brought to bear on the prosecutor whose family had fled the Nazis. Playing on the sense of Jewish persecution, Landis lashed out at her one day in the hallway with a biting, "Schande for the goyim!" James Neal was puzzled until its meaning was explained to him as a Yiddish epithet for "traitor." Neal liked the phrase, and in the hallway hummed it to a Nashville beat, *Schande for the goyim .... Schande for the goyim....* Possibly expecting more indecipherable outbursts from the director, several reporters the next day brought to the hallway Leo Rosten's *Joys of Yiddish*.

The indisputable mistress of the hallway was Deborah "Nadoolman" Landis. Virtually banned by her husband from the prelim two years before (he kept her away, he intimated at the time, because he felt she didn't photograph well) Landis' wife and business partner this time assumed an imposing presence on the 15th floor. She brought pork buns from Chinatown and acted as a kind of social secretary in the affairs of Department 132. With Larry the Bailiff in the courtroom, Aunt Gloria on the judge's elevator, Deborah in the hallway and the phalanx patrolling everywhere, it often appeared to be a question of time before the Criminal Court building, the entire judicial structure, would fall to the *wunderkind* in the *Twilight Zone* case.

Monitoring who came and went, and who was talking to whom, Deborah Landis' chief function appeared to be orchestrating the media. A number of times she joined her husband in taking sudden flight from reporters and photographers, both Landises dashing down the 15th floor emergency stairs as if intent on drawing attention from the press. Craning over the crowd from her great long-legged height, she at times enforced a blackout policy with regard to the press, alerting her husband, for instance, to Folsey's frequent attempts to speak to reporters without John's approval. She decided what days were best for supporters to come. On some days she would encourage visitors to stay home, judging it was better that Lea D'Agostino didn't have a big crowd. Deborah's transparent role in the concealment plot the night of the crash never surfaced even though she and Sue Dugan, the show's costumer, spent time with Myca and Renee in Landis' trailer where the "Vietnamese" were hidden until moments before the 2:20 disaster.

Most of the Hollywood stars in the hallway were familiar faces from Landis movies. Their frequency of visits was in proportion to what Landis had done for them. The careers of stars like Dan Aykroyd and Ralph Bellamy had benefited strongly from the director, being launched in Aykroyd's case (he appeared in five of Landis' eight movies) and resurrected in the case of the 73-year-old Ralph Bellamy with the success of *Trading Places*. It was very nice of the elderly actor to stand behind the troubled young director. Like Vic Morrow, Bellamy appeared grateful to be working again. Personally invited by the director to attend the legal proceedings, Bellamy tried to sell the idea of Landis' concern for safety by telling the journalists in the hallway that once John Landis had rescued him when he fell on the steps of the New York Stock Exchange during filming of *Trading Places*. Bellamy came to the trial several more times, echoing Landis' feelings by grousing that the case was "politically motivated" and "legally upside down."

Bellamy was a favorite with the jurors. They recognized the actor who played FDR in *Sunrise at Campobello* and, not surprisingly, the court burst into uproar when D'Agostino, angered by Bellamy's hallway characterizations of the incident at Indian Dunes, sought to subpoena the venerable movie relic. Many in the prosecutor's own office thought that her attempt to discredit Ralph Bellamy was "tacky." Though the judge immediately quashed the subpoena, it had the effect, as the prosecutor proudly pointed out, of capturing headlines and upstaging the formidable fact of a famous Hollywood star who supported Landis.

The stars who came to the trial were usually brought from Century City to the Criminal Court building and back to Century City in a one-vehicle legal motorcade dubbed by one defense counsel, the "Landismobile." A long white van leased by John Landis, it transported every day for nearly a year the director and his wife, along with James Neal and Jim Sanders, usually along with a guest or possibly one or another lawyer. The arrival of the white van at the building on Temple Street was a Hollywood occasion; it was often possible to catch coming out of the van not only the famous young director but one or more stars.

Dan Aykroyd was one of the better-known names at the trial and a frequent visitor. On his first visit he sported two buttons on his lapel; one button plugged LA's Hard Rock Cafe in which he was an investor, the other button was for *Dragnet*, the movie he was then making. For legal reasons Aykroyd refused to comment on the case other than to say that it concerned an "industrial accident." He spoke in metaphysical terms. "There might be a higher authority involved." In pure Hollywood tones, "I love John," he described the chief defendant as "a superior human being," vowing, 'To go to the wall with him. I pray to God that it ends in a positive outcome."

The visits by other young stars probably went unnoticed by a generation of jurors more attuned to Ralph Bellamy or Don Ameche than to the star of *Into the Night*, Jeff Goldblum, or Michelle Pfeiffer, then filming *The Witches of Eastwick*, or Randy Newman, the "I Love LA" singer/songwriter and now a first-time co-writer on *Three Amigos*, or Tony Edwards, the young actor from *Top Gun*. Even the appearance in the courtroom by Carrie Fisher, Princess Leia of *Star Wars*, who had a role in *Blues Brothers* and had been the real-life girlfriend of Dan Aykroyd, probably escaped the jurors. They might have been hard pressed to identify the awkward, plain-looking girl in the above-the-knee dress as Princess Leia, but they would have known Eddie Fisher and Debbie Reynolds, her famous parents.

Carrie Fisher visited on the same day Dorcey Wingo took the stand, testifying very much against the wishes of Landis, Neal, and Landis' wife. Deborah made sure to introduce the pilot in the courtroom to some Hollywood friends. Carrie Fisher happened to be an idol of Wingo's and he was overwhelmed. "Wow!" he exclaimed as he shook hands with the heroine of *Star Wars*. The actress carried a book on dramatic writing by Lajos Egri. She was in the middle of writing her memoirs of life with the Belushi crowd to be published the following year. In the courtroom Deborah and Carrie sat together and talked about the case.

"It was like an industrial accident," Deborah told Carrie.

She explained how Camomile had "raked his board," which was "like a xylophone … and two explosions went off together."

Carrie Fisher said she had heard from her mother about very gory scenes on movie sets where stuntmen had been "ripped and shredded up." Deborah confided the key problem their side faced in calling another movie director to the stand. "There are all kinds of directors we could call, but if we did have a director testify you never know what she might get him to say." The downside of not calling a director, she explained, "is that during her final argument the prosecutor will be able to say that we couldn't even find one director to testify that what John was doing was all right."

As it happened, the day Carrie attended was a bad one for the prosecution, when yet another witness backfired, an FBI explosives expert whose testimony left an ambiguous impression of supporting Braun's delamination theory. Carrie Fisher never made it to the hallway, not even during recess. Deborah Landis appeared determined to shield her from the press. The end of the day saw her being rushed past reporters out of the courthouse between James Neal and Jim Sanders and safely shut behind the doors of the waiting, revving Landismobile.

A lot of the luminaries visiting the trial were drawn from Hollywood's new generation of studio chiefs and corporate powers. They were quiet and unobtrusive, like Landis' longtime supporter Jeff Katzenberg, nicknamed the "golden retriever," president of Walt Disney's booming film division. Hollywood life went on as usual alongside the trial; Disney had just released *The Color of Money* and as he sat in the courtroom lending support to his embattled friend Katzenberg happily thumbed through the favorable first reviews of Disney's yuppie sequel to *The Hustler*. Landis' best friend, Sean Daniel, attended often and brought lower-ranking Universal execs. A faithful visitor was rotund, balding Bob Weiss, the corpulent *Blues Brothers* producer who was doing *Dragnet* at the time with Dan Aykroyd. One of Hollywood's new female powerbrokers, Dawn Steel, then Paramount production president, came to the courtroom while in the middle of negotiations to replace David Puttnam as the head at Columbia.

Among the visitors from the ranks of Hollywood directors who showed up to offer their moral support was Landis' loudest advocate inside the DGA's executive leadership, Jeremy Kagan (*The Chosen*), and Judith Cates, wife of DGA president Gil Cates and a friend of Deborah Landis, as well as directors Costa-Gavras of *Missing*, "horror master" Larry Cohen, Paul Bartel (*Eating Raoul*), Michael Ritchie (*Fletch*); Tobe Hooper (*Poltergeist, The Texas Chainsaw Massacre*); Miss Piggy's creator, Frank Oz (*Muppets Take Manhattan*) and British television director Jonathan Lynn (*Clue*). Deborah Landis brought a costume designer's perspective to the proceedings. As mistress of the hallway, she helped guide famous Hollywood visitors and kept up a running commentary ("I'm going to write a piece for *Vogue* on what's good and what's not good in a trial." "This afternoon we have a good witness because he loves John." "Lea wears a lot of lavender which is a good color for her"...). The appearance by the famous and glamorous at the trial affected everybody, including the press. It struck the young *Los Angeles Times* reporter whose mother, visiting the trial from Boston, was proudly introduced by her son to Watergate's James Neal. For AP reporter Linda Deutsch it was the time she misidentified John Landis' Uncle Sid as Swifty Lazar in a report circulated to hundreds of newspapers.

The Hollywood glamour was so overpowering that even the prosecutor's assistant Tom Budds began to dream out loud. His *Twilight Zone* investigations constantly threw him in the way of pretty Hollywood women; early in the case, after interviewing Cynthia Nigh one Friday night over a glass of wine, he came back to Kesselman with the glowing report that she was a "dish"; after interviewing Jaqueline Compton, Landis' former driver, he raved to Lea D'Agostino how "foxy" she was. During the trial he openly fantasized whether it might be possible for one of the defense attorneys to fix him up with a date with Carrie Fisher. The names of celebrities were a constant bombardment on Budds, capped with James Neal's promise to get him a signed photograph of President Reagan from his Tennessee friend, Howard Baker. But in the end Budds never had his date with a movie star nor the signed photograph of the chief of state. Only a singular piece of memorabilia was to remind him of his glory days in Hollywood. Two years before the actual trial began, he had turned a blind side to department protocol by removing from the helicopter the colorful nose cone with its painted eagle and outstretched talons. No longer bearing the FLY BY NIGHT legend, the metal cone, he told the NTSB's Don Llorente, would be featured as the top of a barbecue table he planned to build.

Andy Furillo was one of the rare exceptions in refusing to be star-struck. Known for his family ties to baseball, he politely turned down John Landis' offer of a gift baseball book. Local network KNBC-TV's Elizabeth Anderson earned for her solid reporting, muttered, under-the-breath profanities and open sneers from Deborah Landis. The subject of the star-struck syndrome was raised with Neal by one of its dizziest victims, the young *Los Angeles Times* reporter Paul Feldman – wondering if it was proper for Landis to have all the stars show up at the courthouse; he asked the old pro from Nashville whether it was part of the director's scenario for the trial.

"Paul," Neal said, looking pensive, "to answer you honestly, I don't know. My guess is he did not. These people are his friends and I imagine they would call him up and say, 'I'm coming down,' and he'd say, 'Fine,' and he was grateful for that, and if I were on trial being prosecuted by Mizz De Owgustino, or anybody else, I'd be grateful if my friends showed up."

Neal promised to get back to Feldman with an answer.

As part of the trial, the jury members ventured out of the Criminal Court building on three separate occasions. Once they went to visit the Indian Dunes disaster site and on two different occasions, once early in the trial, the other near the end, they left the courtroom to watch the crash footage on the big screen. Each of the excursions was attended by bizarre frills that had come to be expected in the case.

The first viewing of the film was bitterly opposed by the defense. The prosecutor had been able to get permission from the Motion Picture Academy of Arts and Sciences to use its prestigious Samuel B. Goldwyn Theatre in Beverly Hills for the screening. The defense felt out maneuvered. Landis was fuming. Folsey, whose father had been a founding member of the Academy, expressed shock and disdain that the organization would lend its approval. He telephoned his aged father immediately. And whether or not as the result of his complaints, or for other reasons, the two oversize Oscars that ordinarily graced the theatre were removed for the *Twilight Zone* screening.

The director's arrival at the Academy in the Landismobile wasn't anything like the glitter and flashbulbs on Oscar night. Landis was agitated. Inside the theatre he could be heard loudly voicing technical disagreement with the screen presentation. Before the jury and press arrived, he lashed out at the projectionist, "Don't you realize they're trying to put me in jail!" Before the screening took place there had been detailed discussions between the judge and Landis' attorneys. The Hollywood people wanted to be satisfied on all the important technical points, from where the jury should sit to how high the volume should be.

During the showing the jury could be heard taking deep, disbelieving breaths. Afterwards they filed out of the Academy, silent and subdued.

The jury's second excursion, to view the crash site, was arranged with some difficulty. The prosecutor's original idea was to treat the jurors to an elaborate and costly demonstration involving a real exploding village and a low-flying helicopter. In order to prove her point she pursued a zeal for realism that almost matched the director's own. Investigator Jerry Loeb was turned into a UPM and helped her make the office over into a virtual movie production company where the talk was about budgets, scheduling and insurance. While Judge Boren cut back the spectacular, he permitted the prosecutor to take the jury to Indian Dunes; he deferred, however, making the decision as to whether or not he would permit the jurors to see a low-flying helicopter until he first saw the on-site demonstration himself.

It was a critical decision. To have a combat helicopter with its infernal noise hover in the air just over the heads of the jurors was to give them a real feeling for the danger of the scene that was shot on that bedeviled night of July 23, 1982. As a judge, Boren had to consider that it could also be prejudicial: the result was a unique 402 hearing on the bank of the Santa Clara.

An actual court was set up on the sand and gravel shore under the trees. The court reporter sat at her stenography machine facing the bluff. On the shore John and Deborah Landis, both in outdoor wear, sweaters and sturdy boots, stood close together holding hands like newly-weds. The helicopter was brought in before the jury arrived; the grim rotor-driven exhibit came clattering over the cliff in front of the judge, the defendants, their attorneys, and a throng of reporters. Suddenly it dropped to a hover position at the same height Wingo's Huey occupied before it plummeted.

The prosecutor again showed her emotions all too plainly. She visibly recoiled. She made a great demonstration of shielding her eyes from the sand and debris kicked up by the propwash. The sight of Lea D'Agostino cowering, almost prostrate with fear, was noted by Judge Boren who canceled the jury view of the helicopter, persuaded, in part, by the prosecutor's terror-stricken response that the exhibition could be prejudicial.

The actual jury view of the site ended benignly. The jurors would have needed tremendous imagination to picture what had happened on the very site on the night of the final shot five years ago. Without the village, the helicopter, the explosives and the dark night, the bend of the Santa Clara looked like a pleasant picnic ground. The sampan, the No. 4 hut, the dam – none of the structures the jurors had been hearing about in months of trial testimony was there. The spit of sand where Landis directed – the "island" – had been eroded and was barely visible in the shallow river. The smoke burns on the granite wall were washed away and the gas vapors had long since vanished from where the village once stood.

In the final act before resting her case, the prosecutor called for a second, and final, big-screen viewing of the film by the jury. It was held on the old Warner lot in Hollywood. After twice viewing the fatal footage on the big screen, the jurors were as shocked as they had been the first time. The fresh screening again heard their deep, disbelieving gasps. The final master shot in which the helicopter's main rotor blade cuts into Vic Morrow was followed by the same stunned silence and subdued exit.

49

THE STUMBLE

The climax of the trial came on February 18, 1987, with John Landis' surprise appearance as the first and most important defense witness.

As he was the first Hollywood director to stand trial on manslaughter charges there was the feeling of a historic Hollywood precedent. There was a media mob. The courtroom was packed with Landis friends and family: Aunt Gloria, his mother Shirley Levine, Uncle Sid and his wife; Universal's Sean Daniel with Landis' agent Mike Marcus; Dan Goldstine, the Berkeley psychologist, along with the usual flock of junior lawyers and legal secretaries from Joel Behr's office. The throng in the hallway pressed against the doors of Department 132 to get the best seats. Larry the Bailiff tried to calm them: "I don't want you coming in here like a herd of cattle." Meanwhile, he seated Landis' supporters and legal staff first, almost filling the entire first three rows. He acted like a uniformed usher in a theatre showing a new comedy by the husband of Deborah Landis. Standing with the bailiff at the courtroom's entrance she watched the courtroom fill. To a late arrival she shrugged, "I can't give you a seat." For a lot of people, it was strictly SRO.

Neal had been reluctant to let the director take the stand. But after all the name-calling and negative characterizations by the prosecution he realized that the defense opening required a strong response. In a series of meetings immediately preceding the director's appearance Neal tried to bring the other attorneys in line. Marked "confidential," a memo was circulated which listed only John Landis of the five defendants among the small number of defense witnesses to be called. The memo indicated that the singular mention of the director didn't mean that the other four shouldn't testify, but the message was clearly understood that Neal wanted only Landis on the stand.

Although both Neal and Behr found it difficult to control the disparate parts of the defense machine, the five lead lawyers remained united against Lea D'Agostino. Despite internal frictions, they realized that the jury focus would be on Landis. In fact, after a few weeks it was easy to forget that four other defendants were also on trial.

Landis' appearance on the stand was a strongly charged emotional event. Already the feud between the director and D'Agostino who had breathed fire at him for the preceding six months was legendary. Though Neal led off questioning the chief defense witness, it was really Landis' encounter on cross-examination with the Dragon Lady that everyone was intensely curious to see.

As Neal opened his direct examination of the trial's most important witness, he read from a list of questions all typed out in perfect order; obviously there would be no surprises. For the jury it was the first time they saw John Landis without his being bent over a yellow legal pad. It was also the first time they got to hear his piercing nasal voice.

Addressing the witness in a calm, soothing tone, alternating between calling him John and Mr. Landis, Neal's direct examination took the 36-year-old director through a perfectly rehearsed tale in which the hero was Horatio Alger. The jury heard how John Landis got his first job as a mail boy in the studio and did odd jobs like working at Hamburger Hamlet in Westwood. He was a waiter and actor; he also had a "job engraving little signs that go in buildings that say where the doctors are."

The story Landis told at Neal's prompting began with Steven Spielberg telephoning him in March 1982. Spielberg proposed a dinner meeting. They met and discussed various joint projects, one of which was the concept of creating a movie from TV's *Twilight Zone* series. Landis said that after reaching an agreement with Spielberg he went ahead and wrote what would become known as the Landis segment.

Under Neal's supportive questioning Landis mentioned that he was a big fan of Rod Serling. He pointedly remarked to the predominantly minority jury that in his own script he wanted to use the element of fantasy to deal with social issues and that the idea behind his segment was racism as depicted by Bill who lives the lives of his victims. But after distributing the first draft to Spielberg and the Warner people, Landis said he learned that Warner's Lucy Fisher and president Terry Semel had a criticism of the story. Landis said he met with Fisher and Semel numerous times and that at one meeting, which took place at Semel's house, they decided to write an additional scene to "soften" Bill. The witness explained how the concept was written into the June 13, 1982 revision, the third draft.

Then the subject turned to the most controversial and mysterious question in the entire case. Who was truly responsible for having the kids on the set where the dangers of the scene should have seemed obvious to anyone? Landis mentioned pre-production meetings with Frank

Marshall, George Folsey Jr. and Dan Allingham where they discussed the problem of using the children at night. In an account that clashed sharply with what had been spelled out among Frank Marshall's secret communications with Warner Bros.' lawyers, the movie director blithely implicated Spielberg's assistant. Landis testified that Marshall promised he would have someone from his office call the labor board to find out if they could get a waiver for the kids. At a follow-up meeting with the same people present, he testified, Marshall informed the group that the labor board was willing to give a waiver, but only until 8:30 P.M. Since it was still light at that time, Landis said, the waiver would not do them any good.

"We decided to break the law," the director confessed. "We decided wrongly to violate the labor code."

"John, that was wrong," Neal said sternly. "Do you recognize that?"

"Yes."

Hidden in the director's chastened response was his use of the first-person plural pronoun. Neal's mild rebuke substituted the demonstrative for the personal pronoun – "John, that was wrong" – thus conveying the idea of collective blame; even in this most poignant confession there was the devolution of personal responsibility, a tactic designed not so much against his co-defendants who ultimately could be shown to have followed orders given by the director: "*We* decided wrongly to violate the labor code" was aimed at Frank Marshall; and by inference at Steven Spielberg.

Having been thoroughly drilled by his lawyers, having for weeks batted questions shot at him from every angle by Neal and Behr, on the stand the director did exactly as his lawyers told him; and his confession of wrong-doing was immediately amended by a "softening" disclaimer. While failing to honor the letter of the law, he testified, he had acted in its spirit both by explaining to the parents what the scene entailed and by asking them to be on the set as guardians for the children. There never was any suggestion or mention of danger, Landis maintained, and even though he discussed the use of dummies or "small people" with Allingham, it was only in connection with the problem they had with the labor code about night shooting.

One of the strangest stories he told the court was that not until he heard 1st AD Elie Cohn testify at the trial on the "lower, lower" issue – only a few months ago! – did he realize for the first time that maybe those words were spoken. He said he thought the 1st AD gave the cues over his radio to start the machine gun-firing that prompted the explosions. Even stranger was his denial of having ever been told at a June 16, 1982, casting meeting with Mike Fenton and Marci Liroff that the scene was dangerous. "Absolutely not!" It was impossible, he testified, that he could have even told Liroff at the time how the scene was going to be shot. He told the jurors that he didn't even know that he was to shoot the scene with real kids in one take without the use of "inserts," because at that time the budget had not yet been approved by Warner Bros., and he hadn't even made the decision how to film the scene.

The "plan" took up the chief part of Neal's questioning. Certain key phrases, a "safe distance away," "the other side of the river" and "camera platform," were made familiar to the ears of the jurors by being constantly repeated. The director stressed the many meetings and careful preparation of a plan in which the helicopter would be on "the other side of the river" before the final shoreline explosives were detonated. Landis elucidated that once the helicopter was out of the scene on "the other side of the river" it would function as a "camera platform," filming the shoreline explosions going off.

The jurors were informed that what they had seen on the film was mostly "illusion," including the enigmatic last-second incident where Vic falls to his knees in the river and Renee is shaken loose from his grip and dropped into the river just seconds before the crash. Landis said that just before the final scene he told the parents "so they wouldn't be concerned" that Vic was going to stumble. Stating, "I saw Vic fall where we discussed he would fall" literally seconds before the actor was decapitated, he again emphasized the illusionary process of film-making. In the same vein he referred to the 9:30 shot which Jackie Cooper had criticized for showing the kids too close to explosives. The young director explained to the jurors that by using certain camera angles and sound effects it only appeared that Vic and the kids were close to the explosions when actually they were not.

Until the very last moment Neal hammered away that no one, no fire marshals, no helicopter pilot, no special effects men, no one told the director that the scene as planned was unsafe. He rested after his final question. Did Mr. Landis think the scene was safe?

"Yes," the defendant replied firmly.

With Landis' calm performance as a witness, it was easy to forget that his trial testimony was wholly inconsistent with what he had told the NTSB almost five years before, and a year later to the grand jury. The only consistent element was his same blanket refusal to accept any responsibility as a director for what had happened on his set. His trial testimony continued and extended the steam-roller strategy first conceived by Joel

Behr which had successfully leveled every objection for five years. It was the same policy of categorical, across-the-board denial – except that Neal had worked a wonder.

The "gray-haired eminence" had been able to draw out of the chaotic personality the humanly affecting side. There was vast improvement in the movie maker's story-telling technique. Unlike Bill in the script, his creator had evolved and become more sympathetic. Under Neal's gently firm, almost rueful questioning, ran a tone of forgiveness for the prodigal son. Neal skillfully built an evangelical occasion, filled with religious accents from the Bible Belt, with tragedy and joy, sadness and hope. Sometimes a white hanky fluttered from the witness stand and a snuffling sound came through the mike. There were frequent tears from the witness and synchronous ones from a tall, sobbing Hollywood woman in the first row of the gallery who was the young director's suffering wife...

* * *

Everyone had expected the confrontation between Lea D'Agostino and John Landis to be the high point not just of the trial but of the hallway feud between them. But no one had expected the cutting sarcasm of the prosecutor's very first question in the cross-examination.

"Would you like a kleenex, sir?"

The Dragon Lady fluttered a white tissue. The eyes of the witness welled up. Though it had less to do with the case than with the hallway feud, it was dramatic. The offer of a kleenex stated with theatrical effectiveness that she didn't believe the director's words nor his tears.

Continuing in the same merciless vein she asked whether he wasn't a good "story-teller?" And did he not as writer and director use certain techniques to engender sympathy, like having the character cry? And hadn't he himself cried before as an actor?

Landis remained patient and mild. He replied that he had never instructed an actor to cry. He himself had never cried in an acting role except once in his very first movie when he was dressed in ape makeup for the lead role in Schlock! Shot in the end, the monster died, and that was when he cried.

The prosecutor tried to counter the Horatio Alger hero portrayed by Neal with the more pedestrian version of someone who had made it in Hollywood by being very lucky. She mentioned that, besides actually working in Hollywood for years doing bit pieces in 10 or 11 movies, Landis had also been a stuntman in eight movies and in three or four TV shows; he had fallen off a horse, been pushed through a window and hit by a car, but in all of this detailed exposition she barely scratched the surface of the key relationship in his life, satisfied to learn no more than what Landis had said on the stand of meeting Spielberg when he was invited to the Spielberg house for dinner following the success of *Animal House*. Later she would bring up Spielberg one more time, asking the witness about the rivalry between them ("We were not in competition," the director replied).

Under Neal's questioning the rueful format had permitted little scope for the director's fund of film lore. But the prosecutor offered him numerous openings to present the fascination of the consummate fan with Hollywood. Some of the movie stories were of special interest to the ethnically varied jury. Responding to D'Agostino's criticism about his bent for realism in filming, he told of a scene in *Trading Places* to which Paramount objected because it didn't want Don Ameche to call Eddie Murphy "nigger." Landis related how he convinced Paramount to change its mind, pointing out that "nigger" was necessary to show the ugliness of racism.

Of the prior testimony that the Landis defense feared most the witness focused on the statements of the casting agent, Marci Liroff, and even more so, that of the cameraman, Steve Lydecker. On the stand Landis denied Lydecker's testimony in toto. He denied Lydecker's contentions that the helicopter was not supposed to be in the frame of the final shot, or that live ammunition was used in certain scenes, or that he had ever said to Lydecker, "We may lose the helicopter," or that he excoriated one of the electricians for being "chickenshit." He denied "C" Camera assistant Lee Redmond's account of the incident where he told a cameraman to go home if he didn't want to do a dangerous shot. He denied that the Wednesday filming was delayed because of interruptions in certain shots caused by the children's constant giggling. He denied any characterization of himself as using four-letter words and vulgarities or as the "screamer." He also denied the parents' allegations that he had not told them about any helicopter or explosions in connection with the use of their children.

Against this tide of denial, the prosecutor chose his claim that Vic's last-second stumble was planned as conclusive demonstration of the witness's ability to manufacture stories. For trapped by the fall, Vic, the film showed, lost the opportunity to dive for cover. Moreover, there was nothing in the script calling for Vic to trip. Even Landis' friend Elie Cohn had testified that he didn't attend any meeting where a stumble was discussed.

Landis' eyes began to tear.

"Vic is acting!" he cried. "That's why it looks horrendous." He made the decision to have Vic stumble, Landis said "probably during the rehearsal."

One could hear a pin drop during this exchange. The jurors had seen the film and seen Vic's fall. In the courtroom they saw the director leave the stand to indicate on a map where exactly he and Vic had planned the stumble to occur. "I told the kids Vic was going to stumble." He even insisted that he had asked both the parents, and the children, if the children could swim.

The prosecutor caught him with rapid-fire questioning. Did he tell the helicopter pilot about the stumble? Or Dan Allingham who held the light? What about the 1st AD? And why in five years had he never mentioned the stumble? He answered as he did to many questions that pointed up contradictions with his earlier statements, shrugging: he had never been asked.

It would perhaps have been easier to prove from a film maker's viewpoint that the stumble didn't make any film sense. It had no logical necessity. The director of photography's understanding was that Vic was to complete the scene and leave the frame as fast as possible; DP Steve Larner had never heard of a stumble, nor had any of his cameramen. In any event, even allowing that the stumble was planned, it wasn't planned very well because the little girl slipped from Vic's arm into the water. But more importantly, everybody knew it was a one-shot take in which a planned stumble would create too many problems. There was no way for Landis to call it off; there was no contingency plan; if in the event of a stumble the children started to behave unprofessionally, like their giggling on the previous night, and they dropped out of Vic's arm, the shot would be ruined and there was nothing the director could have salvaged.

Landis had already told the court that he had been prepared beforehand for his testimony, but the thoroughness of this drill never ceased to be a revelation. Amazingly he had an answer for everything. He had a ready response to another damning quote which like "lower, lower" had come up in every previous hearing, investigation and judicial proceeding; it concerned the occasion just after the rage scene when in reply to Wingo's complaints about safety he remarked, "You ain't seen nothing yet," promising even bigger fireballs. Landis told the prosecutor that it was his method of joking in order to calm people down.

In the same casual vein, he explained a different sticky question that had tripped up Kathryn Wooten at the prelim. Without admitting that he knew the final shot was dangerous, as he'd done in confidential interviews with his legal phalanx, he resorted to unverifiable movie lore and testified that his call on the bullhorn asking everyone to stand up was a habit he had picked up in Spain, from the "famous" assistant director Jose Ochoa (who used the practice, Landis said, when filming around heavy machinery).

When the prosecutor moved on to show how the movie makers cut corners by doubling up, with Allingham serving both as UPM and 1st AD, Landis denied that it was done for cost-cutting reasons ("It wouldn't be saving that much"). And after his example of Jose Ochoa, he dipped deeper into Hollywood apocrypha to cite the example of someone who had distinguished himself for doing two jobs at once on the set. His name was Tommy Shaw. "Tommy Shaw," the jury learned, "always functioned that way for John Huston." Landis fell back on blanket denial when the questioning turned to a critical photograph that showed the marble-gun shooter standing right next to him, actually Landis' long-time associate, propman Mike Milgrom, the man he had grabbed by the shoulder as Morrow fell to his knees in the final seconds. The director replied that he "was unaware there was anyone firing a marble gun. At only one point was the trial provided the rare instance of hearing mention of the bouffant-crested general of the phalanx. The name surfaced as D'Agostino brought up Landis' controversial NTSB interview which showed him going off the record 25-30 times to talk to a lawyer named Joel Behr. She asked Landis why Behr hadn't taken the opportunity to jog the director's memory in order to make mention of the "camera platform" and "the plan." If the director had failed to mention the helicopter's camera platform role to the NTSB, didn't he have a second chance to explain it a year later during his grand jury appearance?

It was by force of relentless, non-stop, dive-bomb-type questioning that the prosecutor was able to lay bare the cracks in "the plan." Landis said that he'd never been told about the mortars inside the huts center stage to all of the action, nor as a director was it important if he knew. Nor had he heard the discussion the SFX men had testified to in which he was quoted as saying he wanted to see the "huts going up." At another point Landis was stumped and he couldn't tell her how the SFX men would know what the cue for the plan was. He gave up trying to pinpoint the intended location of the chopper according to the plan; it was "somewhere in the middle of the river, I couldn't tell you exactly where now." He resisted any characterization of his set as being dangerous that night; against the most incontrovertible, undeniable and overwhelming evidence, he even insisted "the children were not under a hovering helicopter on my set!!!"

When D'Agostino turned to the elaborate concealment plan that night the director admitted knowing about the fire marshal who was also a child welfare worker. He said he simply told his people after finding out about Tice that there was not much they could do about it. He even implied that the studio teacher knew about their presence – "Tice couldn't have missed the kids." As for George Folsey's role in telling Mrs. Chen and Dr. Le to hush up about the children if they ran into any firemen, Landis distanced himself from the actions of his friend, saying he'd first learned about this story when it was testified to in the courtroom.

Those who had known the director prior to his appearance in court were flabbergasted by his unruffled performance on the witness stand under the prosecutor's merciless questioning. His calmness so puzzled the *Los Angeles Times* reporter who'd come to know him that he asked Neal in the hallway whether Landis had taken a tranquilizer. Neal could only brusquely snort, "You'd have to be a horse's ass to do that."

At the very end of the chief defendant's testimony the prosecutor returned to the story of casting agent Marci Liroff. Nothing seemed to highlight the contradictions in the mass of his testimony more than Liroff's June 16, 1982 handwritten note with the mention of the kids: 2 *Vietnamese kids boy and girl (Chinese, Thai or Korean)*. Again, he couldn't explain the note.

The prosecutor closed her cross-examination with a pointed question. Were his answers in denying knowledge of Liroff's warnings as truthful as the rest of his answers?

"Absolutely!"

* * *

It was one of the strangest ironies that only days before the prosecutor was to begin her long-awaited cross-examination of the director, on February 14, she received a wire from Interpol stating that Frank Marshall's girlfriend had been detained in Spain. Responding to the request from the LA DA's office, Spanish authorities strip-searched Spielberg's partner and treated her like a common fugitive.

Kathleen Kennedy's name was on the Interpol list along with Marshall's. Marshall would be stopped, too, if he tried to enter Spain where he had been spending a lot of time working on Spielberg's *Empire of the Sun*. Suddenly the Interpol message presented the prosecutor with the possibility of finally snaring Marshall.

But it was too late. She had closed the prosecution's phase of the case just a few days before the Interpol wire arrived. Four months had gone by since the district attorney's office first got Interpol to search for Marshall after he skipped England and thumbed his nose at the brisk lady from the embassy who with Budds was waiting to serve him the subpoena. The idea of going after Marshall was no longer practical. So, when, in a panic Marshall's lawyer Rick Rosen called Lea D'Agostino, he was able to persuade the prosecutor to lift the hold on Kathleen Kennedy and inform Interpol that she was no longer needed as a witness in the *Twilight Zone* manslaughter case.

50

"Hello, Wingo"

The end of the prosecutor's cross-examination of John Landis, but for a few remaining questions by opposing counsel, brought to an end the four-day appearance of the chief defendant. Only a few days were left for the other four defendants to decide whether or not to take the stand. Neal planned on calling only a few witnesses before resting his case. Neal's list was small because many of the witnesses called earlier by the prosecution, like Cohn, McLarty or Wooten, had already provided sufficient evidence to support the defense position. Other possible candidates were rejected because on certain key issues they tended to back up dangerous prosecution witnesses like Lydecker or Schuman. That explained, for instance, why Neal did not call the director of photography, Steve Larner, who in a potentially damaging interview with Neal's Jim Sanders on the eve of the trial virtually demolished the defense case when he couldn't recall the use of the helicopter as a "camera platform" in "the plan." Certain statements made by the DP actually focused particular attention on the film makers' pattern of deception, such as Larner's mention of being informed by Folsey that the reason for shooting the children's segment last and late at night was because the production people were trying to make every possible attempt to get waivers. But most seriously damaging would have been the chief photographer's insistence on his understanding at the time of the crash that the helicopter was to be above Lydecker's camera 'B' master shot. This affirmation of Lydecker's testimony, that Landis told him not to worry about the helicopter's position because it was not to be in his shot anyway, would have dealt another mortal blow to the "plan." It would have strengthened D'Agostino's argument that Landis ordered the chopper to fly directly into the SFX explosions in a last-minute, reckless attempt to improve the shot and by inference to those cognizant of the director's ruling obsession, to "out-Spielberg Spielberg."

The few witnesses Neal did put on presented a strikingly odd combination. The single person from the actual Twilight Zone movie set was an obscure gaffer. Neal called Curtis Hanson, the only other movie director besides Jackie Cooper to testify in the case; Hanson (*Losing It, Bedroom Window*), Kathryn Wooten's former husband, was known as sympathetic to the Landis's dilemma. Neal also called a very surprised Andy Furillo who, after sitting in the press gallery for six months, suddenly learned that he was to become a participant in the drama. Another surprise to the prosecution was witness Robert Frasco, Landis' private investigator. Neal's list presented no greater contrast than the "carrot-top" and the executive-looking gumshoe Frasco. Yet both were felt to be important by Neal in order to discredit cameraman Steve Lydecker, the man the phalanx considered to be Landis' most damaging opponent.

Lydecker had been the prosecution's great hope. He had told the jurors of having been brought into the business by his dad at age nine, of having worked as a stunt double; one of his very first jobs, he mentioned, was stunt double in John Wayne's *Wake of the Red Witch*; and of having worked in SFX capacity on *Psycho* and *The Warlords*. With a background in guns and hunting he should have demolished Neal's claim that less lethal "red jets" had been used in the controversial scene disparagingly referred to by the defense as "the banana plant murder." Lydecker was able to identify from memory the type of live ammo Stewart used by the direction of Landis when marble guns failed to produce the desired mayhem in the banana plant scene; ".12 gauge shotgun shells, Remington SP-High Base .00 buck."

Lydecker's report of the director's response to his warning about flying the helicopter too close to the cliff, "So, we lose the helicopter," brought Andy Furillo to the stand. Furillo in an article had quoted the master shot as saying that he believed Landis had been joking. On the stand Furillo's testimony was limited merely to stating whether or not the quote as it appeared in the article was accurate. Neal's questioning of Furillo must have been bewildering to the jury, if only because, joking apart, Landis denied there having been any discussion at all between himself and Lydecker about flying the helicopter too close to the cliff.

Neal called Robert Frasco because the detective had tape-recorded a statement by Lydecker just after the crash which Neal believed favored Landis vis-a-vis the "lower, lower" issue. The detective's appearance was limited solely to discrediting and thereby neutralizing Lydecker. Neither the jury nor the public at large ever heard the true story of the disaster as it was shockingly laid out in Frasco's files. Frasco's testimony consisted of the private eye quoting Lydecker from a lengthy three-hour taped interview done early in the case, brief selections of which were played in open court, in which the cameraman's knowledge of John Landis shouting "lower, lower" was stated as having come from another cameraman, implying that he had not heard it himself.

The only movie director Neal called to the witness stand, Curtis Hanson, was socially close to the Landis circle. Youthful-looking, in his late thirties, he'd dated Folsey's future wife Belinda, and was the nephew of Jack Hanson of the famous Beverly Hills clothier, Jack's, Hollywood's in-place to buy clothes in the 60s. At the trial Neal prompted him to contradict the notes Tom Budds made during his interview with Kathryn Wooten at her Venice Beach home nearly five years before. By his own admission, Hanson had been in and out of the room where the interview took place, yet in his answers he was able to back up with fine detail Kathryn Wooten's trial testimony in which she retracted all the previous statements she had made to Budds about her fears of the explosions and her warnings to Landis.

Neal's final witness was Alan Goldenhar. From a technical standpoint, Goldenhar held an important position on the set as the chief electrician, the gaffer, who set up the crucial lighting for the shots that night. Whenever possible Neal attempted to show that there was always a higher degree of planning on the set than had been indicated by earlier witnesses. The middle-aged gaffer, resembling the jurors in age and manner, in brief and narrow testimony, especially supported Landis' claim of many "meetings." The obscure gaffer left the stand and after six days and four witnesses, in addition to Landis, James Neal rested his case.

Of the remaining four defendants, three had pretty much decided not to testify in the trial. The decision not to let Folsey take the stand, according to Harland Braun, was reached after video-taped rehearsals showed Folsey projecting a weak image. His high, straining, flutey voice came through wavering and uncertain. In any event, Folsey had not been directly involved with the set during the last night's shooting. There was not much he could talk about beyond his role in chaperoning the parents that night, leaving it for the prosecution to determine in how far his actions contributed to deceiving Dr. Le and Mrs. Chen, in addition to shielding them from the inquiring eyes of Jack Tice.

With Allingham the situation was far more complex since, functioning in something like four jobs that night, he had been pivotal to the operation of the set and, in contrast to Folsey, he would have had very much to talk about. More than any other witness he was the prisoner of previous statements that wholly contradicted everything Landis had told the court concerning meetings, planning and rehearsal. When asked at the grand jury in reference to the rage scene, "Did anyone express concern over the helicopter being blasted by water and fire mortars?" Allingham had coyly replied that all he had heard about complaints afterwards was, "Boy, that was a little warm."

Dangerous statements like these, and they were plenty, would become admissible if Allingham took the stand.

The fifth defendant, Paul Stewart, would have presented an only slightly lesser disaster had he decided to appear in his own defense. Stewart previously had informed investigators of his walking the set with the director and showing him where SFX explosives were placed, in sharp contrast to Landis' testimony which held that the director didn't even know there was an explosive under the lethal hut No. 4! Devastating to Landis' "plan," especially one which Landis claimed was actually improved upon after the run-in with explosions during the rage scene, was Stewart's earliest statement, made more than five years ago, revealing that he had not even been informed of the 11:30 near miss! "Nobody ever said anything about the explosions being close to the helicopter," Stewart had recalled, and as far as the so-called "rehearsal" was concerned, Stewart informed the NTSB and police, "They could've flown through ... and they could've been turning the camera and I'd never know." Indeed, except for exchanging a few words with the pilot before the crash, he said he'd never talked with Wingo on the set about the location of the explosives.

Keeping at least three of the four witnesses off the stand was not difficult for Neal. Folsey and Allingham, while technically represented in court by Braun and Levine, still sought their major counsel from Joel Behr and their income from Landis, while Stewart's lawyer Arnie Klein, though distant from Landis' Hollywood lawyers, was a close friend of Braun and subject to his persuasion. Only Dorcey Wingo, the wild card, fighting for his soul, remained outside the orbit of Century City.

Like Folsey, Allingham and Stewart, the pilot represented a Pandora's box of earlier statements that were both inconsistent with the plan and contrary to John Landis' trial testimony. But unlike his three co-defendants the pilot's mouth would not be easily shut and, to the end of keeping him off the stand, a campaign was unleashed whose emotional intensity had not been seen before in the trial. At the time it began, Neal and Wingo's lawyer were at dagger's drawn. In fact, on the day John Landis finished his testimony, Eugene Trope jolted Neal and the others by announcing as a near certainty that Wingo would take the stand.

Neal was furious, according to Braun, while the rest of the defense team "went bananas."

An indication of the fears sparked among the phalanx by the prospect of Wingo's appearance on the stand was their circulation of a super-confidential 12-page memo entitled:

PRIOR STATEMENTS OF DORCEY WINGO – Which May Be Difficult to Overcome

The memo suggested the ease with which the prosecutor could turn against Wingo his previous confessions to investigators. It cited Wingo in statement upon statement which flew directly in the face of John Landis' recent testimony. Each example was followed by pointed comments like, "Contradicts Landis' testimony of numerous meetings between him and Stewart and Wingo"; "Displays Dorcey's total ignorance of special effects," or "Direct contradiction to the testimony of the plan." One statement alone, according to the authors of the memo, appeared almost sufficient to "convict" Landis, Stewart and Wingo, if not Allingham and Folsey. After a thorough analysis of the pilot's prior confessions, they concluded bleakly: "Dorcey is not even aware there are fireballs along the shoreline at all, let alone a plan to turn his helicopter and be a safe distance away before the explosions were set off!"

Obviously, the fears of the defense lawyers would have instantly turned into horror and despair had they known that the pilot had already been speaking in secret to the prosecutor...

At this time, it became impossible to tell by Landis' familiarity with Wingo that not until very recently had he resumed speaking to the pilot after a four-year hiatus. Landis greeted him like a family friend, "Hello, Wingo." Dorcey's wife brought her new-born baby to the trial to be admired by Deborah. The Landises invited the Wingos to Sunday brunch at home on Lloyd Crest. Nevertheless, this onslaught of cordiality fell on stony Oklahoma caution. Despite Wingo's obvious desire still to work in motion pictures, he was being constantly warned by his lawyer to steer clear of the hospitable Landises.

The pilot's own wry comments on the proceedings were contained in the "court-toons" he doodled while sitting through the endless sessions. Landis noted the pilot's work approvingly. Perhaps nothing better illustrated the differences between the cowboy-pilot from Oklahoma and the self-conscious Hollywood auteur than a portrait of Landis which Wingo intended to present him as a gift. Like most of the pilot's art, it contained an element of the grotesque. The movie director criticized this particular "court-toon" for showing him with a "Jewish nose," and Wingo awkwardly retracted the gift and returned to his sketch pad where he solved the dilemma by drawing a portrait, bespectacled and bearded, but with an unexpected touch of surrealism by depicting the likeness without a nose.

The two men were cast from completely different molds. Wingo could never forget that Landis and his people had responded inappropriately after the accident.

"I think John would be a hero to a lot more people had he just said, 'Look, I accept responsibility for the accident because it was my production. I'm the director. I put all the elements together. We all felt we were ready to go and when I yelled, Action! a terrible accident happened, and I will accept responsibility because I was the director on the set.'" These were Wingo's personal feelings to which he clung despite baby gifts and brunch at Lloyd Crest.

Meanwhile, the Landises, John and Deborah, together with Neal and Folsey, lobbied Trope without letup. According to Bill Anderson, Trope's assistant, it was more intense than lobbying legislation on Capitol Hill. Trope even received telephoned pleas from Houston Casualty, the insurance carrier that had hired him, urging at the behest of Warner's attorney not to put Wingo on. George Folsey Jr. with his wife Belinda took Trope and his client to lunch across the street from the courthouse. Neal put in a last-ditch effort after accepting as a certainty that Wingo would appear as a witness in his own defense. According to Trope, Neal approached him with, "Couldn't he just forget that statement, 'Don't be squeamish'!? Couldn't you just have Dorcey 'bend' some of those words?" The Landises, virtually assaulting the pilot on a daily basis, gave reasons why he should stay away from D'Agostino.

"Why subject yourself to the bitch?" Wingo recalled John Landis asking. "She is so loathsome she'll try to trip you up. You really don't need to do it."

"John's right," Deborah chimed. "Why subject yourself?"

* * *

Against this gloomy background of a developing debacle for the defense, Harland Braun presented the only bright spot. Again, he was able to divert everybody's attention from the defendants with a highly unorthodox stratagem. Earlier it had been the delamination theory. This time he revived the ghost of El Gaucho, and against vehement objections from Neal, who feared fresh surprises, Braun brought Gary Kesselman back to the stand as a surprise witness in George Folsey Jr.'s defense. It was Braun's strategy that a fight between the two prosecutors with contradictory accounts over the truth of a star witness would deflect the jury's focus from his client.

In returning to the stand Kesselman was able to explain why during his first appearance six months before he had failed to positively disavow Schuman's allegations; in the meantime, he had been able to consult the handwritten notes of his interview with Donna Schuman, and, finding no reference in these notes concerning any "going to jail" statements, he now felt secure in testifying that no such words from her had ever been spoken to him. For the second time Kesselman became a byword in the DA's office; the ridicule and whispering behind his back got as nasty as it had been in the aftermath of the raid on the taxi-dancing club. It was Braun's aim to exploit this many-sided discord in the DA's office by calling into question the DA's handling of the case in general.

Perhaps the DA's office could have spared itself the embarrassment if it had not initially allowed itself to be swayed by the emotions of the prosecutor. To her superiors, D'Agostino pilloried Kesselman in shrill terms. Avowing her belief in Donna Schuman, she blamed Kesselman's failure to stand behind Schuman on resentment and jealousy for being taken off the case. District attorney Ira Reiner had backed D'Agostino, adding fuel to the fire by giving assurances that Kesselman would be punished for not siding with the prosecution. "He'll never see the inside of a courtroom again as long as I'm in office," Reiner had promised. And in support of D'Agostino, Reiner, without informing her, issued instructions in the very beginning to have the feud between his two DAs analyzed by an unbiased deputy DA in his office. This appointee, acting in the capacity of a special counsel, was to be above the fray and impervious to the publicity attending the trial.

The arbiter selected for this role turned out to be a middle-aged maverick who, after a thorough review of the code of ethics, requested a special meeting with Reiner's deputy Gil Garcetti. At this session he recommended what the DA's office had least expected and least wanted to hear. The special counsel explained that because there was a conflict between two attorneys from the same agency, the office now had a stake in the outcome. Lea D'Agostino and the other high-ranking members of the DA's office in attendance heard Reiner's special appointee express alarm that despite the turn of events the office was still prosecuting the Landis business. From the standpoint of legal ethics, the arbiter maintained, the office could no longer prosecute fairly, and the maverick urged that in order to settle the ethical conflict the DA's office "recuse" itself, that is, remove Lea D'Agostino and turn the case over to the California state attorney general's office for prosecution.

According to one eyewitness at the meeting, the listeners "went white." The district attorney was advised to give up his biggest case! Reiner dismissed the lesson in ethics and thus, by not taking the issue seriously, ultimately aided John Landis. Although Lea D'Agostino played a key role in creating it, the whole Kesselman affair deflected her from the chief defendant and, by going after her predecessor, forced the prosecutor into a two-front battle.

Kesselman returned to the witness stand for the second time on March 10, 1987. Giving bent to their bias, DA investigators had made several attempts over the six-month interim to show that the former prosecutor was lying and had been aware of Donna Schuman's "going to jail" statement. They were unsuccessful and during his second trial appearance, as a defense witness for Folsey! Kesselman was questioned at length by Braun. For certain technical reasons which no juror could be expected to understand, the ethics code required that an attorney other than D'Agostino conduct the interrogation. Thus, in what must have seemed to the jury a disruption of the routine, a complete stranger by the name of Peter Bozanich took D'Agostino's place and with the bird-like prosecutor at his side, without any explanation to the jury, cross-examined Kesselman. Bozanich, like D'Agostino, a deputy district attorney, was the same deputy DA who had originally been offered the job to replace Kesselman, only to decline when his superiors refused to reveal the reasons behind his dismissal.

The exchanges between Kesselman and his questioners in the well of the court produced nothing so memorable as the witness's intense and passionate bearing. When the original prosecutor on the case spoke of his humiliations created by his successor, his indignation filled the room and brought it to a stunned, shamed silence. The emotional power of his testimony produced a confession expressed in lines as haunting as any other spoken in this strange real-life *Twilight Zone* drama. It occurred as Kesselman described how during a meeting D'Agostino had allegedly pressured him into recalling what Schuman had said. "She closed the door so no one could hear her."

Kesselman said she then told him:

"'I'm not important."

"'Donna Schuman is not important."
"'You're not important."
"'Only the case is important,'"
The next day there were headlines.
EX-PROSECUTOR: D'AGOSTINO SUGGESTS PERJURY.

* * *

Braun was gleefully aware that he had the prosecution in a bind. It was Hobson's choice: whatever choice is made it is the wrong choice. If D'Agostino was right, Kesselman's withholding of information meant that he violated the "discovery" rule whereby everything discovered by the prosecutor must be turned over to the defense; and if he was not withholding, as he claimed, then Donna Schuman was making up the story, putting the prosecutor in the untenable position of supporting a witness who was lying under oath. The problem for the DA, however, was not so much the trap laid by Braun but its own inaction. The affair was allowed to simmer for six months and by the time it boiled over in the courtroom it was already far too late. The top prosecutor Ira Reiner did not give the controversy his full attention when it first surfaced, nor did he try and stop Lea D'Agostino, not even after the exposure of the ethical conflict, from going after Kesselman, or suggest a middle ground where the whole thorny question could be avoided. Unbelievably, Reiner did absolutely nothing.

The paralysis only deepened after Kesselman's second appearance. At that point the DA's men became uncomfortably aware that there were too many unanswered questions about the way D'Agostino had handled the Kesselman crisis from its inception. It turned out that she had known at least two weeks before Donna Schuman took the stand about the shocking allegations against the ex-prosecutor! Why didn't she contact Kesselman immediately upon learning of his alleged request to Donna Schuman not to bring up the "going to jail" statement until the trial? Why didn't she tell her superiors as soon as she learned that Kesselman's withholding evidence violated the "discovery" rule?

But what was most puzzling was Kesselman's own motive in appearing as Braun's witness. No question stumped the DA's men so much. Why would Kesselman possibly be untruthful for the sake of Harland Braun, especially since the inside-office speculation held that Kesselman suspected Braun of having used his connections in the DA's office to set up the embarrassing El Gaucho bust, and that the ex-prosecutor even believed it possible that Braun was responsible for having him ultimately removed from the case. This conundrum was perhaps the DA's real introduction to the *Twilight Zone* case; just as the backfiring of the star witness did for D'Agostino, it taught Kessleman that here the unexpected was the rule.

The Kesselman crisis took its heaviest toll on Lea D'Agostino. Her support for Donna Schuman against Kesselman had all the marks of a personal commitment. It had a deeply emotional effect. Her bearing in the courtroom showed how much the decision taxed her self-control. At times during Kesselman's testimony she was barely able to retain her composure. During Kesselman's final appearance her facial gestures and fidgeting became so pronounced that the judge warned that if she didn't control herself, he would have to exclude her from the courtroom.

Kesselman's testimony came through with dignity and poignancy. The intense sincerity of the witness and its gripping effect on the jury was devastating for the prosecution. Kesselman told the jury that the scandal had ruined him. He absolutely denied ever asking or informing any witness to withhold information from the defense for any reason. Donna Schuman, he intimated, was a very good witness but prone to hysteria and dramatics. And, even had Donna Schuman heard a statement like "going to jail" in the first place, hadn't she already admitted that she understood Landis to be joking? How otherwise, Kesselman asked, had she thought it was serious, could she have permitted her husband to go out and recruit the children to work without permits?

By the time Kesselman stepped down the impression was fixed that someone on the prosecution side of the case was not telling the whole story. The prosecution was suddenly saddled with questions it could not explain; and so, rather than being asked to find Landis guilty on manslaughter charges, the jury was sidetracked into questions about the DA's handling of the case. What he had not achieved in the headline-grabbing "Spielberg letter;" and like "delamination" before it, Harland Braun pried open the prosecutor's Pandora's Box of wild emotions. The events followed a scenario not unlike that which resulted in the DeLorean acquittal, ironically, the very dilemma the DA had been most concerned about and which it had hoped to avoid by appointing D'Agostino.

Though Braun did not provoke the Kesselman crisis, once it emptied, he channeled its force and kept it bubbling. The dissension in the courtroom and in the DA's office benefited the entire defense. It was the only time during the trial that John Landis openly praised his former attorney.

"I just want to thank you," he said, according to Braun. "You're the only one who could have pulled this off."

The whole affair created tremendous discord within the prosecutor's immediate circle. Tom Budds was torn by conflicting feelings. On the one hand, he supported the team led by D'Agostino and hoped to give a boost to his career plans as the "winning" investigator in the famous *Twilight Zone* trial. On the other hand, he had over the years become close friends with Kesselman and had come to believe in his integrity.

Personally, Budds saw the conflict between the former and current prosecutors in terms of a personality contest. He didn't think that anyone was lying. "I don't believe that Gary told her that he was going to withhold evidence." But while skeptical of Schuman, and her interpretation of what Kesselman might have said during their interview three years before, Budds was unable to voice these doubts; and, when he was himself called to the witness stand, he did not volunteer these or any of his innermost feelings. He tried not to let friendship and loyalties get in the way. He fulfilled circumspectly his obligations to the prosecutor who was his boss. But he was unhappy to see her own boss, the dour bureaucrat Dick Hecht, openly disdain his friend, often making disparaging remarks about Kesselman.

"I believe what Gary told her," Budds concluded about Kesselman's controversial communication with Donna Schuman, "was what he told all the witnesses: you don't put everything on." Budds believed that Schuman had simply misinterpreted the instruction given to witnesses testifying in a grand jury or preliminary hearing; "You don't present your whole case." Budds also felt that Schuman and D'Agostino had become too chummy so that the prosecutor was swayed and mistakenly elevated Schuman's importance as a witness far beyond its merits, thus locking herself into a no-win position.

The Kesselman crisis, in effect, put the prosecutor on trial. It sapped D'Agostino of energy, it drained her emotionally, it impaired her judgment. It eventually led her to blame Kesselman more than the defendants and, coming as it did near the end of the proceedings, the controversy taxed her credibility in the press, making another "DeLorean" inevitable.

51

A SAFE DISTANCE AWAY

B y the middle of March 1987, as the trial neared the end of its seventh month, the embattled witness with the striking flying man's name took the stand. The defense had looked towards this moment with the abysmal feeling that Dorcey Wingo would be catastrophic. But like Jack Tice, who lost his sting as a witness by appearing after a drab firemen's parade beset by squabbles, Dorcey Wingo's impact was lost against a bleak background of general exhaustion. After Landis' testimony and the Kesselman crisis, and all of the previous 80 witnesses with all of the sheer weight of detail; after the eruption of issue after issue, the constant squabbles and din of clashes, the conundrums and all the bewildering phenomena associated with the *Twilight Zone*, a numbness had set in. People were like plastic, "maxed-out," overcharged with information. The tone in the courtroom was flat, nothing could stir a ripple, not even the long-awaited and potentially most dramatic witness.

A few days before Wingo took the stand on the first day of spring, the entire defense counsel confronted the judge outside the presence of the jury. They requested that he exclude Wingo's previous statements as inadmissible based on the fact that the pilot originally gave these statements after having been told that they would not be used against him in a criminal proceeding. The judge however, citing legal precedent, ruled them admissible for purposes of impeachment, that is, as showing that Wingo had made statements that ran contrary to his testimony at the trial.

As Neal had done with Landis before him, Trope took his client through well-rehearsed paces from the witness stand. They covered his entire flying career from the top secret "crypto" clearance in the still classified Vietnam War "Project Left Bank" to Wingo's peacetime work flying industrial jobs, from fighting fires and lifting mammoth refrigeration systems onto buildings to his involvement in pyrotechnic displays for the *Queen Mary* and Disneyland. After giving a pleasing impression of a skilled pilot and conscientious young veteran trying to break into the movie business, Trope then led the witness into more sensitive areas. He asked the pilot to recall before the jury details of the planning of the fatal shot. At the defense table everyone sighed with relief. In Wingo's temperate reply the catastrophe failed to materialize.

Though Trope had given as his reason for putting Wingo on that he didn't want to see his client painted with the Landis "tarbrush," by and large, Wingo's version of events emerged basically consistent with the testimony given by the director. Only a very close analysis would have revealed the flaws already outlined by the phalanx in its 12-page internal defense memo titled "Prior Inconsistencies of Dorcey Wingo." These were not addressed until the prosecutor began her cross-examination; but the staccato questions and constant reading from transcripts only added to the feeling of numbness and "maxed-out" plastic.

An unnatural lack of verve characterized the prosecutor's treatment of Wingo on the stand. She could still at times sting like the bee that was her emblem and lash sharply with her tongue, but the fire-breathing dragon was fettered by the agreement her office had reached with Trope during the clandestine dismissal negotiations with Wingo just a month before. As a result of these secret negotiations a damaging 124-page transcript of the pilot's most dramatic confessions and critical recollections had been compiled, none of which, as stipulated in the secret agreement with Trope, she could use. Consequently, her cross-examination was limited. Again, by wheeling and dealing she had checkmated herself; like Donna Schuman and Jack Tice, Wingo backfired.

During her cross-examination she berated the pilot like a schoolboy over the discrepancies in his testimony. Without respecting subtleties, she accused him of supporting Landis' recollection of events on the meetings, planning and rehearsal because of his desire to get into show business. Wingo was not a polished witness and in one particularly hot moment during his testimony he forced the lawyers behind the table collectively to bite their tongue as they heard him make astonishing remarks, concerning instructions he claimed he had given Vic Morrow just prior to the crash. The pilot testified to advising Vic that if he heard a change in the sound of the engine to look up as there would be five seconds before the noise changed and the helicopter fell.

"I was depressed to the max that he never looked up," Wingo said, apparently blaming the actor, since Wingo presumed Morrow could have done something about his situation in the five seconds.

During the break the hallway was abuzz with comment.

Braun, standing with his client, said it was foolish of Wingo. Folsey agreed, "What could he have done if he had looked up?"

With characteristic gallows humor Braun quipped with a twinkle that he knew what Vic would have said had he raised his eyes.

"What's that?" Folsey asked.

"Oh, no, another case of heat delamination!"

Later, everyone in the defense squirmed when Wingo repeated the director's "don't-be-squeamish" statement from the stand. But fortunately for Landis it slipped into the record without effect. In the end Wingo's total testimony about the events leading up to the crash spared Landis. It was a much softer characterization than that contained in the account the authorities had received from the pilot during his secret dismissal negotiations.

Trope did not rest after Wingo and his decision to call in several auxiliary witnesses set off fresh consternation among the other four defense lawyers. Privately in the hallway Neal lamented that they needed those witnesses "like tits on a bull."

In some of the trial's most bizarre and incredible testimony, Trope called upon a UCLA psychiatrist to tell the court how posttraumatic stress syndrome may have caused some of the radical memory changes Wingo exhibited on the stand. Trope also called a witness with perhaps the most arcane specialty in the field of specialists, a "helicopter accident reconstruction expert," actually a seasoned helicopter pilot who flew in international aerobatics competition against the Russians. He testified that what Wingo had done was what any other red-blooded helicopter pilot would have done. Although he had no college degree or science credentials, he stated his belief that "delamination" caused the crash. The expert supported the defense contention that debris had not been a critical factor in bringing the helicopter down. He told the jury that a piece of bamboo could not have possibly downed the Huey and, interestingly, in illustration, he mentioned a procedure used in Vietnam whereby the helicopter's main rotor blades were employed like a lawnmower to clear entire swatches of bamboo grove just before landing for rescue emergencies.

The two remaining defendants, Allingham and Stewart, called no witnesses. They put their faith in Neal and Landis in the hope that they would be convincing to the jury and pull the rest along with them.

When Wingo finished testifying it was springtime, the beginning of April, the trial's ninth month. The defense came to a close, leaving only two phases of the case to go to the jury for decision, the rebuttal and final argument.

* * *

While the prosecution plans for rebuttal and final argument were be-ing deliberated in the district attorney's office, Lea D'Agostino remained fixated on Kesselman. She was now obsessed with clearing her name of the charges that she may have solicited another district attorney to com-mit perjury. It became a question of personal integrity; she got hung up on it. She approached Reiner in his office. She told him that with her rep-utation and credibility at stake she wanted to call in additional witnesses to rebut Kesselman. This resulted in a second confrontation between the prosecutor and the district attorney. During the first, over the ill-fated at-tempt to recruit Wingo as a prosecution witness, Reiner had bowed in her favor. But he was no longer in a conciliatory mood. An irritable exchange over Kesselman quickly escalated. Using some four-letter words, Reiner shouted that he was sick and tired of Kesselman.

Present at this clash was the rest of the DA's triumvirate, Gil Garcetti and Dick Hecht. Surprisingly, the unimpressionable supervisor who orig-inally had expressed a degree of skepticism concerning Lea D'Agostino's high-fashion appearance, had turned out in the end most tolerant of her behavior and, unlike his assistant who sometimes walked out during her tirades ("I can't take it anymore!"), Hecht's morale appeared unaffected by similar stormy meetings during which the fiery prosecutor screamed in his office. Only Dick Hecht supported D'Agostino in going after Kes-selman. Reiner, looming his burly boxer physique over the tiny lady with the voice of Lauren Bacall, her golden bee and felt-tip pens, shouted that there was no way of gaining a victory by having DA going against DA. He angrily forbade her calling any witnesses for the rebuttal of Kesselman. The case would have to fly on its own merits, Reiner thundered.

In the same Criminal Court building, meanwhile, Deborah Landis was more than normally visible in her role as hostess of the hallway and unofficial keeper of the court calendar. Toward the end she wore a fash-ionable blue sweater with sunburst spots. Among the women reporters it prompted AP's Linda Deutsch to comment, "I'd never thought I'd see the day when Mrs. Landis shows up in anything but brown or dark blue." It was springtime, even in the criminal court.

In contrast to the other four defendants whose fears and anxieties showed more plainly outside the courtroom, the Landises were thinking ahead of the new home they were planning to buy. Near the end of the trial the director took James Neal to Rock Hudson's hacienda overlooking Beverly Hills and Los Angeles all the way to the Pacific Ocean. It was list-ed at a little over $3 million. Landis was eager to buy the house which had

389

only recently been pictured in headline news as the scene where the actor lay dying pitifully of AIDS. In court, however, the life of the Landises was regulated by what the jury might think. Because of the jury, Deborah told a local radio station reporter, she couldn't wear a lovely gold bracelet she'd been given at Christmas.

To Paul Dandridge of KABC-TV news she tried to convey that the Landises were not like other Hollywood people. One day in the hallway, at a time when the Academy Awards were getting close, Dandridge mentioned to Deborah his own and every LA newsman's dream to go to Spago's and sit at Swifty Lazar's famed post-Oscar gala dinner – the hardest invitation in town.

Deborah said, "I've never been to Spago's."

Several bystanders to this exchange simply scratched their head as if coming from Mrs. Landis it was a strange remark.

The upcoming final arguments set off the final internal battle, appropriately in Joel Behr's Century City office.

Since there were five defendants the problem was the order in which the lawyers would present the jury their final argument as to why their clients should be acquitted. The first and last positions were considered the most critical: the first because it immediately followed the prosecutor's summation, the last because it allowed the speaker to "clean up" the arguments of his predecessors and ultimately in his statements represent the best interests of all five. On the other hand, the last man to speak could just as well torpedo the others by saying something damaging.

Neal chose Leonard Levine, Dan Allingham's lawyer, to end the final arguments over Harland Braun. His choice showed the shift in the power balance that had taken place among the members of the phalanx in the preceding months. LA's link to Nashville had been completed and Braun felt outflanked with Lenny Levine in the delegation from Tennessee. He was infuriated that "Lennybob," whom he had himself brought into the case, had secretly discussed with Neal his plan for final arguments. Braun felt betrayed and fought the southern caucus. He held that his own role in the case was crucial and that Neal still required his skills to pull off an acquittal. A vote was taken in Behr's office and at the last moment "Lennybob" was bumped and Harland Braun got to go last in the arguments.

The prosecutor's relations with John Landis by this time had reached a critical mass. Each encounter between them became an act of mutual belligerence. One of these, ironically set off by a Jewish holiday, became remarkable as the occasion when Lea D'Agostino called John Landis a murderer.

The incident occurred as people poured into the hallway during one of the breaks following one highly vituperative exchange in which the full body of defense attorneys had barked in rare unanimity at the frail prosecutor. Afterwards Lea D'Agostino stood in the hallway with AP's Linda Deutsch and quipped about the hostile courtroom clash, reciting the first of the four ritual Passover questions, Ma-nish tah ha-li-la--ha-zeh ("Why is this day different from any other day?")

Standing nearby, John Landis placed his hands over his ears; reacting violently, he yelled, "How dare you speak Yiddish in front of me!"

(Before the reporters ran off to consult their *Joys of Yiddish* again it was explained to them that the language was not Yiddish but Hebrew). Lea D'Agostino answered with the epithet which made a big story the next day. It was a rare event when the prosecutor muttered "Murderer!" at a Hollywood director. She had been betrayed by her emotions. John Landis had been taunting her for weeks, she offered in explanation of her outburst. She just exploded.

The strain was beginning to tell on everyone, even on Tom Budds. His long-suffering patience was beginning to wear thin and he grew annoyed at his boss. He felt that she was "over-personalizing" the case and getting hung up on the Landis personality. She had a fixation on the "screamer." She would query too many witnesses about whether Landis screamed too much. Once, Budds said, he almost walked out of the courtroom because it got to him. On one occasion he even told her,

"Don't be asking that stupid question. The jury is getting sick of it."

(With the male fraternity in the hallway Budds took it much less seriously and was able to joke, "Landis' wife's jaw dropped when she found out that he was a screamer for the first time in court." Laughing heartily, both Neal and Sanders, winking and leering, ingratiated themselves with D'Agostino's assistant.)

In this final stage of the proceedings Neal stepped out of the shadows of the "gray-haired eminence" and joined in the heckling and harassment of the tiny Dragon Lady. He brought a new macho tone to the innuendo. In the middle of the Kesselman crisis he approached Tom Budds so they would enter the courtroom together. Biting on his unlit Encanto cigar, Neal taunted, "Are you ready to go, Tom? Do you have your instructions from the coach?" As Budds met up with D'Agostino, Neal continued, "This is the first time I ever saw a coach go into the huddle with the quarterback."

Yet the strain was beginning to show even on the seasoned criminal lawyer. A high-priced lawyer is expected to win – and the pressures became crushing in the final weeks. The weekend trips home to Nashville began to take a toll. In the hallway it was rumored that Neal's marriage to Victoria was on the rocks because of his absences due to the trial (the rumors were not far wrong: almost immediately following the 10-month trial Neal separated from his wife). Several times it actually looked as if Neal might not make it back from Nashville to complete the case. One time he fell off a balcony at his Nashville home (he said he had only one drink). On another occasion he returned to the courtroom from a weekend in Tennessee with a large open burn on his hand. One other time he was called home in an emergency because Victoria had fainted (confidentially, Neal explained to the reporters, "She stopped taking her potassium pills").

In the end all the lawyers seemed to stagger around the hallway like punch-drunk boxers. Neal himself at one stage became affected by a strange light-headedness and the same criticism that had been leveled at his client, of behaving inappropriately, could have arguably been made against him. He behaved as if he had discovered an absurdity in the words "safety first," at least when coming from the mouth of "Lennybob," who sort of sang them, attempting to prove with this incantation while cross-examining witnesses that his client, Dan Allingham, by using this slogan, could not have been reckless the night of the crash.

"Safety first," "Safety first."

Neal joked with "Lennybob" about his obsession with the slogan and composed a ditty which he sang and even danced to more than once in the hallway:

He don't fly no helicopter – He just says, safety first.

"Safety first, safety first," the slogan seemed intoxicating to the former Watergate prosecutor.

"On John Landis' next film Dan Allingham is not going to be UPM," he ribbed "Lennybob" mercilessly. "He's going to be the set Crier, yelling, Safety first! Safety first!" Neal's strange fascination with the absurdity led him into committing one of his few indiscretions in the courtroom. It happened just before final arguments began. While the attorneys were sorting out some issues over jury instructions before the judge, Levine asked about a special instruction and, as he always did in connection with his client, happened to preface it with "safety first." He stopped because Neal intervened with seemingly uncontrollable gales of belly laughter.

"Lennybob" lamely addressed the court, "I guess, Mr. Neal finds something funny here. And still Neal couldn't stop. Even the judge gave the famous criminal lawyer a long and quizzical look.

52

THE LIAR'S LIST

With the date of the final argument set for April 21, the media activity again increased. After the long slow winter months, the hallway filled again, bringing back the atmosphere of the trial's opening days with the beetling cameras and reporters swarming everywhere.

John Landis made himself more accessible to the press. He had been reading the trial of Oscar Wilde. In gossipy hallway repartee he finally revealed to the reporters his deep distrust of journalists, singling out Bob Woodward, the author of *Wired*. He told Herb Michaelson of the *Sacramento Bee* and *People*'s Josh Hammer that he had been deceived into granting an interview for the book by Woodward's claim that he didn't have a book contract yet; the author, Landis said indignantly, had even tried to ply him with a little wine before the interview, a method which he understood was designed to loosen his tongue and a typical part of Woodward's journalistic practices. The director defended John Belushi who was depicted on the first page of *Wired* as being slipped cocaine by Landis' very good friend, *Blues Brothers* producer and loyal courtroom visitor, big, balding Bob Weiss. "If he was a pig as depicted in *Wired*," Landis asked with reference to Belushi, "Why did he have so many friends?" The reporters were curious about his hallway admission that he had really punched out a coked-up Belushi on the set of *Blues Brothers*, as reported by Woodward.

To the reporters, Landis seemed eager to convey the impression that Hollywood was behind him in his trial. He privately revealed that the TV newscasts of his four-day appearance on the stand had been videotaped by former Universal president Frank Price and that Price had given him copies of all of the coverage by the different local channels. But there were also days that were clearly one day too many, when it seemed that even in the Landises the nerve failed. One day a process server with a subpoena from Myca's civil lawyer, Ned Good, walked up to Deborah Landis and asked her whether that was her name. (By spending time with the deceased children concealed in her husband's trailer, Deborah Nadoolman

Landis, the show's costume designer, was a direct witness to Myca Les final moments.) She walked hastily away, "I don't think so," and by the time Ned Good's man caught up with her she was standing and shaking between Joel Behr and Disney's "golden retriever," Jeffrey Katzenberg.

On another occasion, after most of the people emptied out of the courtroom, John Landis and his wife remained behind the courtroom doors looking out through the little window into the hall. They could see the clamoring photographers poised for them to come out. Fear and uncertainty were obvious in their faces. They were frozen. Just then a nine-year-old boy, the visiting son of the court clerk, came by on his way out. It was as if a light bulb went on in the director's head. Landis grabbed the kid. "Hey, do you want to be photographed!" – and holding the boy in front of him he created his own shot, an endearing image of someone who really loved kids as he walked out into the blinking cameras. As soon as he got past the newsmen, he let go of the living prop, older and heavier than Myca or Renee, and without a word to the startled boy hastened down the hall to join his wife.

On the day the final arguments began in the latter part of April, the hallway was packed with media but there were surprisingly few friends of the director. According to the hallway grapevine, Deborah Landis had warned her friends to stay away so that the prosecutor wouldn't have a big audience. That day's boycott was effective with the exception of Deborah's mother-in-law, Shirley Levine. She still worked at the Japanese bank in Beverly Hills where she had been unwittingly drawn into her son's scheme by initialing the original "under-the-table" check. She always seemed sad and shy, as if bowed down by the burden of being the mother of a famous son. When Mrs. Levine arrived with John's stepbrother Mark, Deborah intercepted them, and after a whispered exchange they joined the boycott and left the building without having entered the courtroom.

In the courtroom the prosecutor was the first to arrive. Her golden good-luck bee was prominently displayed on her shoulder. When the defense lawyers filed in, they began their harassment without a moment's pause.

"Hello, Lea, you're looking gorgeous today," Braun greeted her; in the hallway he remarked caustically, "I don't know of anyone else who's had the bee as a symbol other than Napoleon." Deborah Landis arrived wearing an expensive turquoise necklace. Her husband wore his courtroom glasses with the shabby wire frame and familiar baggy gray businessman's suit.

It was interesting for the first time in nine months to see the jury come alive for the prosecutor. Until then she had only spoken to witnesses, and if she communicated with the jury it was indirectly through the witness, "Would you please explain to the jury?..." Even her detractors acknowledged her summation to be powerful and gripping.

Basically, D'Agostino's closing argument presented a systematic review focusing on all the contradictions and inconsistencies revealed by witnesses who recalled the events and the crash differently from Landis. She called Landis a "tyrannical dictator." She characterized his actions on the set as "barbaric." She pointed out the many witnesses who had lied to protect themselves or the director and the many friends of Landis who had backed away from what they had said earlier. She talked about the SFX man Jerry Williams, how the physical evidence contradicted his testimony on the stand, showing that he was not even looking up at the helicopter at the time of the crash and, in fact, continued striking his firing board even after the chopper had been hit. She cited Jackie Cooper's 60-year film career in which the film veteran had never once been aware of live ammunition being used on a set.

She said that stunt coordinator Gary McLarty was not telling the truth about why he was up in the helicopter and not on the ground doubling for Vic Morrow; she recalled McLarty's threatening appearance on the stand. "I don't know how many of you thought he was going to get off that witness stand and sock me," she addressed the jurors rhetorically, "but there were a couple of times when it looked like he might very well do that."

As she ran down the witness list, she stated that it was "pathetically obvious" that script girl Kathryn Wooten was "trying to help her friend John Landis," how set designer Richard Sawyer backed off on the size of the explosions and the enormity of the gasoline fumes; and referring to Landis' crying episodes on the stand she showed no mercy. "Any tears he may have are for his own predicament." Attempts to paint John Landis as a "pussy cat" were ridiculed as "one of the biggest jokes of this trial." While mentioning the parents of the children she talked about the innuendos made by the defense suggesting Dr. Le and Mrs. Chen knew about the explosives and low-flying helicopter. She asked the jurors to consider that the parents could hardly be blamed for allowing their children to appear in a Hollywood movie. Wouldn't every parent want their kids, especially in 1982 when "that wonderful movie *E.T.*" was out, in a movie that had Steven Spielberg involved in it? She reminded the jurors of one of the most important instructions they would receive before beginning deliberations.

It related to the credibility of a witness; that is, if a witness was lying on a single item then the jurors should reject all the rest of his testimony.

Her summation was dominated by the issue of lying. Shortly after beginning her argument D'Agostino had put up on the exhibit board next to the witness stand a piece of blank white paper on which she drew a chart. Many of her most devastating statements were made against that background of the board on which so many exhibits had been placed before but which for the three days of her closing argument featured the "Liar's List." She admonished the jurors to remember that, apart from the director's friends, no one lied more than he did. She called Landis an "actor," a "story-teller." The "almost-but- not-quite tears," she again remarked, were for himself.

The prosecutor led off her chart with the names of witnesses who flatly contradicted the director's account in his four days of testimony. It was called, "Persons Lying According to Landis." By the time she was through, the complete list contained the names of 25 people who, if the jurors believed John Landis, would have to be lying–; including the two sets of parents, Cynthia Nigh, Marci Liroff, Steve Lydecker, Randy Robinson and Andy House. Lea D'Agostino tried to show further that the acts of malice didn't stop with the hiring of the kids but continued afterwards, e.g., paying the kids' parents in cash, ignoring helicopter pilot John Gamble's warnings, checking on Jack Tice's location to make sure he couldn't see the children, and George Folsey's instructions to the parents to tell the fire marshals they were friends of the production people.

One continued act of malice, she pointed out, showed George Folsey "was already covering up" within an hour of the accident, quoting his assertion to his former production assistant that they had rehearsed the scene 30 times. "We call film makers dream merchants," the prosecutor remarked trenchantly in the voice which sounded like Lauren Bacall, but "not because they're living in a dream world" – and while Andy House went along because he was intimidated, she reiterated to the jurors that the others, notably Folsey and Allingham, went along willingly; Folsey and Allingham were going to ride on Landis' "coattails to a big movie, because big movies make big bucks!"

The prosecutor hammered away at the "lies" and broke them down into categories. She pointed out to the jurors that there were "real bloopers," e.g., the stories of the meetings and discussions about the huts and the camera platform, or how the helicopter's altitude at 2:20 was at the same level as that during the 2:00 "rehearsal," or that the special effects were not inherently dangerous. Among the "real bloopers" she mentioned Landis' claim of having planned the "stumble," citing the director of photography's testimony that Vic Morrow was not to stumble but supposed to make it across the river as fast as he could. She further demolished Landis' version of a planned stumble with the testimony from SFX man Kevin Quibell who indicated that he stopped firing his squibs because he was surprised when he saw Vic fall.

In a trial which had seen many strange sights one of the strangest occurred in the final hours when Lea D'Agostino made a demonstration of a scientific principle that had made a great impression on her. The NTSB's Don Llorente had taught her the trick. Earlier in her summation she had admitted to the jurors her technical ignorance, but her demonstration was very simple. She held up a potato to the eyes of the amazed citizens in the box, then methodically and with breathless dramatics she fractured it by pushing a straw through it with the merest flick of the finger. It was like a Mr. Wizard trick: by blocking one side of the straw with a finger the straw turns into a pick plunging through the potato. In a last-ditch attempt to address the defense theory that heat delamination and not debris had brought the craft down, she intended to show the jurors how the impact of bamboo debris (the straw) could have fractured the tail rotor (the potato). It turned out to be another miscalculation with an awkward demonstration, better suited for a high-school science fair than a closing argument in one of LA's biggest cases.

The courtroom full of attorneys fell on the potato with a ravenous appetite and at break-time the hallway resounded with cries of "Potato-killer!" For the last time in the trial the prosecutor was engulfed by the familiar rumble of a backfire. The *Los Angeles Times* reporter brought more chuckles by impishly querying if she had any more vegetables up her sleeve. The citizens in the box no longer tried to hide their disapproval. By the expression on their faces, the fractured spud went over like a lead balloon.

In conclusion, the prosecutor poised herself squarely before the two rows of stony-faced arbiters, "Are you going to let them set the standards, these movie makers?" Once more she urged them to bear in mind that Landis who wrote, produced and directed the movie, still refused to accept responsibility. She reminded the jurors that though Hollywood films were an illusion, what had happened at Indian Dunes was not an illusion.

"You're not living in the 'Twilight Zone.'"

* * *

At this critical juncture, while the prosecutor made her final argument, Neal took over the hallway. He kept firm client control and concentrated on dealings with the press. When a newsman asked him what he thought about the prosecutor calling John Landis "barbaric," Neal admitted it "was a sad touch on her part. I've got to assume she misspoke herself. I don't think she meant it."

He kept up morale by being seemingly unconcerned about the outcome. In the hallway Neal talked about his hopes for the trial's speedy conclusion because the Kentucky Derby was only a few days away. He didn't want to miss all the parties. With Stewart's attorney, Arnie Klein, he joked, "I'll make you a wager about how long the jury stays out." Both men pulled out some small bills, then a ten, a twenty. "I'll sweeten the pie," Neal cried. He pulled out a hundred and Arnie matched him. Neal said the jury would be out eight days in deliberation and Arnie said four. (The old pro hit it on the head and won the wager.)

The final arguments were being made against the background of LA's annual Oscar frenzy. The award ceremonies took place right across the street a block away from the courthouse in the Dorothy Chandler Pavilion. Movies and stars, famous and not-famous, were the talk of the movie-obsessed city. The papers blossomed with gossip and every day gave faithful account, almost like a regular feature, on the *Twilight Zone* proceedings.

On the last day of D'Agostino's final argument Miss Piggy's creator, Frank Oz, attended. A client of Joel Behr, he was a good friend of Landis and like him a director and devotee of the new young Hollywood cameo cult (Landis had a bit in Oz's *Muppets Take Manhattan*). Later, in the elevator with the Landises on their way out of the courthouse, Oz heard Landis complain that the lawyers did not object enough to the prosecutor's "long litany of bullshit." Oz expressed his own feelings outside the building, saying he made it a point not to know anything about the case. In his strange disavowal of reality Oz spoke perhaps for a whole generation of young Hollywood movie makers – the reign of baby moguls, boy wonders, kids and muppets – during the film capital's brief era of the Spielberg years. Oz said, "That's not what John needs now. He needs support. He doesn't need more people knowing about the case." Oz didn't care whether or not there were any labor violations. "All I know, I'm here to support John."

Although business could not be quite "as usual" due to Monday-through-Thursday court appearances, the Landis-Folsey team found time during all these proceedings to squeeze out a fresh installment of their rambunctious comic vision. After finishing *Three Amigos*, an untitled "Landis Presentation" was launched with Bob Weiss as producer. It appeared the following year under the title *Amazon Women on the Moon*. Again, it was a movie of segments, a series of jokes, which no one found funny.

Between Hollywood projects and the criminal courtroom, the film director continued to busy himself campaigning for support. Throughout the trial Landis boasted to friends that he had the support of America's greatest living film director. John Huston lay terminally ill of emphysema and would live only two more months; nonetheless, he was prepared to testify in John Landis' behalf "with his last dying breath," according to what Landis had told his Berkeley friend, Dan Goldstine.

Though at the time he had never met Hollywood's living legend, Landis seemed to be telegraphing to the DGA that he was a protege of Huston early in the proceedings. When Landis found out near the end of the trial that the American Lung Association planned to give its National Humanitarian award to Huston, he personally called up the director of the event and asked to be allowed to speak a few words at the ceremony. It was reminiscent of the time he asked Folsey to ask "Barbara and the kids" to let him speak the eulogy for Vic Morrow. He took invitations by storm with a chutzpah not seen since the hero of *What Makes Sammy Run?* established the fictional prototype of the Hollywood pusher and striver. During the second day of the prosecutor's final argument Landis' secretary, Sharon Dolin, brought to the hallway the reply from the American Lung Association. The note read:

> You're sitting at the head of the table tonight.... George and Joel are sitting at another table.

Proudly Landis embellished the story by telling friends that John Huston had personally invited him to accept the award on his behalf. He took Neal to the event at the Beverly Hilton and for the first time was introduced to the grand old man now confined to a wheelchair. During the ceremony John Landis made a short speech introducing the aged movie director whose faith in artistic integrity made him symbolic of Hollywood's lost innocence.

Huston wheezed, barely able to utter a few hoarse croaks.

John Landis, wearing his regular black horn-rim glasses and a tux, had his photograph taken with the dying legend.

* * *

The day following the conclusion of the prosecutor's final argument James Neal prepared to give his own closing statement. It was his forte, the reason he was paid his enormous fee. His final arguments were known to be knockouts.

Neal used all his theatrical flair to make it a truly impressive event. He brought into the courtroom a wooden rostrum. It was set up with the help of the other defense counsel and an easel was placed next to it, both the rostrum and the easel dramatically facing the jury.

While erecting the props Neal spoke mockingly to Lea D'Agostino.

"Hold your ears. Hold your ears."

Neal already exuded a victorious air as he stood facing the empty jury box, casually flipping his index cards on which he had outlined the defense.

"You can see the bald spots; that's what's bothering me."

He turned to Deborah and others in the front row his best form-fitting Hickey Freeman image; he preened himself a little, twirling his glittering glasses and running a hand through his thinning gray hair.

It was like Roman times when a famed orator came to argue in the Forum. With Landis' help people packed the courtroom for Neal's closing statement. Larry the Bailiff was more subdued since receiving a severe reprimand from the judge – no longer could Larry lock up Landis' yellow legal pad inside his desk; no rubber bands, no paper clips, the judge had warned, nothing...

The bailiff discreetly allowed the Landis circle to occupy the front row: Landis' stepbrother Mark, Joel Behr and his wife; Uncle Sid and his wife; Folsey's wife and son and daughter, and Landis' mother Shirley and stepfather Walter. Sprinkled through the other rows was the flock of legal secretaries from Joel Behr's office. Jeremy Kagan, Landis' most loyal DGA supporter, and *Poltergeist* director Tobe Hooper were there, and as usual Ralph Bellamy was nice enough to come. The jurors had probably just seen him on television at the Oscar awards receiving the Academy's humanitarian award (Bellamy's request that Landis present him the award was turned down by Academy executives only too suspect of the motives). Among Landis' friends were the ever-present *Blues Brothers* producer Bob Weiss, as well as the recurrent studio bigwigs, Universal's Sean Daniel, Disney's Jeffrey Katzenberg and Paramount's Dawn Steel. They came to see a silver-tongued $5,000-per-diem orator and their expectations received ample satisfaction. Neal gave a riveting final statement. In his best aw-shucks manner, he held the courtroom spellbound.

As in a gala performance, the audience was treated to a brief warm-up before the main event. Just before Neal began his portion of the final argument his assistant, Jim Sanders, spoke briefly about counts 2 and 4, the child endangerment counts. He reiterated the line taken by the defense throughout the trial, dealing with the theme as to whether or not the scenes were safe, and that if, in fact, they were knowingly unsafe, the burden of proof rested with the prosecutor. Genial and engaging, Sanders was a sprightly overture to the symphony that followed.

By the time Neal reached the rostrum, it was the second time in almost a year that he addressed the jury members directly. However, he was not completely unfamiliar with them. Through selective nodding in the hall and elevator, along with other small telegraphic signals, he had established a tacit rapport. He had been consistent and thorough by adopting strictly the recommendations of the National Jury Project. There was nothing extemporaneous about his final argument. It was prepared on 4x6 index cards which he flipped aside as he covered their contents. Frequently he urged the jury to check him out by looking up pages and lines from the 100-plus volume trial transcript during their deliberations.

Neal opened by saying that the *Twilight Zone* crash had been a tragic accident in a scene which none of the defendants had believed to be dangerous. It was well planned and well-rehearsed; none of those on trial, he told the jurors, was a criminal. Coyly he reminded them of the prosecutor's warning in her closing argument to be wary of being misled by some of the things they could expect to hear from James Neal. Just poppycock, an "old trick." He was an "old prosecutor," he told the jury; he had used that trick himself against the opposition when their case was too strong.

Neal put the case before the jury in the simplest terms – three things: Did John Landis and the others believe the plan for the 2:20 scene to be safe? Was the plan adequately and well-rehearsed? Were there certain unforeseeable events that intervened and caused the tragic accident? In addition, he cited from his own experience the four types of witnesses which the jurors were to keep in mind: those that honestly disagreed; those that wished they had said or done something different; those that were Monday morning quarterbacks; and, finally, liars. Neal had also composed a "liar's list." Not nearly as expansive as D'Agostino's two dozen, his liars numbered four: Donna Schuman, studio/teacher Jack Tice, cameraman Steve Lydecker and hairdresser Virginia Kearns.

Neal called "downright silly" Jack Tice's testimony that there was a cover-up on the set that night to keep him from learning about the kids.

As for Lydecker, he was "not worthy of believing." Jackie Cooper was a "Monday morning quarterback" who drew conclusions about the unsafe conditions on the set only from what he saw on film; he didn't even know, Neal stressed, about "the plan." Neal brought up Frank Marshall and Kathleen Kennedy and pointedly asked why the prosecutor had not called them.

The last of the three issues, the unforeseeable intervening event, concentrated on the argument that James Camomile had prematurely set off his explosives. Bringing his own props to the courtroom, Neal put giant blowups of the actual daily court transcript on the easel, enabling the jury to read four pages of Camomile's poster-size testimony. The gray eminence became magisterial. He delivered a calm sermon; everyone was hypnotized by the soothing words and the glasses he twirled without let-up. He twirled the glasses to point to specific lines in the testimony which were to demonstrate that Camomile had caused the crash. As he wound his two-day summation to a close Neal switched to the moral plane. He sounded a charitable, a Christian duty, to let John Landis off the hook.

And pointing with his glasses in his hands to John Landis, he adjured that the director himself had been injured by the accident; "the scars are deep and ever-lasting," "the tears are genuine." He reproached the director with regard to the violation of the letter of the law itself: "Mr. Landis, you were wrong." Noting the Landis's "two lovely children," he ended, "I suspect when he looks at Rachel and Max, he will remember Renee Chen and Myca Le...

"Members of the jury, we submit that on the proof in this case and that the proof justifies, even requires you to say to Mr. Landis, Mr. Landis, you were wrong; but we know you do not use barbaric tactics. We know you are not a tyrannical dictator. ... We know you are not guilty of the charges in this case."

Procedurally, the prosecutor would get one more chance and have the last word. In parting with the jury Neal said, pointing to his seat, "I will be sitting right over there in agony, because we won't get a chance to answer."

* * *

Neal's final argument came off despite several last-minute obstacles. A sudden illness of the pilot's attorney interrupted the opening pace of his climactic oration. More serious, however, was a sudden show of independence by the attorney for the powder chief. For a brief but fraught interval it threatened the final argument to self-destruct.

Whether Eugene Trope suffered stage fright as he was about to give his own final argument following Neal's or, being the oldest member on the team, he simply succumbed to the strain, his confinement to sickbed with an "inner ear infection" on the second day of Neal's final argument set off a nervous flurry in the court. There was nothing for it but to delay the proceedings till the pilot's attorney recovered.

For Neal those four days while Trope was laid low must have been a purgatory. The train he had linked together and which he, with sheer locomotive power, pulled to its victorious destination threatened to derail due to Paul Stewart's attorney. After the brief glory when Neal patted him on the shoulder for delivering Jimmy Camomile, he had sunk back to being overlooked by the hotshots on the team. But by suddenly objecting that he felt betrayed, Arnie Klein vividly reminded everyone of the key role assigned the powdermen in the "plan." Arnie Klein balked at the manner in which Neal had characterized the "plan" in the opening days of his final argument. He brought home to Neal the leverage he still held over the entire defense contingent.

For Klein the rub started during Landis' testimony. It became pronounced during Neal's final argument. Both the director and his lawyer had outlined to the jury Landis' understanding of a "plan" in which the helicopter was supposed to move to "the other side of the river" and was to become a camera platform across from the village at the time the village was to go up.

Klein objected that this scenario flew in the face of the original agreements he'd made with the other members of the defense, especially with Neal. He had agreed that the special effects crew would testify to their understanding of a "plan" whereby they were to have set off the shoreline explosions once the chopper was a "safe distance away." Klein fell in with Neal and the others by accepting this scenario despite misgivings that in all of the powdermen's previous statements – to the NTSB, to the grand jury, at the prelim – it had never been acknowledged. Klein maintained he had been willing to "live with" this version in the belief that it would be sufficiently compatible with other testimony to be effective in convincing the jury. But after hearing Neal in his final argument relate to the jury his scenario of the "camera platform," arguing that Landis understood the helicopter was to be "across the river" when the village went up, Klein became convinced that the difference between the two versions was so striking that it would be discernible to a jury. In his eyes the brunt of these discrepancies hurt mainly his client, Paul Stewart, who never took the witness stand to explain his understanding of what went wrong at Indian Dunes. Klein felt he'd been "had," and, during a break on Neal's first day of the final argument, he confronted Landis' personal attorney Joel Behr in the hallway.

Arnie Klein was furious. Joel Behr heard him warn that in the remaining portion of his final argument someone must get Neal to change his language in describing "the plan" from "safely across the river" to the original "safe distance away." The latter was the consensus, Klein understood, that had been reached by all of the defense attorneys ten months before. Klein reminded Behr that his own final argument was to follow Neal's. He would ultimately have the last word. The hawk-eyed architect of the phalanx heard the unthinkable. Klein coolly informed him that he could personally sink "Neal's plan." The least of the team, constantly overlooked as a negligible legal quantity, demanded that the famous friend of the Kennedys watch his language.

Joel Behr's tall wavy bouffant, one of the wonders of the trial, tilted as he shook with rage. It seemed to levitate. "His wig shifted by at least six inches," Arnie Klein reckoned.

The slight curly-headed lawyer felt unassailable in the knowledge of a technical hole in Neal's current version of "the plan," a glaring discrepancy which made the position of the helicopter as a camera platform "safely across the river" a cinematic impossibility! Klein had discovered that the airborne camera used by Roger Smith in filming the scene had a wide-angle lens. Due to this feature any filming from the helicopter "across the river" would show entirely too much of the area surrounding the set. Such a wide-angle shot, Klein triumphantly explained, would be useless, proving that Landis could have never formulated any camera platform plan in the first place.

Klein's show of strength in the hallway had the desired result. Soon Deborah Landis came over. During the trial she had not bothered to take much notice of Klein. This time she treated him to a pleasant conversation. And when in the courtroom James Neal resumed his final argument his language reflected the new understanding, removing the helicopter from the "safely-across-the- river" scenario to the position Arnie Klein could live with: a "safe distance away."

* * *

Except for some sharp arguments by Harland Braun, the presentation of the lawyers following Neal was jejune. The statements by Klein, Trope and Levine produced no fresh shocks; they hardly made the scale. Arnie Klein read from a selection of Lewis Carroll's works and informed the jury that his client Paul Stewart was the victim of an Alice-in-Wonderland situation. Dan Allingham's attorney followed, cracking a few jokes and repeating again and again, "Tice knew"; like "safety first" before, which inspired Neal's fit of absurdity to appoint him "town-crier, "Lennybob," by endlessly dinning "Tice knew, Tice knew" tried to fix upon the jury an indelible impression, an echo to remind them during deliberations that the studio teacher Jack Tice knew all along about the kids being on the set. Eugene Trope whom the jurors had mostly seen having his objections overruled, this time surprised them by being able to talk without being called out on something by the judge.

Braun was last. Irrepressible, he took the low road and the high. He informed the jury that the prosecutor wanted to win in order to be invited on the *Johnny Carson Show*. He appealed to the jurors' sense of socio-economic identity. Stressing the anti-racist theme of Bill, he urged that just because it was a Hollywood trial the jurors should not be swayed.

"We shouldn't tear people down just because they make money," Braun advised. He closed his argument by instructing the jury to send a message to Hollywood.

"You're the same, no better, no worse."

53

LAST RITES

O n May 7, 1987, the *Twilight Zone* case for one full day shifted its center of gravity. While on that day Leonard Levine gave his final argument in the familiar 15th floor setting of Department 132 in the downtown Superior Court building, a major development was taking place in the courtroom of a regional branch 20 miles distant in San Fernando. There, Ned Good, representing Myca's parents, and Jerome and Eugene Berchin, the "Berchin brothers," Century City attorneys representing the Chen family, were engaged in highly secret negotiations with the parents and the defendants' lawyers to settle the civil claims before a verdict was reached in the criminal trial downtown.

Many more defendants were represented at this civil action in San Fernando than at the criminal trial; the parents had named among those responsible John Landis and Levitsky Productions, Dan Allingham, Dorcey Wingo, Warner Bros., The Burbank Studios, Bell Helicopter, Paul Stewart, James Camomile, Frank Marshall and Steven Spielberg. Although the defendants had their own internal differences about who was responsible for what share of the settlement, that day saw none of the protracted wrangling characteristic of the previous encounters over money.

Everything was arranged with an almost miraculous dispatch. With more than a dozen lawyers present, the complex negotiations started in the morning and by early afternoon there was an air of excitement in the courthouse as a tentative agreement with the parents was reached. There was a real sense of urgency. Many of the civil lawyers expected a guilty verdict in the criminal case and Ned Good was scheduled to take a deposition from Steven Spielberg on May 9, two days hence. After announcing their progress in chambers to the judge, who was monitoring the sensitive settlement conference, all the lawyers agreed to return to the San Fernando courthouse that evening after consulting with their clients.

The settlement proceedings in San Fernando represented a study in modern American anthropology. Lawyers performed the final death rites over Myca Le and Renee Chen. Like modern-day shamans, the attorneys interpreted the magic of signs and numbers as they negotiated in perplexing legal phrases the price to be paid to the grieving parents. The hallway outside the small courtroom was dotted with threesomes of lawyers standing about and whispering. Among them were Joel Behr; Landis' civil attorney Michael Terhar from Kern, Wooley; and Scott Dunham from O'Melveny & Myers, representing not only Warner Bros., but, as Dunham informed the civil judge, he also had the authority to speak on behalf of Steven Spielberg and Amblin Entertainment.

All of the important discussions were held in chambers outside the presence of spectators. As soon as word leaked out to journalists that settlement discussions were in progress, a gag order was imposed on the proceedings at the request of both sides. It was not until long after the negotiations were secretly concluded that the press ever became aware that the lawyers that day had agreed upon a settlement. In fact, the lawyers agreed among themselves to deliberately mislead the press by telling them that no settlement had been reached and that the civil cases would be continued until September. "This case will drag on till long after the other criminal prosecution is resolved," Ned Good, with a foxy smile, confided to one reporter, adding coyly, "But don't tell anybody I gave you that tip."

Neither the prosecution nor the defense wanted the news of the settlement discussions to leak out to the jury in the criminal trial downtown. The defense worried that news that the case was settled before a verdict was reached might influence the jury to consider the settlement an admission of guilt. To the prosecution, details of a large settlement leaking out might give the jury the impression that the defendants had paid their dues and shouldn't be convicted.

The last rites performed by lawyers in San Fernando was known as a Mandatory Settlement Conference. Under the rules of the court the parents of Myca and Renee were required to be there. Mark Chen and his wife sat quietly and disconsolately on a bench in the hall. For Dr. Daniel and Kim Le the tragedy had created "unlivable conditions" and they had in the meantime divorced. Mrs. Le was now living up near San Jose with her younger son Chris, while Dr. Le remained alone in Los Angeles. Both sets of parents sat in the wings of the courthouse – the Chen family on one side, the Les on the other, while the lawyers buzzed around them. Mrs. Le had reportedly undergone nearly a year-long treatment for mental depression. The Chens had another daughter since Renee's death, and according to the strange calculus of the defense lawyers that meant they should get less in money compensation, since they had not suffered as much as the Les.

In contrast to their short-statured, more freewheeling counterparts in the Criminal Court building downtown, the lawyers at the civil proceedings were all of them tall, straight, button-down corporate types. In-between the courtroom sessions they could be seen flying with their briefcases to hasty hallway consultations and pay phones. The negotiations were so private and confidential that neither the attorneys for the Le nor the Chen family knew what the other was settling for with the defendants.

Among themselves the defendants agreed to settle for a total of $4 million-$2.3 for the Les and $1.7 for the Chens. After intense negotiations between the main defendants and their insurance companies, the payout was divided between Houston Casualty which disbursed the lion's share of $3 million, the Travelers Insurance Company, which paid the $400,000 that was the balance of its $1 million policy with Warner; and Warner itself, which paid $600,000. Before approving the final agreement, O'Melveny's Scott Dunham contacted Howard King, Steven Spielberg's attorney. King gave the nod to the settlement and at 6 P.M. that same day with the courthouse closed to the public, Dunham was back in San Fernando. Warner's O'Melveny lawyer had represented the studio for the entire five years of legal wrangling. He happily reported to the assembled lawyers that Spielberg had agreed with the proposed terms and the conditions involved in accepting the $4 million deal.

Everything remained wrapped in the strictest secrecy. The judge, in fact, at Warner's request, helped bury the whole proceeding by declaring it "non-judicial," ordering the court reporter "not to maintain a record of any of these proceedings in official court files."

54

"It Ended Like a Frank Capra Movie"

Ten days after a final monetary settlement was reached between Landis, Spielberg, Warner Bros, and the parents, almost ten months to the day since the start of the trial, Judge Robert Boren, on May 18, 1987, at last charged the jury and sent it into deliberation. The jury would be out for what would be a total of eight days while the defendants were told to be on two-hours' notice for the verdict.

That morning in the building's cafeteria before going up to the courtroom John Landis, after being reminded by Deborah, for the last time stopped to change his glasses from his regular stylish black pair to the wire-rim pair he wore in court. His wife wore a modish brown suit with an antique ivory broach from her grandmother. Seated in his customary place at the defense table next to James Neal, the director began writing in his yellow legal pad. Referring to himself in his routine "Dear Deborah" letter, he wrote in the aggrieved tone of the victim, "The judge (for the first time) greets a defendant." Landis continued writing while the judge read the jury a complicated series of instructions.

The first day of jury deliberations yielded a surprise to the defense lawyers with the election as jury foreman of the large, loud, dowdy woman who for ten months had been seated in the front row of the jury box. Lois Rogers, a North Hollywood homemaker, was elected on a second ballot, narrowly beating out Bill Fisher, the tall, middle-aged, well-dressed black juror in the back row of the box whom the defense attorneys throughout the case had referred to as the "foreman," certain that when the time came, he would be elected. Bill Fisher with his calm, responsible bearing was a former military man in the Army Corps of Engineers. However, Lois Rogers' daughter had just finished law school and the jurors felt that told in her favor.

Ordinarily, Larry the Bailiff would act as the sole contact between the jury and the outside world during deliberations. But the judge felt constrained to order another sheriff to accompany him. Having been besieged by complaints about the bailiff's rapport with the defendants, the judge felt he had to take this unusual measure in order to guarantee propriety.

After the first day the jury requested to have the testimony of former prosecutor Gary Kesselman and lead witness Donna Schuman reread. They asked for the names of Allingham's former girlfriend, Cynthia Nigh, and casting director Marci Liroff, both of whom had testified to witnessing incidents before the crash which showed that Landis and Folsey knew the scene was dangerous. They asked for a video machine with a frame-by-frame stop-action capability so as to be able to watch the film which previously they'd seen only on the big screen. A few days later they made their last request before announcing the verdict. They wanted to see some exhibits; a map of the set, Camomile's immunity letter and several still photographs that had become exhibits, including the still photo showing Jack Tice with his red fireman's helmet standing next to Paul Stewart during the 2:00 "rehearsal" flight.

After eight days of deliberations, just as Neal had predicted in his wager with Klein, the two-hour notice went out. On Friday, May 29, the defendants were summoned to the courtroom. Due to the short notice only the innermost Landis circle of friends and family, including Universal's Sean Daniel and the unfailing producer Bob Weiss accompanied the chief defendant to his encounter with justice in Department 132. A press mob, however, bristling with cameras and sound equipment trailing coils of wires over the hallway floor already lay in wait. James Neal had brought out his wife Victoria from Nashville; Joel Behr was there with John Diemer. Just before the verdict was announced Judge Boren brought Larry the Bailiff once more into his chamber along with the court reporter and sternly warned them that he didn't want them talking or shaking hands or saying anything at all to the defendants, nothing, no matter what the verdict.

Pandemonium broke out with the Landis circle roaring and cheering as the dowdy homemaker from North Hollywood announced the verdict.

Not guilty to each of the 15 counts.

The judge took the jurors in chambers, thanked them for their endurance and asked if they had any questions. The jurors wanted to know whether he thought they had done the right thing and he told them he couldn't say what he felt one way or the other. Privately, however, the judge felt the defendants were guilty and he had been prepared to sentence John Landis to two years in state prison while being lenient with the others.

In the judge's chamber the jurors made a highly unorthodox request befitting a highly unorthodox trial. They asked whether they could meet with the defendants while still in the jury box and answer questions from the press together. The judge gave his permission and so the pandemonium resumed. The defendants ran to the jury, virtually throwing themselves over the railing of the box. John Landis, Deborah and Neal reached over, pumping hands and uttering cries of flattery to the citizens who blushed from happiness to be in the circle of the rich and famous.

As Neal shook hands with Lois Rogers, her first question to the former Watergate prosecutor was about what John Landis had been writing all these months in his yellow legal pad. Neal replied that he had been writing love letters to his wife. Lois seemed disappointed. "I thought he was writing a new script." Neal just laughed. To the press Lois announced, "You don't prosecute people for unforeseeable accidents." To Deborah Landis she said, "Go home and take care of your two kids."

Another juror intimated, "We felt if they were guilty, they should have had Camomile up there, too." In answer to one question, yet another juror replied, "There was not enough evidence to prove why the accident happened."

Lauretta Hudson, the black juror with the tam-o'-shanter whose position in the jury box placed her closest to the witness stand, embraced Deborah Landis warmly; Deborah, she recalled, said, "'Oh, you don't know how you helped me get through.' She said she would look at me and I would smile. And I did," Lauretta said proudly, oblivious of her juror's duty to have no communication concerning the case with outsiders.

John Landis' friends, the eternal Bob Weiss and Universal's Sean Daniel, stood in the back of the courtroom. As soon as the verdict was read Daniel gave the thumbs-up sign. He and Weiss emotionally congratulated each other.

"It ended like a Frank Capra movie," Daniel said, misty-eyed.

Deborah cried.

Lois Rogers shouted, "We live here. Hollywood is part of our town."

John Landis left the courtroom and waded into the sea of reporters waiting in the hall. He had very few words. With Neal beside him he answered blandly a few shouted questions from the press.

"It was..." he smirked and shrugged, "a trial."

Then he quickly left for a quiet victory celebration that night at the Landis home on Lloyd Crest.

Before the party the Landis cavalcade drove to Joel Behr's office where the director had promised to give an exclusive interview to TV newsman Paul Dandridge of KABC. On camera, Landis painted himself as the victim of political persecution, the misunderstood auteur hounded by un-comprehending authorities, while off-camera he spoke in his usual dis-jointed fashion. From what he told Dandridge it appeared that the deaths on his set had taken place in a true Twilight Zone dimension unrelated to any reality.

"The deaths of Vic Morrow, Renee and Myca had nothing to do with the trial," he told Dandridge. "That was a terrible tragedy. The trial became a separate injustice aimed at the people who were indicted."

At the Landis celebration a few hours later, there were notable absences of several of his co-defendants and their attorneys. Harland Braun, Arnie Klein and Eugene Trope were not invited. Among the guests were direc-tors Jeremy Kagan, Landis' chief lobbyist inside the Director's Guild, and *Poltergeist* producer Tobe Hooper. Sean Daniel and John Landis' moth-er and stepfather were also there. Cold cuts were served. George Folsey made a short speech, thanking all the people who had supported them; he especially thanked James Neal and Jim Sanders to whom he paid the strange compliment, since Neal made $1.8 million out of the case, of hav-ing come all the way from Nashville "to be with us."

Though people were obviously elated, the party was reserved. Sean Daniel again mentioned the "Frank Capra ending" of the trial. On TV they played several times the video of the acquittal taken from the news-cast that evening. The party talk was enlivened by Sean Daniel's amusing story of the new *Dragnet* movie in which they put a character whom they made to look, act and talk like Lea D'Agostino and who even had a bee on her shoulder. Someone jubilantly remarked that Hollywood was getting its revenge.

There were two victory cakes, one with the inscription, "Hooray for our side!" Then Deborah Landis brought out a small box of gold-like met-al bees on a pin. The bees were put on the shoulders of the attorneys. Ev-eryone was amused by Neal's antics. He considered the victory a major one in his career because, as he described it, you had to start out admitting you were wrong and then overcome that.

He pranced around with the pin on his shoulder and sang to much laughter, *I have a bee. I have a bee...*

An acquittal which even the presiding judge conceded privately to have been against his own inclination made people wonder about the reasoning that had led the 12 citizens in the jury box to their decision. Every indication showed that they had been, like many others connect-ed with this strange trial, overwhelmed by Hollywood. But as with most cases, three or four jurors played the most active and vocal role during deliberations.

By most jurors' accounts, in order of importance, they were the foreman, Lois Rogers; Bill Fisher; Chris Bernardo, the most highly educated and youngest of the jurors, a chemist with a master's degree who worked for the state; and Lauretta Hudson, the hip middle-aged black woman with the tam-o-shanter who liked to talk a lot and who, by her own account, was more interested in betting on the ponies at Hollywood Park than she was in being in a movie theatre. For Rogers, Fisher and Bernardo, the inside joke during the lengthy proceeding was how all three were writing a book about the Hollywood trial. Each kidded the other about it with the half-serious suspicion that the other might actually carry off such a venture.

Within days of the verdict the key jurors began to talk openly – and it became possible to penetrate the minds which during the trial had been masked by opaque, almost somnolent expressions.

Apart from being the jury's foreman, Mrs. Rogers conceded that she was also the champion in the marathon sessions of Hollywood Trivial Pursuit which the jury played during the lengthy 402's and other hearings that kept them locked up together in the jury room for so much of the trial. One of the jurors referred to her as "Mrs. Know-it- all." Despite the judge's admonition to the jurors not to watch or listen to any news, Mrs. Rogers did admit inadvertently hearing certain things about the case; and though she never deliberately "fudged" herself, she said others did and had made comments about it. On Donna Schuman her feeling was, "She wasn't telling the truth." She thought the prosecutor's tough examination of Landis, especially the kleenex incident, "a bit much; it wasn't necessary." The blowsy homemaker also wondered aloud how Lea D'Agostino could afford her stylish attire and remarked on her thin figure with obvious envy. "I think that we all wish that we had the wherewithal to get designer clothes.... But we're not jealous"; she advised, "When you got it, flaunt it." Disapprovingly, she noted, "We all saw the bee." Mrs. Rogers also discussed how thin and tall Deborah Landis was "not a beautiful girl but a very good-looking person."

Lois Rogers believed that the "liar's list" used by the prosecutor in her final argument "wasn't fair." She thought casting director Marci Liroff was herself "fibbing" about her claims of having warned Landis of danger and considered the delamination theory more feasible than the debris theory. Jackie Cooper "was trying too hard to please the prosecution," she found.

Mrs. Rogers didn't believe that the Landis people tried to keep Jack Tice from finding the children that night. Nor did she believe the scene to be that dangerous, stating that if not for the fact that it was night, Tice "wouldn't have felt it was dangerous" to shoot the scene as planned. After seeing a photograph of the red-helmeted Tice in one of the trial exhibits, the still photograph showing him standing near the set some twenty minutes before the crash, Mrs. Rogers found it impossible to accept the fact that he didn't know about the kids. Did Landis himself know that a mortar was placed within the much-talked-about "humdinger," the No. 4 hut? She felt that he didn't have to because "he hired experts." Why, she wondered, "should he have to run around to make sure every detail is in place." She further believed the stumble was planned as "a last- minute thing." Like most of her fellow jurors, she expressed the hope that Landis was writing a script about the courtroom drama.

Bill Fisher, nudged out of the foreman's position by one vote, was no slouch on Hollywood trivia himself. He was proudest of his victory in the Hollywood "hangman" game played during the trial where he stumped the other movie buffs on the jury by coming up with the movie title *Mourning Becomes Electra*, with Michael Redgrave, Katina Paxinou and Leo Genn. Fisher, one of the jury's five black members, did most of his growing up in Southern California and remembered his youth in the 40s when there were still segregated theaters in Pasadena. After the verdict he said he was impressed by the fact that Landis knew "Michael" and "Eddie," (Michael Jackson and Eddie Murphy). The most distinguished looking of the jurors, never less than impeccably dressed, Fisher always mentioned the two stars by their first names. "Michael thinks the world of him," Fisher said, meaning Landis, with reference to the *Making of Thriller* video which he'd seen showing Landis directing "Michael." Fisher also loved *Trading Places*, "one of my favorite movies," especially the scene where "Eddie is chased in the club."

Fisher also blamed the whole *Twilight Zone* affair on the special effects man Jimmy Camomile; had he done what he was supposed to, "we probably wouldn't have been here at all." His work in the Army Corps of Engineers had given him some experience with helicopters, he said, and he didn't believe that debris downed the craft. "That helicopter was designed for combat." According to Fisher, Landis was telling the truth, the stumble was planned, Schuman lied, and Landis "was trying to make more money" writing on his yellow pad.

Though he knew that James Neal was a famous Watergate prosecutor, Fisher spoke of him as a "cornpone" with a nice "country delivery ... like

Buddy Ebsen, a hillbilly type, real folksy, he liked to exaggerate a little bit." Like Lois Rogers, he felt Tice had to know about the kids being used in the scene, insisting that the photo of Tice with the red helmet proved the point. He also felt that the parents were told about the explosions and that money played a role in convincing the Les and Chens to overlook the dangers. Of the hyperactive impression the director seemed to convey through the testimony, Fisher talked matter-of-factly like an old movie-hand: that was Hollywood. "I don't know of any director that is not like that. Look at Sam Peckinpah and Stanley Kubrick."

Bill Fisher said that during the trial he discussed *Animal House* and *Blues Brothers* with fellow juror Chris Bernardo. Of this small influential group in the jury's deliberations, Bernardo was the panel's acknowledged film expert, though after the verdict he said he hadn't seen either movie himself. On many days during the trial, Bernardo, a naturalized American citizen from the Philippines, carried an armload of books about Hollywood into the jury room. His edition of *LIFE Goes to the Movies* was a favorite among fellow jurors.

According to Lauretta Hudson, Chris Bernardo was the expert on celebrities. He and Lois Rogers were best at Hollywood hangman. Bernardo recognized Don Ameche and several celebrities in the courtroom. Nevertheless, he mistook one spectator in the courtroom for John Houseman, a mistake often made by jurors, newsmen and spectators during the star-studded trial. With an erudite taste in movies – "foreign movies and movies of an Academy Award calibre" – he decided that Jackie Cooper was merely a "Monday morning quarterback." Just about the only major difference in thinking among the jurors was Chris Bernardo's feeling that he didn't believe the stumble was planned.

One other juror, Beulah "Pat" Wilson, was a devout, bible- toting black woman. Beulah confided that she had a religious experience during the deliberations. She intimated to Bill Fisher that *Blues Brothers* was her favorite movie, even though on the confidential questionnaire the jurors filled out prior to selection she listed her favorite movies as "westerns."

All the jurors were movie buffs. All of them dreamed about being in a movie. Lois Rogers wondered who'd play her part in the movie about the case. Lauretta Hudson, the hip black lady with the tam-o'-shanter, thought Landis while sitting through the trial was writing up a story about it for the new movie. In that event, Fisher gallantly complimented juror Hudson not to be surprised if someone approached her about playing herself.

Epilogue

Washington D.C.
Monday
April 7, 1987
9:00 A.M.

During the ten-month trial nobody knew where Frank Marshall was and not until both the defense and prosecution rested their case in April 1987, did any news surface as to the whereabouts of Steven Spielberg's friend and righthand man.

In a communique from Interpol's Washington office, the Los Angeles district attorney's office was notified that Frank Marshall had been identified by Spanish authorities as he arrived in Spain. He was staying at Madrid's La Caruna. Interpol stated it had made contact with Marshall and ended with the fateful words:

"He's aware of the judicial problems for which he is cited. He says he has already resolved the matter. He took a plane to Seville where he will remain several days at the Hotel Jerez de la Frontera. "Is the witness still wanted?"

EXHIBITS

These are the words painted on the nose of the helicopter before the cover-up began.

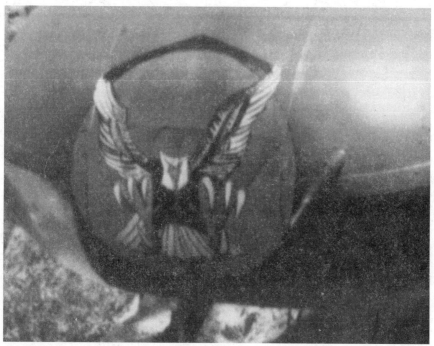

This is the nose of the helicopter with the John Landis logo removed shortly after the crash.

421

These are pre-production illustrations from a large group of drawings that were never turned over to authorities. They were anonymously provided to the author of this book to demonstrate their existence.

John Landis standing under Nite-Sun light at so-called 2AM rehearsal. The director positions the helicopter for a light check using the "eukie stick" (arrow) to serve as a signal to cue the fatal explosion.

The so-called number #4 hut where the square mortar was placed before it brought down the helicopter.

Helicopter focusing Nite-Sun light on Vic & Kids seconds before it crashes on them.

Vic Morrow under the Nite-Sun beam just before stumbling.

Vic Morrow's -stumble,- seconds before fatal SFX explosion that downs the helicopter on him and the kids.

425

Exhibit #35 The photograph taken by the Chapman Crane driver moments before the crash. Pictured from left to right is Jerry Williams (SFX man at his firing board), John Landis (Director), Mike Milgrom (Man who fired marble gun), Vic Morrow & Kids (arrow).

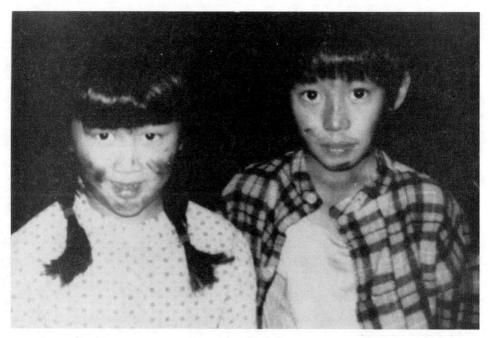

The children, who were illegally hired and hidden on the set, before perishing in the Twilight Zone crash. Left, Renee Shin-Yi Chen. Right, Myca Dinh Le..

The helicopter's fractured rotor blade which investigators concluded was brought down by the special effects explosion originating in Hut #4.

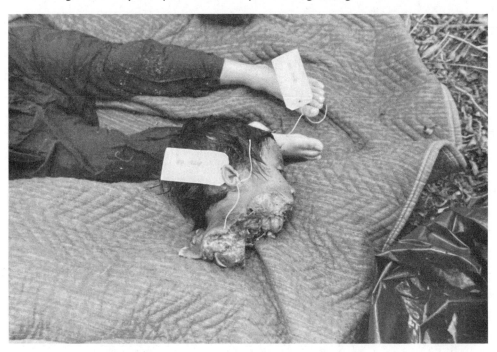

Myca Dinh-Le's decapitated head. The last image his father witnessed before being rushed off the set by Frank Marshall and George Folsey.

427

Vic Morrow's final scene with the doomed children just before the crash.

Moments before the helicopter crash.

Sgt. Budds shocking view of actor Vic Morrow's mangled head in garbage bag hours after the crash.

The remainder of Vic Morrow's mangled torso.

Gary McClarty, the stunt coordinator on the Twilight Zone segment, who never revealed the secret of the "baby dummies.".

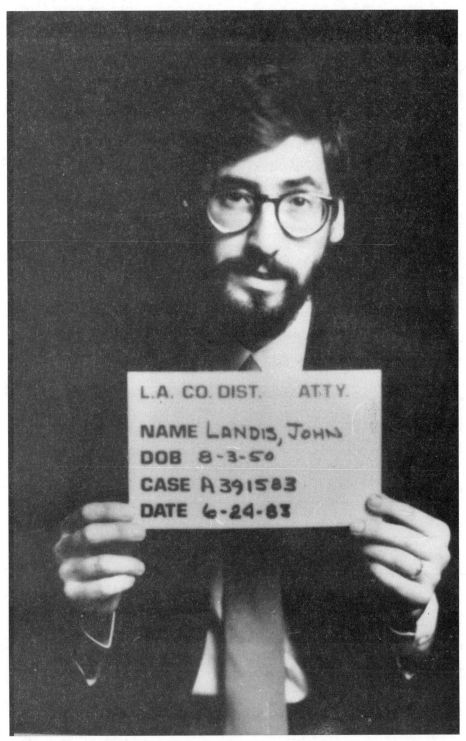

L.A. CO. DIST.   ATTY.

NAME Landis, John
DOB 8-3-50
CASE A 391583
DATE 6-24-83

Director John Landis at the time of his arrest.

Defendant #2 George Folsey Jr., Associate Producer.

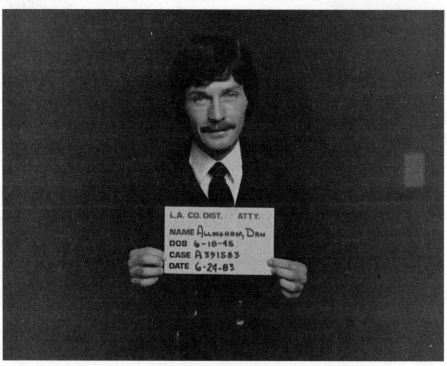

Defendant #3 Dan Allingham, Unit Production Manager (UPM).

Defendant #4 Paul Stewart, Special Effects Chief.

Defendant #5 Dorcey Wingo, Helicopter Pilot.

Gary Kesselman, the initial D.A. prosecutor on the case whose embarrassing ties to the Club El Gaucho ended with his humiliation and removal from the case as lead prosecutor.

Harland Braun (Left), initially the lead criminal attorney on the case, and Joel Behr (Right), Landis' personal attorney.

Lead attorney, James Neal, who commuted to Los Angeles from Memphis during the 10-month Twilight Zone trial.

George Folsey was John Landis' partner and co-defendant in Twilight Zone case.

John Landis consults with his famed Watergate attorney, James Neal, during the trial.

Deborah Landis evading a process server attempting to serve her with a deposition subpoena from the parents of the deceased Vietnamese boy, Myca.

John Landis staged this scene of escorting famed film director, John Houston, in his effort to garner support from his peers in the film industry during the Twilight Zone trial.

Prosecutor Lea DeAugstino (Right), preparing famed Hollywood director, Jackie Cooper (Left) as her expert witness in the case.

Noted Watergate attorney, James Neal, leads client John Landis through the press throng.

Attorney James Neal (Right), offers congratulations to SFX attorney, Arnie Klein, for delivering the needed testimony from the pivotal witness Jimmy Camomile.

John and Deborah Landis bring Trading Place's star, Ralph Bellamy to the trial in the so-called "Landismobile."

Paul Stewart, who many witnesses observed his excessive drinking on the set prior to the fatal shot.

John and Deborah Landis at trial.

Star War's Princess Leia, Carrie Fisher, leaving the Landis courtroom.

Frank Marshal and Kathleen Kennedy. Steven Spielberg's highest ranking officials on the set of the crash that night. Frank Marshal fled the scene and was never interviewed by authorities.

Index